A Northern Romanticism:

Poets of the Confederation

Canadian Critical Editions

General Editors

John Moss and Gerald Lynch

Canadian Critical Editions offer, for academic study and the interested reader, authoritative texts of significant Canadian works within a comprehensive critical setting. Where appropriate, each edition provides extensive biographical and bibliographical background, reprints of documents, commentary to illuminate the context of its creation and the history of its reception, new essays written from a variety of critical perspectives, and a bibliography. These critical editions provide an excellent opportunity for appreciation of the works themselves, for understanding their place in the developing tradition, and for participating in the critical discourse surrounding each work. Making the best accessible, this is the key concept behind Canadian Critical Editions.

Other titles in the Canadian Critical Editions available from Borealis Press

---

Stephen Leacock, *Sunshine Sketches of a Little Town*, editor Gerald Lynch, 1996.

Sarah Jeannette Duncan, *The Imperialist*, editor Thomas E. Tausky, 1996.

Susanna Moodie, *Roughing It in theBush; or, Life in Canada*, editor Elizabeth Thompson, 1997.

John Richardson, *Wacousta*, editor John Moss, 1998.

Early Canadian Short Stories: Short Stories in English Before World War I, editor Misao Dean, 2000.

Titles in Preparation

Stephen Leacock, *Arcadian Adventures with the Idle Rich*, editor David Bentley.

James De Mille, *A Strange Manuscript Found in a Copper Cylinder*, editor Gwendolyn Davies.

Thomas Chandler Haliburton, *The Clockmaker*, editor Carrie MacMillan.

Frances Brooke, *The History of Emily Montague*, editor Laura Moss.

Charles G.D. Roberts, *Charles G.D. Roberts: Animal Stories*, editor Terry Whalen.

Clockwise from top left: Charles G.D. Roberts, Bliss Carman, Duncan Campbell Scott, Archibald Lampman, Isabella Valancy Crawford, and William Wilfred Campbell

A Northern Romanticism: Poets of the Confederation

A Critical Edition

Edited by Tracy Ware

The Tecumseh Press Ltd.
Ottawa, Canada
2000

The Publishers gratefully acknowledge the financial support of the Government of Canada through the Book Publishing Industry Development Program (BPIDP), and of the Ontario Arts Council, for our publishing activities.

Canadian Cataloguing in Publication Program

Main entry under title:

A northern romanticism : poets of the confederation

(Canadian critical editions)
Includes bibliographical references.
ISBN 1-896133-17-7 (bound) - ISBN 1-896133-19-3 (pbk.)

1. Canadian poetry (English)–19th century. 2. Canadian poetry (English)–20th century. I. Ware, Tracy, 1956- II. Series.

PS8291.N67 2000 C811'.5408 C00-900721-0
PR9195.7.N63 2000

cover design by drt 2000

Printed and bound in Canada on acid free paper

Contents

Preface

Around 1880, the writers in this anthology began to write poetry of a calibre not seen before in Canada. Both Isabella Valancy Crawford and William Wilfred Campbell soon emerged as distinctive voices, but the career of the former was curtailed by an early death in 1887, while the latter was an idiosyncratic character whose later career was marred by an enthusiasm for Imperialist ideals and jealousy of his more successful peers (see Hurst). So it was Charles G.D. Roberts who played the vital role. His first volume, *Orion and Other Poems* (1880), showed the young Archibald Lampman new possibilities: "It seemed to me a wonderful thing that such work could be done by a Canadian, by a young man, one of ourselves. It was like a voice from some new paradise of art calling us to be up and doing" (see his vivid account in "Two Canadian Poets" in this anthology). For Duncan Campbell Scott it "connected the poetry of Canada with all that is excellent in English poetry the world over" (see "A Decade of Canadian Poetry" in this anthology). When he published his first volume in 1893, Scott included poems dedicated to Campbell, Bliss Carman, Lampman, and Roberts. At this time, Campbell, Lampman, and Scott were sharing a literary column ("At the Mermaid Inn") for the Toronto *Globe* (see Davies). Shortly after the column ended, Campbell launched an attack on Carman that disrupted the earlier harmony of the group (see Hurst), and the death of Lampman in 1899 marked the end of an era. The four surviving poets would remain active for years, but the last two decades of the nineteenth century were the great years for the writers we have come to identify as the "Confederation poets."

Three factors made Roberts' influence so important: first, Roberts matured so rapidly that his promise must have seemed unlimited. *Orion* is a youthful effort, published when he was twenty, but he wrote his most memorable poem, "The Tantramar Revisited," when he was twenty-three, and many of his best poems appeared in his second book, *In Divers Tones*

(1886). Second, as the bibliographical details in the notes to this anthology attest, Roberts found ready access to the leading American and British periodicals, and so did the Canadian poets who followed him. Third, he was a Classically-trained scholar and a highly articulate critic. The core of his aesthetics was the belief that "Nature becomes significant to man when she is passed through the alembic of his heart. Irrelevant and confusing details having been purged away, what remains is single and vital. It acts either by interpreting, recalling, suggesting, or symbolizing some phase of human feeling" (in "The Poetry of Nature," included in this anthology). Carman agreed when he argued that poetry at its best interprets "for us the beauty of the outward world and the inward mysterious craving of the human mind" (see his essay on Roberts in this anthology). Such an aesthetic is properly called Romantic, and it provided the basis for some of the most familiar poems in this anthology, such as Campbell's "Indian Summer," Lampman's "Among the Timothy," Carman's "Low Tide on Grand Pré," and Scott's "The Height of Land."

This anthology also includes works that might complicate our sense of Confederation poetry. Each of these writers was more than just a regional or nature poet, and none was obsessed about Canadian identity. Roberts and Carman both moved to the United States, and today's readers will be reluctant to follow Campbell in attacking them for doing so. Indeed, the differences between Campbell and the other poets show how little is explained by the existence of common English influences. Like Lampman and Scott, Roberts and Carman were deeply versed in Classical, American, and other literary traditions, and each of these writers showed a measure of "eclectic detachment" (to use A.J.M. Smith's term) in his ability to combine these influences and create anew. Two of the sequences in this anthology indicate their neglected achievements. In the *New York Nocturnes* (1898), which is included in its entirety, Roberts demonstrates that his writing continued to develop after he moved to New York. In this most urban of settings, Roberts finds metaphors for the various stages of an erotic and spiritual quest. In *Sappho* (1905), which is, regrettably, too long for unabridged inclusion, Carman writes with a passionate commitment that might surprise those who know only his nature lyrics.

There is another aspect to the story of Confederation poetry. It involves the international respect that these writers (unlike their Canadianist Modernist successors) enjoyed between 1880 and 1914, the belated national recognition of Roberts and Carman after World War I, and the consequent attacks on the "Maple Leaf" school of poetry led by the young A.J.M. Smith and F.R. Scott. That story is told so well in the critical essays included in this anthology that I can bring my prefatory remarks to a close with a word on the selection and arrangement of texts.

The selection from each of the six poets is prefaced with a brief biographical and critical introduction followed by a list of titles for further reading. Except in the case of sequences, the poems are then arranged chronologically within each section, with the date at the end of the poem being the date of original publication. The notes contain further details about the original periodical publication (if available) and the first (single-authored) book publication of each poem. I have taken the latter as my copy-text, unless otherwise noted, and I have tried to justify any emendations. I have not provided a full list of textual variants, but I have recorded significant changes, and I have attempted to explain allusions and unfamiliar words in the notes.

I am grateful to Gerald Lynch for suggesting this edition and helping with every stage of its production. Queen's University provided funding of two kinds. I thank Suzanne Fortier, Vice-Principal (Research), and B.J. Hutchinson, Director of Research Services, for helping to defray the costs of publication. I thank SSHRC and the Principal's Development Fund and Advisory Research Committee for a grant that enabled me to purchase a computer and hire Sara Jamieson as a research assistant. Her intelligence and industry were a great help throughout. I thank Greg Betts for patiently designing the cover and the frontispiece, and Parks Canada for permission to use Maxime Saint-Amour's "Dandelion Field" as an illustration. I thank Sue Armstrong of the Special Collections and the Learning Technology Unit, Queen's University. The following individuals were helpful in many ways: D.M.R. Bentley, Glenn Clever, Klay Dyer, D.K. Hagel, Bernie Kavanagh, Ross Kilpatrick, Shelley King, Les Monkman, John Moss, Laura Moss, John Pierce, Marilyn Rose, Malcolm Ross, and Frank Tierney. Most of all, I am indebted to my wife, Brenda Reed, who remains the most helpful librarian of them all.

Further Reading on Confederation Poetry in General

Ballstadt, Carl, ed. *The Search for English-Canadian Literature: An Anthology of Critical Articles from the Nineteenth and Early Twentieth Centuries*. Literature of Canada. Toronto: U of Toronto P, 1975.

Bentley, D.M.R. *The Gay] Grey Moose: Essays on the Ecologies and Mythologies of Canadian Poetry, 1690-1990*. Ottawa: U of Ottawa P, 1992.

Bhojwani, Maia. "A Northern Pantheism: Notes on the Confederation Poets and Contemporary Mythographers." *Canadian Poetry: Studies, Documents, Reviews* 9 (1981): 34-49.

Brown, E.K. *On Canadian Poetry*. 1943. Rev. ed. 1944. Ottawa: Tecumseh, 1973.

———. *Responses and Evaluations: Essays on Canada*. Ed. David Staines. New Canadian Library. Toronto: McClelland and Stewart, 1977.

Davies, Barrie, ed. *At the Mermaid Inn: Wilfred Campbell, Archibald Lampman, and Duncan Campbell Scott in* The Globe *1892-93*. Literature of Canada. Toronto: U of Toronto P, 1979.

Daymond, Douglas M., and Leslie G. Monkman, eds. *Towards a Canadian Literature: Essays, Editorials, and Manifestos. Vol. 1 1752-1940*. Ottawa: Tecumseh, 1984. 2 vols.

Doyle, James. "Canadian Poetry and American Magazines, 1885-1905." *Canadian Poetry: Studies, Documents, Reviews* 5 (1979): 73-82.

Glickman, Susan. *The Picturesque and the Sublime: A Poetics of the Canadian Landscape*. Kingston: McGill-Queen's UP, 1998.

Hurst, Alexandra J., ed. *The War Among the Poets: Issues of Plagiarism and Patronage Among the Confederation Poets*. London, ON: Canadian Poetry Press, 1994.

Jones, D.G. *Butterfly on Rock: A Study of Themes and Images in Canadian Literature*. Toronto: U of Toronto P, 1970.

Klinck, Carl F., general ed. *Literary History of Canada: Canadian Literature in English*. Toronto: U of Toronto P, 1965.

McLeod, Les. "Canadian Post-Romanticism: The Context of Late Nineteenth-Century Canadian Poetry." *Canadian Poetry: Studies, Documents, Reviews* 14 (1984): 1-37.

MacMechan, Archibald. *Head-waters of Canadian Literature*. Toronto: McClelland and Stewart, 1924.

McMullen, Lorraine, ed. *Twentieth-Century Essays on Confederation Literature*. Ottawa: Tecumseh, 1976.

Matthews, John P. *Tradition in Exile: A Comparative Study of Social Influences on the Development of Australian and Canadian Poetry in the Nineteenth Century*. Toronto: U of Toronto P, 1962.

Pacey, Desmond. *Ten Canadian Poets: A Group of Biographical and Critical Essays*. Toronto: Ryerson, 1958.

Rashley, R.E. *Poetry in Canada: The First Three Steps*. 1958. Ottawa: Tecumseh, 1979.

Ross, Malcolm. *The Impossible Sum of Our Traditions: Reflections on Canadian Literature*. Toronto: McClelland and Stewart, 1986.

Smith, A.J.M. *Towards a View of Canadian Letters: Selected Critical Essays 1928-71*. Vancouver: UBC P, 1973.

Stevenson, Lionel. *Appraisals of Canadian Literature*. Toronto: Macmillan, 1926.

Woodcock, George, ed. *Colony and Confederation: Early Canadian Poets and their Background*. Vancouver: UBC P, 1974.

Isabella Valancy Crawford (1850-1887)

Isabella Valancy Crawford was born in Dublin in 1850, and came to Canada West in 1858. In the words of her "Autobiographical Sketch," "I was brought to Canada by my parents in my earliest childhood, and have never left the country since that period. I was educated at home, and have never left my home but for about a month, that amount of absence being scattered over all my life" (in Farmiloe vii). What she does not say is that the Crawfords' life in Canada was one of increasing hardship and disgrace. Dorothy Farmiloe's research shows that Crawford's father, a doctor of questionable skills, was an alcoholic and an embezzler. Because of his misdeeds, the family moved from Paisley to Lakefield to Peterborough, where he died in 1875. When her sister Emma died and her brother Stephen moved to Algoma the next year, Crawford and her mother moved to Toronto. For the rest of her life, Crawford supported them by writing poems and stories for Toronto newspapers and American periodicals. At her own expense, she published one collection, *Old Spookses' Pass, Malcolm's Katie, and Other Poems*, in 1884, but she sold only 50 of the 1000 copies. At her death in 1887, she left her most ambitious work incomplete; it was posthumously published as *Hugh and Ion* (1977). Many of her works are still uncollected; the misleadingly titled *Collected Poems* (1905; rpt 1972) is both incomplete and inaccurate (see S.R. MacGillivray's essay in Tierney).

Crawford has long been recognized as apart from the other Confederation poets. As early as 1943, A.J.M. Smith singled out her poems of the Canadian wilderness for praise: "If there is a Canadian poetry that exists as something distinct from English poetry, this—and this almost alone—is it" (see his Introduction to *The Book of Canadian Poetry*). In 1959, James Reaney wrote an influential appreciation of Crawford as a boldly imaginative mythopoeic poet, like Blake or Spenser. While critics disagree about Crawford's merits (see Louis

Dudek's essay in Tierney), the mythopoeic approach is helpful for such poems as "The Dark Stag," "The Lily Bed," "Gisli: the Chieftain," and "Malcolm's Katie," which is not included here because of its length and ready availability elsewhere. As the powerful ending of "Gisli: the Chieftain" shows, Crawford is less interested in retelling Norse myth than in creating her own. In an essay included in this anthology, Germaine Warkentin offers a balanced assessment of Crawford as a poet capable of both undeniable lapses and the sustained brilliance of "Said the Canoe." As a "self-consciously public poet" (Warkentin's term), Crawford also wrote on topical themes, as in "Canada to England" and "War." Finally, she could also write a beautiful pastoral like "The Earth Waxeth Old," in which the distinctive qualities of the Canadian landscape are beside the point.

Further Reading

Bessai, Frank. "The Ambivalence of Love in the Poetry of Isabella Valancy Crawford." *Queen's Quarterly* 77 (1970): 404-18.

Burns, Robert Alan. "Isabella Valancy Crawford." *Canadian Writers and Their Works: Poetry Series*, Volume 1. Eds. Robert Lecker, Jack David, and Ellen Quigley. Toronto: ECW, 1988. 21-71.

———. "The Poet in Her Time: Isabella Valancy Crawford's Social, Economic, and Political Views." *Studies in Canadian Literature* 14:1 (1989): 30-53.

Crawford, Isabella Valancy. *The Collected Poems of Isabella Valancy Crawford*. Ed. John W. Garvin. 1905. Rpt. with introd. by James Reaney. Literature of Canada. Toronto: U of Toronto P, 1972.

———. *Hugh and Ion*. Ed. Glenn Clever. Ottawa: Borealis, 1977.

———. *Malcolm's Katie: A Love Story*. Ed. D.M.R. Bentley. London, ON: Canadian Poetry Press, 1987.

Devereux, Cecily. "Canada and the Epilogue to the *Idylls*: 'The Imperial Connection' in 1873." *Victorian Poetry* 36 (1998): 223-41.

Dunn, Margo. "Crawford's 'Gisli, the Chieftain.'" *Contemporary Verse Two* 2:2 (1976): 48-50.

Farmiloe, Dorothy. *Isabella Valancy Crawford: The Life and the Legends*. Ottawa: Tecumseh, 1983.

Galvin, Elizabeth McNeill. *Isabella Valancy Crawford: We Scarcely Knew Her*. Toronto: Natural Heritage, 1994.

Livesay, Dorothy. "Tennyson's Daughter or Wilderness Child? The Factual and the Literary Background of Isabella Valancy Crawford." *Journal of Canadian Fiction* 2:3 (1973): 161-67.

Ower, John. "Isabella Valancy Crawford: 'The Canoe.'" *Canadian Literature* 34 (1967): 54-62.

Reaney, James. "Isabella Valancy Crawford." *Our Living Tradition, Second and Third Series*. Ed. Robert L. McDougall. Toronto: U of Toronto P, 1959. 268-88.

Ross, Catherine Sheldrick. "Isabella Valancy Crawford's 'Gisli, the Chieftain.'" *Canadian Poetry: Studies, Documents, Reviews* 2 (1978): 28-37.

Tierney, Frank M., ed. *The Crawford Symposium*. Reappraisals: Canadian Writers. Ottawa: U of Ottawa P, 1979.

Canada to England

Gone are the days, old Warrior of the Seas,
When thine armed head, bent low to catch my voice,
Caught but the plaintive sighings of my woods,
And the wild roar of rock-dividing streams,
And the loud bellow of my cataracts,
Bridged with the seven splendours of the bow.
When Nature was a Samson yet unshorn,
Filling the land with solitary might,
Or as the Angel of the Apocalypse,
One foot upon the primeval bowered land,
One foot upon the white mane of the sea,
My voice but faintly swelled the ebb and flow
Of the wild tides and storms that beat upon
Thy rocky girdle,—loud shrieking from the Ind
Ambrosial-breathing furies; from the north
Thundering with Arctic bellows, groans of seas
Rising from tombs of ice disrupted by
The magic kisses of the wide-eyed sun.

The times have won a change. Nature no more
Lords it alone and binds the lonely land
A serf to tongueless solitudes; but Nature's self
Is led, glad captive, in light fetters rich
As music-sounding silver can adorn;
And man has forged them, and our silent God
Behind His flaming worlds smiles on the deed.
"Man hath dominion"—words of primal might;
"Man hath dominion"—thus the words of God.

If destiny is writ on night's dusk scroll,
Then youngest stars are dropping from the hand
Of the Creator, sowing on the sky
My name in seeds of light. Ages will watch
Those seeds expand to suns, such as the tree
Bears on its boughs, which grows in Paradise.

How sounds my voice, my warrior kinsman, now?
Sounds it not like to thine in lusty youth—
A world-possessing shout of busy men,
Veined with the clang of trumpets and the noise
Of those who make them ready for the strife,
And in the making ready bruise its head?
Sounds it not like to thine—the whispering vine,
The robe of summer rustling thro' the fields,
The lowing of the cattle in the meads,
The sound of Commerce, and the music-set,
Flame-brightened step of Art in stately halls,—
All the infinity of notes which chord
The diapason of a Nation's voice?

My infants' tongues lisp word for word with thine;
We worship, wed, and die, and God is named
That way ye name Him,—strong bond between
Two mighty lands when as one mingled cry,
As of one voice, Jehovah turns to hear.
The bonds between us are no subtle links
Of subtle minds binding in close embrace,
Half-struggling for release, two alien lands,
But God's own seal of kindred, which to burst
Were but to dash His benediction from
Our brows. "Who loveth not his kin,
Whose face and voice are his, how shall he love
God whom he hath not seen?"
(1874)

The Roman Rose-Seller

Not from Paestum come my roses; Patrons, see
My flowers are Roman-blown; their nectaries
Drop honey amber, and their petals throw
Rich crimsons on the lucent marble of the shrine
Where snowy Dian lifts her pallid brow,

As crimson lips of Love may seek to warm
A sister glow in hearts as pulseless hewn.
Caesar from Afric wars returns to-day;
Patricians, buy my royal roses; strew
His way knee-deep, as though old Tiber roll'd
A tide of musky roses from his bed to do
A wonder, wond'rous homage. Marcus Lucius, thou
To-day dost wed; buy roses, roses, roses,
To mingle with the nuptial myrtle; look,
I strip the polish'd thorns from the stems,
The nuptial rose should be a stingless flower;
Lucania, pass not by my roses. Virginia,
Here is a rose that has a canker in't, and yet
It is most glorious-dyed and sweeter smells
Than those death hath not touched. To-day they bear
The shield of Claudius with his spear upon it,
Close upon Caesar's chariot—heap, heap it up
With roses such as these; 'tis true he's dead
And there's the canker! but, Romans, he
Died glorious, there's the perfume! and his virtues
Are these bright petals; so buy my roses, Widow.
No Greek-born roses mine. Priestess, priestess!
Thy ivory chariot stay; here's a rose and not
A white one, though thy chaste hands attend
On Vesta's flame. Love's of a colour—be it that
Which ladders Heaven and lives amongst the Gods;
Or like the Daffodil blows all about the earth;
Or, Hesperus-like, is one sole star upon
The solemn sky which bridges some sad life,
So here's a crimson rose: Be thou as pure
As Dian's tears iced on her silver cheek,
And know no quality of love, thou art
A sorrow to the Gods! Oh mighty Love!
I would my roses could but chorus Thee.
No roses of Persepolis are mine. Helot, here—
I give thee this last blossom: A bee as red
As Hybla's golden toilers sucked its sweets;

A butterfly, wing'd like to Eros, nipp'd
Its new-pinked leaves; the sun, bright despot, stole
The dew night gives to all. Poor slave, methinks
A bough of cypress were as gay a gift, and yet
It hath some beauty left! a little scarlet—for
The Gods love all; a little perfume, for there is no life,
Poor slave, but hath its sweetness. Thus I make
My roses Oracles. O hark! the cymbals beat
In god-like silver bursts of sound; I go
To see great Ceasar leading Glory home,
From Campus Martius to the Capitol!
(1874)

War

Shake, shake the earth with giant tread,
  Thou red-maned Titan bold;
For every step a man lies dead,
  A cottage hearth is cold.
Take up the babes with mailed hands,
  Transfix them with thy spears,
Spare not the chaste young virgin-bands,
  Tho' blood may be their tears.

Beat down the corn, tear up the vine,
  The waters turn to blood;
And if the wretch for bread doth whine,
  Give him his kin for food.
Aye, strew the dead to saddle girth,
  They make so rich a mould,
Thoul't thus enrich the wasted earth—
  They'll turn to yellow gold.

On with thy thunders, shot and shell,
  Send screaming, featly hurl'd;

Science has made them in her cell,
  To *civilize* the world.
Not, not alone where Christian men
  Pant in the well-arm'd strife;
But seek the jungle-throttled glen—
  The savage has a life.

He has a soul—so priests will say—
  Go! save it with thy sword;
Thro' his rank forests force thy way,
  Thy war cry, "For the Lord!"
Rip up his mines, and from his strands
  Wash out the gold with blood—
Religion raises blessing hands,
  "War's evil worketh good!"

When striding o'er the conquer'd land,
  Silence thy rolling drum,
And led by white-robed choiring bands
  With loud "*Te Deum*" come.
Seek the grim chancel, on its wall
  Thy blood-stiff banner hang;
They lie who say thy blood is gall,
  Thy tooth the serpent's fang.

See! the white Christ is lifted high,
  Thy conqu'ring sword to bless;
Smiles the pure monarch of the sky—
  Thy king can do no less.
Drink deep with him the festal wine,
  Drink with him drop for drop;
If, like the sun, his throne doth shine,
  Thou art that throne's prop.

If spectres wait upon the bowl,
  Thou needs not be afraid,
Grin hell-hounds for thy bold black soul,
  His purple be thy shade.
Go! feast with Commerce, be her spouse;
  She loves thee, thou art hers—
For thee she decks her board and house,
  Then how may others curse

If she, mild-seeming matron, leans
  Upon thine iron neck,
And leaves with thee her household scenes
  To follow at thy beck—
Bastard in brotherhood of kings,
  Their blood runs in thy veins,
For them the crowns, the sword that swings,
  For thee to hew their chains.

For thee the rending of the prey—
  They, jackals to the lion,
Tread after in the gory way
  Trod by the mightier scion.
O slave! that slayest other slaves,
  O'er vassals crowned, a king!
War, build high thy throne with graves,
  High as the vulture's wing!
(1879)

The Camp of Souls

My white canoe, like the silvery air
  O'er the River of Death that darkly rolls
When the moons of the world are round and fair,
  I paddle back from the "Camp of Souls."

When the wishton-wish in the low swamp grieves
Come the dark plumes of red "Singing Leaves."

Two hundred times have the moons of spring
  Rolled over the bright bay's azure breath
Since they decked me with plumes of an eagle's wing,
  And painted my face with the "paint of death,"
And from their pipes o'er my corpse there broke
The solemn rings of the blue "last smoke."

Two hundred times have the wintry moons
  Wrapped the dead earth in a blanket white;
Two hundred times have the wild sky loons
  Shrieked in the flush of the golden light
Of the first sweet dawn, when the summer weaves
Her dusky wigwam of perfect leaves.

Two hundred moons of the falling leaf
  Since they laid my bow in my dead right hand
And chanted above me the "song of grief"
  As I took my way to the spirit land;
Yet when the swallow the blue air cleaves
Come the dark plumes of red "Singing Leaves."

White are the wigwams in that far camp,
  And the star-eyed deer on the plains are found;
No bitter marshes or tangled swamp
  In the Manitou's happy hunting-ground!
And the moon of summer forever rolls

Above the red men in their "Camp of Souls."
Blue are its lakes as the wild dove's breast,
  And their murmurs soft as her gentle note;
As the calm, large stars in the deep sky rest,
  The yellow lilies upon them float;
And canoes, like flakes of the silvery snow,
Thro' the tall, rustling rice-beds come and go.

Green are its forests; no warrior wind
  Rushes on war trail the dusk grove through,
With leaf-scalps of tall trees mourning behind;
  But South Wind, heart friend of Great Manitou,
When ferns and leaves with cool dews are wet,
Blows flowery breaths from his red calumet.

Never upon them the white frosts lie,
  Nor glow their green boughs with the "paint of death";
Manitou smiles in the crystal sky,
  Close breathing above them His life-strong breath;
And He speaks no more in fierce thunder sound,
So near is His happy hunting-ground.

Yet often I love, in my white canoe,
  To come to the forests and camps of earth:
'Twas there death's black arrow pierced me through;
  'Twas there my red-browed mother gave me birth;
There I, in the light of a young man's dawn,
Won the lily heart of dusk "Springing Fawn."

And love is a cord woven out of life,
  And dyed in the red of the living heart;
And time is the hunter's rusty knife,
  That cannot cut the red strands apart:
And I sail from the spirit shore to scan
Where the weaving of that strong cord began.

But I may not come with a giftless hand,
  So richly I pile, in my white canoe,
Flowers that bloom in the spirit land,
  Immortal smiles of Great Manitou.
When I paddle back to the shores of earth
I scatter them over the white man's hearth.

For love is the breath of the soul set free;
  So I cross the river that darkly rolls,

That my spirit may whisper soft to thee
  Of *thine* who wait in the "Camp of Souls."
When the bright day laughs, or the wan night grieves,
Come the dusky plumes of red "Singing Leaves."
(1880)

The Earth Waxeth Old

When yellow-lock'd and crystal ey'd
  I dream'd green woods among;
Where tall trees waved from side to side,
And in their green breasts deep and wide,
I saw the building blue jay hide,
  O, then the earth was young!

The winds were fresh and brave and bold,
  The red sun round and strong;
No prophet voice chill, loud and cold,
Across my woodland dreamings roll'd,
"The green earth waxeth sere and old,
  That once was fair and young!"

I saw in scarr'd and knotty bole,
  The fresh'ning of the sap;
When timid spring gave first small dole,
Of sunbeams thro' bare boughs that stole,
I saw the bright'ning blossoms roll,
  From summer's high pil'd lap.

And where an ancient oak tree lay
  The forest stream across,
I mus'd above the sweet shrill spray,
I watch'd the speckl'd trout at play,
I saw the shadows dance and sway
  On ripple and on moss.

I pull'd the chestnut branches low,
  As o'er the stream they hung,
To see their bursting buds of snow—
I heard the sweet spring waters flow—
My heart and I we did not know
  But that the earth was young!

I joy'd in solemn woods to see,
  Where sudden sunbeams clung,
On open space of mossy lea,
The violet and anemone,
Wave their frail heads and beckon me—
  Sure then the earth was young!

I heard the fresh wild breezes birr,
  New budded boughs among,
I saw the deeper tinting stir
In the green tassels of the fir,
I heard the pheasant rise and whirr,
  Above her callow young.

I saw the tall fresh ferns prest,
  By scudding doe and fawn;
I saw the grey dove's swelling breast,
Above the margin of her nest;
When north and south and east and west
  Roll'd all the red of dawn.

At eventide at length I lay,
  On grassy pillow flung;
I saw the parting bark of day,
With crimson sails and shrouds all gay,
With golden fires drift away,
  The billowy clouds among.

I saw the stately planets sail
  On that blue ocean wide;

I saw blown by some mystic gale,
Like silver ship in elfin tale,
That bore some damsel rare and pale,
  The moon's slim crescent glide.

And ev'ry throb of spring that shook
  The rust'ling boughs among,
That filled the silver vein of brook,
That lit with bloom the mossy nook,
Cried to my boyish bosom: "Look!
  How fresh the earth and young!"

The winds were fresh, the days as c[lear]
  As crystals set in gold.
No shape, with prophet-mantle drear,
Thro' those old woods came drifting near,
To whisper in my wond'ring ear,
  "The green earth waxeth old."
(1883)

The Dark Stag

A startled stag, the blue-grey Night,
  Leaps down beyond black pines.
Behind—a length of yellow light—
  The hunter's arrow shines:
His moccasins are stained with red,
  He bends upon his knee,
From covering peaks his shafts are sped,
The blue mists plume his mighty head,—
   Well may the swift Night flee!

The pale, pale Moon, a snow-white doe,
  Bounds by his dappled flank:
They beat the stars down as they go,
  Like wood-bells growing rank.

The winds lift dewlaps from the ground,
  Leap from the quaking reeds;
Their hoarse bays shake the forests round,
With keen cries on the track they bound,—
  Swift, swift the dark stag speeds!

Away! his white doe, far behind,
  Lies wounded on the plain;
Yells at his flank the nimblest wind,
  His large tears fall in rain;
Like lily-pads, small clouds grow white
  About his darkling way;
From his bald nest upon the height
The red-eyed eagle sees his flight;
He falters, turns, the antlered Night,—
  The dark stag stands at bay!

His feet are in the waves of space;
  His antlers broad and dun
He lowers; he turns his velvet face
  To front the hunter, Sun;
He stamps the lilied clouds, and high
  His branches fill the west.
The lean stork sails across the sky,
The shy loon shrieks to see him die,
  The winds leap at his breast.

Roar the rent lakes as thro' the wave
  Their silver warriors plunge,
As vaults from core of crystal cave
  The strong, fierce muskallunge;
Red torches of the sumach glare,
  Fall's council-fires are lit;
The bittern, squaw-like, scolds the air;
The wild duck splashes loudly where
  The rustling rice-spears knit.

Shaft after shaft the red Sun speeds:
  Rent the stag's dappled side,
His breast, fanged by the shrill winds, bleeds,
  He staggers on the tide;
He feels the hungry waves of space
  Rush at him high and blue;
Their white spray smites his dusky face,
Swifter the Sun's fierce arrows race
  And pierce his stout heart thro'.

His antlers fall; once more he spurns
  The hoarse hounds of the day;
His blood upon the crisp blue burns,
  Reddens the mounting spray;
His branches smite the wave—with cries
  The loud winds pause and flag—
He sinks in space—red glow the skies,
The brown earth crimsons as he dies,
  The strong and dusky stag.
(1883)

The Canoe

My masters twain made me a bed
Of pine-boughs resinous, and cedar;
Of moss, a soft and gentle breeder
Of dreams of rest; and me they spread
With furry skins, and laughing said,
"Now she shall lay her polish'd sides,
As queens do rest, or dainty brides,
Our slender lady of the tides!"

My masters twain their camp-soul lit,
Streamed incense from the hissing cones,
Large, crimson flashes grew and whirled[;]
Thin, golden nerves of sly light curl'd

Round the dun camp, and rose faint zones,
Half way about each grim bole knit,
Like a shy child that would bedeck
With its soft clasp a Brave's red neck;
Yet sees the rough shield on his breast,
The awful plumes shake on his crest,
And fearful drops his timid face,
Nor dares complete the sweet embrace.

Into the hollow hearts of brakes,
Yet warm from sides of does and stags,
Pass'd to the crisp dark river flags;
Sinuous, red as copper snakes,
Sharp-headed serpents, made of light,
Glided and hid themselves in night.

My masters twain, the slaughter'd deer
Hung on fork'd boughs—with thongs of leather.
Bound were his stiff, slim feet together—
His eyes like dead stars cold and drear;
The wand'ring firelight drew near
And laid its wide palm, red and anxious,
On the sharp splendor of his branches;
On the white foam grown hard and sere
  On flank and shoulder.
Death—hard as breast of granite boulder,
  And under his lashes
Peer'd thro' his eyes at his life's grey ashes.

My masters twain sang songs that wove
(As they burnish'd hunting blade and rifle)
A golden thread with a cobweb trifle—
Loud of the chase, and low of love.

"O Love, art thou a silver fish?
Shy of the line and shy of gaffing,
Which we do follow, fierce, yet laughing,

Casting at thee the light-wing'd wish,
And at the last shall we bring thee up
From the crystal darkness under the cup
  Of lily folden,
  On broad leaves golden?

"O Love! art thou a silver deer,
Swift thy starr'd feet as wing of swallow,
While we with rushing arrows follow;
And at the last shall we draw near,
And over thy velvet neck cast thongs—
Woven of roses, of stars, of songs?
  New chains all moulden
  Of rare gems olden!"

They hung the slaughter'd fish like swords
On saplings slender— like scimitars
Bright, and ruddied from new-dead wars,
Blaz'd in the light—the scaly hordes.

They pil'd up boughs beneath the trees,
Of cedar-web and green fir tassel;
Low did the pointed pine tops rustle,
The camp fire blush'd to the tender breeze.

The hounds laid dew-laps on the ground,
With needles of pine[,] sweet, soft and rusty—
Dream'd of the dead stag stout and lusty;
A bat by the red flames wove its round.

The darkness built its wigwam walls
Close round the camp, and at its curtain
Press'd shapes, thin woven and uncertain,
As white locks of tall waterfalls.
(1884)

Isabella Valancy Crawford

The Lily Bed

His cedar paddle, scented, red,
He thrust down through the lily bed;

Cloaked in a golden pause he lay,
Locked in the arms of the placid bay.

Trembled alone his bark canoe
As shocks of bursting lilies flew

Thro' the still crystal of the tide,
And smote the frail boat's birchen side;

Or, when beside the sedges thin
Rose the sharp silver of a fin;

Or when, a wizard swift and cold,
A dragon-fly beat out in gold

And jewels all the widening rings
Of waters singing to his wings;

Or, like a winged and burning soul,
Dropped from the gloom an oriole

On the cool wave, as to the balm
Of the Great Spirit's open palm

The freed soul flies. And silence clung
To the still hours, as tendrils hung,

In darkness carven, from the trees,
Sedge-buried to their burly knees.

Stillness sat in his lodge of leaves;
Clung golden shadows to its eaves,

And on its cone-spiced floor, like maize,
Red-ripe, fell sheaves of knotted rays.

The wood, a proud and crested brave;
Bead-bright, a maiden, stood the wave.

And he had spoke his soul of love
With voice of eagle and of dove.

Of loud, strong pines his tongue was made;
His lips, soft blossoms in the shade,

That kissed her silver lips—hers cool
As lilies on his inmost pool—

Till now he stood, in triumph's rest,
His image painted in her breast.

One isle 'tween blue and blue did melt,—
A bead of wampum from the belt

Of Manitou—a purple rise
On the far shore heaved to the skies.

His cedar paddle, scented, red,
He drew up from the lily bed;

All lily-locked, all lily-locked,
His light bark in the blossoms rocked.

Their cool lips round the sharp prow sang,
Their soft clasp to the frail sides sprang,

With breast and lip they wove a bar.
Stole from her lodge the Evening Star;

With golden hand she grasped the mane
Of a red cloud on her azure plain.

It by the peaked, red sunset flew;
Cool winds from its bright nostrils blew.

They swayed the high, dark trees, and low
Swept the locked lilies to and fro.

With cedar paddle, scented, red,
He pushed out from the lily bed.
(1884)

The Hidden Room

I marvel if my heart,
Hath any room apart,
Built secretly its mystic walls within;
With subtly warded key

Ne'er yielded unto me—
Where even I have surely never been.

Ah, surely I know all
The bright and cheerful hall
With the fire ever red upon its hearth;
My friends dwell with me there,
Nor comes the step of Care
To sadden down its music and its mirth.

Full well I know as mine,
The little cloister'd shrine
No foot but mine alone hath ever trod;
There come the shining wings—
The face of one who brings
The pray'rs of men before the throne of God.

And many know full well,
The busy, busy cell,
Where I toil at the work I have to do,
Nor is the portal fast,
Where stand phantoms of the past,
Or grow the bitter plants of darksome rue.

I know the dainty spot
(Ah, who doth know it not?)
Where pure young Love his lily-cradle made;
And nestled some sweet springs
With lily-spangled wings—
Forget-me-nots upon his bier I laid.

Yet marvel I, my soul,
Know I thy very whole,
Or dost thou hide a chamber still from me?
Is it built upon the wall?
Is it spacious? is it small?
Is it God, or man, or I who holds the key?
(1884)

Gisli: the Chieftain

[Part I]

To the Goddess Lada prayed
Gisli, holding high his spear
Bound with buds of spring, and laughed
All his heart to Lada's ear.

Damp his yellow beard with mead,
Loud the harps clang'd thro['] the day;
With bruised breasts triumphant rode
Gisli's galleys in the bay.

Bards sang in the banquet hall,
  Set in loud verse Gisli's fame,
On their lips the war gods laid
  Fire to chaunt their warrior's name.

To the Love-queen Gisli pray'd,
  Buds upon his tall spear's tip;
Laughter in his broad blue eyes,
  Laughter on his bearded lip.

To the Spring-queen Gisli pray'd,
  She, with mystic distaff slim,
Spun her hours of love and leaves,
  Made the stony headlands dim—

Dim and green with tender grass,
  Blew on ice-fields with red mouth;
Blew on lovers['] hearts; and lured
  White swans from the blue-arched south.

To the Love-queen Gisli pray'd,
  Groan'd far icebergs tall and blue
As to Lada's distaff slim,
  All their ice-locked fires flew.

To the Love-queen Gisli prayed,
  She, with red hands, caught and spun
Yellow flames from crater lips,
  Long flames from the waking sun.

To the Love-queen Gisli prayed,
  She with loom and beam and spell,
All the subtle fires of earth
  Wove, and wove them strong and well.

To the Spring-queen Gisli prayed,
  Low the sun the pale sky trod;

Mute her ruddy hand she raised
  Beckon'd back the parting God.

To the Love-queen Gisli prayed—
  Weft and woof of flame she wove—
Lada, Goddess of the Spring!
  Lada, Goddess strong of Love!

Sire of the strong chieftain's prayer,
  Victory with his pulse of flame;
Mead its mother—loud he laughed,
  Calling on great Lada's name.

"Goddess Lada—Queen of Love!
  "Here stand I and quaff to thee—
"Deck for thee with buds my spear—
  "Give a comely wife to me!

"Blow not to my arms a flake
  "Of crisp snow in maiden guise;
"Mists of pallid hair and tips
  " Of long ice-spears in her eyes!

"When my death-sail skims the foam—
  "Strain my oars on Death's black sea—
"When my foot the "Glass-Hill" seeks—
  "Such a maid may do for me!

"Now, O Lada, mate the flesh!
  "Mate the fire and flame of life,
"Tho' the soul go still unwed,
  "Give the flesh its fitting wife!

"As the galley runs between,
  "Skies with billows closely spun;
"Feeling but the wave that leaps
  "Closest to it in the sun

"Throbs but to the present kiss
  "Of the wild lips of the sea;
"Thus a man joys in his life—
  "Nought of the Beyond knows he!

"Goddess! here I cast bright buds,
  "Spicy pine boughs at thy feet;
"Give the flesh its fitting mate
  "Life is strong and life is sweet![”]

To the Love-queen Gisli pray'd—
  Weft and woof of flame she wove:
Lada, Goddess of the Spring—
  Lada, Goddess strong of Love!

Part II

From harpings and sagas and mirth of the town,
Great Gisli, the chieftain[,] strode merrily down.

His ruddy beard stretch'd in the loom of the wind,
His shade like a dusky God striding behind.

Gylfag, his true hound, to his heel glided near,
Sharp-fang'd, lank and red as a blood-rusted spear.

As crests of the green bergs flame white in the sky,
The town on its sharp hill shone brightly and high.

In fiords roared the ice [shields;] below the dumb
    stroke
Of the Sun's red hammer rose blue mist like smoke.

It clung to the black pines, and clung to the bay—
The galleys of Gisli grew ghosts of the day.

It followed the sharp wings of swans, as they rose—
It fell to the wide jaws of swift riven floes;

It tam'd the wild shriek of the eagle—grew dull
The cries, in its foldings, of osprey and gull.

"Arouse thee, bold wind," shouted Gisli "and drive
"Floe and Berg out to sea as bees from a hive.

"Chase this woman-lipped haze at top of thy speed,
"It cloys to the soul as the tongue cloys with mead!

"Come, buckle thy sharp spear again to thy breast!
"Thy galley hurl forth from the seas of the West.

"With the long, hissing oars, beat loud the north sea.
"The sharp gaze of day give the eagles and me.

"No cunning mists shrouding the sea and the sky,
"Or the brows of the great Gods, bold wind, love I!

"As Gylfag, my hound, lays his fangs in the flank
"Of a grey wolf, shadowy, leather-thew'd, lank.

"Bold wind, chase the blue mist, thy prow in its hair,
"Sun, speed thy keen shafts thro' the breast of the air![”]

Part III

The shouting of Gisli, the chieftain,
Rock'd the blue hazes, and cloven
In twain by sharp prow of the west wind,
To north and to south fled the thick mist.

As in burnish'd walls of Valhalla,
In cleft of the mist stood the chieftain,

And up to the blue shield of Heaven,
Flung the loud shaft of his laughter.

Smote the mist, with shrill spear the swift wind,
Grey shapes fled like ghosts on the Hell way;
Bay'd after their long locks hoarse Gylfag,
Stared at them, triumphant, the eagles.

To mate and to eaglets, the eagle
Shriek'd, "Gone is my foe of the deep mist,
"Rent by the vast hands of the kind Gods,
"Who know the knife-pangs of our hunger!"

Shrill whistled the wind as his dun wings
Strove with it feather by feather;
Loud grated the rock as his talons
Spurned slowly its breast; and his red eyes

Like fires seemed to flame in the swift wind,
At his sides the darts of his hunger—
At his ears the shriek of his eaglets—
In his breast the love of the quarry.

Unfurl'd to the northward and southward
His wings broke the air, and to eastward
His breast gave its iron; and God-ward
Pierc'd the shrill voice of his hunger.

Bared were his great sides as he laboured
Up the first steep blue of the broad sky;
His gaze on the fields of his freedom,
To the Gods spoke the prayers of his gyres.

Bared were his vast sides as he glided
Black in the sharp blue of the north sky;
Black over the white of the tall cliffs,
Black over the arrow of Gisli.

The Song of the Arrow

What know I,
As I bite the blue veins of the throbbing sky;
To the quarry's breast,
Hot from the sides of the sleek smooth nest?

What know I
Of the will of the tense bow from which I fly!
What the need or jest
That feathers my flight to its bloody rest.

What know I
Of the will of the bow that speeds me on high?
What doth the shrill bow
Of the hand on its singing soul-string know?

Flame-swift speed I—
And the dove and the eagle shriek out and die;
Whence comes my sharp zest
For the heart of the quarry? the Gods know best.

Deep pierc'd the red gaze of the eagle—
The breast of a cygnet below him;
Beneath his dun wing from the eastward
Shrill-chaunted the long shaft of Gisli!

Beneath his dun wing from the westward
Shook a shaft that laugh'd in its biting—
Met in the fierce breast of the eagle
The arrows of Gisli and Brynhild!

Part IV

A ghost along the Hell-way sped,
The Hell-shoes shod his misty tread;
A phantom hound beside him sped.

Beneath the spandrils of the Way,
Worlds roll'd to-night—from night to day;
In space's ocean Suns were spray.

Group'd worlds, eternal eagles, flew;
Swift comets fell like noiseless dew;
Young earths slow budded in the blue.

The waves of space inscrutable,
With awful pulses rose and fell—
Silent and godly—terrible.

Electric souls of strong Suns laid,
Strong hands along the awful shade
That God about His God-work made.

Ever from all ripe worlds did break
Men's voices, as when children speak,
Eager and querulous and weak.

And pierc'd to the All-worker thro'
His will that veil'd Him from the view[:]
"What hast thou done? What dost thou do?"

And ever from His heart did flow
Majestical, the answer low—
The benison "Ye shall not know![")]

The wan ghost on the Hell-way sped,
Nor yet Valhalla's lights were shed
Upon the white brow of the Dead.

Nor sang within his ears the roll
Of trumpets calling to his soul;
Nor shone wide portals of the goal.

His spear grew heavy on his breast,
Dropp'd, like a star[,] his golden crest;
Far, far the vast Halls of the Blest!

His heart grown faint, his feet grown weak,
He scal'd the knit mists of a peak,
That ever parted grey and bleak.

And, as by unseen talons nipp'd,
To deep Abysses slowly slipp'd;
Then, swift as thick smoke strongly ripp'd

By whirling winds from ashy ring,
Of dank weeds blackly smoldering,
The peak sprang upward, quivering

And perdurable, set its face
Against the pulsing breast of space
But for a moment; to its base

Refluent roll'd the crest new sprung,
In clouds with ghastly lightnings stung,—
Faint thunders to their black feet clung.

His faithful hound ran at his heel—
His thighs and breast were bright with steel—
He saw the awful Hellway reel.

But far along its bleak peaks rang
A distant trump—its airy clang
Like light through deathly shadows sprang.

He knew the blast—the voice of love!
Cleft lay the throbbing peak above
Sail'd light, wing'd like a silver dove.

On strove the toiling ghost, his soul
Stirr'd like strong mead in wassail bowl,
That quivers to the shout of "Skoal!"

Strode from the mist close-curv'd and cold
As is a writhing dragon's fold;
A warrior with shield of gold.

A sharp blade glitter'd at his hip,
Flamed like a star his lance's tip;
His bugle sang at bearded lip.

Beneath his golden sandals flew
Stars from the mist as grass flings dew;
Or red fruit falls from the dark yew.

As under shelt'ring wreaths of snow
The dark blue north flowers richly blow—
Beneath long locks of silver glow

Clear eyes, that burning on a host
Would win a field at sunset lost,
Ere stars from Odin's hand were toss'd.

He stretch'd his hand, he bowed his head;
The wan ghost to his bosom sped—
Dead kiss'd the bearded lips of Dead!

"What dost thou here, my youngest born?
"Thou—scarce yet fronted with life's storm—
"Why art thou from the dark earth torn?

"When high Valhalla puls'd and rang
"With harps that shook as grey bards sang—
"'Mid the loud joy I heard the clang

"Of Death's dark doors—to me alone
"Smote in thy awful dying groan—
"My soul recall'd its blood and bone.

"Viewless the cord which draws from far
"To the round sun some mighty star;
"Viewless the strong-knit soul-cords are!

"I felt thy dying gasp—thy soul
"Towards mine a kindred wave in roll,
"I left the harps—I left the bowl.

"I sought the Hellway—I—the blest;
"That thou, new death-born son should rest
"Upon the strong rock of my breast.

"What dost thou here, young, fair and bold?
"Sleek with youth's gloss thy locks of gold;
"Thy years by flow'rs might yet be told!

"What dost thou at the ghostly goal,
"While yet thy years were to thy soul,
"As mead yet shallow in the bowl?"

His arm about the pale ghost cast,
The warrior blew a clear, loud blast;
Like frighten'd wolves the mists fled past.

Grew firm the way; worlds flame to light
The awful peak that thrusts its height,
With swift throbs upward, like a flight

Of arrows from a host close set
Long meteors pierc'd its breast of jet—
Again the trump his strong lips met—

And at its blast blew all the day,
In broad winds on the awful Way;
Sun smote at Sun across the grey;

As reindeer smite the high-pil'd snow
To find the green moss far below—
They struck the mists thro' which did glow

Bright vales— and on a sea afar,
Lay at a sunlit harbour bar,
A galley gold-sail'd like a star!

Spake the pale ghost as onward sped
Heart press'd to heart the valiant dead;
Soft the green paths beneath their tread.

"I loved, this is my tale, and died—
"The fierce chief hunger'd for my bride—
"The spear of Gisli pierc'd my side!

"And she—her love fill'd all my need—
"Her vows were sweet and strong as mead;
"Look, father—doth my heart still bleed?

"I built her round with shaft and spear,
"I kept her mine for one brief year—
"She laugh'd above my blood-stain'd bier!

"Upon a far and ice-peak'd coast
"My galleys by long winds were toss'd—
"There Gisli feasted with his host

"Of warriors triumphant—he
"Strode out from harps and revelry;
"And sped his shaft above the sea!

“Look, father, doth my heart bleed yet?
“His arrow Brynhild’s arrow met—
“My galleys anchor’d in their rest.

“Again their arrows meet—swift lies
“That pierc’d me from their smiling eyes;
“How fiercely hard a man’s heart dies!

“She false—he false! There came a day
“Pierc’d by the fierce chief’s spear I lay—
“My ghost rose shrieking from its clay.

“I saw on Brynhild’s golden vest
“The shining locks of Gisli rest;
“I sought the Hell-way to the Blest.

“Father, put forth thy hand and tear
“Their twin shafts from my heart, all bare
“To thee—they rankle death-like there.[”]

* * *

Said the voice of Evil to the ear of Good,
  “Clasp thou my strong, right hand,
“Nor shall our clasp be known or understood
  “By any in the land.

“I, the dark giant, rule strongly on the earth,
  “Yet thou, bright one, and I
“Sprang from the one great mystery—at one birth
  “We looked upon the sky!

“I labour at my bleak, my stern toil[,] accurs’d
  “Of all mankind— nor stay,
“To rest, to murmur ‘I hunger!’ or ‘I thirst!’
  “Nor for my joy delay.

"My strength pleads strongly with thee; doth any beat
"With hammer and with stone[,]
"Past tools[,] to use them to his deep defeat—
"To turn them on his throne?

"Then I of God the mystery—toil thou with me
"Brother; but in the sight
"Of men who know not, I, the stern son shall be
"Of Darkness—Thou of Light!"
(1884)

William Wilfred Campbell (1860-1918)

William Wilfred Campbell is well summarized by Carl F. Klinck: "Rugged and self-reliant, yet imaginative and reverent, he fought his way through earthly storms without forgetting the sublime" (17). Born in 1860 in Canada West, Campbell was the son and grandson of Anglican clergymen. His family moved to Wiarton in 1872, and the scenery around Lake Huron and Georgian Bay appears in many of his best poems. After working briefly as a teacher and studying at the University of Toronto, Campbell entered first Wycliffe College (Toronto Anglican divinity school) then Episcopal Theological School (Cambridge, Massachusetts). He graduated and was ordained in 1885, then served various parishes in New England, New Brunswick, and Ontario. He frequently published poems in the most prestigious American journals, and his first substantial collection, *Lake Lyrics and Other Poems*, appeared in 1889. In 1891 Campbell moved to Ottawa and joined the Civil Service, having left "$1,200 a year and a rectory to live a richer life at $500 a year" (see Klinck 49). His struggles to retain his faith are reflected in a controversial *Mermaid Inn* column (in the Toronto *Globe*) on the "mythic" status of the Bible and in the poems in *The Dread Voyage* (1893). In 1895, he initiated the "war among the poets" when he publicly accused Carman of "log-rolling" and plagiarism. As Alexandra J. Hurst argues, however, Campbell was "prone to a jealousy of his more successful peers" (xxiii). After he published *Beyond the Hills of Dream* with Houghton Mifflin of Boston in 1899, his interest in Imperialism caused him to turn away from American culture. His growing faith in Empire and his own spiritualism ("Calvinism without creeds," in Klinck's phrase—see 257) are apparent in the 1905 *Collected Poems*, much of which was written in the previous five years. Andrew Carnegie was so impressed with the book that he ordered a special edition for his libraries. In the last fifteen years before his death in 1918, he was active as a novelist, anthologist, and popular historian in addition to his work as a civil servant and as a poet. His closet dramas were collected in *Poetical Tragedies* (1908), while *Sagas of Vaster Britain* and his anthology, *The Oxford Book of Canadian Verse*, appeared in 1914.

The restlessness that is evident in any summary of Campbell's life also appears in his poetry. As Terry Whalen has argued, Campbell "often explored different and contradictory perspectives in different poems of the same collection" ("Poetry of Celebration" 29). Strong interests in nature poetry, history, Classical mythology, and folklore pervade his work; his early career is notable for the quiet nature poems set in his beloved lake region, while his work after 1900 is increasingly marked by the Imperial theme. Posterity has been harsher on Campbell than on the other Confederation poets, even Carman, but generally speaking the *Lake Lyrics* have endured better than the *Sagas of Vaster Britain.* When the characters in Alice Munro's "The Ottawa Valley" recite poetry, they remember "Indian Summer," not "The Lazarus of Empire." Nonetheless, Campbell's occasional poems had an immediate response from a large audience, and so this selection includes "The Dead Leader," Campbell's elegy for John A. Macdonald, as well as "Bereavement of the Fields," his elegy for Archibald Lampman. It also includes "The Mother," which caused a stir in both the U.S. and Canada after it appeared in *Harper's* in 1891, and two fine poems on mythical subjects, "Pan the Fallen" and "Phaethon." As Lampman wrote in a July 5, 1897 letter to E.W. Thomson, "He is a rum card—Campbell—but he has the power of making himself felt."

Further Reading

Bentley, D.M.R. "'Along the Line of Smoky Hills': further Steps Towards an Ecological Poetics." *Canadian Poetry: Studies, Documents, Reviews* 26 (1990): v-xix.

Boone, Laurel, ed. "The Collected Poems of William Wilfred Campbell." Diss. U of New Brunswick, 1981.

———. "Wilfred Campbell Reconsidered." *Canadian Literature* 94 (1982): 67-82.

Campbell, William Wilfred. *Selected Poetry and Essays*. Ed. Laurel Boone. Waterloo: Wilfrid Laurier UP, 1987.

Fisher IV, Benjamin Franklin. "King Arthur Plays from the 1890s." *Victorian Poetry* 28: 3-4 (1990): 153-76.

Hurst, Alexandra J., ed. *The War Among the Poets: Issues of Plagiarism and Patronage Among the Confederation Poets*. London ON: Canadian Poetry Press, 1994.

Klinck, Carl F. *Wilfred Campbell: A Study in Late Provincial Victorianism*. 1942. Ottawa: Tecumseh, 1977.

Knister, Raymond. "The Poetical Works of Wilfred Campbell." *Queen's Quarterly* 31 (1924): 435-49. *The First Day of Spring: Stories and Other Prose*. Ed. Peter Stevens. Literature of Canada. Toronto: U of Toronto P, 1976. 440-54.

Ower, John. "Portraits of the Landscape as Poet: Canadian Nature as Aesthetic Symbol in Three Confederation Writers." *Journal of Canadian Studies* 6 (1971): *27-32. Twentieth-Century Essays on Confederation Literature*. Ed. Lorraine McMullen. Ottawa: Tecumseh, 1976. 140-51.

Whalen, Terry. "Wilfred Campbell: The Poetry of Celebration and Harmony," "The Poetry of Doubt," "The Poetry of Mysticism," *Journal of Canadian Poetry* 1:2 (1978): 27-41; 2:2 (1979): 35-47; 3:1 (1980): 39-61.

Wicken, George. "William Wilfred Campbell." *Canadian Writers and Their Works, Poetry Series: Volume Two*. Ed. Robert Lecker, Jack David, and Ellen Quigley. Downsview ON: ECW, 1983. 25-74.

William Wilfred Campbell

Indian Summer

Along the line of smoky hills
  The crimson forest stands,
And all the day the blue-jay calls
  Throughout the autumn lands.

Now by the brook the maple leans
  With all his glory spread,
And all the sumachs on the hills
  Have turned their green to red.

Now by great marshes wrapt in mist,
  Or past some river's mouth,
Throughout the long, still autumn day
  Wild birds are flying south.
(1881)

The Winter Lakes

Out in a world of death far to the northward lying,
  Under the sun and the moon, under the dusk and the
      day;
Under the glimmer of stars and the purple of sunsets
      dying,
  Wan and waste and white, stretch the great lakes away.

Never a bud of spring, never a laugh of summer,
  Never a dream of love, never a song of bird;
But only the silence and white, the shores that grow
      chiller and dumber,
  Wherever the ice winds sob, and the griefs of winter
      are heard.

Crags that are black and wet out of the grey lake
      looming,

Under the sunset's flush and the pallid, faint glimmer of dawn;
Shadowy, ghost-like shores, where midnight surfs are booming
Thunders of wintry woe over the spaces wan.

Lands that loom like spectres, whited regions of winter,
Wastes of desolate woods, deserts of water and shore;
A world of winter and death, within these regions who enter,
Lost to summer and life, go to return no more.

Moons that glimmer above, waters that lie white under,
Miles and miles of lake far out under the night;
Foaming crests of waves, surfs that shoreward thunder,
Shadowy shapes that flee, haunting the spaces white.

Lonely hidden bays, moon-lit, ice-rimmed, winding,
Fringed by forests and crags, haunted by shadowy shores;
Hushed from the outward strife, where the mighty surf is grinding
Death and hate on the rocks, as sandward and landward it roars.
(1889)

Vapor and Blue

Domed with the azure of heaven,
Floored with a pavement of pearl,
Clothed all about with a brightness
Soft as the eyes of a girl,

Girt with a magical girdle,
Rimmed with a vapor of rest—

These are the inland waters,
These are the lakes of the west.

Voices of slumberous music,
Spirits of mist and of flame,
Moonlit memories left here
By gods who long ago came,

And vanishing left but an echo
In silence of moon-dim caves,
Where haze-wrapt the August night slumbers,
Or the wild heart of October raves.

Here where the jewels of nature
Are set in the light of God's smile;
Far from the world's wild throbbing,
I will stay me and rest me awhile.

And store in my heart old music,
Melodies gathered and sung
By the genies of love and of beauty
When the heart of the world was young.
(1889)

How One Winter Came in the Lake Region

For weeks and weeks the autumn world stood still,
Clothed in the shadow of a smoky haze;
The fields were dead, the wind had lost its will,
And all the lands were hushed by wood and hill,
In those grey, withered days.

Behind a mist the blear sun rose and set,
At night the moon would nestle in a cloud;
The fisherman, a ghost, did cast his net;

The lake its shores forgot to chafe and fret,
  And hushed its caverns loud.

Far in the smoky woods the birds were mute,
  Save that from blackened tree a jay would scream,
Or far in swamps the lizard's lonesome lute
Would pipe in thirst, or by some gnarlèd root
  The tree-toad trilled his dream.

From day to day still hushed the season's mood,
  The streams stayed in their runnels shrunk and dry;
Suns rose aghast by wave and shore and wood,
And all the world, with ominous silence, stood
  In weird expectancy:

When one strange night the sun like blood went down,
  Flooding the heavens in a ruddy hue;
Red grew the lake, the sere fields parched and brown,
Red grew the marshes where the creeks stole down,
  But never a wind-breath blew.

That night I felt the winter in my veins,
  A joyous tremor of the icy glow;
And woke to hear the north's wild vibrant strains,
While far and wide, by withered woods and plains,
  Fast fell the driving snow.
(1890)

Pan the Fallen

He wandered into the market
  With pipes and goatish hoof;
He wandered in a grotesque shape,
  And no one stood aloof.
For the children crowded round him,
  The wives and greybeards, too,

To crack their jokes and have their mirth,
And see what Pan would do.

The Pan he was they knew him,
Part man, but mostly beast,
Who drank, and lied, and snatched what bones
Men threw him from their feast;
Who seemed in sin so merry,
So careless in his woe,
That men despised, scarce pitied him,
And still would have it so.

He swelled his pipes and thrilled them,
And drew the silent tear;
He made the gravest clack with mirth
By his sardonic leer.
He blew his pipes full sweetly
At their amused demands,
And caught the scornful, earth-flung pence
That fell from careless hands.

He saw the mob's derision,
And took it kindly, too,
And when an epithet was flung,
A coarser back he threw;
But under all the masking
Of a brute, unseemly part,
I looked, and saw a wounded soul,
And a god-like, breaking heart.

And back of the elfin music,
The burlesque, clownish play,
I knew a wail that the weird pipes made,
A look that was far away,—
A gaze into some far heaven
Whence a soul had fallen down;
But the mob only saw the grotesque beast
And the antics of the clown.

For scant-flung pence he paid them
  With mirth and elfin play,
Till, tired for a time of his antics queer,
  They passed and went their way;
Then there in the empty market
  He ate his scanty crust,
And, tired face turned to heaven, down
  He laid him in the dust.

And over his wild, strange features
  A softer light there fell,
And on his worn, earth-driven heart
  A peace ineffable.
And the moon rose over the market,
  But Pan the beast was dead;
While Pan the god lay silent there,
  With his strange, distorted head.

And the people, when they found him,
  Stood still with awesome fear.
No more they saw the beast's rude hoof,
  The furtive, clownish leer;
But the lightest spirit in that audience
  Went silent from the place,
For they knew the look of a god released
  That shone from his dead face.
(1890)

The Mother

It was April, blossoming spring,
They buried me, when the birds did sing;

Earth, in clammy wedging earth,
They banked my bed with a black, damp girth.

Under the damp and under the mould,
I kenned my breasts were clammy and cold.

Out from the red beams, slanting and bright,
I kenned my cheeks were sunken and white.

I was a dream, and the world was a dream,
And yet I kenned all things that seem.

I was a dream, and the world was a dream,
But you cannot bury a red sunbeam.

For though in the under-grave's doom-night
I lay all silent and stark and white,

Yet over my head I seemed to know
The murmurous moods of wind and snow,

The snows that wasted, the winds that blew,
The rays that slanted, the clouds that drew

The water-ghosts up from lakes below,
And the little flower-souls in earth that grow.

Under earth, in the grave's stark night,
I felt the stars and the moon's pale light.

I felt the winds of ocean and land
That whispered the blossoms soft and bland.

Though they had buried me dark and low,
My soul with the season's seemed to grow.

II

I was a bride in my sickness sore,
I was a bride nine months and more.

From throes of pain they had buried me low,
For death had finished a mother's woe.

But under the sod, in the grave's dread doom,
I dreamed of my baby in glimmer and gloom.

I dreamed of my babe, and I kenned that his rest
Was broken in wailings on my dead breast.

I dreamed that a rose-leaf hand did cling:
Oh, you cannot bury a mother in spring.

When the winds are soft and the blossoms are red
She could not sleep in her cold earth-bed.

I dreamed of my babe for a day and a night,
And then I rose in my grave-clothes white.

I rose like a flower from my damp earth-bed
To the world of sorrowing overhead.

Men would have called me a thing of harm,
But dreams of my babe made me rosy and warm.

I felt my breasts swell under my shroud;
No stars shone white, no winds were loud;

But I stole me past the graveyard wall,
For the voice of my baby seemed to call;

And I kenned me a voice, though my lips were dumb:
Hush, baby, hush! for mother is come.

I passed the streets to my husband's home;
The chamber stairs in a dream I clomb;

I heard the sound of each sleeper's breath,
Light waves that break on the shores of death.

I listened a space at my chamber door,
Then stole like a moon-ray over its floor.

My babe was asleep on a stranger arm,
"O baby, my baby, the grave is so warm,

"Though dark and so deep, for mother is there!
O come with me from the pain and care!

"O come with me from the anguish of earth,
Where the bed is banked with a blossoming girth,

"Where the pillow is soft and the rest is long,
And mother will croon you a slumber-song,

"A slumber-song that will charm your eyes
To a sleep that never in earth-song lies!

"The loves of earth your being can spare,
But never the grave, for mother is there."

I nestled him soft to my throbbing breast,
And stole me back to my long, long rest.

And here I lie with him under the stars,
Dead to earth, its peace and its wars;

Dead to its hates, its hopes, and its harms,
So long as he cradles up soft in my arms.

And heaven may open its shimmering doors,
And saints make music on pearly floors,

And hell may yawn to its infinite sea,
But they never can take my baby from me.

For so much a part of my soul he hath grown
That God doth know of it high on His throne.

And here I lie with him under the flowers
That sun-winds rock through the billowy hours,

With the night-airs that steal from the murmuring sea,
Bringing sweet peace to my baby and me.
(1891)

The Dead Leader

(*Written on the day of Sir John A. Macdonald's Funeral, June 10th, 1891*)

Let the sad drums mutter low,
And the serried ranks move slow,
And the thousand hearts beat hushed along the street;
For a mighty heart is still,
And a great, unconquered will
Hath passed to meet the conqueror all must meet.

Outworn without assoil
From a great life's lengthened toil,
Laurelled with a half a century's fame;
From the care and adulation
To the heart-throb of the nation
He hath passed to be a memory and a name.

With banners draped and furled,
'Mid the sorrow of a world,
We lay him down with fitting pomp and state;
With slumber in his breast,
To his long, eternal rest
We lay him down, this man who made us great.

Him of the wider vision,
Who had one hope, elysian,
To mould a mighty empire toward the west:
Who through the hostile years,
'Mid the wrangling words, like spears,
Still bore this titan vision in his breast.

God gave this highest honor
To the nation, that upon her
He was spared to lay the magic of his hand;
Then to live to see the greatness
Of his noble work's completeness,
Then to pass to rest beloved by his land.

We stand at death's dim gates
Where his mighty soul awaits
Somewhere the long, long silence of the years.
And the marble of his lips
Doth all our woe eclipse,
Death's awful peace rolls back upon our tears.

Greater than all sorrow
That our hearts can borrow,
Loftier than our fleeting, human praise;
He hath calmness, great and grim,
That death hath granted him,
The wisest and the mightiest of our days.

Let the sad drums mutter low,
And the serried ranks move slow,

And the thousand hearts beat hushed along the street;
  For a mighty heart is still,
  And a great, unconquered will
Hath passed to meet the conqueror all must meet.
(1891)

The Dread Voyage

Trim the sails the weird stars under—
Past the iron hail and thunder,
Past the mystery and the wonder,
  Sails our fated bark;
Past the myriad voices hailing,
Past the moaning and the wailing,
The far voices failing, failing,
  Drive we to the dark.

Past the headlands grim and sombre,
Past the shores of mist and slumber,
Leagues on leagues no man may number,
  Soundings none can mark;
While the olden voices calling,
One by one behind are falling;
Into silence dread, appalling,
  Drift we to the dark.

Far behind, the sad eyes yearning,
Hands that wring for our returning,
Lamps of love yet vainly burning:
  Past the headlands stark!
Through the wintry snows and sleeting,
On our pallid faces beating,
Through the phantom twilight fleeting,
  Drive we to the dark.

Without knowledge, without warning,
Drive we to no lands of morning;
Far ahead no signals horning
  Hail our nightward bark.
Hopeless, helpless, weird, outdriven,
Fateless, friendless, dread, unshriven,
For some race-doom unforgiven,
  Drive we to the dark.

Not one craven or unseemly;
In the flare-light gleaming dimly,
Each ghost-face is watching grimly:
  Past the headlands stark!
Hearts wherein no hope may waken,
Like the clouds of night wind-shaken,
Chartless, anchorless, forsaken,
  Drift we to the dark.
(1893)

Morning on the Shore

The lake is blue with morning; and the sky
  Sweet, clear, and burnished as an orient pearl.
  High in its vastness, scream and skim and whirl
White gull-flocks where the gleaming beaches die
Into dim distance, where great marshes lie.
  Far in ashore the woods are warm with dreams,
  The dew-wet road in ruddy sunlight gleams,
The sweet, cool earth, the clear blue heaven on high.

Across the morn a carolling school-boy goes,
Filling the world with youth to heaven's stair;
  Some chattering squirrel answers from his tree;
But down beyond the headland, where ice-floes
Are great in winter, pleading in mute prayer,
  A dead, drowned face stares up immutably.
(1893)

An August Reverie

There is an autumn sense subdues the air,
  Though it is August and the season still
A part of summer, and the woodlands fair.
  I hear it in the humming of the mill,
I feel it in the rustling of the trees,
That scarcely shiver in the passing breeze.

'Tis but a touch of Winter ere his time,
  A presaging of sleep and icy death,
When skies are rich and fields are in their prime,
  And heaven and earth commingle in a breath:—
When hazy airs are stirred with gossamer wings,
And in shorn fields the shrill cicada sings.

So comes the slow revolving of the year,
  The glory of nature ripening to decay,
When in those paths by which, through loves austere,
  All men and beasts and blossoms find their way,
By steady easings of the spirit's dream,
From sunlight past the pallid starlight's beam.

Nor should the spirit sorrow as it passes,
  Declining slowly by the heights it came;
We are but brothers to the birds and grasses,
  In our brief coming and our end the same—
And though we glory, god-like in our day,
Perchance some kindred law their lives obey.

There are a thousand beauties gathered round,
  The sounds of waters falling over-night,
The morning scents that steamed from the fresh ground,
  The hair-like streaming of the morning light
Through early mists and dim, wet woods where brooks
Chatter, half-seen, down under mossy nooks.

The ragged daisy starring all the fields,
  The buttercup abrim with pallid gold,
The thistle and burr-flowers hedged with prickly shields,
  All common weeds the draggled pastures hold,
With shrivelled pods and leaves, are kin to me,
Like-heirs of earth and her maturity.

They speak a silent speech that is their own,
  These wise and gentle teachers of the grass;
And when their brief and common days are flown,
  A certain beauty from the year doth pass:—

A beauty of whose light no eye can tell,
Save that it went; and my heart knew it well.

I may not know each plant as some men know them,
  Like children gather beasts and birds to tame;
But I went 'mid them as the winds that blow them,
  From childhood's hour, and loved without a name:—
There is more beauty in a field of weeds,
Than in all blooms the hothouse garden breeds.

For they are nature's children, in their faces
  I see that sweet obedience to the sky
That marks these dwellers of the wilding places,
  Who with the season's being live and die;
Knowing no love but of the wind and sun,
Who still are nature's when their life is done.

They are a part of all the haze-filled hours,
  The happy, happy world all drenched with light,
The far-off, chiming click-clack of the mowers,
  And yon blue hills whose mists elude my sight,
And they to me will ever bring in dreams
Far mist-clad heights and brimming rain-fed streams.

In this dream August air, whose ripened leaf,
  Pausing before it puts death's glories on,

Deepens its green, and the half-garnered sheaf
  Gladdens the haze-filled sunlight; love hath gone
Beyond the material, trembling like a star,
To those sure heights where all thought's glories are.

And Thought, that is the greatness of this earth,
  And man's most inmost being, soars and soars,
Beyond the eye's horizon's outmost girth,
  Garners all beauty, on all mystery pores:—
Like some ethereal fountain in its flow,
Finds heavens where the senses may not go.
(1893)

Bereavement of the Fields

(*In Memory of Archibald Lampman, who died February 10, 1899*)

Soft fall the February snows, and soft
Falls on my heart the snow of wintry pain;
For never more, by wood or field or croft,
Will he we knew walk with his loved again;
No more, with eyes adream and soul aloft,
In those high moods where love and beauty reign,
Greet his familiar fields, his skies without a stain.

Soft fall the February snows, and deep,
Like downy pinions from the moulting breast
Of all the mothering sky, round his hushed sleep,
Flutter a million loves upon his rest,
Where once his well-loved flowers were fain to peep,
With adder-tongue and waxen petals prest,
In young spring evenings reddening down the west.

Soft fall the February snows, and hushed
Seems life's loud action, all its strife removed,
Afar, remote, where grief itself seems crushed,

And even hope and sorrow are reproved;
For he whose cheek erstwhile with hope was flushed,
And by the gentle haunts of being moved,
Hath gone the way of all he dreamed and loved.

Soft fall the February snows, and lost,
This tender spirit gone with scarce a tear,
Ere, loosened from the dungeons of the frost,
Wakens with yearnings new the enfranchised year,
Late winter-wizened, gloomed, and tempest-tost;
And Hesper's gentle, delicate veils appear,
When dream anew the days of hope and fear.

And Mother Nature, she whose heart is fain,
Yea, she who grieves not, neither faints nor fails,
Building the seasons, she will bring again
March with rudening madness of wild gales,
April and her wraiths of tender rain,
And all he loved,—this soul whom memory veils,
Beyond the burden of our strife and pain.

Not his to wake the strident note of song,
Nor pierce the deep recesses of the heart,
Those tragic wells, remote, of might and wrong;
But rather, with those gentler souls apart,
He dreamed like his own summer days along,
Filled with the beauty born of his own heart,
Sufficient in the sweetness of his song.

Outside this prison-house of all our tears,
Enfranchised from our sorrow and our wrong,
Beyond the failure of our days and years,
Beyond the burden of our saddest song,
He moves with those whose music filled his ears,
And claimed his gentle spirit from the throng,—
Wordsworth, Arnold, Keats, high masters of his song.

Like some rare Pan of those old Grecian days,
Here in our hours of deeper stress reborn,
Unfortunate thrown upon life's evil ways,
His inward ear heard ever that satyr horn
From Nature's lips reverberate night and morn,
And fled from men and all their troubled maze,
Standing apart, with sad, incurious gaze.

And now, untimely cut, like some sweet flower
Plucked in the early summer of its prime,
Before it reached the fulness of its dower,
He withers in the morning of our time;
Leaving behind him, like a summer shower,
A fragrance of earth's beauty, and the chime
Of gentle and imperishable rhyme.

Songs in our ears of winds and flowers and buds
And gentle loves and tender memories
Of Nature's sweetest aspects, her pure moods,
Wrought from the inward truth of intimate eyes
And delicate ears of him who harks and broods,
And, nightly pondering, daily grows more wise,
And dreams and sees in mighty solitudes.

Soft fall the February snows, and soft
He sleeps in peace upon the breast of her
He loved the truest; where, by wood and croft,
The wintry silence folds in fleecy blur
About his silence, while in glooms aloft
The mighty forest fathers, without stir,
Guard well the rest of him, their rare sweet worshipper.
(1899)

The Lazarus of Empire

The Celt, he is proud in his protest,
  The Scot, he is calm in his place,
For each has a word in the ruling and doom
  Of the Empire that honors his race;
And the Englishman, doggèd and grim,
  Looks the world in the face as he goes,
And he holds a proud lip, for he sails his own ship,
  And he cares not for rivals nor foes:—
But lowest and last, with his areas vast,
  And horizon so servile and tame,
Sits the poor beggar Colonial
  Who feeds on the crumbs of her fame.

He knows no place in her councils,
  He holds no part in the word
That girdles the world with its thunders
  When the fiat of Britain is heard:—
He beats no drums to her battles,
  He gives no triumphs her name,
But lowest and last, with his areas vast,
  He feeds on the crumbs of her fame.

How long, O how long, the dishonor,
  The servile and suppliant place?
Are we Britons who batten upon her,
  Or degenerate sons of the race?
It is souls that make nations, not numbers,
  As our forefathers proved in the past.
Let us take up the burden of empire,
  Or nail our own flag to the mast.
Doth she care for us, value us, want us,
  Or are we but pawns in the game;
Where lowest and last, with our areas vast,
  We feed on the crumbs of her fame?
(1899)

Phaethon

I Phaethon: dwelling in that golden house,
Which Hephaistos did build for my great sire,
Old Helios, king of glowing heaven and day;
Knowing this life but mortal in its span,
Hedged in by puling youth and palsied age,
Where poor men crawl like insects, knowing pain
And mighty sorrow to the gates of death;
Besought the god my father by his love,
To grant me that which I did long for most
Of all things great in earth and heaven and sea,
The which he granting in his mighty love,—
Of all things splendid under the splendid sky
Built of old by toil of ancient gods,
To me the dearest; for one round golden day,
To stand in his great chariot built of fire,
And chase the rosy hours from dawn to dusk,
Guiding his fleeting steeds o'er heaven's floors.
He gave to me.—No god yet brake his word.—
Speaking to me in sorrow: "O my son,
Know what thy foolish pride hath made for thee.
That mortal life which is to men a span,
From childhood unto youth, and manhood's prime,
Reaching on out to happy olden age,
For thee must shrink into one woeful day.
For, O my son, impetuous in thy pride,
Who would be as the gods and ape their ways,
And sacrilegious leave thy mortal bounds,—
Know thou must die upon that baleful day,
That terrible day of days thou mountest up
To ride that chariot never mortal rode,
And drive those steeds that never man hath driven.["]
Then I: "My father, know me, thine own son,
Better to me to live one day a god,
Going out in some great flame of death,
Than live this weary life of common men,

Misunderstood, misunderstanding still,
Half wakeful, moving dimly in a dream,
Confused, phantasmic, men call history;
Chasing the circles of the perishing suns,
The summers and dim winters, hating all,
Heart-eaten for a longing ne'er attained,
Despising all things named of earth or heaven,
Or mortal birth that they should ever be;
Knowing within this mystery of my being,
This curbed heredity, lies a latent dream
Of some old vanished, banished, lease of being,
When life was life and man's soul lived its hour,
Uncurbed, uncabined, like the mighty gods,
Vast, splendid, capable, and heraclean,
To drain the golden beaker of his days."
Thus I: "My father, I am over weary,
Chained in this summer-plot of circumstance,
Beaten by fearful custom, childish, chidden,
Hounded of cruel wolves of superstition,
And rounded by a petty wall of time,
Plodding the dreary years that wend their round,
Aping the sleeping, sensual life of beasts,
Fearful of all things, dreading mostly death,
Past pain and age and all their miseried end,
Where all must rot, who smile and weep and sleep,
And be a part of all this grim corruption.
Nay, better to me than the long-measured draught,
Trickling out through many anxious years,
Iron-eaten, haggard, to the place of death—
To drain my flagon of life in one glad draught,—
To live, to love, aspire, and dare all things;
Be all I am and others ought to be,
Real man or demi-god, to blossom my rose,
To scale my heights, to live my vastest dream,
To climb, to be, and then, if chance my fate,
To greatly fall."

Then my great father, laden
With woe divine: "My son, take thou thy way;
As thou hast chosen, thus 'twill be to thee;"
And passing, darkened down his godlike face,
And shadowed splendor thence forevermore.
'T was night ambrosial down the orient meads,
With stars like winking pearls far-studding heaven,
And dews all glorious on the bending stem,
Odorous, passionate as the rose of sleep
Half-budded on the throbbing heart of night,
And in the east a glowing sapphire gloomed;
When I awoke and lifted up mine eyes,
And saw through rose and gold and vermeil dyes,
And splendid mists of azure hung with pearl,
Half-hid, half-seen, as life would apprehend,
As in a sleep, the presence of dim death
And fate and terrible gods, the car of day.

Like morn within the morning, glad, it hung,
Light hid in light, swift blinding all who saw,
Dazzled, its presence; motionless though vibrate,
Where it did swing athwart the deep-welled night,
The heart of morning in the folds of dark,
Pulsating sleep, and conquering death with life;
So glowed its glory, folded, cloud in cloud,
Gold within azure, purple shut in gold,
The bud of morning pulsing ere it break,
And spill its splendors many vermeil-dyed,
Reddening Ocean to his outmost rim.

Here charmèd dreams and drowsèd magic hung,
And wingèd hopes and rosy joys afloat
Filled all the air, and I was quick aware
That this was life, and this mine hour supreme,
To seize and act and be one with the gods.
So dreamed I reckless when to think, to act,
And moved, elate, with swift life-flaming step

Athwart the meadow's budding asphodels,
Song on my lip, and life at heart and eye,
Exultant, breathing flame of pride and power.

Joy rose and sang, a bird, across the fields,
Hope's rosy wings shot trembling to the blue,
And Courage with dauntless steps before me went,
Brushing the veils of fierce cobwebby fires.
And there, before me, sprawled grim ancient Power,
A hideous ethiope, huge in sodden sleep,
The golden reins clutched in his titan hands.
I snatched, leaped, shouted; morning rose in flame,
And ashweed paled to lily, lily blushed
To ruddy crocus, crocus flamed to rose,
And out of all, borne on the floors of light,
I floated, gloried, up the orient walls,
And all things woke, and sang of conquering day.

Higher, yet higher, out of fiery mists,
Filling those meadows of the dew-built dawn,
Gloried and glorying, power clutched in my hand,
Wreathed about in terrible splendors, I drave,
Glowing, the dawn's gold coursers, champing steam
Of snow and pearly foam from golden bridles,
Forged in blue eidolon forges of the night,
Beaten on steely anvils of the stars.
These, champing, reared their fetlocks; breathing flame,
In red, dew-draining lances, thundered on,
'Whelming night, as golden stair by stair
They climbed the glimmering bridgeway of the day.
Far under, wreathed in mists, old ocean swayed;
And, cyclops-like, the bearded mountains hung.
Vast shining rivers with their brimming floors
And broad curved courses gleamed and glanced and
shone,
And loneliness and gloom and gray despair
With sombre hauntings fled to shuddering night
Hidden in caves and coral glooms of seas.

Low down the east the morn's ambrosial meads
Sank in soft splendors. Sphering out below,
Gilded in morning, anchored the patient earth,
Mountain and valley, ocean and wide plain,
Opening to dawn's young footsteps where we wheeled,
And blossomed wide the rosebud of the day.
Glory was mine, but greater, sense of power,
Nor marred by fear, as loftier we climbed,
With glinting hoofs, that clanged the azure bridge
That arched from dawning up to flaming noon.
Dauntless my soul, and fiery-glad my heart,
And "vastness," "vastness," sang through all my being,
As gloved with adamant I guided on
The day's red coursers up their flaming hill,
To reach the mighty keystone of the day.

All things conspired to build my upward road:
The fitful winds of morning, the soft clouds,
That fleece-like swept my cheek, the azure glint
Of ocean swaying, restless, on his rim,
Where slept the continents like a serpent curled
In sleep, leviathan, huge, about the world.

Then sudden all my waking turned to dream,
A madness wherein, hideous, all things hung.
Thought fled confused, and awful apprehension
Shadowed my spirit, power and reason fled;
And, maddening, day's red coursers thundered on,
Uncurbed, unguided by my palsied hand.
Then with loud ruin, blundering from the bridge,
Through space went swaying, now high up, now down,
Scattering conflagration and fierce death
O'er earth's shrunk verges where their scorchings
scarred.

Time fled in terror, forests shriveled up,
Ocean drew back in shudderings to his caves,
Huge mountains shook and rumbled to their base,

Great streams dried up, old cities smoked and fell,
And all life met confusion and despair,
And dread annihilation.
Then the Gods,
Pitying wrecked nature, in their sudden vengeance,
Me, impious, hurled from out my dizzying height.
Time vanished, reason swooned, then left her throne,
And darkness wrapt me as I shuddering fell,
Oblivion-clouded, to the plunging seas.
Ocean received me, folding in his deeps,
Cooling and emerald. Here in coral dreams
I rest and cure me, never wholly waking,
Filled with one splendor, fumbling in a dream,
As waves do fumble all about a cave,
For one clear memory of that one high day.

I failed, was mortal; where I climbed I fell.
But all else little matters; life was mine,
I dreamed, I dared, I grappled with, I fell;
And here I live it over in my dreams.
All things may pass, decline, and come to naught,
Death 'whelm life as day engulfed in dark,
But I have greatly lived, have greatly dared,
And death will never wholly wrap me round
And black me in its terrors. I am made
One with the future, dwelling in the dreams
And memories dread of envious gods and men.
(1899)

Nature

Nature, the dream that wraps us round,
One comforting and saving whole;
And as the clothes to the body of man,
The mantle of the soul.

Nature, the door that opens wide
  From this close, fetid house of ill;
That lifts from curse of street to vast
  Receding hill on hill.

Nature, the mood, now sweet of night,
  Now grand and splendid, large of day;
From vast skyline and cloudy towers,
  To stars in heaven that stray.

Nature, the hope, the truth, the gleam,
  Beyond this bitter cark and dole;
Whose walls the infinite weft of dream,
  Whose gift is to console.
(1905)

Charles G.D. Roberts (1860-1943)

Charles G.D. Roberts was the acknowledged leader of the Confederation poets. He was born in Douglas, New Brunswick in 1860, the son of a rector and the cousin of Bliss Carman. He grew up on a glebe farm near Sackville and the Tantramar marshes that figure so memorably in his poetry. *Orion and Other Poems* appeared when he was twenty and Headmaster at Chatham Grammar School; it collected poems that he had written as an undergraduate at the University of New Brunswick, and it had a vital influence on his contemporaries. After moving to Toronto in 1883 to work as an editor of *The Week*, Roberts returned to the Maritimes to teach English, economics, and French at King's College in Windsor, Nova Scotia, from 1885 to 1895. These were his most productive years as a poet, but, as we know from John Coldwell Adams' biography, Roberts was involved in several extramarital affairs even then. In 1895 he quit King's and moved to Fredericton, ostensibly in order to devote himself to his writing, but actually, in Adams' words, "embarking upon a course that would nearly end his career as a poet" (65). In 1897, he left his family for New York and thereafter turned increasingly to prose, especially to the animal stories that were both lucrative and sensationally popular. He moved to London in 1907, lied about his age to serve in World War I, and received a commission as first lieutenant of the 16th Battalion of the King's (Liverpool) Regiment. After returning to Canada in 1925, he finally found time for poetry among other activities, but his finances had long been insecure. As Adams reveals, Roberts was too poor to attend the Investiture or pay for his own Letters Patent when he was knighted in 1935. A pension granted by Prime Minister Bennett helped make Roberts' last years more comfortable. He remarried in 1943, to Joan Montgomery, fifty years his junior, and died later that year.

In a summary that has been too readily accepted, Desmond Pacey described Roberts' poetic career as "a rapid development, a sudden decline, a long silence, and a late revival" (35). The development is already underway in *Orion* (see Early), while *In Divers Tones* (1886) contains some of Roberts' best poems, including "The Pipes of Pan," "The Tantramar Revisited," and the early sonnets. As the title of that volume indicates, Roberts was still a poet of occasional lyrics and diverse interests. With *Songs of the Common Day* (1893), the commitments to Romantic nature poetry and Maritime rural life are fused in two ambitious works: the twenty-six sonnets that form the titular sequence; and "Ave! An Ode for the Centenary of Shelley's Birth." Both of these works should be read in the context of Roberts' incisive critical essays, especially "The Poetry of Nature" (included in this anthology). There Roberts divides nature poetry "into two main classes: that which deals with pure description, and that which treats of nature in some one of its many relations with humanity." At first some of the sonnets might seem like examples of the first and humbler class, until we recognize their place in a sequence that follows the seasonal cycle and moves towards a religious perspective on common life. This anthology also includes, as a challenge to Pacey's summary, the seventeen poems that form the *New York Nocturnes* sequence (1898). At the very least, these poems reveal that Roberts was more than a regional poet. Furthermore, D.M.R. Bentley has demonstrated that this sequence explores the complex issues of the 1890s, and that Roberts balances the claims of erotic passion and religious idealism in "a heterodox vision of sanctified earthly love" (in Clever 58). Whether or not we agree with Pacey about Roberts' decline, there is no doubt about the "long silence" after *The Book of the Rose* (1903). When he returned to poetry during the last two decades of his life, Roberts was once again a poet of "diverse tones." The following selection focusses on the poems written in the last two decades of the nineteenth century, and it ends with "Two Rivers," in which Roberts summarizes the divided interests of his long career.

Further Reading

Adams, John Coldwell. *Sir Charles God Damn: The Life of Sir Charles G.D. Roberts.* Toronto: U of Toronto P, 1986.

Bentley, D.M.R. "Roberts's 'Series of Sonnets' in *Songs of the Common Day.*" *Dalhousie Review* 69 (1989): 393-412.

Boone, Laurel, ed. *The Collected Letters of Charles G.D. Roberts.* Fredericton: Goose Lane, 1989.

Cappon, James. *Charles G.D. Roberts and the Influences of His Time.* 1905. Ottawa: Tecumseh, 1975.

Clever, Glenn. ed. *The Sir Charles G.D. Roberts Symposium.* Reappraisals: Canadian Writers. Ottawa: U of Ottawa P, 1984.

Cogswell, Fred. "Charles G.D. Roberts." *Canadian Writers and Their Works, Poetry Series: Volume Two.* Eds. Robert Lecker, Jack David, and Ellen Quigley. Downsview, ON: ECW, 1983. 187-232.

Early, L.R. "'An Old-World Radiance': Roberts' *Orion and Other Poems.*" *Canadian Poetry: Studies, Documents, Reviews* 8 (1981): 8-32.

Glickman, Susan. *The Picturesque and the Sublime: A Poetics of the Canadian Landscape.* Montreal: McGill-Queen's UP, 1998.

Jackel, David. "Roberts' 'Tantramar Revisited': Another View." *Canadian Poetry: Studies, Documents, Reviews* 5 (1979): 41-56.

Keith, W.J. *Charles G.D. Roberts.* Studies in Canadian Literature. Toronto: Copp Clark, 1969.

MacMillan, Carrie, ed. *The Proceedings of the Sir Charles G.D. Roberts Symposium, Mount Allison University.* Halifax: Nimbus, 1984.

Mathews, Robin. "Charles G.D. Roberts and the Destruction of the Canadian Imagination." *Journal of Canadian Fiction* 1 (1972): 47-56. Rpt. as "Charles G. D. Roberts: Father of Canadian Poetry." *Canadian Literature: Surrender or Revolution.* Ed. Gail Dexter. Toronto: Steel Rail, 1978. 45-62.

Pacey, Desmond. "Sir Charles G.D. Roberts." *Ten Canadian Poets: A Group of Biographical and Critical Essays.* Toronto: Ryerson, 1958. 34-58.

Pomeroy. E.M. *Sir Charles G.D. Roberts: A Biography*. Toronto: Ryerson, 1943.

Precosky, Don. "'The Need that Irks': Roberts' Sonnets in *Songs of the Common Day*." *Canadian Poetry: Studies, Documents, Reviews* 22 (1988): 22-31.

Roberts, Charles G.D. *The Collected Poems of Sir Charles G.D. Roberts: A Critical Edition*. Eds. Desmond Pacey and Graham Adams. Wolfville, N.S.: Wombat, 1985.

———. *Selected Poetry and Critical Prose*. Ed. W.J. Keith. Literature of Canada. Toronto: U of Toronto P, 1974.

Strong, William. "Charles G.D. Roberts' 'The Tantramar Revisited.'" *Canadian Poetry: Studies, Documents, Reviews* 3 (1978): 26-37.

Ware, Tracy. "Remembering It All Well: 'The Tantramar Revisited.'" *Studies in Canadian Literature* 8 (1983): 221-37.

Ode to Drowsihood

Breather of honeyed breath upon my face!
  Teller of balmy tales! Weaver of dreams!
  Sweet conjurer of palpitating gleams
And peopled shadows trooping into place
    In purple streams
Between the drooped lid and the drowsy eye!
  Moth-winged seducer, dusky-soft and brown,
Of bubble gifts and bodiless minstrelsy
  Lavish enough! Of rest the restful crown!
At whose behest are closed the lips that sigh,
  And weary heads lie down.

Thee, Nodding Spirit! Magic Comforter!
  Thee, with faint mouth half speechless, I invoke,
  And straight uplooms through the dead centuries' smoke
The agèd Druid in his robe of fur,
    Beneath the oak
Where hang uncut the paly mistletoes.
  The mistletoe dissolves to Indian willow,
Glassing its red stems in the stream that flows
  Through the broad interval; a lazy billow
Flung from my oar lifts the long grass that grows
  To be the Naiad's pillow.

The startled meadow-hen floats off, to sink
  Into remoter shades and ferny glooms;
  The great bees drone about the thick pea-blooms;
The linkéd bubblings of the bobolink,
    With warm perfumes
From the broad-flowered wild parsnip, drown my brain;
  The grackles bicker in the alder boughs;
The grasshoppers pipe out their thin refrain
  That with intenser heat the noon endows:

Then thy weft weakens, and I wake again
  Out of my dreamful drowse.

Ah! fetch thy poppy-baths, juices exprest
  In fervid sunshine, where the Javan palm
  Stirs scarce awakened from its odorous calm
By the enervate wind, that sinks to rest
    Amid the balm
And sultry silence, murmuring, half asleep,
  Cool fragments of the ocean's foamy roar,
And of the surge's mighty sobs that keep
  Forever yearning up the golden shore,
Mingled with song of Nereids that leap
  Where the curled crests downpour.

Who sips thy wine may float in Baiae's skies,
  Or flushed Maggiore's ripples, mindless made
  Of storming troubles hard to be allayed.
Who eats thy berries, for his ears and eyes
    May vineyard shade
Melt with soft Tuscan, glow with arms and lips
  Cream-white and crimson, making mock at reason.
Thy balm on brows by care uneaten drips;
  I have thy favors, but I fear thy treason.
Fain would I hold thee by the dusk wing-tips
  Against a grievous season.
(1879)

To Fredericton in May-Time

This morning, full of breezes and perfume,
  Brimful of promise of midsummer weather,
  When bees and birds and I are glad together,
Breathes of the full-leaved season, when soft gloom
Chequers thy streets, and thy close elms assume
  Round roof and spire the semblance of green billows;

Yet now thy glory is the yellow willows,
The yellow willows, full of bees and bloom.

Under their dusty blossoms blackbirds meet,
And robins pipe amid the cedars nigher;
Thro' the still elms I hear the ferry's beat;
The swallows chirp about the towering spire;
The whole air pulses with its weight of sweet;
Yet not quite satisfied is my desire!
(1881)

In the Afternoon

Wind of the summer afternoon,
Hush, for my heart is out of tune!

Hush, for thou movest restlessly
The too light sleeper, Memory!

Whate'er thou hast to tell me, yet
'Twere something sweeter to forget,—

Sweeter than all thy breath of balm
An hour of unremembering calm!

Blowing over the roofs, and down
The bright streets of this inland town,

These busy crowds, these rocking trees—
What strange note hast thou caught from these?

A note of waves and rushing tides,
Where past the dikes the red flood glides,

To brim the shining channels far
Up the green plains of Tantramar.

Once more I sniff the salt, I stand
On the long dikes of Westmoreland;

I watch the narrowing flats, the strip
Of red clay at the water's lip;

Far off the net-reels, brown and high,
And boat-masts slim against the sky;

Along the ridges of the dikes
Wind-beaten scant sea-grass, and spikes

Of last year's mullein; down the slopes
To landward, in the sun, thick ropes

Of blue vetch, and convolvulus,
And matted roses glorious.

The liberal blooms o'erbrim my hands;
I walk the level, wide marsh-lands;

Waist-deep in dusty-blossomed grass
I watch the swooping breezes pass

In sudden, long, pale lines, that flee
Up the deep breast of this green sea.

I listen to the bird that stirs
The purple tops, and grasshoppers

Whose summer din, before my feet
Subsiding, wakes on my retreat.

Again the droning bees hum by;
Still-winged, the gray hawk wheels on high;

I drink again the wild perfumes,
And roll, and crush the grassy blooms.

Blown back to olden days, I fain
Would quaff the olden joys again;

But all the olden sweetness not
The old unmindful peace hath brought.

Wind of this summer afternoon,
Thou hast recalled my childhood's June;

My heart—still is it satisfied
By all the golden summer-tide?

Hast thou one eager yearning filled,
Or any restless throbbing stilled,

Or hast thou any power to bear
Even a little of my care?—

Ever so little of this weight
Of weariness canst thou abate?

Ah, poor thy gift indeed, unless
Thou bring the old child-heartedness,—

And such a gift to bring is given,
Alas, to no wind under heaven!

Wind of the summer afternoon,
Be still; my heart is not in tune.

Sweet is thy voice; but yet, but yet—
Of all 'twere sweetest to forget!
(1882)

The Tantramar Revisited

Summers and summers have come, and gone with the flight of the swallow;
Sunshine and thunder have been, storm, and winter, and frost;
Many and many a sorrow has all but died from remembrance,
Many a dream of joy fall'n in the shadow of pain.
Hands of chance and change have marred, or moulded, or broken,
Busy with spirit or flesh, all I most have adored;
Even the bosom of Earth is strewn with heavier shadows,—
Only in these green hills, aslant to the sea, no change!
Here where the road that has climbed from the inland valleys and woodlands,
Dips from the hill-tops down, straight to the base of the hills,—
Here, from my vantage-ground, I can see the scattering houses,
Stained with time, set warm in orchards, meadows, and wheat,
Dotting the broad bright slopes outspread to southward and eastward,
Wind-swept all day long, blown by the south-east wind.
Skirting the sunbright uplands stretches a riband of meadow,
Shorn of the labouring grass, bulwarked well from the sea,
Fenced on its seaward border with long clay dikes from the turbid
Surge and flow of the tides vexing the Westmoreland shores.
Yonder, toward the left, lie broad the Westmoreland marshes,—
Miles on miles they extend, level, and grassy, and dim,

Clear from the long red sweep of flats to the sky in the distance,
Save for the outlying heights, green-rampired Cumberland Point;
Miles on miles outrolled, and the river-channels divide them,—
Miles on miles of green, barred by the hurtling gusts.
Miles on miles beyond the tawny bay is Minudie.
There are the low blue hills; villages gleam at their feet.
Nearer a white sail shines across the water, and nearer
Still are the slim, gray masts of fishing boats dry on the flats.
Ah, how well I remember those wide red flats, above tide-mark
Pale with scurf of the salt, seamed and baked in the sun!
Well I remember the piles of blocks and ropes, and the net-reels
Wound with the beaded nets, dripping and dark from the sea!
Now at this season the nets are unwound; they hang from the rafters
Over the fresh-stowed hay in upland barns, and the wind
Blows all day through the chinks, with the streaks of sunlight, and sways them
Softly at will; or they lie heaped in the gloom of a loft.

Now at this season the reels are empty and idle; I see them
Over the lines of the dikes, over the gossiping grass.
Now at this season they swing in the long strong wind, thro' the lonesome
Golden afternoon, shunned by the foraging gulls.
Near about sunset the crane will journey homeward above them;
Round them, under the moon, all the calm night long,

Winnowing soft gray wings of marsh-owls wander and wander,
Now to the broad, lit marsh, now to the dusk of the dike.
Soon, thro' their dew-wet frames, in the live keen freshness of morning,
Out of the teeth of the dawn blows back the awakening wind.

Then, as the blue day mounts, and the low-shot shafts of the sunlight
Glance from the tide to the shore, gossamers jewelled with dew
Sparkle and wave, where late sea-spoiling fathoms of drift-net
Myriad-meshed, uploomed sombrely over the land.

Well I remember it all. The salt raw scent of the margin;
While, with men at the windlass, groaned each reel, and the net,
Surging in ponderous lengths, uprose and coiled in its station;
Then each man to his home,—well I remember it all!

Yet, as I sit and watch, this present peace of the landscape,—
Stranded boats, these reels empty and idle, the hush,
One gray hawk slow-wheeling above yon cluster of haystacks,—
More than the old-time stir this stillness welcomes me home.
Ah the old-time stir, how once it stung me with rapture,—
Old-time sweetness, the winds freighted with honey and salt!
Yet will I stay my steps and not go down to the marsh-land,—
Muse and recall far off, rather remember than see,—

Lest on too close sight I miss the darling illusion,
Spy at their task even here the hands of chance and
change.
(1883)

The Pipes of Pan

Ringed with the flocking of hills, within shepherding
watch of Olympus,
Tempe, vale of the gods, lies in green quiet withdrawn;
Tempe, vale of the gods, deep-couched amid woodland
and woodland,
Threaded with amber of brooks, mirrored in azure of
pools,
All day drowsed with the sun, charm-drunken with
moonlight at midnight,
Walled from the world forever under a vapour of
dreams,—
Hid by the shadows of dreams, not found by the curious
footstep,
Sacred and secret forever, Tempe, vale of the gods.

How through the cleft of its bosom, goes sweetly the
water Penëus!
How by Penëus the sward breaks into saffron and blue!
How the long slope-floored beech-glades mount to the
wind-wakened uplands,
Where, through flame-berried ash, troop the hoofed
Centaurs at morn!
Nowhere greens a copse but the eye-beams of Artemis
pierce it.
Breathes no laurel her balm but Phoebus' fingers caress.
Springs no bed of wild blossom but limbs of dryad
have pressed it.
Sparkle the nymphs, and the brooks chime with shy
laughter and calls.

Here is a nook. Two rivulets fall to mix with Penëus,
Loiter a space, and sleep, checked and choked by the reeds.
Long grass waves in the windless water, strown with the lote-leaf;

Twist thro' dripping soil great alder roots, and the air
Glooms with the dripping tangle of leaf-thick branches, and stillness
Keeps in the strange-coiled stems, ferns, and wet-loving weeds.
Hither comes Pan, to this pregnant earthy spot, when his piping
Flags; and his pipes outworn breaking and casting away,
Fits new reeds to his mouth with the weird earth-melody in them,
Piercing, alive with a life able to mix with the god's.
Then, as he blows, and the searching sequence delights him, the goat-feet
Furtive withdraw; and a bird stirs and flutes in the gloom
Answering. Float with the stream the outworn pipes, with a whisper,—
"What the god breathes on, the god never can wholly evade!"
God-breath lurks in each fragment forever. Dispersed by Penëus
Wandering, caught in the ripples, wind-blown hither and there,
Over the whole green earth and globe of sea they are scattered,
Coming to secret spots, where in a visible form
Comes not the god, though he come declared in his workings. And mortals
Straying at cool of morn, or bodeful hasting at eve,
Or in the depths of noonday plunged to shadiest coverts,
Spy them, and set to their lips; blow, and fling them away!

Ay, they fling them away,—but never wholly! Thereafter
Creeps strange fire in their veins, murmur strange tongues in their brain,
Sweetly evasive; a secret madness takes them,—a charm-struck
Passion for woods and wild life, the solitude of the hills.
Therefore they fly the heedless throngs and traffic of cities,
Haunt mossed caverns, and wells bubbling ice-cool; and their souls
Gather a magical gleam of the secret of life, and the god's voice
Calls to them, not from afar, teaching them wonderful things.
(1886)

The Poet is Bidden to Manhattan Island

Dear Poet, quit your shady lanes
  And come where more than lanes are shady.
Leave Phyllis to the rustic swains
  And sing some Knickerbocker lady.
O hither haste, and here devise
  Divine *ballades* before unuttered.
Your poet's eyes *must* recognize
  The side on which your bread is buttered!

Dream not I tempt you to forswear
  One pastoral joy, or rural frolic.
I call you to a city where
  The most urbane are most bucolic.
'Twill charm your poet's eyes to find
  Good husbandmen in brokers burly;—
Their stock is ever on their mind;
  To water it they rise up early.

Things you have sung, but ah, not seen—
  Things proper to the age of Saturn—
Shall greet you here; for we have been
  Wrought quaintly, on the Arcadian pattern.
Your poet's lips will break in song
  For joy, to see at last appearing
The bulls and bears, a peaceful throng,
  While a lamb leads them—to the shearing!

And metamorphoses, of course,
  You'll mark in plenty, *à la* Proteus:
A bear become a little horse—
  Presumably from too much throat-use!
A thousandfold must go untold;
  But, should you miss your farm-yard sunny,
And miss your ducks and drakes, behold
  We'll make you ducks and drakes—of money!

Greengrocers here are fairly read.
  And should you set your heart upon them,
We lack not beets—but some are dead,
  While others have policemen on them.
And be the dewfall dear to you,
  Possess your poet's soul in patience!
Your *notes* shall soon be falling dew,—
  Most mystical of transformations!

Your heart, dear Poet, surely yields;
  And soon you'll leave your uplands flowery,
Forsaking fresh and bowery fields,
  For "pastures new"—upon the Bowery!
You've piped at home, where none could pay,
  Till now, I trust, your wits are riper.
Make no delay, but come this way,
  And pipe for them that pay the piper!
(1886)

Charles G.D. Roberts

Ave!

(*An Ode for the Shelley Centenary, 1892*)

I

O tranquil meadows, grassy Tantramar,
  Wide marshes ever washed in clearest air,
Whether beneath the sole and spectral star
  The dear severity of dawn you wear,
Or whether in the joy of ample day
  And speechless ecstasy of growing June
You lie and dream the long blue hours away
    Till nightfall comes too soon,
Or whether, naked to the unstarred night,
You strike with wondering awe my inward sight,—

II

You know how I have loved you, how my dreams
  Go forth to you with longing, though the years
That turn not back like your returning streams
  And fain would mist the memory with tears,
Though the inexorable years deny
  My feet the fellowship of your deep grass,
O'er which, as o'er another, tenderer sky,
    Cloud phantoms drift and pass,—
You know my confident love, since first, a child,
Amid your wastes of green I wandered wild.

III

Inconstant, eager, curious, I roamed;
  And ever your long reaches lured me on;
And ever o'er my feet your grasses foamed,
  And in my eyes your far horizons shone.
But sometimes would you (as a stillness fell
  And on my pulse you laid a soothing palm),
Instruct my ears in your most secret spell;

And sometimes in the calm
Initiate my young and wondering eyes
Until my spirit grew more still and wise.

IV

Purged with high thoughts and infinite desire
I entered fearless the most holy place,
Received between my lips the secret fire,
The breath of inspiration on my face.
But not for long these rare illumined hours,
The deep surprise and rapture not for long.
Again I saw the common, kindly flowers,
Again I heard the song
Of the glad bobolink, whose lyric throat
Pealed like a tangle of small bells afloat.

V

The pounce of mottled marsh-hawk on his prey;
The flicker of sand-pipers in from sea
In gusty flocks that puffed and fled; the play
Of field-mice in the vetches;—these to me
Were memorable events. But most availed
Your strange unquiet waters to engage
My kindred heart's companionship; nor failed
To grant this heritage,—
That in my veins forever must abide
The urge and fluctuation of the tide.

VI

The mystic river whence you take your name,
River of hubbub, raucous Tantramar,
Untamable and changeable as flame,
It called me and compelled me from afar,
Shaping my soul with its impetuous stress.
When in its gaping channel deep withdrawn

Its waves ran crying of the wilderness
  And winds and stars and dawn,
How I companioned them in speed sublime,
Led out a vagrant on the hills of Time!

VII

And when the orange flood came roaring in
 From Fundy's tumbling troughs and tide-worn caves,
While red Minudie's flats were drowned with din
 And rough Chignecto's front oppugned the waves,
How blithely with the refluent foam I raced
 Inland along the radiant chasm, exploring
The green solemnity with boisterous haste;
  My pulse of joy outpouring
To visit all the creeks that twist and shine
From Beauséjour to utmost Tormentine.

VIII

And after, when the tide was full, and stilled
 A little while the seething and the hiss,
And every tributary channel filled
 To the brim with rosy streams that swelled to kiss
The grass-roots all a-wash and goose-tongue wild
 And salt-sap rosemary,—then how well content
I was to rest me like a breathless child
 With play-time rapture spent,—
To lapse and loiter till the change should come
And the great floods turn seaward, roaring home.

IX

And now, O tranquil marshes, in your vast
 Serenity of vision and of dream,
Wherethrough by every intricate vein have passed
 With joy impetuous and pain supreme
The sharp fierce tides that chafe the shores of earth

In endless and controlless ebb and flow,
Strangely akin you seem to him whose birth
One hundred years ago
With fiery succour to the ranks of song
Defied the ancient gates of wrath and wrong.

X

Like yours, O marshes, his compassionate breast,
Wherein abode all dreams of love and peace,
Was tortured with perpetual unrest.
Now loud with flood, now languid with release,
Now poignant with the lonely ebb, the strife
Of tides from the salt sea of human pain
That hiss along the perilous coasts of life
Beat in his eager brain;
But all about the tumult of his heart
Stretched the great calm of his celestial art.

XI

Therefore with no far flight, from Tantramar
And my still world of ecstasy, to thee,
Shelley, to thee I turn, the avatar
Of Song, Love, Dream, Desire and Liberty;
To thee I turn with reverent hands of prayer
And lips that fain would ease my heart of praise,
Whom chief of all whose brows prophetic wear
The pure and sacred bays
I worship, and have worshipped since the hour
When first I felt thy bright and chainless power.

XII

About thy sheltered cradle, in the green
Untroubled groves of Sussex, brooded forms
That to the mother's eye remained unseen,—
Terrors and ardours, passionate hopes, and storms

Of fierce retributive fury, such as jarred
  Ancient and sceptred creeds, and cast down kings,
And oft the holy cause of Freedom marred,
    With lust of meaner things,
With guiltless blood, and many a frenzied crime
Dared in the face of unforgetful Time.

XIII

The star that burns on revolution smote
  Wild heats and change on thine ascendant sphere,
Whose influence thereafter seemed to float
  Through many a strange eclipse of wrath and fear,
Dimming awhile the radiance of thy love.
  But still supreme in thy nativity,
All dark, invidious aspects far above,
    Beamed one clear orb for thee,—
The star whose ministrations just and strong
Controlled the tireless flight of Dante's song.

XIV

With how august contrition, and what tears
  Of penitential unavailing shame,
Thy venerable foster-mother hears
  The sons of song impeach her ancient name,
Because in one rash hour of anger blind
  She thrust thee forth in exile, and thy feet
Too soon to earth's wild outer ways consigned,—
    Far from her well-loved seat,
Far from her studious halls and storied towers
And weedy Isis winding through his flowers.

XV

And thou, thenceforth the breathless child of change,
  Thine own Alastor, on an endless quest
Of unimagined loveliness, didst range,

Urged ever by the soul's divine unrest.
Of that high quest and that unrest divine
Thy first immortal music thou didst make,
Inwrought with fairy Alp, and Reuss, and Rhine,
And phantom seas that break
In soundless foam along the shores of Time,
Prisoned in thine imperishable rhyme.

XVI

Thyself the lark melodious in mid-heaven;
Thyself the Protean shape of chainless cloud,
Pregnant with elemental fire, and driven
Through deeps of quivering light, and darkness loud
With tempest, yet beneficent as prayer;
Thyself the wild west wind, relentless strewing
The withered leaves of custom on the air,
And through the wreck pursuing
O'er lovelier Arnos, more imperial Romes,
Thy radiant visions to their viewless homes.

XVII

And when thy mightiest creation thou
Wert fain to body forth,—the dauntless form,
The all-enduring, all-forgiving brow
Of the great Titan, flinchless in the storm
Of pangs unspeakable and nameless hates,
Yet rent by all the wrongs and woes of men,
And triumphing in his pain, that so their fates
Might be assuaged,—oh then
Out of that vast compassionate heart of thine
Thou wert constrained to shape the dream benign.

XVIII

—O Baths of Caracalla, arches clad
In such transcendent rhapsodies of green

That one might guess the sprites of spring were glad
For your majestic ruin, yours the scene,
The illuminating air of sense and thought;
And yours the enchanted light, O skies of Rome,
Where the giant vision into form was wrought;
Beneath your blazing dome
The intensest song our language ever knew
Beat up exhaustless to the blinding blue!—

XIX

The domes of Pisa and her towers superb,
The myrtles and the ilexes that sigh
O'er San Giuliano, where no jars disturb
The lonely aziola's evening cry,
The Serchio's sun-kissed waters,—these conspired
With Plato's theme occult, with Dante's calm
Rapture of mystic love, and so inspired
Thy soul's espousal psalm,
A strain of such elect and pure intent
It breathes of a diviner element.

XX

Thou on whose lips the word of Love became
A rapt evangel to assuage all wrong,
Not Love alone, but the austerer name
Of Death engaged the splendours of thy song.
The luminous grief, the spacious consolation
Of thy supreme lament, that mourned for him
Too early haled to that still habitation
Beneath the grass-roots dim,—
Where his faint limbs and pain-o'erwearied heart
Of all earth's loveliness became a part,

XXI

But where, thou sayest, himself would not abide,—
  Thy solemn incommunicable joy
Announcing Adonais has not died,
  Attesting Death to free but not destroy,
All this was as thy swan-song mystical.
  Even while the note serene was on thy tongue
Thin grew the veil of the Invisible,
    The white sword nearer swung,—
And in the sudden wisdom of thy rest
Thou knewest all thou hadst but dimly guessed.

XXII

—Lament, Lerici, mourn for the world's loss!
  Mourn that pure light of song extinct at noon!
Ye waves of Spezzia that shine and toss
  Repent that sacred flame you quenched too soon!
Mourn, Mediterranean waters, mourn
  In affluent purple down your golden shore!
Such strains as his, whose voice you stilled in scorn,
    Our ears may greet no more,
Unless at last to that far sphere we climb
Where he completes the wonder of his rhyme!

XXIII

How like a cloud she fled, thy fateful bark,
  From eyes that watched to hearts that waited, till
Up from the ocean roared the tempest dark—
  And the wild heart love waited for was still!
Hither and thither in the slow, soft tide,
  Rolled seaward, shoreward, sands and wandering shells
And shifting weeds thy fellows, thou didst hide
    Remote from all farewells,
Nor felt the sun, nor heard the fleeting rain,
Nor heeded Casa Magni's quenchless pain.

XXIV

Thou heedest not? Nay, for it was not thou,
  That blind, mute clay relinquished by the waves
Reluctantly at last, and slumbering now
  In one of kind earth's most compassionate graves!
Not thou, not thou,—for thou wert in the light
  Of the Unspeakable, where time is not.
Thou sawest those tears; but in thy perfect sight
    And thy eternal thought
Were they not even now all wiped away
In the reunion of the infinite day!

XXV

There face to face thou sawest the living God
  And worshipedst, beholding Him the same
Adored on earth as Love, the same whose rod
  Thou hadst endured as Life, whose secret name
Thou now didst learn, the healing name of Death.
  In that unroutable profound of peace,
Beyond experience of pulse and breath,
    Beyond the last release
Of longing, rose to greet thee all the lords
Of Thought, with consummation in their words.

XXVI

He of the seven cities claimed, whose eyes,
  Though blind, saw gods and heroes, and the fall
Of Ilium, and many alien skies,
  And Circe's Isle; and he whom mortals call
The Thunderous, who sang the Titan bound
  As thou the Titan victor; the benign
Spirit of Plato; Job; and Judah's crowned
    Singer and seer divine;
Omar; the Tuscan; Milton vast and strong;
And Shakespeare, captain of the host of Song.

XXVII

Back from the underworld of whelming change
 To the wide-glittering beach thy body came;
And thou didst contemplate with wonder strange
 And curious regard thy kindred flame,
Fed sweet with frankincense and wine and salt,
 With fierce purgation search thee, soon resolving
Thee to the elements of the airy vault
  And the far spheres revolving,
The common waters, the familiar woods,
And the great hills' inviolate solitudes.

XXVIII

Thy close companions there officiated
 With solemn mourning and with mindful tears;—
The pained, imperious wanderer unmated
 Who voiced the wrath of those rebellious years;
Trelawney, lion-limbed and high of heart;
 And he, that gentlest sage and friend most true,
Whom Adonais loved. With these bore part
  One grieving ghost, that flew

Hither and thither through the smoke unstirred
In wailing semblance of a wild white bird.

XXIX

O heart of fire, that fire might not consume,
 For ever glad the world because of thee;
Because of thee for ever eyes illume
 A more enchanted earth, a lovelier sea!
O poignant voice of the desire of life,
 Piercing our lethargy, because thy call
Aroused our spirits to a nobler strife
  Where base and sordid fall,

For ever past the conflict and the pain
More clearly beams the goal we shall attain!

XXX

And now once more, O marshes, back to you
  From whatsoever wanderings, near or far,
To you I turn with joy forever new,
  To you, O sovereign vasts of Tantramar!
Your tides are at the full. Your wizard flood,
  With every tribute stream and brimming creek,
Ponders, possessor of the utmost good,
    With no more left to seek;—
But the hour wanes and passes; and once more
Resounds the ebb with destiny in its roar.

XXXI

So might some lord of men, whom force and fate
  And his great heart's unvanquishable power
Have thrust with storm to his supreme estate,
  Ascend by night his solitary tower
High o'er the city's lights and cries uplift.
  Silent he ponders the scrolled heaven to read
And the keen stars' conflicting message sift,
    Till the slow signs recede,
And ominously scarlet dawns afar
The day he leads his legions forth to war.
(1892)

Marsyas

A little grey hill-glade, close-turfed, withdrawn
Beyond resort or heed of trafficking feet,
Ringed round with slim trunks of the mountain ash,
Through the slim trunks and scarlet bunches flash—
Beneath the clear chill glitterings of the dawn—

Far off, the crests, where down the rosy shore
The Pontic surges beat.
The plains lie dim below. The thin airs wash
The circuit of the autumn-coloured hills,
And this high glade, whereon
The satyr pipes, who soon shall pipe no more.
He sits against the beech-tree's mighty bole,—
He leans, and with persuasive breathing fills
The happy shadows of the slant-set lawn.
The goat-feet fold beneath a gnarlèd root;
And sweet, and sweet the note that steals and thrills
From slender stops of that shy flute.
Then to the goat-feet comes the wide-eyed fawn
Hearkening; the rabbits fringe the glade, and lay
Their long ears to the sound;
In the pale boughs the partridge gather round,
And quaint hern from the sea-green river reeds;
The wild ram halts upon a rocky horn
O'erhanging; and, unmindful of his prey,
The leopard steals with narrowed lids to lay
His spotted length along the ground.
The thin airs wash, the thin clouds wander by,
And those hushed listeners move not. All the morn
He pipes, soft-swaying, and with half-shut eye,
In rapt content of utterance,—
                                        nor heeds
The young God standing in his branchy place,
The languor on his lips, and in his face,
Divinely inaccessible, the scorn.
(1893)

Charles G.D. Roberts

From Songs of the Common Day

The Furrow

How sombre slope these acres to the sea
  And to the breaking sun! The sun-rise deeps
  Of rose and crocus, whence the far dawn leaps,
Gild but with scorn their grey monotony.

The glebe rests patient for its joy to be.
  Past the salt field-foot many a dim wing sweeps;
  And down the field a first slow furrow creeps,
Pledge of near harvests to the unverdured lea.

With clank of harness tramps the serious team—
  The sea air thrills their nostrils. Some wise crows
  Feed confidently behind the ploughman's feet.
In the early chill the clods fresh cloven steam,
  And down its griding path the keen share goes:
  So, from a scar, best flowers the future's sweet.
(1890)

The Sower

A brown, sad-coloured hillside, where the soil
  Fresh from the frequent harrow, deep and fine,
  Lies bare; no break in the remote sky-line,
Save where a flock of pigeons streams aloft,
Startled from feed in some low-lying croft,
  Or far-off spires with yellow of sunset shine;
  And here the Sower, unwittingly divine,
Exerts the silent forethought of his toil.

Alone he treads the glebe, his measured stride
  Dumb in the yielding soil; and though small joy
  Dwell in his heavy face, as spreads the blind

Pale grain from his dispensing palm aside,
  This plodding churl grows great in his employ;—
  Godlike, he makes provision for mankind.
(1884)

The Waking Earth

With shy bright clamour the live brooks sparkle and
    run.
  Freed flocks confer about the farmstead ways.
  The air's a wine of dreams and shining haze,
Beaded with bird-notes thin,—for Spring's begun!
The sap flies upward. Death is over and done.
  The glad earth wakes; the glad light breaks; the days
  Grow round, grow radiant. Praise for the new life!
    Praise
For bliss of breath and blood beneath the sun!

What potent wizardry the wise earth wields,
To conjure with a perfume! From bare fields
  The sense drinks in a breath of furrow and sod.
And lo, the bound of days and distance yields;
  And fetterless the soul is flown abroad,
  Lord of desire and beauty, like a God!
(1889)

The Cow Pasture

I see the harsh, wind-ridden, eastward hill,
  By the red cattle pastured, blanched with dew;
 The small, mossed hillocks where the clay gets through;
The grey webs woven on milkweed tops at will.
The sparse, pale grasses flicker, and are still.
  The empty flats yearn seaward. All the view

Is naked to the horizon's utmost blue;
And the bleak spaces stir me with strange thrill.

Not in perfection dwells the subtler power
To pierce our mean content, but rather works
Through incompletion, and the need that irks,—
Not in the flower, but effort toward the flower.
When the want stirs, when the soul's cravings urge,
The strong earth strengthens, and the clean heavens purge.
(1893)

Frogs

Here in the red heart of the sunset lying,
My rest an islet of brown weeds blown dry,
I watch the wide bright heavens, hovering nigh,
My plain and pools in lucent splendours dyeing.
My view dreams over the rosy wastes, descrying
The reed-tops fret the solitary sky;
And all the air is tremulous to the cry
Of myriad frogs on mellow pipes replying.

For the unrest of passion here is peace,
And eve's cool drench for midday soil and taint.
To tired ears how sweetly brings release
This limpid babble from life's unstilled complaint;
While under tired eyelids lapse and faint
The noon's derisive visions—fade and cease.
(1888)

The Salt Flats

Here clove the keels of centuries ago
 Where now unvisited the flats lie bare.
 Here seethed the sweep of journeying waters, where
No more the tumbling floods of Fundy flow,
And only in the samphire pipes creep slow
 The salty currents of the sap. The air
Hums desolately with wings that seaward fare,
Over the lonely reaches beating low.

The wastes of hard and meagre weeds are thronged
With murmurs of a past that time has wronged;
 And ghosts of many an ancient memory
Dwell by the brackish pools and ditches blind,
In these low-lying pastures of the wind,
 These marshes pale and meadows by the sea.
(1891)

The Pea-Fields

These are the fields of light, and laughing air,
 And yellow butterflies, and foraging bees,
 And whitish, wayward blossoms winged as these,
And pale green tangles like a seamaid's hair.
Pale, pale the blue, but pure beyond compare,
 And pale the sparkle of the far-off seas,
 A-shimmer like these fluttering slopes of peas,
And pale the open landscape everywhere.

From fence to fence a perfumed breath exhales
 O'er the bright pallor of the well-loved fields,—
My fields of Tantramar in summer-time;
 And, scorning the poor feed their pasture yields,
Up from the bushy lots the cattle climb,
 To gaze with longing through the grey, mossed rails.
(1891)

The Mowing

This is the voice of high midsummer's heat.
 The rasping vibrant clamour soars and shrills
 O'er all the meadowy range of shadeless hills,
As if a host of giant cicadae beat
The cymbals of their wings with tireless feet,
 Or brazen grasshoppers with triumphing note
 From the long swath proclaimed the fate that smote
The clover and timothy-tops and meadowsweet.

The crying knives glide on; the green swath lies.
 And all noon long the sun, with chemic ray,
 Seals up each cordial essence in its cell,
That in the dusky stalls, some winter's day,
 The spirit of June, here prisoned by his spell,
 May cheer the herds with pasture memories.
(1890)

Buckwheat

This smell of home and honey on the breeze,
 This shimmer of sunshine woven in white and pink
 That comes, a dream from memory's visioned brink,
Sweet, sweet and strange across the ancient trees,—
It is the buckwheat, boon of the later bees,
 Its breadths of heavy-headed bloom appearing
 Amid the blackened stumps of this high clearing,
Freighted with cheer of comforting auguries.

But when the blunt, brown grain and red-ripe sheaves,
Brimming the low log barn beyond the eaves,
 Crisped by the first frost, feel the thresher's flail,
Then flock the blue wild-pigeons in shy haste
 All silently down Autumn's amber trail,
To glean at dawn the chill and whitening waste.
(1893)

The Potato Harvest

A high bare field, brown from the plough, and borne
  Aslant from sunset; amber wastes of sky
  Washing the ridge; a clamour of crows that fly
In from the wide flats where the spent tides mourn
To yon their rocking roosts in pines wind-torn;
  A line of grey snake-fence, that zigzags by
  A pond, and cattle; from the homestead nigh
The long deep summonings of the supper horn.

Black on the ridge, against that lonely flush,
  A cart, and stoop-necked oxen; ranged beside
    Some barrels; and the day-worn harvest-folk,
Here emptying their baskets, jar the hush
  With hollow thunders. Down the dusk hillside
    Lumbers the wain; and day fades out like smoke.
(1886)

The Oat-Threshing

A little brown old homestead, bowered in trees
  That o'er the Autumn landscape shine afar,
  Burning with amber and with cinnabar.
A yellow hillside washed in airy seas
Of azure, where the swallow drops and flees.
  Midway the slope, clear in the beaming day,
  A barn by many seasons beaten grey,
Big with the gain of prospering husbandries.

In billows round the wide red welcoming doors
  High piles the golden straw; while from within,
  Where plods the team amid the chaffy din,
The loud pulsation of the thresher soars,
  Persistent as if earth could not let cease
  This happy proclamation of her peace.
(1893)

The Autumn Thistles

The morning sky is white with mist, the earth
  White with the inspiration of the dew.
  The harvest light is on the hills anew,
And cheer in the grave acres' fruitful girth.
Only in this high pasture is there dearth,
  Where the gray thistles crowd in ranks austere,
  As if the sod, close-cropt for many a year,
Brought only bane and bitterness to birth.

But in the crisp air's amethystine wave
  How the harsh stalks are washed with radiance now,
  How gleams the harsh turf where the crickets lie
Dew-freshened in their burnished armour brave!
  Since earth could not endure nor heaven allow
  Aught of unlovely in the morn's clear eye.
(1891)

The Pumpkins in the Corn

Amber and blue, the smoke behind the hill,
  Where in the glow fades out the Morning Star,
  Curtains the Autumn cornfield, sloped afar,
And strikes an acrid savour on the chill.
The hilltop fence shines saffron o'er the still
  Unbending ranks of bunched and bleaching corn
  And every pallid stalk is crisp with morn,
Crisp with the silver Autumn morns distil.

Purple the narrowing valleys stretched between
  The spectral shooks, a purple harsh and cold,
  But spotted, where the gadding pumpkins run,
With bursts of blaze that startle the serene
  Like sudden voices,—globes of orange bold,
  Elate to mimic the unrisen sun.
(1893)

The Winter Fields

Winds here, and sleet, and frost that bites like steel.
The low bleak hill rounds under the low sky.
Naked of flock and fold the fallows lie,
Thin streaked with meagre drift. The gusts reveal
By fits the dim grey snakes of fence, that steal
Through the white dusk. The hill-foot poplars sigh,
While storm and death with winter trample by,
And the iron fields ring sharp, and blind lights reel.

Yet in the lonely ridges, wrenched with pain,
Harsh solitary hillocks, bound and dumb,
Grave glebes close-lipped beneath the scourge and chain,
Lurks hid the germ of ecstasy,—the sum
Of life that waits on summer, till the rain
Whisper in April and the crocus come.
(1890)

The Flight of the Geese

I hear the low wind wash the softening snow,
The low tide loiter down the shore. The night
Full filled with April forecast, hath no light.
The salt wave on the sedge-flat pulses slow.
Through the hid furrows lisp in murmurous flow
The thaw's shy ministers; and hark! The height
Of heaven grows weird and loud with unseen flight
Of strong hosts prophesying as they go!

High through the drenched and hollow night their wings
Beat northward hard on winter's trail. The sound
Of their confused and solemn voices, borne
Athwart the dark to their long Arctic morn,

Comes with a sanction and an awe profound,
A boding of unknown, foreshadowed things.
(1890)

The Vengeance of Gluskâp
(A Micmac Legend)

Gluskâp, the friend and father of his race,
With help in need went journeying three days' space.

His village slept, and took no thought of harm,
Secure beneath the shadow of his arm.

But wandering wizards watched his outward path,
And marked his fenceless dwelling for their wrath.

They came upon the tempest's midnight wings,
With shock of thunder and the lightning's slings,
And flame, and hail, and all disastrous things.

When home at length the hero turned again,
His huts were ashes and his servants slain;
And o'er the ruin wept a slow, great rain.

He wept not; but he cried a mighty word
Across the wandering sea, and the sea heard.

Then came great whales, obedient to his hand,
And bare him to the demon-haunted land,

Where, in malign morass and ghostly wood
And grim cliff-cavern, lurked the evil brood.

And scarce the avenger's foot had touched their coast
Ere horror seized on all the wizard host,
And in their hiding-places hushed the boast.

He grew and gloomed before them like a cloud,
And his eye drew them till they cried aloud,

And withering like spent flame before his frown
They ran forth in a madness and fell down.

Rank upon rank they lay without a moan,—
His finger touched them, and their hearts grew stone.

All round the coasts he heaped their stiffened clay;
And the sea-mews wail o'er them to this day.
(1894)

The New York Nocturnes (1898)

The Ideal

To Her, when life was little worth,
  When hope, a tide run low,
Between dim shores of emptiness
  Almost forgot to flow,—

Faint with the city's fume and stress
  I came at night to Her.
Her cool white fingers on my face—
  How wonderful they were!

More dear they were to fevered lids
  Than lilies cooled in dew.
They touched my lips with tenderness,
  Till life was born anew.

The city's clamour died in calm;
  And once again I heard
The moon-white woodland stillnesses
  Enchanted by a bird;

The wash of far, remembered waves;
  The sigh of lapsing streams;
And one old garden's lilac leaves
  Conferring in their dreams.

A breath from childhood daisy fields
  Came back to me again,
Here in the city's weary miles
  Of city-wearied men.
(1898)

Ω Θεοί, τίς ἀρα Κύπρις, ἤ τίς ἵμερος τοῦδε ξυνῄψατο

In the Crowd

I walk the city square with thee.
  The night is loud; the pavements roar.
Their eddying mirth and misery
Encircle thee and me.

The street is full of lights and cries.
  The crowd but brings thee close to me.
I only hear thy low replies;
I only see thine eyes.
(1898)

Night in a Down-town Street

Not in the eyed, expectant gloom,
  Where soaring peaks repose
And incommunicable space
  Companions with the snows;

Not in the glimmering dusk that crawls
  Upon the clouded sea,
Where bourneless wave on bourneless wave
  Complains continually;

Not in the palpable dark of woods
  Where groping hands clutch fear,
Does Night her deeps of solitude
  Reveal unveiled as here.

The street is a grim cañon carved
  In the eternal stone,
That knows no more the rushing stream
  It anciently has known.

The emptying tide of life has drained
  The iron channel dry.
Strange winds from the forgotten day
  Draw down, and dream, and sigh.

The narrow heaven, the desolate moon
  Made wan with endless years,
Seem less immeasurably remote
  Than laughter, love, or tears.
(1897)

At the Railway Station

Here the night is fierce with light,
  Here the great wheels come and go,
Here are partings, waitings, meetings,
  Mysteries of joy and woe.

Here is endless haste and change,
  Here the ache of streaming eyes,

Radiance of expectant faces,
  Breathless askings, brief replies.

Here the jarred, tumultuous air
  Throbs and pauses like a bell,
Gladdens with delight of greeting,
  Sighs and sorrows with farewell.

Here, ah, here with hungry eyes
  I explore the passing throng.
Restless I await your coming
  Whose least absence is so long.

Faces, faces pass me by,
  Meaningless, and blank, and dumb,
Till my heart grows faint and sickens
  Lest at last you should not come.

Then—I see you. And the blood
  Surges back to heart and brain.
Eyes meet mine,—and Heaven opens.
  You are at my side again.
(1898)

Nocturnes of the Honeysuckle

I

Forever shed your sweetness on the night,
Dear honeysuckle, flower of our delight!

Forever breathe the mystery of that hour
When her hand touched me, lightlier than a flower,—

And life became forever strange and sweet,
A gift to lay with worship at her feet.

II

Oh, flower of the honeysuckle,
  Tell me how often the long night through
She turns in her dream to the open window,
  She turns in her dream to you.

Oh, flower of the honeysuckle,
  Tell me how tenderly out of the dew
You breathe her a dream of that night of wonder
  When life was fashioned anew.

Oh, flower of the honeysuckle,
  Tell me how long ere, the sweet night through,
She will turn not to you but to me in the darkness,
  And dream and desire come true.
(1898)

My Garden

I have a garden in the city's grime
Where secretly my heart keeps summer time;

Where blow such airs of rapture on my eyes
As those blest dreamers know in Paradise,

Who after lives of longing come at last
Where anguish of vain love is overpast.

When the broad noon lies shadeless on the street,
And traffic roars, and toilers faint with heat,

Where men forget that ever woods were green,
The wonders of my garden are not seen.

Only at night the magic doors disclose
Its labyrinths of lavender and rose;

And honeysuckle, white beneath its moon,
Whispers me softly thou art coming soon;

And led by Love's white hand upon my wrist
Beside its glimmering fountains I keep tryst.

O Love, this moving fragrance on my hair,—
Is it thy breath, or some enchanted air

From far, uncharted realms of mystery
Which I have dreamed of but shall never see?

O Love, this low, wild music in my ears,
Is it the heart-beat of thy hopes and fears,

Or the faint cadence of some fairy song
On winds of boyhood memory blown along?

O Love, what poignant ecstasy is this
Upon my lips and eyes? Thy touch,—thy kiss.
(1898)

Presence

Dawn like a lily lies upon the land
Since I have known the whiteness of your hand.
Dusk is more soft and more mysterious where
Breathes on my eyes the perfume of your hair.
Waves at your coming break in livelier blue;
And solemn woods are glad because of you.
Brooks of your laughter learn their liquid notes.
Birds to your voice attune their pleading throats.
Fields to your feet grow smoother and more green;
And happy blossoms tell where you have been.
(1898)

Twilight on Sixth Avenue

Over the tops of the houses
Twilight and sunset meet.
The green, diaphanous dusk
Sinks to the eager street.

Astray in the tangle of roofs
Wanders a wind of June.
The dial shines in the clock-tower
Like the face of a strange-scrawled moon.

The narrowing lines of the houses
Palely begin to gleam,
And the hurrying crowds fade softly
Like an army in a dream.

Above the vanishing faces
A phantom train flares on
With a voice that shakes the shadows,—
Diminishes, and is gone.

And I walk with the journeying throng
In such a solitude
As where a lonely ocean
Washes a lonely wood.
(1895)

The Street Lamps

Eyes of the city,
Keeping your sleepless watch from sun to sun,
Is it for pity
You tremble, seeing innocence undone;

Or do you laugh, to think men thus should set
Spies on the folly day would fain forget?
(1898)

In Darkness

I have faced life with courage,—but not now!
O Infinite, in this darkness draw thou near.
Wisdom alone I asked of thee, but thou
Hast crushed me with the awful gift of fear.
(1898)

In the Solitude of the City

Night; and the sound of voices in the street.
Night; and the happy laughter where they meet,
The glad boy lover and the trysting girl.
But thou—but thou—I cannot find thee, Sweet!

Night; and far off the lighted pavements roar.
Night; and the dark of sorrow keeps my door.
I reach my hand out trembling in the dark.
Thy hand comes not with comfort any more.

O Silent, Unresponding! If these fears
Lie not, nor other wisdom come with years,
No day shall dawn for me without regret,
No night go uncompanioned by my tears.
(1898)

A Nocturne of Exile

Out of this night of lonely noise,
 The city's crowded cries,
Home of my heart, to thee, to thee
 I turn my longing eyes.

Years, years, how many years I went
 In exile wearily,
Before I lifted up my face
 And saw my home in thee.

I had come home to thee at last.
 I saw thy warm lights gleam.
I entered thine abiding joy,—
 Oh, was it but a dream?

Ere I could reckon with my heart
 The sum of our delight,
I was an exile once again
 Here in the hasting night.

Thy doors were shut; thy lights were gone
 From my remembering eyes.—
Only the city's endless throng!
 Only the crowded cries!
(1898)

A Street Vigil

Here is the street
Made holy by the passing of her feet,—
 The little, tender feet, more sweet than myrrh,
 Which I have washed with tears for love of her.

Here she has gone
Until the very stones have taken on
  A glory from her passing, and the place
  Is tremulous with memory of her face.

Here is the room
That holds the light to lighten all my gloom.
  Beyond that blank white window she is sleeping
  Who hath my hope, my health, my fame, in keeping.

A little peace
Here for a little, ere my vigil cease
  And I turn homeward, shaken with the strife
  Of hope that struggles hopeless, sick for life.

Surely the power
That lifted me from darkness that one hour
  To a dear heaven whereof no word can tell
  Not wantonly will thrust me back to hell.
(1898)

A Nocturne of Trysting

Broods the hid glory in its sheath of gloom
Till strikes the destined hour, and bursts the bloom,
A rapture of white passion and perfume.

    So the long day is like a bud
      That aches with coming bliss,
    Till flowers in light the wondrous night
      That brings me to thy kiss.

Then, with a thousand sorrows forgotten in one hour,
  In thy pure eyes and at thy feet I find at last my goal;

And life and hope and joy seem but a faint prevision
  Of the flower that is thy body and the flame that is thy soul.
(1898)

In a City Room

O city night of noises and alarms,
  Your lights may flare, your cables clang and rush,
But in the sanctuary of my love's arms
  Your blinding tumult dies into a hush.

My doors are surged about with your unrest;
  Your plangent cares assail my realm of peace;
But when I come unto her quiet breast
  How suddenly your jar and clamour cease!

Then even remembrance of your strifes and pains
  Diminishes to a ghost of sorrows gone,
Remoter than a dream of last year's rains
  Gusty against my window in the dawn.
(1898)

A Nocturne of Consecration

I talked about you, Dear, the other night,
Having myself alone with my delight.
Alone with dreams and memories of you,
All the divine-houred summer stillness through
I talked of life, of love the always new,
Of tears, and joy,—yet only talked of you.

To the sweet air
That breathed upon my face
The spirit of lilies in a leafy place,

Your breath's caress, the lingering of your hair,
I said—"In all your wandering through the dusk,
Your waitings on the marriages of flowers
Through the long, intimate hours
When soul and sense, desire and love confer,
You must have known the best that God has made.
What do you know of Her?"

Said the sweet air—
"Since I have touched her lips,
Bringing the consecration of her kiss,
Half passion and half prayer,
And all for you,
My various lore has suffered an eclipse.
I have forgot all else of sweet I knew."

To the wise earth,
Kind, and companionable, and dewy cool,
Fair beyond words to tell, as you are fair,
And cunning past compare
To leash all heaven in a windless pool,
I said—"The mysteries of death and birth
Are in your care.
You love, and sleep; you drain life to the lees;
And wonderful things you know.
Angels have visited you, and at your knees
Learned what I learn forever at her eyes,
The pain that still enhances Paradise.
You in your breast felt her first pulses stir;
And you have thrilled to the light touch of her feet,
Blindingly sweet.
Now make me wise with some new word of Her."

Said the wise earth—
"She is not all my child.
But the wild spirit that rules her heart-beats wild

Is of diviner birth
And kin to the unknown light beyond my ken.
All I can give to Her have I not given?
Strength to be glad, to suffer, and to know;
The sorcery that subdues the souls of men;
The beauty that is as the shadow of heaven;
The hunger of love
And unspeakable joy thereof.
And these are dear to Her because of you.
You need no word of mine to make you wise
Who worship at her eyes
And find there life and love forever new!"

To the white stars,
Eternal and all-seeing,
In their wide home beyond the wells of being,
I said—"There is a little cloud that mars
The mystical perfection of her kiss.
Mine, mine, She is,
As far as lip to lip, and heart to heart,
And spirit to spirit when lips and hands must part,
Can make her mine. But there is more than this,—
More, more of Her to know.
For still her soul escapes me unaware,
To dwell in secret where I may not go.
Take, and uplift me. Make me wholly Hers."

Said the white stars, the heavenly ministers,—
"This life is brief, but it is only one.
Before to-morrow's sun
For one or both of you it may be done.
This love of yours is only just begun.
Will all the ecstasy that may be won
Before this life its little course has run
At all suffice
The love that agonizes in your eyes?

Therefore be wise.
Content you with the wonder of love that lies
Between her lips and underneath her eyes.
If more you should surprise,
What would be left to hope from Paradise?
In other worlds expect another joy
Of Her, which blundering fate shall not annoy,
Nor time nor change destroy."

So, Dear, I talked the long, divine night through,
And felt you in the chrismal balms of dew.
The thing then learned
Has ever since within my bosom burned—
One life is not enough for love of you.
(1897)
(end of *New York Nocturnes* sequence)

The Skater

My glad feet shod with the glittering steel
I was the god of the winged heel.

The hills in the far white sky were lost;
The world lay still in the wide white frost;

And the woods hung hushed in their long white dream
By the ghostly, glimmering, ice-blue stream.

Here was a pathway, smooth like glass,
Where I and the wandering wind might pass

To the far-off palaces, drifted deep,
Where Winter's retinue rests in sleep.

I followed the lure, I fled like a bird,
Till the startled hollows awoke and heard

A spinning whisper, a sibilant twang,
As the stroke of the steel on the tense ice rang;

And the wandering wind was left behind
As faster, faster I followed my mind;

Till the blood sang high in my eager brain,
And the joy of my flight was almost pain.

Then I stayed the rush of my eager speed
And silently went as a drifting seed,—

Slowly, furtively, till my eyes
Grew big with the awe of a dim surmise,

And the hair of my neck began to creep
At hearing the wilderness talk in sleep.

Shapes in the fir-gloom drifted near.
In the deep of my heart I heard my fear;

And I turned and fled, like a soul pursued,
From the white, inviolate solitude.
(1901)

The Unknown City

There lies a city inaccessible,
Where the dead dreamers dwell.

Abrupt and blue, with many a high ravine
And soaring bridge half seen.
With many an iris cloud that comes and goes

Over the ancient snows,
The imminent hills environ it, and hold
Its portals from of old,
That grief invade not, weariness, nor war,
Nor anguish evermore.
White-walled and jettied on the peacock tide,
With domes and towers enskied,
Its battlements and balconies one sheen
Of ever-living green,
It hears the happy dreamers turning home
Slow-oared across the foam.

Cool are its streets with waters musical
And fountains' shadowy fall.
With orange and anemone and rose,
And every flower that blows
Of magic scent or unimagined dye,
Its gardens shine and sigh.
Its chambers, memoried with old romance
And faëry circumstance,—
From any window love may lean some time
For love that dares to climb.

This is that city babe and seer divined
With pure, believing mind.
This is the home of unachieved emprize.
Here, here the visioned eyes
Of them that dream past any power to do,
Wake to the dream come true.
Here the high failure, not the level fame,
Attests the spirit's aim.
Here is fulfilled each hope that soared and sought
Beyond the bournes of thought.
The obdurate marble yields; the canvas glows;
Perfect the column grows;
The chorded cadence art could ne'er attain

Crowns the imperfect strain;
And the great song that seemed to die unsung
Triumphs upon the tongue.
(1903)

Philander's Song

(From "The Sprightly Pilgrim")

I sat and read Anacreon.
  Moved by the gay, delicious measure
I mused that lips were made for love
  And love to charm a poet's leisure.

And as I mused a maid came by
  With something in her look that caught me.
Forgotten was Anacreon's line,
  But not the lesson he had taught me.
(1927)

To a Certain Mystic

Sometimes you saw what others could not see.
  Sometimes you heard what no one else could hear:—
A light beyond the unfathomable dark,
  A voice that sounded only to your ear.

And did you, voyaging the tides of vision
  In your lone shallop, steering by what star,
Catch hints of some Elysian fragrance, wafted
  On winds impalpable, from who knows how far?

And did dawn show you driftage from strange continents
  Of which we dream but no man surely knows,—

Some shed gold leafage from the Tree Eternal,
  Some petals of the Imperishable Rose?

And did you once, Columbus of the spirit,
  Essay the crossing of that unknown sea,
Really touch land beyond the mists of rumour
  And find new lands where they were dreamed to be?

Ah, why brought you not back the word of power,
  The charted course, the unambiguous sign,
Or even some small seed, whence we might grow
  A flower unmistakably divine?

But you came empty-handed, and your tongue
  Babbled strange tidings none could wholly trust.
And if we half believed you, it was only
  Because we would, and not because we must.
(1931)

Two Rivers

[*The Tantramar and the St. John*]

Two rivers are there hold my heart
  And neither would I leave.
When I would stay with one too long
  The other tugs my sleeve.

For both are in my blood and bone
  And will be till I die.
Along my veins their argument
  Goes on incessantly.

The one, inconstant as the wind
  And fickle as the foam,

Disturbs my soul with strange desires
  And pricks my feet to roam.

The other, a strong and tranquil flood
  With stars upon its breast,
Would win me back from wandering
  And snare desire with rest.

II. The Tantramar

To you, my moon-led Tantramar,
  I turn, who taught my feet to range,—
You and the vagrant moon conspiring,
  Twin arbiters of change,—

To you I turn, my Tantramar.
  A wide-eyed boy I played beside
Your wastes of wind-swept green and chased
  Your ever-changing tide.

I watched your floods come tumbling in
  To fill your inland creeks remote,
Assail your prisoning dykes, and set
  Your long marsh grass afloat.

I watched your venturing floods at full
  Falter and halt, turn and retreat,
And race with laughter back to sea,
  Mocking their own defeat.

Far up to Midgic's farms you flow
  And there for a brief space rest your fill,
Then back past Sackville's studious halls
  To Westcock on her hill.

Draining your vast red channels bare
  To shine like copper in the sun
You tremble down the gleaming chasm
  And whimper as you run;

But, soon repenting your dismay,
  With challenging roar you surge again
To brim your dykes and reassume
  Your lordship of the plain.

. . . .

Across the estranging, changing years,
  Blind puppet of my restless star,
In discontent content alone,
  You urge and drive me, Tantramar.

III. The St. John

To you I turn again, St. John,
  Great river, constant tide,—return
With a full heart to you, beside
  Whose green banks I was born.

A babe I left you, and a youth
  Returned to you, ancestral stream,
Where sits my city, Fredericton,
  A jewel in a dream.

Your broad tide sweeps her storied shores
  Where loyalties and song were bred,
And that green hill where sleeps the dust
  Of my beloved dead.

From many a distant source withdrawn
  You drain your waters,—from the wash

Of Temiscouata's waves, and lone
  Swamps of the Allegash,—

From many a far and nameless lake
  Where rain-birds greet the showery noon
And dark moose pull the lily pads
  Under an alien moon.

Full-fed from many a confluent stream
  Your fortunate waters dream toward sea,—
And reach the barrier heights that hold
  Your calm estates in fee.

In that strait gate you stand on guard
  While Fundy's floods, without surcease,
In giant wrath assault in vain
  The portals of your peace.

Outside, reared on that iron rock
  Where first the Ships of Freedom came,
Sits the proud city, foam begirt,
  That bears your name and fame,—

Saint John, rock-bound, rock-ribbed, secure,
  To her stern birthright constant still,
She fronts the huge o'er mastering tides
  And bends them to her will.

. . . .

Dear and great River, when my feet
  Have wearied of the endless quest,
Heavy with sleep I will come back
  To your calm shores for rest.
(1937)

Archibald Lampman (1861-99)

Archibald Lampman was born in 1861 at Morpeth, Canada West. Like Roberts and Campbell, he was the son of an Anglican clergyman. After a year at Parrytown, the family moved to Gore's Landing on Rice Lake, an experience that proved a mixed blessing: Lampman loved the area and met Susanna Moodie and Catherine Parr Traill, but in 1868 he contracted rheumatic fever, which permanently weakened his heart. The family moved to Cobourg in 1874, and Lampman finished his schooling at Trinity College, Port Hope. In 1879 he entered Trinity College, Toronto, where he distinguished himself socially and intellectually. He later wrote a memorable account (see "Two Canadian Poets" in this anthology) of his excitement at reading Roberts' *Orion* as an undergraduate, and he responded by writing his own poems for *Rouge et Noir*, the Trinity College journal. After a brief attempt at teaching, he moved to Ottawa in 1883 to work in the Post Office Department. He remained there for the rest of his life, and while he often lamented the bureaucratic routine, he did not pursue jobs at Cornell and Boston when the opportunity arose. He published his first collection, *Among the Millet*, privately in 1888; a second collection, *Lyrics of Earth*, was published in Boston in 1896, while a third, *Alcyone*, was with the publisher at the time of Lampman's death at the age of 37 in 1899.

Lampman has been more consistently admired than the other Confederation poets, even by writers who reacted against the nineteenth century. For instance, Louis Dudek calls Lampman "the first fundamental critic of our culture and our political life" (in Granowski 198), while Raymond Souster calls Lampman's poetry "the best we have" (in his poem "A Letter to Archibald Lampman"). No doubt his death in 1899 shielded Lampman from the unfair demand (sometimes made of Roberts and Carman) that his writing conform to Modernist values, but there are three more important reasons for his status. First, his style in his best work is so precise and so effective that its virtues are undeniable. Second, while his best poems are his short nature lyrics, it is not hard to see that nature for Lampman is less important than human nature. He wrote that his intention "for instance in writing 'Among the Timothy' was not in the first place to describe a landscape, but to describe the effect of a few hours spent among the summer fields on a mind in a troubled or despondent condition. The description of the landscape was really an accessory to my plan" (qtd. in Doyle 40). Third, his socialism (see "The Land of Pallas") and scepticism (see "To an Ultra Protestant") distinguish him from his Confederation peers, and so R.E. Rashley's argument (see his essay in this anthology) that the choice of a natural setting constitutes an implicit criticism of society is particularly effective for Lampman. His other virtues are discussed in the essays by E.K. Brown, Malcolm Ross, and D.M.R. Bentley in this anthology. Together, they show that such poems as "Heat," "Among the Timothy," "Morning on the Lièvres," "The City of the End of Things," and many of the sonnets are still among the best written in Canada.

Further Reading

Arnold, Richard. "'The Clearer Self': Lampman's Transcendental-Visionary Development." *Canadian Poetry: Studies, Documents, Reviews* 8 (1981): 33-55.

Ball, Eric. "Life 'Only Sweet': The Significance of the Sequence in Lampman's *Lyrics of Earth*." Two Parts. *Canadian Poetry: Studies, Documents, Reviews* 25 (1989): 1-20; 26 (1990): 19-42.

Beattie, Munro. "Archibald Lampman." *Our Living Tradition, First Series*. Ed. Claude Bissell. Toronto: U of Toronto P, 1957. 63-88.

Bentley, D.M.R. "Watchful Dreams and Sweet Unrest: An Essay on the Vision of Archibald Lampman." Two Parts. *Studies in Canadian Literature* 6 (1981): 188-210; 7 (1982): 5-26.

Brown, E.K. "Archibald Lampman." *On Canadian Poetry*. 1943. Rev. ed. 1944. Ottawa: Tecumseh, 1973. 88-118.

Compton, Anne. "The Poet-Impressionist: Some Landscapes by Archibald Lampman." *Canadian Poetry: Studies, Documents, Reviews* 34 (1994): 33-56.

Archibald Lampman

Connor, Carl Y. *Archibald Lampman: Canadian Poet of Nature.* 1929. Ottawa: Borealis, 1977.

Davies, Barrie. "Lampman and Religion." *Canadian Literature* 56 (1973): 40-60. *Colony and Confederation: Early Canadian Poets and Their Background.* Ed. George Woodcock. Vancouver: UBC P, 1974. 103-23.

Doyle, James. "Archibald Lampman and Hamlin Garland." *Canadian Poetry: Studies, Documents, Reviews* 16 (1985): 38-46.

Early, L.R. *Archibald Lampman.* Twayne's World Authors. Boston: Twayne, 1986.

———. "Archibald Lampman." *Canadian Writers and Their Works, Poetry Series: Volume Two.* Eds. Robert Lecker, Jack David, and Ellen Quigley. Downsview, ON: ECW, 1983. 135-85.

Gnarowski, Michael, ed. *Archibald Lampman.* Critical Views on Canadian Writers. Toronto: Ryerson, 1970.

Kennedy, Margaret. "Lampman and the Canadian Thermopylae: 'At the Long Sault: May, 1660.'" *Canadian Poetry: Studies, Documents, Reviews* 1 (1977): 54-59.

Lampman, Archibald. *The Essays and Reviews of Archibald Lampman.* Ed. D.M.R. Bentley. London, ON: Canadian Poetry Press, 1996.

———. *The Poems of Archibald Lampman.* Ed. Duncan Campbell Scott. Toronto: Morang, 1900. *The Poems of Archibald Lampman (including At the Long Sault).* Introd. Margaret Coulby Whitridge. Literature of Canada. Toronto: U of Toronto P, 1974.

———. *Selected Poetry.* Ed. Michael Gnarowski. Ottawa: Tecumseh, 1990.

Lynn, Helen, ed. *An Annotated Edition of the Correspondence Between Archibald Lampman and Edward William Thomson (1890-1898).* Ottawa: Tecumseh, 1980.

McMullen, Lorraine, ed. *The Lampman Symposium.* Re-appraisals: Canadian Writers. Ottawa: U of Ottawa P, 1976.

Mezei, Kathy. "Lampman Among the Timothy." *Canadian Poetry: Studies, Documents, Reviews* 5 (1979): 57-72.

Pacey, Desmond. "Archibald Lampman." *Ten Canadian Poets: A Group of Biographical and Critical Essays.* Toronto: Ryerson, 1958. 114-40.

Scott, Duncan Campbell. Introd. *Lyrics of Earth: Sonnets and Ballads.* By Lampman. Ed. Scott. Toronto: Musson, 1925. 3-47.

The Railway Station

The darkness brings no quiet here, the light
No waking: ever on my blinded brain
The flare of lights, the rush, and cry, and strain,
The engines' scream, the hiss and thunder smite:
I see the hurrying crowds, the clasp, the flight,
Faces that touch, eyes that are dim with pain:
I see the hoarse wheels turn, and the great train
Move labouring out into the bourneless night.
So many souls within its dim recesses,
So many bright, so many mournful eyes:
Mine eyes that watch grow fixed with dreams and guesses;
What threads of life, what hidden histories,
What sweet or passionate dreams and dark distresses,
What unknown thoughts, what various agonies!
(1887)

In October

Along the waste, a great way off, the pines,
Like tall slim priests of storm, stand up and bar
The low long strip of dolorous red that lines
The under west, where wet winds moan afar.
The cornfields all are brown, and brown the meadows
With the blown leaves' wind-heapèd traceries,
And the brown thistle stems that cast no shadows,
And bear no bloom for bees.

As slowly earthward leaf by red leaf slips,
The sad trees rustle in chill misery,
A soft strange inner sound of pain-crazed lips,
That move and murmur incoherently;
As if all leaves, that yet have breath, were sighing,

With pale hushed throats, for death is at the door,
So many low soft masses for the dying
Sweet leaves that live no more.

Here I will sit upon this naked stone,
Draw my coat closer with my numbèd hands,
And hear the ferns sigh, and the wet woods moan,
And send my heart out to the ashen lands;
And I will ask myself what golden madness,
What balmèd breaths of dreamland spicery,
What visions of soft laughter and light sadness
Were sweet last month to me.

The dry dead leaves flit by with thin weird tunes,
Like failing murmurs of some conquered creed,
Graven in mystic markings with strange runes,
That none but stars and biting winds may read;
Here I will wait a little; I am weary,
Not torn with pain of any lurid hue,
But only still and very gray and dreary,
Sweet sombre lands, like you.
(1888)

Among the Timothy

Long hours ago, while yet the morn was blithe,
Nor sharp athirst had drunk the beaded dew,
A reaper came, and swung his cradled scythe
Around this stump, and, shearing slowly, drew
Far round among the clover, ripe for hay,
A circle clean and grey;
And here among the scented swathes that gleam,
Mixed with dead daisies, it is sweet to lie
And watch the grass and the few-clouded sky,
Nor think but only dream.

For when the noon was turning, and the heat
  Fell down most heavily on field and wood,
I too came hither, borne on restless feet,
  Seeking some comfort for an aching mood.
  Ah, I was weary of the drifting hours,
    The echoing city towers,
The blind grey streets, the jingle of the throng,
  Weary of hope that like a shape of stone
  Sat near at hand without a smile or moan,
    And weary most of song.

And those high moods of mine that sometime made
  My heart a heaven, opening like a flower,
A sweeter world where I in wonder strayed,
  Begirt with shapes of beauty and the power
  Of dreams that moved through that enchanted clime
    With changing breaths of rhyme,
Were all gone lifeless now like those white leaves,
  That hang all winter, shivering dead and blind
  Among the sinewy beeches in the wind,
    That vainly calls and grieves.

Ah! I will set no more mine overtaskèd brain
  To barren search and toil that beareth nought,
Forever following with sorefooted pain
  The crossing pathways of unbournèd thought;
  But let it go, as one that hath no skill,
    To take what shape it will,
An ant slow-burrowing in the earthy gloom,
  A spider bathing in the dew at morn,
  Or a brown bee in wayward fancy borne
    From hidden bloom to bloom.

Hither and thither o'er the rocking grass
  The little breezes, blithe as they are blind,
Teasing the slender blossoms pass and pass,
  Soft-footed children of the gipsy wind,

To taste of every purple-fringèd head
  Before the bloom is dead;
And scarcely heed the daisies that, endowed
 With stems so short they cannot see, up-bear
 Their innocent sweet eyes distressed, and stare
  Like children in a crowd.

Not far to fieldward in the central heat,
 Shadowing the clover, a pale poplar stands
With glimmering leaves that, when the wind comes, beat
 Together like innumerable small hands,
 And with the calm, as in vague dreams astray,
  Hang wan and silver-grey;
Like sleepy maenads, who in pale surprise,
 Half-wakened by a prowling beast, have crept
 Out of the hidden covert, where they slept,
  At noon with languid eyes.

The crickets creak, and through the noonday glow,
 That crazy fiddler of the hot mid-year,
The dry cicada plies his wiry bow
 In long-spun cadence, thin and dusty sere:
 From the green grass the small grasshoppers' din
  Spreads soft and silvery thin:
And ever and anon a murmur steals
 Into mine ears of toil that moves alway,
 The crackling rustle of the pitch-forked hay
  And lazy jerk of wheels.

And so I lie and feel the soft hours wane,
 To wind and sun and peaceful sound laid bare,
That aching dim discomfort of the brain
 Fades off unseen, and shadowy-footed care
 Into some hidden corner creeps at last
  To slumber deep and fast;
And gliding on, quite fashioned to forget,
 From dream to dream I bid my spirit pass

Out into the pale green ever-swaying grass
To brood, but no more fret.

And hour by hour among all shapes that grow
Of purple mints and daisies gemmed with gold
In sweet unrest my visions come and go;
I feel and hear and with quiet eyes behold;
And hour by hour, the ever-journeying sun,
In gold and shadow spun,
Into mine eyes and blood, and through the dim
Green glimmering forest of the grass shines down,
Till flower and blade, and every cranny brown,
And I are soaked with him.
(1888)

Among the Millet

The dew is gleaming in the grass,
The morning hours are seven,
And I am fain to watch you pass,
Ye soft white clouds of heaven.

Ye stray and gather, part and fold;
The wind alone can tame you;
I think of what in time of old
The poets loved to name you.

They called you sheep, the sky your sward,
A field without a reaper;
They called the shining sun your lord,
The shepherd wind your keeper.

Your sweetest poets I will deem
The men of old for moulding
In simple beauty such a dream,

  And I could lie beholding,
Where daisies in the meadow toss,
  The wind from morn till even,
Forever shepherd you across
  The shining field of heaven.
(1888)

Morning on the Lièvres

Far above us where a jay
Screams his matins to the day,
Capped with gold and amethyst,
Like a vapour from the forge
Of a giant somewhere hid,
Out of hearing of the clang
Of his hammer, skirts of mist
Slowly up the woody gorge
Lift and hang.

Softly as a cloud we go,
Sky above and sky below,
Down the river, and the dip
Of the paddles scarcely breaks,
With the little silvery drip
Of the water as it shakes
From the blades, the crystal deep
Of the silence of the morn,
Of the forest yet asleep,
And the river reaches borne
In a mirror, purple grey,
Sheer away
To the misty line of light,
Where the forest and the stream
In the shadow meet and plight,
Like a dream.

From amid a stretch of reeds,
Where the lazy river sucks
All the water as it bleeds
From a little curling creek,
And the muskrats peer and sneak
In around the sunken wrecks
Of a tree that swept the skies
Long ago,
On a sudden seven ducks
With a splashy rustle rise,
Stretching out their seven necks,
One before, and two behind,
And the others all arow,
And as steady as the wind
With a swivelling whistle go,
Through the purple shadow led,
Till we only hear their whir
In behind a rocky spur,
Just ahead.
(1888)

Between the Rapids

The point is turned; the twilight shadow fills
  The wheeling stream, the soft receding shore,
And on our ears from deep among the hills
  Breaks now the rapid's sudden quickening roar.
Ah yet the same, or have they changed their face,
  The fair green fields, and can it still be seen,
The white log cottage near the mountain's base,
  So bright and quiet, so home-like and serene?
Ah, well I question, for as five years go,
How many blessings fall, and how much woe.

Aye there they are, nor have they changed their cheer,
The fields, the hut, the leafy mountain brows;
Across the lonely dusk again I hear
The loitering bells, the lowing of the cows,
The bleat of many sheep, the stilly rush
Of the low whispering river, and through all,
Soft human tongues that break the deepening hush
With faint-heard song or desultory call:
Oh comrades hold; the longest reach is past;
The stream runs swift, and we are flying fast.

The shore, the fields, the cottage just the same,
But how with them whose memory makes them
sweet?
Oh if I called them, hailing name by name,
Would the same lips the same old shouts repeat?
Have the rough years, so big with death and ill,
Gone lightly by and left them smiling yet?
Wild black-eyed Jeanne whose tongue was never still,
Old wrinkled Picaud, Pierre and pale Lisette,
The homely hearts that never cared to range,
While life's wide fields were filled with rush and
change.

And where is Jacques, and where is Verginie?
I cannot tell; the fields are all a blur.
The lowing cows whose shapes I scarcely see,
Oh do they wait and do they call for her?
And is she changed, or is her heart still clear
As wind or morning, light as river foam?
Or have life's changes borne her far from here,
And far from rest, and far from help and home?
Ah comrades, soft, and let us rest awhile,
For arms grow tired with paddling many a mile.

The woods grow wild, and from the rising shore
The cool wind creeps, the faint wood odours steal;

Like ghosts adown the river's blackening floor
  The misty fumes begin to creep and reel.
Once more I leave you, wandering toward the night,
  Sweet home, sweet heart, that would have held me in;
Whither I go I know not, and the light
  Is faint before, and rest is hard to win.
Ah sweet ye were and near to heaven's gate;
But youth is blind and wisdom comes too late.

Blacker and loftier grow the woods, and hark!
  The freshening roar! The chute is near us now,
And dim the canyon grows, and inky dark
  The water whispering from the birchen prow.
One long last look, and many a sad adieu,
  While eyes can see and heart can feel you yet,
I leave sweet home and sweeter hearts to you,
  A prayer for Picaud, one for pale Lisette,
A kiss for Pierre, my little Jacques, and thee,
A sigh for Jeanne, a sob for Verginie.

Oh, does she still remember? Is the dream
  Now dead, or has she found another mate?
So near, so dear; and ah, so swift the stream;
  Even now perhaps it were not yet too late.
But oh, what matter; for before the night
  Has reached its middle, we have far to go:
Bend to your paddles, comrades; see, the light
  Ebbs off apace; we must not linger so.
Aye thus it is! Heaven gleams and then is gone:
Once, twice, it smiles, and still we wander on.
(1888)

Archibald Lampman

The Frogs

I

Breathers of wisdom won without a quest,
  Quaint uncouth dreamers, voices high and strange,
  Flutists of lands where beauty hath no change,
And wintry grief is a forgotten guest,
Sweet murmurers of everlasting rest,
  For whom glad days have ever yet to run,
  And moments are as aeons, and the sun
But ever sunken half-way toward the west.

Often to me who heard you in your day,
  With close wrapt ears, it could not choose but seem
That earth, our mother, searching in what way,
  Men's hearts might know her spirit's inmost dream,
    Ever at rest beneath life's change and stir,
    Made you her soul, and bade you pipe for her.

II

In those mute days when spring was in her glee,
  And hope was strong, we knew not why or how,
  And earth, the mother, dreamed with brooding brow,
Musing on life, and what the hours might be,
When love should ripen to maternity,
  Then like high flutes in silvery interchange
  Ye piped with voices still and sweet and strange,
And ever as ye piped, on every tree

The great buds swelled; among the pensive woods
  The spirits of first flowers awoke and flung
From buried faces the close fitting hoods,
  And listened to your piping till they fell,
  The frail spring-beauty with her perfumed bell,
The wind-flower, and the spotted adder-tongue.

III

All the day long, wherever pools might be
  Among the golden meadows, where the air
  Stood in a dream, as it were moorèd there
Forever in a noon-tide reverie,
Or where the birds made riot of their glee
  In the still woods, and the hot sun shone down,
  Crossed with warm lucent shadows on the brown
Leaf-paven pools, that bubbled dreamily.

Or far away in whispering river meads
  And watery marshes where the brooding noon,
  Full with the wonder of its own sweet boon,
Nestled and slept among the noiseless reeds,
  Ye sat and murmured, motionless as they,
  With eyes that dreamed beyond the night and day.

IV

And when day passed and over heaven's height,
  Thin with the many stars and cool with dew,
  The fingers of the deep hours slowly drew
The wonder of the ever-healing night,
No grief or loneliness or wrapt delight
  Or weight of silence ever brought to you
  Slumber or rest; only your voices grew
More high and solemn; slowly with hushed flight

Ye saw the echoing hours go by, long-drawn,
  Nor ever stirred, watching with fathomless eyes,
  And with your countless clear antiphonies
Filling the earth and heaven, even till dawn,
  Last-risen, found you with its first pale gleam,
  Still with soft throats unaltered in your dream.

V

And slowly as we heard you, day by day,
  The stillness of enchanted reveries
  Bound brain and spirit and half-closèd eyes,
In some divine sweet wonder-dream astray;
To us no sorrow or upreared dismay
  Nor any discord came, but evermore
  The voices of mankind, the outer roar,
Grew strange and murmurous, faint and far away.

Morning and noon and midnight exquisitely,
  Wrapt with your voices, this alone we knew,
Cities might change and fall, and men might die,
  Secure were we, content to dream with you,
    That change and pain are shadows faint and fleet,
    And dreams are real, and life is only sweet.
(1888)

Heat

From plains that reel to southward, dim,
  The road runs by me white and bare;
Up the steep hill it seems to swim
  Beyond, and melt into the glare.
Upward halfway, or it may be
  Nearer the summit, slowly steals
A hay-cart, moving dustily
  With idly clacking wheels.

By his cart's side the wagoner
  Is slouching slowly at his ease,
Half-hidden in the windless blur
  Of white dust puffing to his knees.
This wagon on the height above,
  From sky to sky on either hand,
Is the sole thing that seems to move
  In all the heat-held land.

Beyond me in the fields the sun
  Soaks in the grass and hath his will;
I count the marguerites one by one;
  Even the buttercups are still.
On the brook yonder not a breath
  Disturbs the spider or the midge.
The water-bugs draw close beneath
  The cool gloom of the bridge.

Where the far elm-tree shadows flood
  Dark patches in the burning grass,
The cows, each with her peaceful cud,
  Lie waiting for the heat to pass.
From somewhere on the slope near by
  Into the pale depth of the noon
A wandering thrush slides leisurely
  His thin revolving tune.

In intervals of dreams I hear
  The cricket from the droughty ground;
The grass-hoppers spin into mine ear
  A small innumerable sound.
I lift mine eyes sometimes to gaze:
  The burning sky-line blinds my sight:
The woods far off are blue with haze:
  The hills are drenched in light.

And yet to me not this or that
  Is always sharp or always sweet;
In the sloped shadow of my hat
  I lean at rest, and drain the heat;
Nay more, I think some blessèd power
  Hath brought me wandering idly here:
In the full furnace of this hour
  My thoughts grow keen and clear.
(1888)

Winter Hues Recalled

Life is not all for effort: there are hours
When fancy breaks from the exacting will,
And rebel thought takes schoolboy's holiday,
Rejoicing in its idle strength. 'Tis then,
And only at such moments, that we know
The treasure of hours gone—scenes once beheld,
Sweet voices and words bright and beautiful,
Impetuous deeds that woke the God within us,
The loveliness of forms and thoughts and colors,
A moment marked and then as soon forgotten.
These things are ever near us, laid away,
Hidden and waiting the appropriate times,
In the quiet garner-house of memory.
There in the silent unaccounted depth,
Beneath the heated strainage and the rush
That teem the noisy surface of the hours,
All things that ever touched us are stored up,
Growing more mellow like sealed wine with age;
We thought them dead, and they are but asleep.
In moments when the heart is most at rest
And least expectant, from the luminous doors,
And sacred dwelling place of things unfeared,
They issue forth, and we who never knew
Till then how potent and how real they were,
Take them, and wonder, and so bless the hour.

Such gifts are sweetest when unsought. To me,
As I was loitering lately in my dreams,
Passing from one remembrance to another,
Like him who reads upon an outstretched map,
Content and idly happy, there rose up,
Out of that magic well-stored picture house,
No dream, rather a thing most keenly real,
The memory of a moment, when with feet
Arrested and spellbound, and captured eyes,

Made wide with joy and wonder, I beheld
The spaces of a white and wintery land
Swept with the fire of sunset, all its width
Vale, forest, town, and misty eminence,
A miracle of color and of beauty.

I had walked out, as I remember now,
With covered ears, for the bright air was keen,
To southward up the gleaming snow-packed fields,
With the snowshoer's long rejoicing stride,
Marching at ease. It was a radiant day
In February, the month of the great struggle
'Twixt sun and frost, when with advancing spears,
The glittering golden vanguard of the spring
Holds the broad winter's yet unbroken rear
In long-closed wavering contest. Thin pale threads
Like streaks of ash across the far off blue
Were drawn, nor seemed to move. A brooding silence
Kept all the land, a stillness as of sleep;
But in the east the grey and motionless woods,
Watching the great sun's fiery slow decline,
Grew deep with gold. To westward all was silver.
An hour had passed above me; I had reached
The loftiest level of the snow-piled fields,
Clear eyed, but unobservant, noting not
That all the plain beneath me and the hills
Took on a change of color splendid, gradual,
Leaving no spot the same; nor that the sun
Now like a fiery torrent overflamed
The great line of the west. Ere yet I turned
With long stride homeward, being heated
With the loose swinging motion, weary too,
Nor uninclined to rest, a buried fence,
Whose topmost log just shouldered from the snow,
Made me a seat, and thence with heated cheeks,
Grazed by the northwind's edge of stinging ice,
I looked far out upon the snow-bound waste,

The lifting hills and intersecting forests,
The scarce marked courses of the buried streams,
And as I looked lost memory of the frost,
Transfixed with wonder, overborne with joy.
I saw them in their silence and their beauty,
Swept by the sunset's rapid hand of fire,
Sudden, mysterious, every moment deepening
To some new majesty of rose or flame.
The whole broad west was like a molten sea
Of crimson. In the north the light-lined hills
Were veiled far off as with a mist of rose
Wondrous and soft. Along the darkening east
The gold of all the forests slowly changed
To purple. In the valley far before me,
Low sunk in sapphire shadows, from its hills,
Softer and lovelier than an opening flower,
Uprose a city with its sun-touched towers,
A bunch of amethysts.

Like one spell-bound
Caught in the presence of some god, I stood,
Nor felt the keen wind and the deadly air,
But watched the sun go down, and watched the gold
Fade from the town and the withdrawing hills,
Their westward shapes athwart the dusky red
Freeze into sapphire, saw the arc of rose
Rise ever higher in the violet east,
Above the frore front of the uprearing night
Remorsefully soft and sweet. Then I awoke
As from a dream, and from my shoulders shook
The warning chill, till then unfelt, unfeared.
(1888)

In November

With loitering step and quiet eye,
Beneath the low November sky,
I wandered in the woods, and found
A clearing, where the broken ground
Was scattered with black stumps and briers,
And the old wreck of forest fires.
It was a bleak and sandy spot,
And, all about, the vacant plot
Was peopled and inhabited
By scores of mulleins long since dead.
A silent and forsaken brood
In that mute opening of the wood,
So shrivelled and so thin they were,
So gray, so haggard, and austere,
Not plants at all they seemed to me,
But rather some spare company
Of hermit folk, who long ago,
Wandering in bodies to and fro,
Had chanced upon this lonely way,
And rested thus, till death one day
Surprised them at their compline prayer,
And left them standing lifeless there.

There was no sound about the wood
Save the wind's secret stir. I stood
Among the mullein-stalks as still
As if myself had grown to be
One of their sombre company,
A body without wish or will.
And as I stood, quite suddenly,
Down from a furrow in the sky
The sun shone out a little space
Across that silent sober place,
Over the sand heaps and brown sod,

The mulleins and dead goldenrod,
And passed beyond the thickets gray,
And lit the fallen leaves that lay,
Level and deep within the wood,
A rustling yellow multitude.

And all around me the thin light,
So sere, so melancholy bright,
Fell like the half-reflected gleam
Or shadow of some former dream;
A moment's golden reverie
Poured out on every plant and tree
A semblance of weird joy, or less,
A sort of spectral happiness;
And I, too, standing idly there,
With muffled hands in the chill air,
Felt the warm glow about my feet,
And shuddering betwixt cold and heat,
Drew my thoughts closer, like a cloak,
While something in my blood awoke,
A nameless and unnatural cheer,
A pleasure secret and austere.
(1890)

A Sunset at Les Eboulements

Broad shadows fall. On all the mountain side
The scythe-swept fields are silent. Slowly home
By the long beach the high-piled hay-carts come,
Splashing the pale salt shallows. Over wide
Fawn-coloured wastes of mud the slipping tide,
Round the dun rocks and wattled fisheries,
Creeps murmuring in. And now by twos and threes,
O'er the slow spreading pools with clamorous chide,
Belated crows from strip to strip take flight.

Soon will the first star shine; yet ere the night
Reach onward to the pale-green distances,
The sun's last shaft beyond the gray sea-floor
Still dreams upon the Kamouraska shore,
And the long line of golden villages.
(1891)

Comfort of the Fields

What would'st thou have for easement after grief,
  When the rude world hath used thee with despite,
  And care sits at thine elbow day and night,
Filching thy pleasures like a subtle thief?
To me, when life besets me in such wise,
'Tis sweetest to break forth, to drop the chain,
  And grasp the freedom of this pleasant earth,
    To roam in idleness and sober mirth,
Through summer airs and summer lands, and drain
The comfort of wide fields unto tired eyes.

By hills and waters, farms and solitudes,
  To wander by the day with wilful feet;
  Through fielded valleys wide with yellowing wheat;
Along gray roads that run between deep woods,
Murmurous and cool; through hallowed slopes of pine,
  Where the long daylight dreams, unpierced, unstirred,
  And only the rich-throated thrush is heard;
By lonely forest brooks that froth and shine
  In bouldered crannies buried in the hills;
By broken beeches tangled with wild vine,
  And log-strewn rivers murmurous with mills.

In upland pastures, sown with gold, and sweet
  With the keen perfume of the ripening grass,
  Where wings of birds and filmy shadows pass,

Spread thick as stars with shining marguerite;
To haunt old fences overgrown with brier,
  Muffled in vines, and hawthorns, and wild cherries,
  Rank poisonous ivies, red-bunched elder-berries,
And pièd blossoms to the heart's desire,
  Gray mullein towering into yellow bloom,
  Pink-tasseled milkweed, breathing dense perfume,
And swarthy vervain, tipped with violet fire.

To hear at eve the bleating of far flocks,
  The mud-hen's whistle from the marsh at morn;
  To skirt with deafened ears and brain o'erborne
Some foam-filled rapid charging down its rocks
With iron roar of waters; far away
  Across wide-reeded meres, pensive with noon,
  To hear the querulous outcry of the loon;
To lie among deep rocks, and watch all day
  On liquid heights the snowy clouds melt by;
Or hear from wood-capped mountain-brows the jay
  Pierce the bright morning with his jibing cry.

To feast on summer sounds; the jolted wains,
  The thresher humming from the farm near by,
  The prattling cricket's intermittent cry,
The locust's rattle from the sultry lanes;
Or in the shadow of some oaken spray,
  To watch, as through a mist of light and dreams,
  The far-off hay-fields, where the dusty teams
Drive round and round the lessening squares of hay,
  And hear upon the wind, now loud, now low,
With drowsy cadence half a summer's day,
  The clatter of the reapers come and go.

Far violet hills, horizons filmed with showers,
  The murmur of cool streams, the forest's gloom,
  The voices of the breathing grass, the hum
Of ancient gardens overbanked with flowers:

Thus, with a smile as golden as the dawn,
  And cool fair fingers radiantly divine,
  The mighty mother brings us in her hand,
For all tired eyes and foreheads pinched and wan,
Her restful cup, her beaker of bright wine:
  Drink, and be filled, and ye shall understand!
(1892)

An Autumn Landscape

No wind there is that either pipes or moans;
  The fields are cold and still; the sky
    Is covered with a blue-gray sheet
    Of motionless cloud; and at my feet
  The river, curling softly by,
Whispers and dimples round its quiet gray stones.

Along the chill green slope that dips and heaves
  The road runs rough and silent, lined
    With plum-trees, misty and blue-gray,
    And poplars pallid as the day,
  In masses spectral, undefined,
Pale greenish stems half hid in dry gray leaves.

And on beside the river's sober edge
  A long fresh field lies black. Beyond,
    Low thickets gray and reddish stand,
    Stroked white with birch; and near at hand,
  Over a little steel-smooth pond,
Hang multitudes of thin and withering sedge.

Across a waste and solitary rise
  A ploughman urges his dull team,
    A stooped gray figure with prone brow
    That plunges bending to the plough

With strong, uneven steps. The stream
Rings and re-echoes with his furious cries.

Sometimes the lowing of a cow, long-drawn,
Comes from far off; and crows in strings
Pass on the upper silences.
A flock of small gray goldfinches,
Flown down with silvery twitterings,
Rustle among the birch-cones and are gone.

This day the season seems like one that heeds,
With fixèd ear and lifted hand,
All moods that yet are known on earth,
All motions that have faintest birth,
If haply she may understand
The utmost inward sense of all her deeds.
(1892)

On the Companionship with Nature

Let us be much with Nature; not as they
That labour without seeing, that employ
Her unloved forces, blindly without joy;
Nor those whose hands and crude delights obey
The old brute passion to hunt down and slay;
But rather as children of one common birth,
Discerning in each natural fruit of earth
Kinship and bond with this diviner clay.
Let us be with her wholly at all hours,
With the fond lover's zest, who is content
If his ear hears, and if his eye but sees;
So shall we grow like her in mould and bent,
Our bodies stately as her blessèd trees,
Our thoughts as sweet and sumptuous as her flowers.
(1892)

September

Now hath the summer reached her golden close,
  And, lost amid her corn-fields, bright of soul,
Scarcely perceives from her divine repose
  How near, how swift, the inevitable goal:
Still, still, she smiles, though from her careless feet
  The bounty and the fruitful strength are gone,
  And through the soft long wondering days goes on
The silent sere decadence sad and sweet.

The kingbird and the pensive thrush are fled,
  Children of light, too fearful of the gloom;
The sun falls low, the secret word is said,
  The mouldering woods grow silent as the tomb;
Even the fields have lost their sovereign grace,
  The cone-flower and the marguerite; and no more,
  Across the river's shadow-haunted floor,
The paths of skimming swallows interlace.

Already in the outland wilderness
  The forests echo with unwonted dins;
In clamorous gangs the gathering woodmen press
  Northward, and the stern winter's toil begins.
Around the long low shanties, whose rough lines
  Break the sealed dreams of many an unnamed lake,
  Already in the frost-clear morns awake
The crash and thunder of the falling pines.

Where the tilled earth, with all its fields set free,
  Naked and yellow from the harvest lies,
By many a loft and busy granary,
  The hum and tumult of the threshers rise;
There the tanned farmers labor without slack,
  Till twilight deepens round the spouting mill,

Feeding the loosened sheaves, or with fierce will,
Pitching waist-deep upon the dusty stack.

Still a brief while, ere the old year quite pass,
Our wandering steps and wistful eyes shall greet
The leaf, the water, the beloved grass;
Still from these haunts and this accustomed seat
I see the wood-wrapt city, swept with light,
The blue long-shadowed distance, and, between,
The dotted farm-lands with their parcelled green,
The dark pine forest and the watchful height.

I see the broad rough meadow stretched away
Into the crystal sunshine, wastes of sod,
Acres of withered vervain, purple-gray,
Branches of aster, groves of goldenrod;
And yonder, toward the sunlit summit, strewn
With shadowy boulders, crowned and swathed with weed,
Stand ranks of silken thistles, blown to seed,
Long silver fleeces shining like the noon.

In far-off russet cornfields, where the dry
Gray shocks stand peaked and withering, half concealed
In the rough earth, the orange pumpkins lie,
Full-ribbed; and in the windless pasture-field
The sleek red horses o'er the sun-warmed ground
Stand pensively about in companies,
While all around them from the motionless trees
The long clean shadows sleep without a sound.

Under cool elm-trees floats the distant stream,
Moveless as air; and o'er the vast warm earth
The fathomless daylight seems to stand and dream,
A liquid cool elixir—all its girth

Bound with faint haze, a frail transparency,
Whose lucid purple barely veils and fills
The utmost valleys and the thin last hills,
Nor mars one whit their perfect clarity.

Thus without grief the golden days go by,
So soft we scarcely notice how they wend,
And like a smile half happy, or a sigh,
The summer passes to her quiet end;
And soon, too soon, around the cumbered eaves
Sly frosts shall take the creepers by surprise,
And through the wind-touched reddening woods shall rise
October with the rain of ruined leaves.
(1893)

Indian Summer

The old gray year is near his term in sooth,
And now with backward eye and soft-laid palm
Awakens to a golden dream of youth,
A second childhood lovely and most calm,
And the smooth hour about his misty head
An awning of enchanted splendour weaves,
Of maples, amber, purple and rose-red,
And droop-limbed elms down-dropping golden leaves.
With still half-fallen lids he sits and dreams
Far in a hollow of the sunlit wood,
Lulled by the murmur of thin-threading streams,
Nor sees the polar armies overflood
The darkening barriers of the hills, nor hears
The north-wind ringing with a thousand spears.
(1893)

Archibald Lampman

The City of the End of Things

Beside the pounding cataracts
Of midnight streams unknown to us
'Tis builded in the leafless tracts
And valleys huge of Tartarus.
Lurid and lofty and vast it seems;
It hath no rounded name that rings,
But I have heard it called in dreams
The City of the End of Things.

Its roofs and iron towers have grown
None knoweth how high within the night,
But in its murky streets far down
A flaming terrible and bright
Shakes all the stalking shadows there,
Across the walls, across the floors,
And shifts upon the upper air
From out a thousand furnace doors;
And all the while an awful sound
Keeps roaring on continually,
And crashes in the ceaseless round
Of a gigantic harmony.
Through its grim depths re-echoing
And all its weary height of walls,
With measured roar and iron ring,
The inhuman music lifts and falls.
Where no thing rests and no man is,
And only fire and night hold sway;
The beat, the thunder and the hiss
Cease not, and change not, night nor day.

And moving at unheard commands,
The abysses and vast fires between,
Flit figures that with clanking hands
Obey a hideous routine;

They are not flesh, they are not bone,
They see not with the human eye,
And from their iron lips is blown
A dreadful and monotonous cry;
And whoso of our mortal race
Should find that city unaware,
Lean Death would smite him face to face,
And blanch him with its venomed air:
Or caught by the terrific spell,
Each thread of memory snapt and cut,
His soul would shrivel and its shell
Go rattling like an empty nut.

It was not always so, but once,
In days that no man thinks upon,
Fair voices echoed from its stones,
The light above it leaped and shone:
Once there were multitudes of men,
That built that city in their pride,
Until its might was made, and then
They withered age by age and died.
But now of that prodigious race,
Three only in an iron tower,
Set like carved idols face to face,
Remain the masters of its power;
And at the city gate a fourth,
Gigantic and with dreadful eyes,
Sits looking toward the lightless north,
Beyond the reach of memories;
Fast rooted to the lurid floor,
A bulk that never moves a jot,
In his pale body dwells no more,
Or mind, or soul,—an idiot!
But sometime in the end those three
Shall perish and their hands be still,
And with the master's touch shall flee
Their incommunicable skill.

A stillness absolute as death
Along the slacking wheels shall lie,
And, flagging at a single breath,
The fires shall moulder out and die.
The roar shall vanish at its height,
And over that tremendous town
The silence of eternal night
Shall gather close and settle down.
All its grim grandeur, tower and hall,
Shall be abandoned utterly,
And into rust and dust shall fall
From century to century;
Nor ever living thing shall grow,
Or trunk of tree, or blade of grass;
No drop shall fall, no wind shall blow,
Nor sound of any foot shall pass:
Alone of its accursèd state,
One thing the hand of Time shall spare,
For the grim Idiot at the gate
Is deathless and eternal there.
(1894)

To an Ultra Protestant

Why rage and fret thee; only let them be:
The monkish rod, the sacerdotal pall,
Council and convent, Pope and Cardinal,
The black priest and his holy wizardry.
Nay dread them not, for thought and liberty
Spread ever faster than the foe can smite,
And these shall vanish as the starless night
Before a morning mightier than the sea.
But what of thee and thine? That battle cry?
Those forms and dogmas that thou rear'st so high?
Those blasts of doctrine and those vials of wrath?

Thy hell for most and heaven for the few?
That narrow, joyless and ungenerous path?
What then of these? Ah, they shall vanish too!
(1894)

To a Millionaire

The world in gloom and splendour passes by,
And thou in the midst of it with brows that gleam,
A creature of that old distorted dream
That makes the sound of life an evil cry.
Good men perform just deeds, and brave men die,
And win not honour such as gold can give,
While the vain multitudes plod on, and live,
And serve the curse that pins them down: But I
Think only of the unnumbered broken hearts,
The hunger and the mortal strife for bread,
Old age and youth alike mistaught, misfed,
By want and rags and homelessness made vile,
The griefs and hates, and all the meaner parts
That balance thy one grim misgotten pile.
(1894)

Beauty

Only the things of Beauty shall endure.
While man goes woeful, wasting his brief day,
From Truth and Love and Nature far astray,
Lo! Beauty, the lost goal, the unsought cure;
For how can he whom Beauty hath made sure,
Who hath her law and sovereign creed by heart,
Be proud, or pitiless, play the tyrant's part,
Be false, or envious, greedy or impure.
Nay! she will gift him with a golden key

To unlock every virtue. Name not ye,
As once, "the good, the beautiful, the true,"
For these are but three names for one sole thing;
Or rather Beauty is the perfect ring
That circles and includes the other two.
(1894)

Alcyone

In the silent depth of space,
Immeasurably old, immeasurably far,
Glittering with a silver flame
Through eternity,
Rolls a great and burning star,
With a noble name,
   Alcyone!

In the glorious chart of heaven
It is marked the first of seven;
'Tis a Pleiad:
And a hundred years of earth
With their long-forgotten deeds have come and gone,
Since that tiny point of light,
Once a splendour fierce and bright,
Had its birth
In the star we gaze upon.
It has travelled all that time—
Thought has not a swifter flight—
Through a region where no faintest gust
Of life comes ever, but the power of night
Dwells stupendous and sublime,
Limitless and void and lonely,
A region mute with age, and peopled only
With the dead and ruined dust
Of worlds that lived eternities ago.

Man! when thou dost think of this,
And what our earth and its existence is,
The half-blind toils since life began,
The little aims, the little span,
With what passion and what pride,
And what hunger fierce and wide,
Thou dost break beyond it all,
Seeking for the spirit unconfined
In the clear abyss of mind
A shelter and a peace majestical.
For what is life to thee,
Turning toward the primal light,
With that stern and silent face,
If thou canst not be
Something radiant and august as night,
Something wide as space?
Therefore with a love and gratitude divine
Thou shalt cherish in thine heart for sign
A vision of the great and burning star,
Immeasurably old, immeasurably far,
Surging forth its silver flame
Through eternity;
And thine inner heart shall ring and cry
With the music strange and high,
The grandeur of its name
   Alcyone!
(1895)

White Pansies

Day and night pass over, rounding,
  Star and cloud and sun,
Things of drift and shadow, empty
  Of my dearest one.

Soft as slumber was my baby,
  Beaming bright and sweet;
Daintier than bloom or jewel
  Were his hands and feet.

He was mine, mine all, mine only,
  Mine and his the debt;
Earth and Life and Time are changers;
  I shall not forget.

Pansies for my dear one—heartsease—
  Set them gently so;
For his stainless lips and forehead,
  Pansies white as snow.

Would that in the flower-grown little
  Grave they dug so deep,
I might rest beside him, dreamless,
  Smile no more, nor weep.
(1897)

The Largest Life

I

I lie upon my bed and hear and see.
The moon is rising through the glistening trees;
And momently a great and sombre breeze,
With a vast voice returning fitfully,
Comes like a deep-toned grief, and stirs in me,
Somehow, by some inexplicable art,
A sense of my soul's strangeness, and its part
In the dark march of human destiny.
What am I, then, and what are they that pass

Yonder, and love and laugh, and mourn and weep?
What shall they know of me, or I, alas!
Of them? Little. At times, as if from sleep,
We waken to this yearning passionate mood,
And tremble at our spiritual solitude.

II

Nay, never once to feel we are alone,
While the great human heart around us lies:
To make the smile on other lips our own,
To live upon the light in others' eyes:
To breathe without a doubt the limpid air
Of that most perfect love that knows no pain:
To say—I love you—only, and not care
Whether the love come back to us again,
Divinest self-forgetfulness, at first
A task, and then a tonic, then a need;
To greet with open hands the best and worst,
And only for another's wound to bleed:
This is to see the beauty that God meant,
Wrapped round with life, ineffably content.

III

There is a beauty at the goal of life,
A beauty growing since the world began,
Through every age and race, through lapse and strife
Till the great human soul complete her span.
Beneath the waves of storm that lash and burn,
The currents of blind passion that appall,
To listen and keep watch till we discern
The tide of sovereign truth that guides it all;
So to address our spirits to the height,
And so attune them to the valiant whole,
That the great light be clearer for our light,

And the great soul the stronger for our soul:
To have done this is to have lived, though fame
Remember us with no familiar name.
(1899)

The Land of Pallas

Methought I journeyed along ways that led for ever
  Throughout a happy land where strife and care were
    dead,
And life went by me flowing like a placid river
  Past sandy eyots where the shifting shoals make head.

A land where beauty dwelt supreme, and right, the
    donor
  Of peaceful days; a land of equal gifts and deeds,
Of limitless fair fields and plenty had with honour;
  A land of kindly tillage and untroubled meads,

Of gardens, and great fields, and dreaming rose-
    wreathed alleys,
  Wherein at dawn and dusk the vesper sparrows sang;
Of cities set far off on hills down vista'd valleys,
  And floods so vast and old, men wist not whence they
    sprang,

Of groves, and forest depths, and fountains softly
    welling,
  And roads that ran soft-shadowed past the open doors
Of mighty palaces and many a lofty dwelling,
  Where all men entered and no master trod their floors.

A land of lovely speech, where every tone was
    fashioned
  By generations of emotion high and sweet,

Of thought and deed and bearing lofty and impassioned;
A land of golden calm, grave forms, and fretless feet.

And every mode and saying of that land gave token
Of limits where no death or evil fortune fell,
And men lived out long lives in proud content unbroken,
For there no man was rich, none poor, but all were well.

And all the earth was common, and no base contriving
Of money of coined gold was needed there or known,
But all men wrought together without greed or striving,
And all the store of all to each man was his own.

From all that busy land, grey town, and peaceful village,
Where never jar was heard, nor wail, nor cry of strife,
From every laden stream and all the fields of tillage,
Arose the murmur and the kindly hum of life.

At morning to the fields came forth the men, each neighbour
Hand linked to other, crowned, with wreaths upon their hair,
And all day long with joy they gave their hands to labour,
Moving at will, unhastened, each man to his share.

At noon the women came, the tall fair women, bearing
Baskets of wicker in their ample hands for each,
And learned the day's brief tale, and how the fields were faring,
And blessed them with their lofty beauty and blithe speech.

And when the great day's toil was over, and the shadows
Grew with the flocking stars, the sound of festival
Rose in each city square, and all the country meadows,
Palace, and paven court, and every rustic hall.

Beside smooth streams, where alleys and green gardens meeting
Ran downward to the flood with marble steps, a throng
Came forth of all the folk, at even, gaily greeting,
With echo of sweet converse, jest, and stately song.

In all their great fair cities there was neither seeking
For power of gold, nor greed of lust, nor desperate pain
Of multitudes that starve, or, in hoarse anger breaking,
Beat at the doors of princes, break and fall in vain.

But all the children of that peaceful land, like brothers,
Lofty of spirit, wise, and ever set to learn
The chart of neighbouring souls, the bent and need of others,
Thought only of good deeds, sweet speech, and just return.

And there there was no prison, power of arms, nor palace,
Where prince or judge held sway, for none was needed there;
Long ages since the very names of fraud and malice
Had vanished from men's tongues, and died from all men's care.

And there there were no bonds of contract, deed, or marriage,
No oath, nor any form, to make the word more sure,

For no man dreamed of hurt, dishonour, or miscarriage,
Where every thought was truth, and every heart was pure.

There were no castes of rich or poor, of slave or master,
Where all were brothers, and the curse of gold was dead,
But all that wise fair race to kindlier ends and vaster
Moved on together with the same majestic tread.

And all the men and women of that land were fairer
Than even the mightiest of our meaner race can be;
The men like gentle children, great of limb, yet rarer
For wisdom and high thought, like kings for majesty.

And all the women through great ages of bright living,
Grown goodlier of stature, strong, and subtly wise,
Stood equal with the men, calm counsellors, ever giving
The fire and succour of proud faith and dauntless eyes.

And as I journeyed in that land I reached a ruin,
The gateway of a lonely and secluded waste,
A phantom of forgotten time and ancient doing,
Eaten by age and violence, crumbled and defaced.

On its grim outer walls the ancient world's sad glories
Were recorded in fire; upon its inner stone,
Drawn by dead hands, I saw, in tales and tragic stories,
The woe and sickness of an age of fear made known.

And lo, in that grey storehouse, fallen to dust and rotten,
Lay piled the traps and engines of forgotten greed,

The tomes of codes and canons, long disused, forgotten,
The robes and sacred books of many a vanished creed.

An old grave man I found, white-haired and gently spoken,
Who, as I questioned, answered with a smile benign,
'Long years have come and gone since these poor gauds were broken,
Broken and banished from a life made more divine.

'But still we keep them stored as once our sires deemed fitting,
The symbol of dark days and lives remote and strange,
Lest o'er the minds of any there should come unwitting
The thought of some new order and the lust of change.

'If any grow disturbed, we bring them gently hither,
To read the world's grim record and the sombre lore
Massed in these pitiless vaults, and they returning thither,
Bear with them quieter thoughts, and make for change no more.'

And thence I journeyed on by one broad way that bore me
Out of that waste, and as I passed by tower and town
I saw amid the limitless plain far out before me
A long low mountain, blue as beryl, and its crown

Was capped by marble roofs that shone like snow for whiteness,
Its foot was deep in gardens, and that blossoming plain

Seemed in the radiant shower of its majestic brightness
A land for gods to dwell in, free from care and pain.

And to and forth from that fair mountain like a river
Ran many a dim grey road, and on them I could see
A multitude of stately forms that seemed for ever
Going and coming in bright bands; and near to me

Was one that in his journey seemed to dream and linger,
Walking at whiles with kingly step, then standing still,
And him I met and asked him, pointing with my finger,
The meaning of the palace and the lofty hill.

Whereto the dreamer: 'Art thou of this land, my brother,
And knowest not the mountain and its crest of walls,
Where dwells the priestless worship of the all-wise mother?
That is the hill of Pallas; those her marble halls!

'There dwell the lords of knowledge and of thought increasing,
And they whom insight and the gleams of song uplift;
And thence as by a hundred conduits flows unceasing
The spring of power and beauty, an eternal gift.'

Still I passed on until I reached at length, not knowing
Whither the tangled and diverging paths might lead,
A land of baser men, whose coming and whose going
Were urged by fear, and hunger, and the curse of greed.

I saw the proud and fortunate go by me, faring
In fatness and fine robes, the poor oppressed and slow,

The faces of bowed men, and piteous women bearing
The burden of perpetual sorrow and the stamp of woe.

And tides of deep solicitude and wondering pity
Possessed me, and with eager and uplifted hands
I drew the crowd about me in a mighty city,
And taught the message of those other kindlier lands.

I preached the rule of Faith and brotherly Communion,
The law of Peace and Beauty and the death of Strife,
And painted in great words the horror of disunion,
The vainness of self-worship, and the waste of life.

I preached, but fruitlessly; the powerful from their stations
Rebuked me as an anarch, envious and bad,
And they that served them with lean hands and bitter patience
Smiled only out of hollow orbs, and deemed me mad.

And still I preached, and wrought, and still I bore my message,
For well I knew that on and upward without cease
The spirit works for ever, and by Faith and Presage
That somehow yet the end of human life is Peace.
(1899)

Winter Uplands

The frost that stings like fire upon my cheek,
The loneliness of this forsaken ground,
The long white drift upon whose powdered peak
I sit in the great silence as one bound;
The rippled sheet of snow where the wind blew
Across the open fields for miles ahead;

The far-off city towered and roofed in blue
A tender line upon the western red;
The stars that singly, then in flocks appear,
Like jets of silver from the violet dome,
So wonderful, so many and so near,
And then the golden moon to light me home—
The crunching snowshoes and the stinging air,
And silence, frost and beauty everywhere.
(1900)

Epitaph on a Rich Man

He made himself a great name in his day,
A glittering fellow on the world's hard way,
He tilled and seeded and reaped plentifully
From the black soil of human misery;
He won great riches, and they buried him
With splendour that the people's want makes grim;
But some day he shall not be called to mind
Save as the curse and pestilence of his kind.
(1943)

At the Long Sault: May, 1660

Under the day-long sun there is life and mirth
  In the working earth,
And the wonderful moon shines bright
  Through the soft spring night,
The innocent flowers in the limitless woods are
    springing
  Far and away
  With the sound and the perfume of May,
And ever up from the south the happy birds are
    winging,

The waters glitter and leap and play
While the grey hawk soars.

But far in an open glade of the forest set
Where the rapid plunges and roars,
Is a ruined fort with a name that men forget,—
A shelterless pen
With its broken palisade,
Behind it, musket in hand,
Beyond message or aid
In this savage heart of the wild,
Mere youngsters, grown in a moment to men,
Grim and alert and arrayed,
The comrades of Daulac stand.
Ever before them, night and day,
The rush and skulk and cry
Of foes, not men but devils, panting for prey;
Behind them the sleepless dream
Of the little frail-walled town, far away by the plunging
stream,
Of maiden and matron and child,
With ruin and murder impending, and none but they
To beat back the gathering horror
Deal death while they may,
And then die.

Day and night they have watched while the little plain
Grew dark with the rush of the foe, but their host
Broke ever and melted away, with no boast
But to number their slain;
And now as the days renew
Hunger and thirst and care
Were they never so stout, so true,
Press at their hearts; but none
Falters or shrinks or utters a coward word,
Though each setting sun

Brings from the pitiless wild new hands to the Iroquois horde,
And only to them despair.

Silent, white-faced, again and again
Charged and hemmed round by furious hands,
Each for a moment faces them all and stands
In his little desperate ring; like a tired bull moose
Whom scores of sleepless wolves, a ravening pack,
Have chased all night, all day
Through the snow-laden woods, like famine let loose;
And he turns at last in his track
Against a wall of rock and stands at bay;
Round him with terrible sinews and teeth of steel
They charge and recharge; but with many a furious plunge and wheel,
Hither and thither over the trampled snow,
He tosses them bleeding and torn;
Till, driven, and ever to and fro
Harried, wounded and weary grown,
His mighty strength gives way
And all together they fasten upon him and drag him down.

So Daulac turned him anew
With a ringing cry to his men
In the little raging forest glen,
And his terrible sword in the twilight whistled and slew.
And all his comrades stood
With their backs to the pales, and fought
Till their strength was done;
The thews that were only mortal flagged and broke
Each struck his last wild stroke,
And they fell one by one,
And the world that had seemed so good
Passed like a dream and was naught.

And then the great night came
With the triumph-songs of the foe and the flame
Of the camp-fires.
Out of the dark the soft wind woke,
The song of the rapid rose alway
And came to the spot where the comrades lay,
Beyond help or care,
With none but the red men round them
To gnash their teeth and stare.

All night by the foot of the mountain
  The little town lieth at rest,
The sentries are peacefully pacing;
  And neither from East nor from West

Is there rumour of death or of danger;
  None dreameth tonight in his bed
That ruin was near and the heroes
  That met it and stemmed it are dead.

But afar in the ring of the forest,
  Where the air is so tender with May
And the waters are wild in the moonlight,
  They lie in their silence of clay.

The numberless stars out of heaven
  Look down with a pitiful glance;
And the lilies asleep in the forest
  Are closed like the lilies of France.
(1943)

Bliss Carman (1861-1929)

Bliss Carman had the greatest international recognition among the Confederation poets. To give two examples, the young Wallace Stevens turned to Carman when he "felt the need for poetry" (qtd. in Bentley, "Minor" v), while Ezra Pound said that Carman "is by drowning" (qtd. by Mary B. McGillivray in Lynch 7). Car about the only living American poet who would not improve man was born in Fredericton, and, like his cousin Charles G.D. Roberts, he studied at the University of New Brunswick. After graduating in 1881 he attended Oxford and Edinburgh universities without earning a degree from either, then returned to the University of New Brunswick to receive an M.A. in 1884. After the deaths of both parents in the next two years, Carman started graduate work in English at Harvard in 1886. Again he did not earn a degree, but the encounters with such scholars as Josiah Royce, George Santayana, and Francis Child, and such students as Richard Hovey, had an enduring influence. In his interests in contemporary experimental writers like Paul Verlaine, in mysticism, and in the cult of the book as an aesthetic object, Carman carried the enthusiasms of Harvard into his career as a man of letters (see Schlereth). That career was underway before Carman went to Harvard, for he wrote "Low Tide on Grand Pré" before leaving New Brunswick. From 1890, he worked as an editor for various periodicals, beginning with the *Independent* (New York) and including *The Atlantic Monthly* and *The Chap-Book*. He published his first collection of poetry, *Low Tide on Grand Pré*, in 1893. It was followed by *Songs from Vagabondia* (1894), the first of three popular collections of light verse on which he collaborated with Hovey; *Behind the Arras* (1895), *Ballads of Lost Haven* (1897), *Sappho: One Hundred Lyrics* (1905), and many other books, including several collections of prose. His colourful life as a bachelor was moderated by his steady involvement with a married woman, Mary Perry King, from 1896 to his death in 1929 (see Gundy,

"Kennerley"). In the last years of his life, he toured Canada as a lecturer, and so he was celebrated here long after he had produced his best work.

Carman's international acclaim has been less influential than the attacks on Carman mounted by such young Modernists as F.R. Scott and A.J.M. Smith in the 1920s. Later, Smith came to realize that when Carman "gives expression to the Lucretian sense of tears at the heart of things his writing takes on a simplicity and grandeur that is unmistakable" (137-38). That aspect of Carman is most evident at the beginning of his career, especially in the two volumes that dominate the selection in this anthology: *Low Tide on Grand Pré* and *Sappho.* The eight pieces from the former show a lyric genius with the themes of love and longing, while the twenty poems from the latter show Carman at his most passionate and his most impersonal, as he adopts the persona of Sappho to express his own "Unitrinian" philosophy (see Bentley 32). "In the Heart of the Hills," "The Grave-Tree," and "To P.V." reveal Carman's skills as an elegist, while "The Ships of St. John" and "A Vagabond Song" are forceful examples of the qualities that made Carman so popular. The gentle affirmations in much of his later work, such as "Vestigia," ignore the tensions that made his earlier poems so distinctive, but he continued to write memorable poems until the end of his career.

Further Reading

Bentley, D.M.R. "Preface: Minor Poets of a Superior Order." *Canadian Poetry: Studies, Documents, Reviews* 14 (1984): v-viii.

———. "Threefold in Wonder: Bliss Carman's *Sappho: One Hundred Lyrics*." *Canadian Poetry: Studies, Documents, Reviews* 17 (1985): 29-58.

Cappon, James. *Bliss Carman and the Literary Currents and Influences of His Time.* Toronto: Ryerson, 1930.

Carman, Bliss. *The Poems of Bliss Carman.* Ed. John Robert Sorfleet. New Canadian Library. Toronto: McClelland and Stewart, 1976.

Gundy, H. Pearson, ed. "Kennerley on Carman." *Canadian Poetry: Studies, Documents, Reviews* 14 (1984): 69-74.

———, ed. *Letters of Bliss Carman.* Kingston: McGill-Queen's, 1981.

Lynch, Gerald, ed. *Bliss Carman: A Reappraisal.* Reappraisals: Canadian Writers. Ottawa: U of Ottawa P, 1990.

Miller, Muriel. *Bliss Carman: A Portrait.* Toronto: Ryerson, 1935.

———. *Bliss Carman: Quest & Revolt.* St. John's: Jesperson, 1985.

Pacey, Desmond. "Bliss Carman." *Ten Canadian Poets: A Group of Biographical and Critical Essays.* Toronto: Ryerson, 1958. 59-113.

———. "Bliss Carman: A Reappraisal." *Northern Review* 3:3 (1950): 2-10.

Ross, Malcolm. "Bliss Carman and the Poetry of Mystery: A Defence of the Personal Fallacy." *The Impossible Sum of Our Traditions: Reflections on Canadian Literature.* Toronto: McClelland and Stewart, 1986. 43-66.

Schlereth, Wendy Clauson. *The Chap-Book: A Journal of American Intellectual Life in the 1890s.* Ann Arbor: UMI, 1982.

Smith, A.J.M. "The Fredericton Poets." *Twentieth-Century Essays on Confederation Literature.* Ed. Lorraine McMullen. Ottawa: Tecumseh, 1976. 128-39.

Sorfleet, John Robert. "Transcendentalist, Mystic, Evolutionary Idealist: Bliss Carman, 1886-1894." *Colony and Confederation: Early Canadian Poets and Their Background.* Ed. George Woodcock. Vancouver: UBC P, 1974. 189-210.

Stephens, Donald. *Bliss Carman.* Twayne's World Authors. New York: Twayne, 1966.

Surette, Leon. "Ezra Pound, Bliss Carman, and Richard Hovey." *Canadian Poetry: Studies, Documents, Reviews* 43 (1998): 44-69.

Ware, Tracy, ed. "Arthur Symons' Reviews of Bliss Carman." *Canadian Poetry: Studies, Documents, Reviews* 37 (1995): 100-13.

———. "The Integrity of Carman's *Low Tide on Grand Pré.*" *Canadian Poetry: Studies, Documents, Reviews* 14 (1984): 38-52.

Whalen, Terry. "Bliss Carman." *Canadian Writers and Their Works, Poetry Series: Volume Two.* Eds. Robert Lecker, Jack David, and Ellen Quigley. Downsview, ON: ECW, 1983. 77-132.

from *Low Tide on Grand Pré* (1893; 1895)

Low Tide on Grand Pré

The sun goes down, and over all
  These barren reaches by the tide
Such unelusive glories fall,
  I almost dream they yet will bide
  Until the coming of the tide.

And yet I know that not for us,
  By any ecstasy of dream,
He lingers to keep luminous
  A little while the grievous stream,
  Which frets, uncomforted of dream—

A grievous stream, that to and fro
  Athrough the fields of Acadie
Goes wandering, as if to know
  Why one beloved face should be
  So long from home and Acadie.

Was it a year or lives ago
  We took the grasses in our hands,
And caught the summer flying low
  Over the waving meadow lands,
  And held it there between our hands?

The while the river at our feet—
  A drowsy inland meadow stream—
At set of sun the after-heat
  Made running gold, and in the gleam
  We freed our birch upon the stream.

There down along the elms at dusk
  We lifted dripping blade to drift,
Through twilight scented fine like musk,

Where night and gloom awhile uplift,
Nor sunder soul and soul adrift.

And that we took into our hands
Spirit of life or subtler thing—
Breathed on us there, and loosed the bands
Of death, and taught us, whispering,
The secret of some wonder-thing.

Then all your face grew light, and seemed
To hold the shadow of the sun;
The evening faltered, and I deemed
That time was ripe, and years had done
Their wheeling underneath the sun.

So all desire and all regret,
And fear and memory, were naught;
One to remember or forget
The keen delight our hands had caught;
Morrow and yesterday were naught.

The night has fallen, and the tide . . . .
Now and again comes drifting home,
Across these aching barrens wide,
A sigh like driven wind or foam:
In grief the flood is bursting home.
(1887)

A Windflower

Between the roadside and the wood,
Between the dawning and the dew,
A tiny flower before the sun,
Ephemeral in time, I grew.

And there upon the trail of spring,
  Not death nor love nor any name
Known among men in all their lands
  Could blur the wild desire with shame.

But down my dayspan of the year
  The feet of straying winds came by;
And all my trembling soul was thrilled
  To follow one lost mountain cry.

And then my heart beat once and broke
  To hear the sweeping rain forebode
Some ruin in the April world,
  Between the woodside and the road.

To-night can bring no healing now;
  The calm of yesternight is gone;
Surely the wind is but the wind,
  And I a broken waif thereon.
(1889)

In Lyric Season

The lyric April time is forth
  With lyric mornings, frost and sun;
  From leaguers vast of night undone
Auroral mild new stars are born.

And ever at the year's return,
  Along the valleys gray with rime,
  Thou leadest as of old, where time
Can naught but follow to thy sway.

The trail is far through leagues of spring,
  And long the quest to the white core

Of harvest quiet, yet once more
I gird me to the old unrest.

I know I shall not ever meet
Thy still regard across the year,
And yet I know thou wilt draw near,
When the last hour of pain and loss

Drifts out to slumber, and the deeps
Of nightfall feel God's hand unbar
His lyric April, star by star,
And the lost twilight land reveal.
(1888)

The Pensioners

We are the pensioners of Spring,
And take the largess of her hand
When vassal warder winds unbar
The wintry portals of her land;

The lonely shadow-girdled winds,
Her seraph almoners, who keep
This little life in flesh and bone
With meagre portions of white sleep.

Then all year through with starveling care
We go on some fool's idle quest,
And eat her bread and wine in thrall
To a fool's shame with blind unrest.

Until her April train goes by,
And then because we are the kin
Of every hill flower on the hill
We must arise and walk therein.

Because her heart as our own heart,
  Knowing the same wild upward stir,
Beats joyward by eternal laws,
  We must arise and go with her;

Forget we are not where old joys
  Return when dawns and dreams retire;
Make grief a phantom of regret,
  And fate the henchman of desire;

Divorce unreason from delight;
  Learn how despair is uncontrol,
Failure the shadow of remorse,
  And death a shudder of the soul.

Yea, must we triumph when she leads.
  A little rain before the sun,
A breath of wind on the road's dust,
  The sound of trammeled brooks undone,

Along red glinting willow stems
  The year's white prime, on bank and stream
The haunting cadence of no song
  And vivid wanderings of dream,

A range of low blue hills, the far
  First whitethroat's ecstasy unfurled:
And we are overlords of change,
  In the glad morning of the world,

Though we should fare as they whose life
  Time takes within his hands to wring
Between the winter and the sea,
  The weary pensioners of Spring.
(1889)

Carnations in Winter

Your carmine flakes of bloom to-night
 The fire of wintry sunsets hold;
Again in dreams you burn to light
 A far Canadian garden old.

The blue north summer over it
 Is bland with long ethereal days;
The gleaming martins wheel and flit
 Where breaks your sun down orient ways.

There, when the gradual twilight falls,
 Through quietudes of dusk afar,
Hermit antiphonal hermit calls
 From hills below the first pale star.

Then in your passionate love's foredoom
 Once more your spirit stirs the air,
And you are lifted through the gloom
 To warm the coils of her dark hair.
(1888)

A Sea-Drift

As the seaweed swims the sea
 In the ruin after storm,
Sunburnt memories of thee
 Through the twilight float and form.

And desire, when thou art gone,
 Roves his desolate domain,
As the meadow-birds at dawn
 Haunt the spaces of the rain.
(1894)

The Eavesdropper

In a still room at hush of dawn,
  My Love and I lay side by side
And heard the roaming forest wind
  Stir in the paling autumn-tide.

I watched her earth-brown eyes grow glad
  Because the round day was so fair;
While memories of reluctant night
  Lurked in the blue dusk of her hair.

Outside, a yellow maple tree,
  Shifting upon the silvery blue
With tiny multitudinous sound,
  Rustled to let the sunlight through.

The livelong day the elvish leaves
  Danced with their shadows on the floor;
And the lost children of the wind
  Went straying homeward by our door.

And all the swarthy afternoon
  We watched the great deliberate sun
Walk through the crimsoned hazy world,
  Counting his hilltops one by one.

Then as the purple twilight came
  And touched the vines along our eaves,
Another Shadow stood without
  And gloomed the dancing of the leaves.

The silence fell on my Love's lips;
  Her great brown eyes were veiled and sad
With pondering some maze of dream,
  Though all the splendid year was glad.

Restless and vague as a gray wind
  Her heart had grown, she knew not why.
But hurrying to the open door,
  Against the verge of western sky

I saw retreating on the hills,
  Looming and sinister and black,
The stealthy figure swift and huge
  Of One who strode and looked not back.
(1893)

In Apple Time

The apple harvest days are here,
  The boding apple harvest days,
  And down the flaming valley ways,
The foresters of time draw near.

Through leagues of bloom I went with Spring,
  To call you on the slopes of morn,
  Where in imperious song is borne
The wild heart of the goldenwing.

I roamed through alien summer lands,
  I sought your beauty near and far;
  To-day, where russet shadows are,
I hold your face between my hands.

On runnels dark by slopes of fern,
  The hazy undern sleeps in sun.
  Remembrance and desire, undone,
From old regret to dreams return.

The apple harvest time is here,
  The tender apple harvest time;

A sheltering calm, unknown at prime,
Settles upon the brooding year.
(1888)

End of poems from *Low Tide on Grand Pré*

In the Heart of the Hills

In the warm blue heart of the hills
My beautiful, beautiful one
Sleeps where he laid him down
Before the journey was done.

All the long summer day
The ghosts of noon draw nigh,
And the tremulous aspens hear
The footing of winds go by.

Down to the gates of the sea,
Out of the gates of the west,
Journeys the whispering river
Before the place of his rest.

The road he loved to follow
When June came by his door,
Out through the dim blue haze
Leads, but allures no more.

The trailing shadows of clouds
Steal from the slopes and are gone;
The myriad life in the grass
Stirs, but he slumbers on;

The inland wandering tern
Skreel as they forage and fly;

His loons on the lonely reach
Utter their querulous cry;

Over the floating lilies
A dragon-fly tacks and steers;
Far in the depth of the blue
A martin settles and veers;

To every roadside thistle
A gold-brown butterfly clings;
But he no more companions
All the dear vagrant things.

The strong red journeying sun,
The pale and wandering rain,
Will roam on the hills forever
And find him never again.

Then twilight falls with the touch
Of a hand that soothes and stills,
And a swamp-robin sings into light
The lone white star of the hills.

Alone in the dusk he sings,
And a burden of sorrow and wrong
Is lifted up from the earth
And carried away in his song.

Alone in the dusk he sings,
And the joy of another day
Is folded in peace and borne
On the drift of years away.

But there in the heart of the hills
My beautiful weary one
Sleeps where he laid him down;
And the large sweet night is begun.
(1892)

The Grave-Tree

Let me have a scarlet maple
For the grave-tree at my head,
With the quiet sun behind it,
In the years when I am dead.

Let me have it for a signal,
Where the long winds stream and stream,
Clear across the dim blue distance,
Like a horn blown in a dream;

Scarlet when the April vanguard
Bugles up the laggard Spring,
Scarlet when the bannered Autumn,
Marches by unwavering.

It will comfort me with honey
When the shining rifts and showers
Sweep across the purple valley
And bring back the forest flowers.

It will be my leafy cabin,
Large enough when June returns
And I hear the golden thrushes
Flute and hesitate by turns.

And in fall, some yellow morning,
When the stealthy frost has come,
Leaf by leaf it will befriend me
As with comrades going home.

Let me have the Silent Valley
And the hill that fronts the east,
So that I can watch the morning
Redden and the stars released.

Leave me in the Great Lone Country,
For I shall not be afraid
With the shy moose and the beaver
There within my scarlet shade.

I would sleep, but not too soundly,
Where the sunning partridge drums,
Till the crickets hush before him
When the Scarlet Hunter comes.

That will be in warm September,
In the stillness of the year,
When the river-blue is deepest
And the other world is near.

When the apples burn their reddest
And the corn is in the sheaves,
I shall stir and waken lightly
At a footfall in the leaves.

It will be the Scarlet Hunter
Come to tell me time is done;
On the idle hills forever
There will stand the idle sun.

There the wind will stay to whisper
Many wonders to the reeds;
But I shall not fear to follow
Where my Scarlet Hunter leads.

I shall know him in the darkling
Murmur of the river bars,
While his feet are on the mountains
Treading out the smoldering stars.

I shall know him, in the sunshine
Sleeping in my scarlet tree,

Long before he halts beside it
Stooping down to summon me.

Then fear not, my friends, to leave me
In the boding autumn vast;
There are many things to think of
When the roving days are past.

Leave me by the scarlet maple,
When the journeying shadows fail,
Waiting till the Scarlet Hunter
Pass upon the endless trail.
(1892)

By the Aurelian Wall

In Memory of John Keats

By the Aurelian Wall,
Where the long shadows of the centuries fall
From Caius Cestius' tomb,
A weary mortal seeking rest found room
For quiet burial,

Leaving among his friends
A book of lyrics.
Such untold amends
A traveller might make
In a strange country, bidden to partake
Before he farther wends;

Who shyly should bestow
The foreign reed-flute they had seen him blow
And finger cunningly,
On one of the dark children standing by,
Then lift his cloak and go.

The years pass. And the child
Thoughtful beyond his fellows, grave and mild,
Treasures the rough-made toy,
Until one day he blows it for clear joy,
And wakes the music wild.

His fondness makes it seem
A thing first fashioned in delirious dream,
Some god had cut and tried,
And filled with yearning passion, and cast aside
On some far woodland stream,—

After long years to be
Found by the stranger and brought over sea,
A marvel and delight
To ease the noon and pierce the dark blue night,
For children such as he.

He learns the silver strain
Wherewith the ghostly houses of gray rain
And lonely valleys ring,
When the untroubled whitethroats make the spring
A world without a stain;

Then on his river reed,
With strange and unsuspected notes that plead
Of their own wild accord
For utterances no bird's throat could afford,
Lifts it to human need.

His comrades leave their play,
When calling and compelling far away
By river-slope and hill,
He pipes their wayward footsteps where he will,
All the long lovely day.

Even his elders come.
"Surely the child is elvish," murmur some,
And shake the knowing head;
"Give us the good old simple things instead,
Our fathers used to hum."

Others at the open door
Smile when they hear what they have hearkened for
These many summers now,
Believing they should live to learn somehow
Things never known before.

But he can only tell
How the flute's whisper lures him with a spell,
Yet always just eludes
The lost perfection over which he broods;
And how he loves it well.

Till all the country-side,
Familiar with his piping far and wide,
Has taken for its own
That weird enchantment down the evening blown,—
Its glory and its pride.

And so his splendid name,
Who left the book of lyrics and small fame
Among his fellows then,
Spreads through the world like autumn—who knows when?—
Till all the hillsides flame.

Grand Pré and Margaree
Hear it upbruited from the unresting sea;
And the small Gaspareau,
Whose yellow leaves repeat it, seems to know
A new felicity.

Even the shadows tall,
Walking at sundown through the plain, recall
A mound the grasses keep,
Where once a mortal came and found long sleep
By the Aurelian Wall.
(1893)

A Vagabond Song

There is something in the autumn that is native to my
blood—
Touch of manner, hint of mood;
And my heart is like a rhyme,
With the yellow and the purple and the crimson keeping
time.

The scarlet of the maples can shake me like a cry
Of bugles going by.
And my lonely spirit thrills
To see the frosty asters like a smoke upon the hills.

There is something in October sets the gypsy blood astir;
We must rise and follow her,
When from every hill of flame
She calls and calls each vagabond by name.
(1895)

To P.V.

So they would raise your monument,
Old vagabond of lovely earth?
Another answer without words
To Humdrum's, "What are poets worth?"

Not much we gave you when alive,
Whom now we lavishly deplore,—
A little bread, a little wine,
A little caporal—no more.

Here in our lodging of a day
You roistered till we were appalled;
Departing, in your room we found
A string of golden verses scrawled.

The princely manor-house of art,
A vagrant artist entertains;
And when he gets him to the road,
Behold, a princely gift remains.

Abashed, we set your name above
The purse-full patrons of our board;
Remind newcomers with a nudge,
"Verlaine took once what we afford!"

The gardens of the Luxembourg,
Spreading beneath the brilliant sun,
Shall be your haunt of leisure now
When all your wander years are done.

There you shall stand, the very mien
You wore in Paris streets of old,
And ponder what a thing is life,
Or watch the chestnut blooms unfold.

There you will find, I dare surmise,
Another tolerance than ours,
The loving-kindness of the grass,
The tender patience of the flowers.

And every year, when May returns
To bring the golden age again,

And hope comes back with poetry
In your loved land across the Seine,

Some youth will come with foreign speech,
Bearing his dream from over sea,
A lover of your flawless craft,
Apprenticed to your poverty.

He will be mute before you there,
And mark those lineaments which tell
What stormy unrelenting fate
Had one who served his art so well.

And there be yours, the livelong day,
Beyond the mordant reach of pain,
The little gospel of the leaves,
The *Nunc dimittis* of the rain!
(1896)

From Sappho: One Hundred Lyrics (1903)

III

Power and beauty and knowledge,—
Pan, Aphrodite, or Hermes,—
Whom shall we life-loving mortals
  Serve and be happy?

Lo, now your garlanded altars,
Are they not goodly with flowers?
Have ye not honour and pleasure
  In lovely Lesbos?

Will ye not, therefore, a little
Hearten, impel, and inspire

One who adores, with a favour
  Threefold in wonder?

IV

I

O Pan of the evergreen forest,
Protector of herds in the meadows,
Helper of men at their toiling,—
Tillage and harvest and herding,—
How many times to frail mortals
  Hast thou not hearkened!

Now even I come before thee
With oil and honey and wheat bread,
Praying for strength and fulfilment
Of human longing, with purpose
Ever to keep thy great worship
  Pure and undarkened.

II

O Hermes, master of knowledge,
Measure and number and rhythm,
Worker of wonders in metal,
Moulder of malleable music,
So often the giver of secret
  Learning to mortals!

Now even I, a fond woman,
Frail and of small understanding,
Yet with unslakable yearning
Greatly desiring wisdom,
Come to the threshold of reason
  And the bright portals.

III

And thou, sea-born Aphrodite,
In whose beneficent keeping
Earth with her infinite beauty,
Colour and fashion and fragrance,
Glows like a flower with fervour
   Where woods are vernal!

Touch with thy lips and enkindle
This moon-white delicate body,
Drench with the dew of enchantment
This mortal one, that I also
Grow to the measure of beauty
   Fleet yet eternal.

VI

Peer of the gods he seems,
Who in thy presence
Sits and hears close to him
Thy silver speech-tones
And lovely laughter.

Ah, but the heart flutters
Under my bosom,
When I behold thee
Even a moment;
Utterance leaves me;

My tongue is useless;
A subtle fire
Runs through my body;
My eyes are sightless,
And my ears ringing;

I flush with fever,
And a strong trembling
Lays hold upon me;
Paler than grass am I,
Half dead for madness.

Yet must I, greatly
Daring, adore thee,
As the adventurous
Sailor makes seaward
For the lost sky-line

And undiscovered
Fabulous islands,
Drawn by the lure of
Beauty and summer
And the sea's secret.

VII

The Cyprian came to thy cradle,
When thou wast little and small,
And said to the nurse who rocked thee,
"Fear not thou for the child:

"She shall be kindly favoured,
And fair and fashioned well,
As befits the Lesbian maidens
And those who are fated to love."

Hermes came to thy cradle,
Resourceful, sagacious, serene,
And said, "The girl must have knowledge,
To lend her freedom and poise.

"Naught will avail her beauty,
If she have not wit beside.

She shall be Hermes' daughter,
Passing wise in her day."

Great Pan came to thy cradle,
With calm of the deepest hills,
And smiled, "They have forgotten
The veriest power of life.

"To kindle her shapely beauty,
And illumine her mind withal,
I give to the little person
The glowing and craving soul."

XVIII

The courtyard of her house is wide
And cool and still when day departs.
Only the rustle of leaves is there
  And running water.

And then her mouth, more delicate
Than the frail wood-anemone,
Brushes my cheek, and deeper grow
  The purple shadows.

XXIII

I loved thee, Atthis, in the long ago,
When the great oleanders were in flower
In the broad herded meadows full of sun.
And we would often at the fall of dusk
Wander together by the silver stream,
When the soft grass-heads were all wet with dew
And purple-misted in the fading light.
And joy I knew and sorrow at thy voice,
And the superb magnificence of love,—
The loneliness that saddens solitude,

And the sweet speech that makes it durable,—
The bitter longing and the keen desire,
The sweet companionship through quiet days
In the slow ample beauty of the world,
And the unutterable glad release
Within the temple of the holy night.
O Atthis, how I loved thee long ago
In that fair perished summer by the sea!

XXXIV

"Who was Atthis?" men shall ask,
When the world is old, and time
Has accomplished without haste
The strange destiny of men.

Haply in that far-off age
One shall find these silver songs,
With their human freight, and guess
What a lover Sappho was.

XLI

Phaon, O my lover,
What should so detain thee,

Now the wind comes walking
Through the leafy twilight?

All the plum leaves quiver
With the coolth and darkness,

After their long patience
In consuming ardour.

And the moving grasses
Have relief; the dew-drench

Comes to quell the parching
Ache of noon they suffered.

I alone of all things
Fret with unsluiced fire.

And there is no quenching
In the night for Sappho,

Since her lover Phaon
Leaves her unrequited.

XLV

Softer than the hill fog to the forest
Are the loving hands of my dear lover,
When she sleeps beside me in the starlight
And her beauty drenches me with rest.

As the quiet mist enfolds the beech-trees,
Even as she dreams her arms enfold me,
Half awaking with a hundred kisses
On the scarlet lily of her mouth.

LIV

How soon will all my lovely days be over,
And I no more be found beneath the sun,—
Neither beside the many-murmuring sea,
Nor where the plain winds whisper to the reeds,
Nor in the tall beech-woods among the hills
Where roam the bright-lipped oreads, nor along
The pasture sides where berry-pickers stray
And harmless shepherds pipe their sheep to fold!

For I am eager, and the flame of life
Burns quickly in the fragile lamp of clay.

Passion and love and longing and hot tears
Consume this mortal Sappho, and too soon
A great wind from the dark will blow upon me,
And I be no more found in the fair world,
For all the search of the revolving moon
And patient shine of everlasting stars.

LV

Soul of sorrow, why this weeping?
What immortal grief hath touched thee
With the poignancy of sadness,—
   Testament of tears?

Have the high gods deigned to show thee
Destiny, and disillusion
Fills thy heart at all things human,
   Fleeting and desired?

Nay, the gods themselves are fettered
By one law which links together
Truth and nobleness and beauty,
   Man and stars and sea.

And they only shall find freedom
Who with courage rise and follow
Where love leads beyond all peril,
   Wise beyond all words.

LXI

There is no more to say now thou art still,
There is no more to do now thou art dead,
There is no more to know now thy clear mind
Is back returned unto the gods who gave it.

Now thou art gone the use of life is past,
The meaning and the glory and the pride,
There is no joyous friend to share the day
And on the threshold no awaited shadow.

LXXVI

Ye have heard how Marsyas,
In the folly of his pride,
Boasted of a matchless skill,—
When the great god's back was turned;

How his fond imagining
Fell to ashes cold and grey,
When the flawless player came
In serenity and light.

So it was with those I loved
In the years ere I loved thee.
Many a saying sounds like truth,
Until Truth itself is heard.

Many a beauty only lives
Until Beauty passes by,
And the mortal is forgot
In the shadow of the god.

LXXXII

Over the roofs the honey-coloured moon,
With purple shadows on the silver grass,

And the warm south wind on the curving sea,
While we two, lovers past all turmoil now,

Watch from the window the white sails come in,
Bearing what unknown ventures safe to port!

So falls the hour of twilight and of love
With wizardry to loose the hearts of men,

And there is nothing more in this great world
Than thou and I and the blue dome of dusk.

LXXXIV

Soft was the wind in the beech-trees;
Low was the surf on the shore;
In the blue dusk one planet
Like a great sea-pharos shone.

But nothing to me were the sea-sounds,
The wind and the yellow star,
When over my breast the banner
Of your golden hair was spread.

LXXXVII

Hadst thou with all thy loveliness been true,
Had I with all my tenderness been strong,
We had not made this ruin out of life,
This desolation in a world of joy,
My poor Gorgo.

Yet even the high gods at times do err;
Be therefore thou not overcome with woe,
But dedicate anew to greater love
An equal heart, and be thy radiant self
Once more, Gorgo.

LXXXVIII

As on a morn a traveller might emerge
From the deep green seclusion of the hills,
By a cool road through forest and through fern,

Little frequented, winding, followed long
With joyous expectation and day-dreams,
And on a sudden turning a great rock
Covered with frondage, dark with dripping water,
Behold the seaboard full of surf and sound,
With all the space and glory of the world
Above the burnished silver of the sea,—

Even so it was upon that first spring day
When time that is a devious path for men
Led me all lonely to thy door at last;
And all thy splendid beauty gracious and glad
(Glad as bright colour, free as wind or air,
And lovelier than racing seas of foam)
Bore sense and soul and mind at once away
To a pure region where the gods might dwell,
Making of me, a vagrant child before,
A servant of joy at Aphrodite's will.

XCII

Like a red lily in the meadow grasses,
Swayed by the wind and burning in the sunlight,
I saw you where the city chokes with traffic
Bearing among the passers-by your beauty,
Unsullied, wild, and delicate as a flower.
And then I knew past doubt or peradventure
Our loved and mighty Eleusinian mother
Had taken thought of me for her pure worship,
And of her favour had assigned my comrade
For the Great Mysteries,—knew I should find you
When the dusk murmured with its new-made lovers,
And we be no more foolish but wise children
And well content partake of joy together,
As she ordains and human hearts desire.

XCIII

When in the spring the swallows all return,
And the bleak bitter sea grows mild once more,
With all its thunders softened to a sigh;

When to the meadows the young green comes back,
And swelling buds put forth on every bough,
With wild-wood odours on the delicate air;

Ah, then, in that so lovely earth wilt thou
With all thy beauty love me all one way,
And make me all thy lover as before?

Lo, where the white-maned horses of the surge,
Plunging in thunderous onset to the shore,
Trample and break and charge along the sand!

C

Once more the rain on the mountain,
Once more the wind in the valley,
With the soft odours of springtime
And the long breath of remembrance,
   O Lityerses!

Warm is the sun in the city.
On the street corners with laughter
Traffic the flower-girls. Beauty
Blossoms once more for thy pleasure
   In many places.

Gentlier now falls the twilight,
With the slim moon in the pear-trees;
And the green frogs in the meadows
Blow on shrill pipes to awaken
   Thee, Lityerses.

Gladlier now crimson morning
Flushes fair-built Mitylene,—
Portico, temple, and column,—
Where the young garlanded women
   Praise thee with singing.

Ah, but what burden of sorrow
Tinges their slow stately chorus,
Though spring revisits the glad earth?
Wilt thou not wake to their summons,
   O Lityerses?

Shall they then never behold thee,—
Nevermore see thee returning
Down the blue cleft of the mountains,
Nor in the purple of evening
   Welcome thy coming?

Nevermore answer thy glowing
Youth with their ardour, nor cherish
With lovely longing thy spirit,
Nor with soft laughter beguile thee,
   O Lityerses?

Heedless, assuaged, art thou sleeping
Where the spring sun cannot find thee,
Nor the wind waken, nor woodlands
Bloom for thy innocent rapture
   Through golden hours?

Hast thou no passion nor pity
For thy deserted companions?
Never again will thy beauty
Quell their desire nor rekindle,
   O Lityerses?

Nay, but in vain their clear voices
Call thee. Thy sensitive beauty
Is become part of the fleeting
Loveliness, merged in the pathos
   Of all things mortal.

In the faint fragrance of flowers,
On the sweet draft of the sea-wind,
Linger strange hints now that loosen
Tears for thy gay gentle spirit,
   O Lityerses!

The World Voice

I heard the summer sea
Murmuring to the shore
Some endless story of a wrong
The whole world must deplore.

I heard the mountain wind
Conversing with the trees
Of an old sorrow of the hills,
Mysterious as the sea's.

And all that haunted day
It seemed that I could hear
The echo of an ancient speech
Ring in my listening ear.

And then it came to me,
That all that I had heard
Was my own heart in the sea's voice
And the wind's lonely word.
(1915)

Vestigia

I took a day to search for God,
And found Him not. But as I trod
By rocky ledge, through woods untamed,
Just where one scarlet lily flamed,
I saw His footprint in the sod.

Then suddenly, all unaware,
Far off in the deep shadows, where
A solitary hermit thrush
Sang through the holy twilight hush—
I heard His voice upon the air.

And even as I marvelled how
God gives us Heaven here and now,
In a stir of wind that hardly shook
The poplar leaves beside the brook—
His hand was light upon my brow.

At last with evening as I turned
Homeward, and thought what I had learned
And all that there was still to probe—
I caught the glory of His robe
Where the last fires of sunset burned.

Back to the world with quickening start
I looked and longed for any part
In making saving Beauty be . . .
And from that kindling ecstasy
I knew God dwelt within my heart.
(1921)

Bliss Carman

The Ships of Saint John

Where are the ships that I used to know,
  That came to port on the Fundy tide
Half a century ago,
  In beauty and stately pride?

In they would come past the beacon light,
  With the sun on gleaming sail and spar,
Folding their wings like birds in flight
  From countries strange and far.

Schooner and brig and barkentine,
  I watched them slow as the sails were furled,
And wondered what cities they must have seen
  On the other side of the world.

Frenchman and Britisher and Dane,
  Yankee, Spaniard and Portugee,
And many a home ship back again
  With her stories of the sea.

Calm and victorious, at rest
  From the relentless, rough sea-play,
The wild duck on the river's breast
  Was not more sure than they.

The creatures of a passing race,
  The dark spruce forests made them strong,
The sea's lore gave them magic grace,
  The great winds taught them song.

And God endowed them each with life—
  His blessing on the craftsman's skill—
To meet the blind unreasoned strife
  And dare the risk of ill.

Not mere insensate wood and paint
  Obedient to the helm's command,
But often restive as a saint
  Beneath the Heavenly hand.

All the beauty and mystery
  Of life were there, adventure bold,
Youth, and the glamour of the sea
  And all its sorrows old.

And many a time I saw them go
  Out on the flood at morning brave,
As the little tugs had them in tow,
  And the sunlight danced on the wave.

There all day long you could hear the sound
  Of the caulking iron, the ship's bronze bell,
And the clank of the capstan going round
  As the great tides rose and fell.

The sailors' songs, the Captain's shout,
  The boatswain's whistle piping shrill,
And the roar as the anchor chain runs out,—
  I often hear them still.

I can see them still, the sun on their gear,
  The shining streak as the hulls careen,
And the flag at the peak unfurling,—clear
  As a picture on a screen.

The fog still hangs on the long tide-rips,
  The gulls go wavering to and fro,
But where are all the beautiful ships
  I knew so long ago?
(1921)

Victoria

Where the traveller looks from Saanich,
Fair is the sight he sees,
A gracious imperial city
Guarding the gates of the seas,
With a robe of golden English broom
Spreading about her knees.

Lovely, with old-world leisure
Gracing her modest state,
In youthful pride of dominion
She sits by the Western gate,
Watching the liners come and go
Through Juan de Fuca Strait.

She is crowned with ivy and laurel
Fresh with an ageless spring;
Tales of the East and news of the North
Her sheltered sea-lanes bring;
And all her beauteous days go by,
Soft as a gray gull's wing.

Child of the strong adventure,
Bred to the clean and fine,
With touch of the velvet tropics
And eyes with the Northern shine,
Never to be forgotten—
Last of the Sea-Kings' line.
(1925)

Duncan Campbell Scott (1862-1947)

Duncan Campbell Scott was born in Ottawa in 1862. His father's duties as a Methodist minister forced the family to move several times to various towns in Ontario and Quebec, but Scott returned to Ottawa in 1879 to work in the Department of Indian Affairs, after having been hired by John A. Macdonald. So like Crawford, but unlike the other Confederation poets, Scott did not receive a university education. He told E.K. Brown that "It never occurred to me to write a line of prose or poetry until I was about twenty-five—and after I had met Archibald Lampman" (qtd. in Brown, "Memoir" 115). That meeting happened in the 1880s, and towards the end of that decade Scott's poems and stories began to appear in American and Canadian periodicals. His first book, *The Magic House and Other Poems*, was published in 1893; subsequent collections appeared at regular intervals for the next five decades. In 1905-06, according to Stan Dragland, Scott's "life and work were at a pinnacle of sorts" (*Floating* 19) when Scott travelled extensively in Northern Ontario while negotiating Treaty 9; some of his most ambitious poems derive from these travels. But in 1907, Scott's daughter died while the family was in Europe, and his grief (expressed in "The Closed Door") was profound. In 1913, Scott was appointed Deputy Superintendent General, and as such he was effectively the head of Indian Affairs until his retirement in 1932 (Titley 13). After his first wife died in 1929, Scott married Elise Aylen in 1931, and they travelled extensively in Europe and North America for the next decade. He continued to write until his death in 1947, with three books appearing that year.

Current interest is understandably focussed on Scott's representations of Canada's First Nations. It is therefore surprising to realize that, in Leon Slonim's calculation, only about a dozen of Scott's approximately 400 poems "have anything to do with Indians" (1 n). Whereas earlier admirers such as Brown found a sympathetic attitude in both the government career and the poetry, today's readers face the problem raised by Dragland: "how to reconcile Scott's attractive and apparently humane poems and stories about Indians . . . with the dreadful legacy of his administration of Indian Affairs" (*Floating* 5). Critics like John Flood and Lisa Salem are less convinced that the poems are "humane," but Dragland's criticism shows that the attitudes in "A Scene at Lake Manitou" and "Lines in Memory of Edmund Morris" are quite different from those in "Watkwenies" and "The Forsaken." In any case, we should remember Gary Geddes' warning about the "failure to see [Scott] within the context of the nineteenth century, where most of his best verse belongs" (in Dragland, *Scott: A Book* 165). So while Scott's related interests in the remote landscapes of the North and in freer poetic forms won him admirers among some Modern Canadian writers, he was also concerned with issues of faith and doubt throughout his career. As he told Brown, "I have left the religion of my youth behind me . . . but I have gone not into the United Church, but into the wilderness, and I do not feel at all lost in it" (qtd. in Brown, "Memoir" 129-30).

Further Reading

Bentley, D.M.R. "The Onondaga Madonna: A Sonnet of Rare Beauty." *CV II* 3:2 (1977): 28-29.

———. "Duncan Campbell Scott and Maurice Maeterlinck." *Studies in Canadian Literature* 21:2 (1996): 104-19.

Brown, E.K. "Duncan Campbell Scott: A Memoir." *Selected Poems of Duncan Campbell Scott*. Ed. Brown. Toronto: Ryerson, 1951. xi-xliii. *Responses and Evaluations: Essays on Canada*. Ed. David Staines. New Canadian Library. Toronto: McClelland and Stewart, 1977. 112-44.

Dragland, Stan, ed. *Duncan Campbell Scott: A Book of Criticism*. Ottawa: Tecumseh, 1974.

———. *Floating Voice: Duncan Campbell Scott and the Literature of Treaty 9*. Concord, ON: Anansi, 1994.

Flood, John. "The Duplicity of D.C. Scott and the James Bay Treaty." *Black Moss*, Second Series, 2 (1976): 50-63.

Johnston, Gordon. "Duncan Campbell Scott." *Canadian Writers and Their Works: Poetry Series, Volume Two*. Ed. Robert Lecker, Jack

David, and Ellen Quigley. Downsview, ON: ECW, 1983. 235-89.

Jones, D.G. *Butterfly on Rock: A Study of Themes and Images in Canadian Literature*. Toronto: U of Toronto P, 1970.

Kilpatrick, R.S. "Scott's 'Night Hymns on Lake Nipigon': 'Matins' in the Northern Midnight." *Canadian Poetry: Studies, Documents, Reviews* 14 (1984): 64-68.

Lynch, Gerald. "An Endless Flow: D.C. Scott's Indian Poems." *Studies in Canadian Literature* 7 (1982): 27-54.

McDougall, Robert L., ed. *The Poet and the Critic: A Literary Correspondence Between D.C. Scott and E.K. Brown*. Ottawa: Carleton UP, 1983.

Meckler, Lee B. "Rabbit-Skin Robes and Mink-Traps: Indian and European in 'The Forsaken.'" *Canadian Poetry: Studies, Documents, Reviews* 1 (1977): 60-65.

Roberts, Carolyn. "Words After Music: A Musical Reading of Scott's 'Night Hymns on Lake Nipigon.'" *Canadian Poetry: Studies, Documents, Reviews* 8 (1981): 56-63.

Salem, Lisa. "'Her Blood is Mingled With Her Ancient Foes': The Concepts of Blood, Race and 'Miscegenation' in the Poetry and Short Fiction of Duncan Campbell Scott." *Studies in Canadian Literature* 18 (1993): 99-117.

Scott, Duncan Campbell. *Selected Poetry*. Ed. Glenn Clever. Ottawa: Tecumseh, 1974.

Simpson, Janice. "Healing the Wound: Cultural Compromise in D.C. Scott's 'A Scene at Lake Manitou.'" *Canadian Poetry: Studies, Documents, Reviews* 18 (1986): 66-76.

Slonim, Leon. "A Critical Edition of the Poems of Duncan Campbell Scott." Diss. Toronto, 1978.

Stich, K.P., ed. *The Duncan Campbell Scott Symposium*. Re-appraisals: Canadian Writers. Ottawa: U of Ottawa P, 1980.

Stow, Glenys. "The Wound Under the Feathers: Scott's Discontinuities." *Colony and Confederation: Early Canadian Poets and Their Background*. Ed. George Woodcock. Vancouver: UBC P, 1974. 161-77.

Titley, E. Brian. *A Narrow Vision: Duncan Campbell Scott and the Administration of Indian Affairs in Canada*. Vancouver: UBC P, 1986.

Ware, Tracy. "The Beginnings of Duncan Campbell Scott's Poetic Career." *English Studies in Canada* 16 (1990): 215-31.

Weis, Lyle. "D.C. Scott's View of History and the Indians." *Canadian Literature* 111 (1986): 27-40.

Duncan Campbell Scott

The Magic House

In her chamber, whereso'er
 Time shall build the walls of it,
Melodies shall minister,
 Mellow sounds shall flit
Through a dusk of musk and myrrh.

Lingering in the spaces vague,
 Like the breath within a flute,
Winds shall move along the stair;
 When she walketh mute
Music meet shall greet her there.

Time shall make a truce with Time,
 All the languid dials tell
Irised hours of gossamer,
 Eve perpetual
Shall the night or light defer.

From her casement she shall see
 Down a valley wild and dim,
Swart with woods of pine and fir;
 Shall the sunsets swim
Red with untold gold to her.

From her terrace she shall see
 Lines of birds like dusky motes
Falling in the heated glare;
 How an eagle floats
In the wan unconscious air.

From her turret she shall see
 Vision of a cloudy place,
Like a group of opal flowers
 On the verge of space,
Or a town, or crown of towers.

From her garden she shall hear
  Fall the cones between the pines;
She shall seem to hear the sea,
  Or behind the vines
Some small noise, a voice may be.

But no thing shall habit there,
  There no human foot shall fall,
No sweet word the silence stir,
  Naught her name shall call,
Nothing come to comfort her.

But about the middle night,
  When the dusk is loathèd most,
Ancient thoughts and words long said,
  Like an alien host,
There shall come unsummonèd.

With her forehead on her wrist
  She shall lean against the wall
And see all the dream go by;
  In the interval
Time shall turn Eternity.

But the agony shall pass—
  Fainting with unuttered prayer,
She shall see the world's outlines
  And the weary glare
And the bare unvaried pines.
(1890)

Duncan Campbell Scott

The Reed-Player

To B.C.

By a dim shore where water darkening
  Took the last light of spring,
I went beyond the tumult, hearkening
  For some diviner thing.

Where the bats flew from the black elms like leaves,
  Over the ebon pool
Brooded the bittern's cry, as one that grieves
  Lands ancient, bountiful.

I saw the fireflies shine below the wood,
  Above the shallows dank,
As Uriel from some great altitude,
  The planets rank on rank.

And now unseen along the shrouded mead
  One went under the hill;
He blew a cadence on his mellow reed,
  That trembled and was still.

It seemed as if a line of amber fire
  Had shot the gathered dusk,
As if had blown a wind from ancient Tyre
  Laden with myrrh and musk.

He gave his luring note amid the fern;
  Its enigmatic fall
Haunted the hollow dusk with golden turn
  And argent interval.

I could not know the message that he bore,
  The springs of life from me
Hidden; his incommunicable lore
  As much a mystery.

And as I followed far the magic player
  He passed the maple wood,
And when I passed the stars had risen there,
  And there was solitude.
(1890)

At Scarboro' Beach

The wave is over the foaming reef
  Leaping alive in the sun,
Seaward the opal sails are blown
  Vanishing one by one.

'Tis leagues around the blue sea curve
  To the sunny coast of Spain,
And the ships that sail so deftly out
  May never come home again.

A mist is wreathed round Richmond point,
  There's a shadow on the land,
But the sea is in the splendid sun,
  Plunging so careless and grand.

The sandpipers trip on the glassy beach,
  Ready to mount and fly;
Whenever a ripple reaches their feet
  They rise with a timorous cry.

Take care, they pipe, take care, take care,
  For this is the treacherous main,
And though you may sail so deftly out,
  You may never come home again.
(1893)

Duncan Campbell Scott

In the Country Churchyard

To the Memory of My Father

This is the acre of unfathomed rest,
These stones, with weed and lichen bound, enclose
No active grief, no uncompleted woes,
But only finished work and harboured quest,
And balm for ills;
And the last gold that smote the ashen west
Lies garnered here between the harvest hills.

This spot has never known the heat of toil,
Save when the angel with the mighty spade
Has turned the sod and built the house of shade;
But here old chance is guardian of the soil;
Green leaf and grey,
The barrows blossom with the tangled spoil,
And God's own weeds are fair in God's own way.

Sweet flowers may gather in the ferny wood:
Hepaticas, the morning stars of spring;
The bloodroots with their milder ministering,
Like planets in the lonelier solitude;
And that white throng,
Which shakes the dingles with a starry brood,
And tells the robin his forgotten song.

These flowers may rise amid the dewy fern,
They may not root within this antique wall,
The dead have chosen for their coronal,
No buds that flaunt of life and flare and burn;
They have agreed,
To choose a beauty puritan and stern,
The universal grass, the homely weed.

This is the paradise of common things,
The scourged and trampled here find peace to grow,
The frost to furrow and the wind to sow,
The mighty sun to time their blossomings;
And now they keep
A crown reflowering on the tombs of kings,
Who earned their triumph and have claimed their sleep.

Yea, each is here a prince in his own right,
Who dwelt disguised amid the multitude,
And when his time was come, in haughty mood,
Shook off his motley and reclaimed his might;
His sombre throne
In the vast province of perpetual night,
He holds secure, inviolate, alone.

The poor forgets that ever he was poor,
The priest has lost his science of the truth,
The maid her beauty, and the youth his youth,
The statesman has forgot his subtle lure,
The old his age,
The sick his suffering, and the leech his cure,
The poet his perplexed and vacant page.

These swains that tilled the uplands in the sun
Have all forgot the field's familiar face,
And lie content within this ancient place,
Whereto when hands were tired their thought would run
To dream of rest,
When the last furrow was turned down, and won
The last harsh harvest from the earth's patient breast.

O dwellers in the valley vast and fair,
I would that calling from your tranquil clime,
You make a truce for me with cruel time;
For I am weary of this eager care
That never dies;

I would be born into your tranquil air,
  Your deserts crowned and sovereign silences.

I would, but that the world is beautiful,
 And I am more in love with the sliding years,
 They have not brought me frantic joy or tears,
But only moderate state and temperate rule;
  Not to forget
This quiet beauty, not to be Time's fool,
  I will be man a little longer yet.

For lo, what beauty crowns the harvest hills!—
 The buckwheat acres gleam like silver shields;
 The oats hang tarnished in the golden fields;
Between the elms the yellow wheat-land fills;
  The apples drop
Within the orchard, where the red tree spills,
  The fragrant fruitage over branch and prop.

The cows go lowing through the lovely vale;
 The clarion peacock warns the world of rain,
 Perched on the barn a gaudy weather-vane;
The farm lad holloes from the shifted rail,
  Along the grove
He beats a measure on his ringing pail,
  And sings the heart-song of his early love.

There is a honey scent along the air;
 The hermit thrush has tuned his fleeting note.
 Among the silver birches far remote
His spirit voice appeareth here and there,
  To fail and fade,
A visionary cadence falling fair,
  That lifts and lingers in the hollow shade.

And now a spirit in the east, unseen,
 Raises the moon above her misty eyes,

And travels up the veiled and starless skies,
Viewing the quietude of her demesne;
Stainless and slow,
I watch the lustre of her planet's sheen,
From burnished gold to liquid silver flow.
And now I leave the dead with you, O night;
You wear the semblance of their fathomless state,
For you we long when the day's fire is great,
And when stern life is cruellest in his might,
Of death we dream:
A country of dim plain and shadowy height,
Crowned with strange stars and silences supreme:

Rest here, for day is hot to follow you,
Rest here until the morning star has come,
Until is risen aloft dawn's rosy dome,
Based deep on buried crimson into blue,
And morn's desire
Has made the fragile cobweb drenched with dew
A net of opals veiled with dreamy fire.
(1893)

The Cup

Here is pleasure; drink it down.
Here is sorrow; drain it dry.
Tilt the goblet, don't ask why.
Here is madness; down it goes.
Here's a dagger and a kiss,
Don't ask what the reason is.
Drink your liquor, no one knows;
Drink it bravely like a lord.
Do not roll a coward eye,
Pain and pleasure is one sword
Hacking out your destiny;
Do not say, "It is not just."

That word won't apply to life;
You must drink because you must;
Tilt the goblet, cease the strife.
Here at last is something good,
Just to warm your flagging blood.
Don't take breath—
At the bottom of the cup
Here is death:
Drink it up.
(1894)

The Onondaga Madonna

She stands full-throated and with careless pose,
This woman of a weird and waning race,
The tragic savage lurking in her face,
Where all her pagan passion burns and glows;
Her blood is mingled with her ancient foes,
And thrills with war and wildness in her veins;
Her rebel lips are dabbled with the stains
Of feuds and forays and her father's woes.

And closer in the shawl about her breast,
The latest promise of her nation's doom,
Paler than she her baby clings and lies,
The primal warrior gleaming from his eyes;
He sulks, and burdened with his infant gloom,
He draws his heavy brows and will not rest.
(1894)

The Piper of Arll

There was in Arll a little cove
Where the salt wind came cool and free:
A foamy beach that one would love,
If he were longing for the sea.

A brook hung sparkling on the hill,
The hill swept far to ring the bay;
The bay was faithful, wild or still,
To the heart of the ocean far away.

There were three pines above the comb
That, when the sun flared and went down,
Grew like three warriors reaving home
The plunder of a burning town.

A piper lived within the grove,
Tending the pasture of his sheep;
His heart was swayed with faithful love,
From the springs of God's ocean clear and deep.

And there a ship one evening stood,
Where ship had never stood before;
A pennon bickered red as blood,
An angel glimmered at the prore.

About the coming on of dew,
The sails burned rosy, and the spars
Were gold, and all the tackle grew
Alive with ruby-hearted stars.

The piper heard an outland tongue,
With music in the cadenced fall;
And when the fairy lights were hung,
The sailors gathered one and all,

And leaning on the gunwales dark,
Crusted with shells and dashed with foam,
With all the dreaming hills to hark,
They sang their longing songs of home.

When the sweet airs had fled away,
The piper, with a gentle breath,

Moulded a tranquil melody
Of lonely love and longed-for death.

When the fair sound began to lull,
From out the fireflies and the dew,
A silence held the shadowy hull,
Until the eerie tune was through.

Then from the dark and dreamy deck
An alien song began to thrill;
It mingled with the drumming beck,
And stirred the braird upon the hill.

Beneath the stars each sent to each
A message tender, till at last
The piper slept upon the beach,
The sailors slumbered round the mast.

Still as a dream till nearly dawn,
The ship was bosomed on the tide;
The streamlet, murmuring on and on,
Bore the sweet water to her side.

Then shaking out her lawny sails,
Forth on the misty sea she crept;
She left the dawning of the dales,
Yet in his cloak the piper slept.

And when he woke he saw the ship,
Limned black against the crimson sun;
Then from the disc he saw her slip,
A wraith of shadow—she was gone.

He threw his mantle on the beach,
He went apart like one distraught,
His lips were moved—his desperate speech
Stormed his inviolable thought.

He broke his human-throated reed,
And threw it in the idle rill;
But when his passion had its mead,
He found it in the eddy still.

He mended well the patient flue,
Again he tried its varied stops;
The closures answered right and true,
And starting out in piercing drops,

A melody began to drip
That mingled with a ghostly thrill
The vision-spirit of the ship,
The secret of his broken will.

Beneath the pines he piped and swayed,
Master of passion and of power;
He was his soul and what he played,
Immortal for a happy hour.

He, singing into nature's heart,
Guiding his will by the world's will,
With deep, unconscious, childlike art
Had sung his soul out and was still.

And then at evening came the bark
That stirred his dreaming heart's desire;
It burned slow lights along the dark
That died in glooms of crimson fire.

The sailors launched a sombre boat,
And bent with music at the oars;
The rhythm throbbing every throat,
And lapsing round the liquid shores,

Was that true tune the piper sent,
Unto the wave-worn mariners,

When with the beck and ripple blent
He heard that outland song of theirs.

Silent they rowed him, dip and drip,
The oars beat out an exequy,
They laid him down within the ship,
They loosed a rocket to the sky.

It broke in many a crimson sphere
That grew to gold and floated far,
And left the sudden shore-line clear,
With one slow-changing, drifting star.

Then out they shook the magic sails,
That charmed the wind in other seas,
From where the west line pearls and pales,
They waited for a ruffling breeze.

But in the world there was no stir,
The cordage slacked with never a creak,
They heard the flame begin to purr
Within the lantern at the peak.

They could not cry, they could not move,
They felt the lure from the charmed sea;
They could not think of home or love
Or any pleasant land to be.

They felt the vessel dip and trim,
And settle down from list to list;
They saw the sea-plain heave and swim
As gently as a rising mist.

And down so slowly, down and down,
Rivet by rivet, plank by plank;
A little flood of ocean flown
Across the deck, she sank and sank.

From knee to breast the water wore,
It crept and crept; ere they were ware
Gone was the angel at the prore,
They felt the water float their hair.

They saw the salt plain spark and shine,
They threw their faces to the sky;
Beneath a deepening film of brine
They saw the star-flash blur and die.

She sank and sank by yard and mast,
Sank down the shimmering gradual dark;
A little drooping pennon last
Showed like the black fin of a shark.

And down she sank till, keeled in sand,
She rested safely balanced true,
With all her upward gazing band,
The piper and the dreaming crew.

And there, unmarked of any chart,
In unrecorded deeps they lie,
Empearled within the purple heart
Of the great sea for aye and aye.

Their eyes are ruby in the green
Long shaft of sun that spreads and rays,
And upward with a wizard sheen
A fan of sea-light leaps and plays.

Tendrils of or and azure creep,
And globes of amber light are rolled,
And in the gloaming of the deep
Their eyes are starry pits of gold.

And sometimes in the liquid night
The hull is changed, a solid gem,

That glows with a soft stony light,
The lost prince of a diadem.

And at the keel a vine is quick,
That spreads its bines and works and weaves
O'er all the timbers veining thick
A plenitude of silver leaves.
(1895)

Watkwenies

Vengeance was once her nation's lore and law:
When the tired sentry stooped above the rill,
Her long knife flashed, and hissed, and drank its fill;
Dimly below her dripping wrist she saw,
One wild hand, pale as death and weak as straw,
Clutch at the ripple in the pool; while shrill
Sprang through the dreaming hamlet on the hill,
The war-cry of the triumphant Iroquois.

Now clothed with many an ancient flap and fold,
And wrinkled like an apple kept till May,
She weighs the interest-money in her palm,
And, when the Agent calls her valiant name,
Hears, like the war-whoops of her perished day,
The lads playing snow-snake in the stinging cold.
(1898)

Night Hymns on Lake Nipigon

Here in the midnight, where the dark mainland and
 island
Shadows mingle in shadow deeper, profounder,
Sing we the hymns of the churches, while the dead water
 Whispers before us.

Thunder is travelling slow on the path of the lightning;
One after one the stars and the beaming planets
Look serene in the lake from the edge of the storm-cloud,
Then have they vanished.

While our canoe, that floats dumb in the bursting thunder,
Gathers her voice in the quiet and thrills and whispers,
Presses her prow in the star-gleam, and all her ripple
Lapses in blackness.

Sing we the sacred ancient hymns of the churches,
Chanted first in old-world nooks of the desert,
While in the wild, pellucid Nipigon reaches
Hunted the savage.

Now have the ages met in the Northern midnight,
And on the lonely, loon-haunted Nipigon reaches
Rises the hymn of triumph and courage and comfort,
Adeste Fideles.

Tones that were fashioned when the faith brooded in darkness,
Joined with sonorous vowels in the noble Latin,
Now are married with the long-drawn Ojibwa,
Uncouth and mournful.

Soft with the silver drip of the regular paddles
Falling in rhythm, timed with the liquid, plangent
Sounds from the blades where the whirlpools break and are carried
Down into darkness;

Each long cadence, flying like a dove from her shelter
Deep in the shadow, wheels for a throbbing moment,

Poises in utterance, returning in circles of silver
    To nest in the silence.

All wild nature stirs with the infinite, tender
Plaint of a bygone age whose soul is eternal,
Bound in the lonely phrases that thrill and falter
    Back into quiet.

Back they falter as the deep storm overtakes them,
Whelms them in splendid hollows of booming thunder,
Wraps them in rain, that, sweeping, breaks and onrushes
    Ringing like cymbals.
(1900)

The Ghost's Story

All my life long I heard the step
  Of some one I would know,
Break softly in upon my days
  And lightly come and go.

A foot so brisk I said must bear
  A heart that's clean and clear;
If that companion blithe would come,
  I should be happy here.

But though I waited long and well,
  He never came at all,
I grew aweary of the void,
  Even of the light foot-fall.

From loneliness to loneliness
  I felt my spirit grope—
At last I knew the uttermost,
  The loneliness of hope.

And just upon the border land,
  Where flesh and spirit part,
I knew the secret foot-fall was
  The beating of my heart.
(1902)

The Forsaken

I

Once in the winter,
Out on a lake
In the heart of the north-land,
Far from the Fort
And far from the hunters,
A Chippewa woman
With her sick baby,
Crouched in the last hours
Of a great storm.
Frozen and hungry,
She fished through the ice
With a line of the twisted
Bark of the cedar,
And a rabbit-bone hook
Polished and barbed;
Fished with the bare hook
All through the wild day,
Fished and caught nothing;
While the young chieftain
Tugged at her breasts,
Or slept in the lacings
Of the warm *tikanagan*.
All the lake-surface
Streamed with the hissing
Of millions of iceflakes,
Hurled by the wind;

Behind her the round
Of a lonely island
Roared like a fire
With the voice of the storm
In the deeps of the cedars.
Valiant, unshaken,
She took of her own flesh,
Baited the fish-hook,
Drew in a gray-trout,
Drew in his fellow,
Heaped them beside her,
Dead in the snow.
Valiant, unshaken,
She faced the long distance,
Wolf-haunted and lonely,
Sure of her goal
And the life of her dear one;
Tramped for two days,
On the third in the morning,
Saw the strong bulk
Of the Fort by the river,
Saw the wood-smoke
Hang soft in the spruces,
Heard the keen yelp
Of the ravenous huskies
Fighting for whitefish:
Then she had rest.

II

Years and years after,
When she was old and withered,
When her son was an old man
And his children filled with vigour,
They came in their northern tour on the verge of winter,
To an island in a lonely lake.
There one night they camped, and on the morrow

Gathered their kettles and birch-bark
Their rabbit-skin robes and their mink-traps,
Launched their canoes and slunk away through the islands,
Left her alone forever,
Without a word of farewell,
Because she was old and useless,
Like a paddle broken and warped,
Or a pole that was splintered.
Then, without a sigh,
Valiant, unshaken,
She smoothed her dark locks under her kerchief,
Composed her shawl in state,
Then folded her hands ridged with sinews and corded with veins,
Folded them across her breasts spent with the nourishing of children,
Gazed at the sky past the tops of the cedars,
Saw two spangled nights arise out of the twilight,
Saw two days go by filled with the tranquil sunshine,
Saw, without pain, or dread, or even a moment of longing:
Then on the third great night there came thronging and thronging
Millions of snowflakes out of a windless cloud;
They covered her close with a beautiful crystal shroud,
Covered her deep and silent.
But in the frost of the dawn,
Up from the life below,
Rose a column of breath
Through a tiny cleft in the snow,
Fragile, delicately drawn,
Wavering with its own weakness,
In the wilderness a sign of the spirit,
Persisting still in the sight of the sun
Till day was done.

Then all light was gathered up by the hand of God and
hid in His breast,
Then there was born a silence deeper than silence,
Then she had rest.
(1903)

On the Way to the Mission

They dogged him all one afternoon,
Through the bright snow,
Two whitemen servants of greed;
He knew that they were there,
But he turned not his head;
He was an Indian trapper;
He planted his snow-shoes firmly,
He dragged the long toboggan
Without rest.

The three figures drifted
Like shadows in the mind of a seer;
The snow-shoes were whisperers
On the threshold of awe;
The toboggan made the sound of wings,
A wood-pigeon sloping to her nest.

The Indian's face was calm.
He strode with the sorrow of fore-knowledge,
But his eyes were jewels of content
Set in circles of peace.

They would have shot him;
But momently in the deep forest,
They saw something flit by his side:
Their hearts stopped with fear.
Then the moon rose.

They would have left him to the spirit,
But they saw the long toboggan
Rounded well with furs,
With many a silver fox-skin,
With the pelts of mink and of otter.
They were the servants of greed;
When the moon grew brighter
And the spruces were dark with sleep,
They shot him.
When he fell on a shield of moonlight
One of his arms clung to his burden;
The snow was not melted:
The spirit passed away.

Then the servants of greed
Tore off the cover to count their gains;
They shuddered away into the shadows,
Hearing each the loud heart of the other.
Silence was born.

There in the tender moonlight,
 As sweet as they were in life,
Glimmered the ivory features,
 Of the Indian's wife.

In the manner of Montagnais women
 Her hair was rolled with braid;
Under her waxen fingers
 A crucifix was laid.

He was drawing her down to the Mission,
 To bury her there in spring,
When the bloodroot comes and the windflower
 To silver everything.

But as a gift of plunder
 Side by side were they laid,

The moon went on to her setting
 And covered them with shade.
(1905)

An Impromptu

Here in the pungent gloom
Where the tamarac roses glow
And the balsam burns its perfume,
A vireo turns his slow
Cadence, as if he gloated
Over the last phrase he floated;
Each one he moulds and mellows
Matching it with its fellows:
So have you noted
How the oboe croons,
The canary-throated,
In the gloom of the violoncellos
And bassoons.

But afar in the thickset forest
I hear a sound go free,
Crashing the stately neighbours
The pine and the cedar tree,
Horns and harps and tabors,
Drumming and harping and horning
In savage minstrelsy—
It wakes in my soul a warning
Of the wind of destiny.

My life is soaring and swinging
In triple walls of quiet,
In my heart there is rippling and ringing
A song with melodious riot,
When a fateful thing comes nigh it
A hush falls, and then

I hear in the thickset world
The wind of destiny hurled
On the lives of men.
(1906)

Lines in Memory of Edmund Morris

Dear Morris—here is your letter—
Can my answer reach you now?
Fate has left me your debtor,
You will remember how;
For I went away to Nantucket,
And you to the Isle of Orleans,
And when I was dawdling and dreaming
Over the ways and means
Of answering, the power was denied me,
Fate frowned and took her stand;
I have your unanswered letter
Here in my hand.
This—in your famous scribble,
It was ever a cryptic fist,
Cuneiform or Chaldaic
Meanings held in a mist.

Dear Morris, (now I'm inditing
And poring over your script)
I gather from the writing,
The coin that you had flipt,
Turned tails; and so you compel me
To meet you at Touchwood Hills:
Or, mayhap, you are trying to tell me
The sum of a painter's ills:
Is that Phimister Proctor
Or something about a doctor?
Well, nobody knows, but Eddie,
Whatever it is I'm ready.

For our friendship was always fortunate
In its greetings and adieux,
Nothing flat or importunate,
Nothing of the misuse
That comes of the constant grinding
Of one mind on another.
So memory has nothing to smother,
But only a few things captured
On the wing, as it were, and enraptured.
Yes, Morris, I am inditing—
Answering at last it seems,
How can you read the writing
In the vacancy of dreams?

I would have you look over my shoulder
Ere the long, dark year is colder,
And mark that as memory grows older,
The brighter it pulses and gleams.
And if I should try to render
The tissues of fugitive splendour
That fled down the wind of living,
Will they read it some day in the future,
And be conscious of an awareness
In our old lives, and the bareness
Of theirs, with the newest passions
In the last fad of the fashions?

. . . .

How often have we risen without daylight
When the day star was hidden in mist,
When the dragon-fly was heavy with dew and sleep,
And viewed the miracle pre-eminent, matchless,
The prelusive light that quickens the morning.
O crystal dawn, how shall we distill your virginal
freshness
When you steal upon a land that man has not sullied
with his intrusion,
When the aboriginal shy dwellers in the broad solitudes

Are asleep in their innumerable dens and night haunts
Amid the dry ferns, in the tender nests
Pressed into shape by the breasts of the Mother birds?
How shall we simulate the thrill of announcement
When lake after lake lingering in the starlight
Turn their faces toward you,
And are caressed with the salutation of colour?

How shall we transmit in tendril-like images,
The tenuous tremor in the tissues of ether,
Before the round of colour buds like the dome of a shrine,
The preconscious moment when love has fluttered in the bosom,
Before it begins to ache?

How often have we seen the even
Melt into the liquidity of twilight,
With passages of Titian splendour,
Pellucid preludes, exquisitely tender,
Where vanish and revive, thro' veils of the ashes of roses,
The crystal forms the breathless sky discloses.

The new moon a slender thing,
In a snood of virgin light,
She seemed all shy on venturing
Into the vast night.

Her own land and folk were afar,
She must have gone astray,
But the gods had given a silver star,
To be with her on the way.

. . . .

I can feel the wind on the prairie
And see the bunch-grass wave,
And the sunlights ripple and vary

The hill with Crowfoot's grave,
Where he "pitched off" for the last time
In sight of the Blackfoot Crossing,
Where in the sun for a pastime
You marked the site of his tepee
With a circle of stones. Old Napiw
Gave you credit for that day.
And well I recall the weirdness
Of that evening at Qu'Appelle,
In the wigwam with old Sakimay,
The keen, acrid smell,
As the kinnikinick was burning;
The planets outside were turning,
And the little splints of poplar

Flared with a thin, gold flame.
He showed us his painted robe
Where in primitive pigments
He had drawn his feats and his forays,
And told us the legend
Of the man without a name,
The hated Blackfoot,
How he lured the warriors,
The young men, to the foray
And they never returned.
Only their ghosts
Goaded by the Blackfoot
Mounted on stallions:
In the night time
He drove the stallions
Reeking into the camp;
The women gasped and whispered,
The children cowered and crept,
And the old men shuddered
Where they slept.
When Sakimay looked forth
He saw the Blackfoot,

And the ghosts of the warriors,
And the black stallions
Covered by the night wind
As by a mantle.

. . . .

I remember well a day,
When the sunlight had free play,
When you worked in happy stress,
While grave Ne-Pah-Pee-Ness
Sat for his portrait there,
In his beaded coat and his bare
Head, with his mottled fan
Of hawk's feathers, A Man!
Ah Morris, those were the times
When you sang your inconsequent rhymes
Sprung from a careless fountain:
"He met her on the mountain,
"He gave her a horn to blow,
"And the very last words he said to her
"Were, 'Go 'long, Eliza, go.'"

Foolish,—but life was all,
And under the skilful fingers
Contours came at your call—
Art grows and time lingers;—
But now the song has a change
Into something wistful and strange.
And one asks with a touch of ruth
What became of the youth
And where did Eliza go?
He met her on the mountain,
He gave her a horn to blow,
The horn was a silver whorl
With a mouthpiece of pure pearl,
And the mountain was all one glow,
With gulfs of blue and summits of rosy snow.
The cadence she blew on the silver horn

Was the meaning of life in one phrase caught,
And as soon as the magic notes were born,
She repeated them once in an afterthought.
They heard in the crystal passes,
The cadence, calling, calling,
And faint in the deep crevasses,
The echoes falling, falling.
They stood apart and wondered;
Her lips with a wound were aquiver,
His heart with a sword was sundered,
For life was changed forever
When he gave her the horn to blow:
But a shadow arose from the valley,
Desolate, slow and tender,
It hid the herdsmen's chalet,
Where it hung in the emerald meadow,
(Was death driving the shadow?)
It quenched the tranquil splendour
Of the colour of life on the glow-peaks,
Till at the end of the even,
The last shell-tint on the snow-peaks
Had passed away from the heaven.
And yet, when it passed, victorious,
The stars came out on the mountains,
And the torrents gusty and glorious,
Clamoured in a thousand fountains,
And even far down in the valley,
A light re-discovered the chalet.
The scene that was veiled had a meaning,
So deep that none might know;
Was it here in the morn on the mountain,
That he gave her the horn to blow?

. . . .

Tears are the crushed essence of this world,
The wine of life, and he who treads the press
Is lofty with imperious disregard
Of the burst grapes, the red tears and the murk.

But nay! that is a thought of the old poets,
Who sullied life with the passional bitterness
Of their world-weary hearts. We of the sunrise,
Joined in the breast of God, feel deep the power
That urges all things onward, not to an end,
But in an endless flow, mounting and mounting,
Claiming not overmuch for human life,
Sharing with our brothers of nerve and leaf
The urgence of the one creative breath,—
All in the dim twilight—say of morning,
Where the florescence of the light and dew
Haloes and hallows with a crown adorning
The brows of life with love; herein the clue,
The love of life—yea, and the peerless love
Of things not seen, that leads the least of things
To cherish the green sprout, the hardening seed;
Here leans all nature with vast Mother-love,
Above the cradled future with a smile.
Why are there tears for failure, or sighs for weakness,
While life's rhythm beats on? Where is the rule
To measure the distance we have circled and clomb?
Catch up the sands of the sea and count and count
The failures hidden in our sum of conquest.
Persistence is the master of this life;
The master of these little lives of ours;
To the end—effort—even beyond the end.

Here, Morris, on the plains that we have loved,
Think of the death of Akoose, fleet of foot,
Who, in his prime, a herd of antelope
From sunrise, without rest, a hundred miles
Drove through rank prairie, loping like a wolf,
Tired them and slew them, ere the sun went down.
Akoose, in his old age, blind from the smoke
Of tepees and the sharp snow light, alone
With his great-grandchildren, withered and spent,
Crept in the warm sun along a rope

Stretched for his guidance. Once when sharp autumn
Made membranes of thin ice upon the sloughs,
He caught a pony on a quick return
Of prowess and, all his instincts cleared and quickened,
He mounted, sensed the north and bore away
To the Last Mountain Lake where in his youth
He shot the sand-hill-cranes with his flint arrows.
And for these hours in all the varied pomp
Of pagan fancy and free dreams of foray
And crude adventure, he ranged on entranced,
Until the sun blazed level with the prairie,
Then paused, faltered and slid from off his pony.
In a little bluff of poplars, hid in the bracken,
He lay down; the populace of leaves
In the lithe poplars whispered together and trembled,
Fluttered before a sunset of gold smoke,
With interspaces, green as sea water,
And calm as the deep water of the sea.

There Akoose lay, silent amid the bracken,
Gathered at last with the Algonquin Chieftains.
Then the tenebrous sunset was blown out,
And all the smoky gold turned into cloud wrack.
Akoose slept forever amid the poplars,
Swathed by the wind from the far-off Red Deer
Where dinosaurs sleep, clamped in their rocky tombs.
Who shall count the time that lies between
The sleep of Akoose and the dinosaurs?
Innumerable time, that yet is like the breath
Of the long wind that creeps upon the prairie
And dies away with the shadows at sundown.

. . . .

What we may think, who brood upon the theme,
Is, when the old world, tired of spinning, has fallen
Asleep, and all the forms, that carried the fire
Of life, are cold upon her marble heart—
Like ashes on the altar—just as she stops,

That something will escape of soul or essence,—
The sum of life, to kindle otherwhere:
Just as the fruit of a high sunny garden,
Grown mellow with autumnal sun and rain,
Shrivelled with ripeness, splits to the rich heart,
And looses a gold kernel to the mould,
So the old world, hanging long in the sun,
And deep enriched with effort and with love,
Shall, in the motions of maturity,
Wither and part, and the kernel of it all
Escape, a lovely wraith of spirit, to latitudes
Where the appearance, throated like a bird,
Winged with fire and bodied all with passion,
Shall flame with presage, not of tears, but joy.
(1915)

The Height of Land

Here is the height of land:
The watershed on either hand
Goes down to Hudson Bay
Or Lake Superior;
The stars are up, and far away
The wind sounds in the wood, wearier
Than the long Ojibway cadence
In which Potàn the Wise
Declares the ills of life
And Chees-que-ne-ne makes a mournful sound
Of acquiescence. The fires burn low
With just sufficient glow
To light the flakes of ash that play
At being moths, and flutter away
To fall in the dark and die as ashes:
Here there is peace in the lofty air,
And Something comes by flashes
Deeper than peace;—

The spruces have retired a little space
And left a field of sky in violet shadow
With stars like marigolds in a water-meadow.

Now the Indian guides are dead asleep;
There is no sound unless the soul can hear
The gathering of the waters in their sources.

We have come up through the spreading lakes
From level to level,—
Pitching our tents sometimes over a revel
Of roses that nodded all night,
Dreaming within our dreams,
To wake at dawn and find that they were captured
With no dew on their leaves;
Sometimes mid sheaves
Of bracken and dwarf-cornel, and again
On a wide blue-berry plain
Brushed with the shimmer of a bluebird's wing;
A rocky islet followed
With one lone poplar and a single nest
Of white-throat-sparrows that took no rest
But sang in dreams or woke to sing,—
To the last portage and the height of land—:
Upon one hand
The lonely north enlaced with lakes and streams,
And the enormous targe of Hudson Bay,
Glimmering all night
In the cold arctic light;
On the other hand
The crowded southern land
With all the welter of the lives of men.
But here is peace, and again
That Something comes by flashes
Deeper than peace,—a spell
Golden and inappellable
That gives the inarticulate part

Of our strange being one moment of release
That seems more native than the touch of time,
And we must answer in chime;
Though yet no man may tell
The secret of that spell
Golden and inappellable.

Now are there sounds walking in the wood,
And all the spruces shiver and tremble,
And the stars move a little in their courses.
The ancient disturber of solitude
Breathes a pervasive sigh,
And the soul seems to hear
The gathering of the waters at their sources;
Then quiet ensues and pure starlight and dark;
The region-spirit murmurs in meditation,
The heart replies in exaltation
And echoes faintly like an inland shell
Ghost tremors of the spell;
Thought reawakens and is linked again
With all the welter of the lives of men.

Here on the uplands where the air is clear
We think of life as of a stormy scene,—
Of tempest, of revolt and desperate shock;
And here, where we can think, on the bright uplands
Where the air is clear, we deeply brood on life
Until the tempest parts, and it appears
As simple as to the shepherd seems his flock:
A Something to be guided by ideals—
That in themselves are simple and serene—
Of noble deed to foster noble thought,
And noble thought to image noble deed,
Till deed and thought shall interpenetrate,
Making life lovelier, till we come to doubt
Whether the perfect beauty that escapes
Is beauty of deed or thought or some high thing

Mingled of both, a greater boon than either:
Thus we have seen in the retreating tempest
The victor-sunlight merge with the ruined rain,
And from the rain and sunlight spring the rainbow.

The ancient disturber of solitude
Stirs his ancestral potion in the gloom,
And the dark wood
Is stifled with the pungent fume
Of charred earth burnt to the bone
That takes the place of air.
Then sudden I remember when and where,—
The last weird lakelet foul with weedy growths
And slimy viscid things the spirit loathes,
Skin of vile water over viler mud
Where the paddle stirred unutterable stenches,
And the canoes seemed heavy with fear,
Not to be urged toward the fatal shore
Where a bush fire, smouldering, with sudden roar
Leaped on a cedar and smothered it with light
And terror. It had left the portage-height
A tangle of slanted spruces burned to the roots,
Covered still with patches of bright fire
Smoking with incense of the fragrant resin
That even then began to thin and lessen
Into the gloom and glimmer of ruin.

'Tis overpast. How strange the stars have grown;
The presage of extinction glows on their crests
And they are beautified with impermanence;
They shall be after the race of men
And mourn for them who snared their fiery pinions,
Entangled in the meshes of bright words.

A lemming stirs the fern and in the mosses
Eft-minded things feel the air change, and dawn
Tolls out from the dark belfries of the spruces.

How often in the autumn of the world
Shall the crystal shrine of dawning be rebuilt
With deeper meaning! Shall the poet then,
Wrapped in his mantle on the height of land,
Brood on the welter of the lives of men
And dream of his ideal hope and promise
In the blush sunrise? Shall he base his flight
Upon a more compelling law than Love
As Life's atonement; shall the vision
Of noble deed and noble thought immingled
Seem as uncouth to him as the pictograph
Scratched on the cave side by the cave-dweller
To us of the Christ-time? Shall he stand
With deeper joy, with more complex emotion,
In closer commune with divinity,
With the deep fathomed, with the firmament charted,
With life as simple as a sheep-boy's song,
What lies beyond a romaunt that was read
Once on a morn of storm and laid aside
Memorious with strange immortal memories?
Or shall he see the sunrise as I see it
In shoals of misty fire the deluge-light
Dashes upon and whelms with purer radiance,
And feel the lulled earth, older in pulse and motion,
Turn the rich lands and the inundant oceans
To the flushed color, and hear as now I hear
The thrill of life beat up the planet's margin
And break in the clear susurrus of deep joy
That echoes and reëchoes in my being?
O Life is intuition the measure of knowledge
And do I stand with heart entranced and burning
At the zenith of our wisdom when I feel
The long light flow, the long wind pause, the deep
Influx of spirit, of which no man may tell
The Secret, golden and inappellable?
(1916)

The Closed Door

The dew falls and the stars fall,
The sun falls in the west,
But never more
Through the closed door,
Shall the one that I loved best
Return to me:
A salt tear is the sea,
All earth's air is a sigh,
But they never can mourn for me
With my heart's cry,
For the one that I loved best
Who caressed me with her eyes,
And every morning came to me,
With the beauty of sunrise,
Who was health and wealth and all,
Who never shall answer my call,
While the sun falls in the west,
The dew falls and the stars fall.
(1916)

The Fragment of a Letter

You will recall, of all those magic nights
One when we floated on the sunset lights,
In all the mirrored crimson from the flare;
Not knowing whether we were led by air
Or by secret impulse of the lake.
We watched the youthful darkness swiftly take
The burning mountain-chain of fretted colour
And drench it with his dream of dusk;—duller
It grew and duller, to a high coast of ashes.
The impalpable sheet lightning fled in flashes,
Signalling, in a vivid instant code,
The approach of another wonder-episode

Of beauty, ever stealing nigh and nigher,
And then we were aware of the still fire
Of the Great Moon!

We neared a shadowy island where we lay
And watched the faint illusive moonlight play
Along the shore whereon our tents were pitched.
The silver-birches like live things bewitched
By malice jealous of their beauty, stood
Upon the liquid threshold of the wood.
Then quick upon the dark, like knocks of fate,
There fell three axe-strokes, and then clear, elate
Came back the echoes true to tune and time,
Three axe-strokes—rhythmed and matched in rhyme;
Then a leaf-comment died away in murmurs.
The smoke of our camp-fire amid the firs
Like a tall ghost rose up below the moon.
The enchanted water joined an antiphonal rune
In labials and liquids with the rocky shoal
Where we were moored by pressure of the breeze,
That barely chafed our bark canoe, and stole
Like a wing-flutter through the hazel-trees.
Hidden above there, half asleep, a thrush
Spoke a few silver words upon the hush,—
Then paused self-charmed to silence.

'Tis winged impromptu and the occasion strange
That gives to beauty its full power and range.
The bird was nature; and his casual giving,
Us to ourselves—for what we gain from living,
When we possess our souls or seem to own,
Is not the peak of knowledge, but the tone
Of feeling; is not the problem solved, but just
The hope of solving opened out and thrust
A little further into the spirit air;
But whether there be demonstration there
We know not; no more than the growing vines

When they commission their young eager bines
To find amid the void a clinging-spot
Know whether it be really there or not.

The bird is silent in the groves that grow
Around the past; still the reflections are
That fluttered from his song, and long ago
The tranquil evening ended with a star.
Nothing of all remains but pure romance,
A magic space wherein the mind can dwell,
Above the touch of tedium or of chance
Where fragile thoughts are irrefrangible.
Still the young Time is guardian of that space,
Trembling with unstained beauty through and through,
Where shoots of memory radiate and enlace
Bright as the sun-point in a globe of dew;
Until old Time sables the crystal door,
We may re-enter there,—once more, once more.
(1921)

En Route

The train has stopped for no apparent reason
In the wilds;
A frozen lake is level and fretted over
With rippled wind lines;
The sun is burning in the South; the season
Is winter trembling at a touch of spring.
A little hill with birches and a ring
Of cedars—all so still, so pure with snow—
It seems a tiny landscape in the moon.
Long wisps of shadow from the naked birches
Lie on the white in lines of cobweb-grey;
From the cedar roots the snow has shrunk away,
One almost hears it tinkle as it thaws.
Traces there are of wild things in the snow—

Partridge at play, tracks of the foxes' paws
That broke a path to sun them in the trees.
They're going fast where all impressions go
On a frail substance—images like these,
Vagaries the unconscious mind receives
From nowhere, and lets go to nothingness
With the lost flush of last year's autumn leaves.
(1930)

Chiostro Verde

Here in the old Green Cloister
At Santa Maria Novella
The grey well in the centre
Is dry to the granite curb;
No splashing will ever disturb
The cool depth of the shaft.
In the stone-bordered quadrangle
Daisies, in galaxy, spangle
The vivid cloud of grass.
Four young cypresses fold
Themselves in their mantles of shadow
Away from the sun's hot gold;
And roses revel in the light,
Hundreds of roses; if one could gather
The flush that fades over the Arno
Under Venus at sundown
And dye a snow-rose with the colour,
The ghost of the flame on the snow
Might give to a painter the glow
Of these roses.
Above the roof of the cloister
Rises the rough church wall
Worn with the tides of Time.
The burnished pigeons climb
And slide in the shadowed air,

Wing-whispering everywhere,
Coo and murmur and call
From their nooks in the crannied wall.
Then on the rustling space,
Falling with delicate grace,
Boys' voices from the far off choir,
The full close of a phrase,
A cadence of Palestrina
Or something of even older days,—
No words—only the tune.
It dies now—too soon.
Will music forever die,
The soul bereft of its cry,
And no young throats
Vibrate to clear new notes?
While the cadence was hovering in air
The pigeons were flying
In front of the seasoned stone,
Visiting here and there,
Cooing from the cool shade
Of their nooks in the wall;
Who taught the pigeons their call
Their murmurous music?
Under the roof of the cloister
A few frescoes are clinging
Made by Paolo Uccello,
Once they were clear and mellow
Now they have fallen away
To a dull green-gray,
What has not fallen will fall;
Of all colour bereft
Will nothing at last be left
But a waste wall?
Will painting forever perish,
Will no one be left to cherish
The beauty of life and the world,
Will the soul go blind of the vision?

Who painted those silver lights in the daisies
That sheen in the grass-cloud
That hides their stars or discloses,
Who stained the bronze-green shroud
Wrapping the cypress
Who painted the roses?
(1935)

A Scene at Lake Manitou

In front of the fur-trader's house at Lake Manitou
Indian girls were gathering the hay,
Half labour and half play;
So small the stony field
And light the yield
They gathered it up in their aprons,
Racing and chasing,
And laughing loud with the fun
Of building the tiny cocks.
The sun was hot on the rocks.
The lake was all shimmer and tremble
To the bronze-green islands of cedar and pines;
In the channel between the water shone
Like an inset of polished stone;
Beyond them a shadowy trace
Of the shore of the lake
Was lost in the veil of haze.

Above the field on the rocky point
Was a cluster of canvas tents,
Nearly deserted, for the women had gone
Berry-picking at dawn
With most of the children.
Under the shade of a cedar screen
Between the heat of the rock and the heat of the sun,
The Widow Frederick

Whose Indian name means Stormy Sky,
Was watching her son Matanack
In the sunlight die,
As she had watched his father die in the sunlight.
Worn out with watching,
She gazed at the far-off islands
That seemed in a mirage to float
Moored in the sultry air.
She had ceased to hear the breath in Matanack's throat
Or the joy of the children gathering the hay.
Death, so near, had taken all sound from the day,
And she sat like one that grieves
Unconscious of grief.

With a branch of poplar leaves
She kept the flies from his face,
And her mind wandered in space
With the difficult past
When her husband had faded away;
How she had struggled to live
For Matanack four years old;
Triumphant at last!

She had taught him how and where
To lay the rabbit snare,
And how to set
Under the ice, the net,
The habits of shy wild things
Of the forest and marsh;
To his inherited store
She had added all her lore;
He was just sixteen years old
A hunter crafty and bold;
But there he lay,
And his life with its useless cunning
Was ebbing out with the day.
Fitfully visions rose in her tired brain,

Faded away, and came again and again.
She remembered the first day
He had gone the round of the traps alone,
She saw him stand in the frosty light
Two silver-foxes over his shoulder.
She heard the wolves howl,
Or the hoot of a hunting owl,
Or saw in a sunlit gap
In the woods, a mink in the trap;
Mingled with thoughts of Nanabojou
And the powerful Manitou
That lived in the lake;
Mingled with thoughts of Jesus
Who raised a man from the dead,
So Father Pacifique said.

Suddenly something broke in her heart.
To save him, to keep him forever!
She had prayed to their Jesus,
She had called on Mary His mother
To save him, to keep him forever!
The Holy Water and the Scapular!
She had used all the Holy Water
Father Pacifique had given her;
He had worn his Scapular
Always, and for months had worn hers too;
There was nothing more to be done
That Christians could do.

Now she would call on the Powers of the Earth and the
    Air,
The Powers of the Water;
She would give to the Manitou
That lived in the lake
All her treasured possessions,
And He would give her the lad.
The children heard her scream,

The trader and the loafing Indians
Saw her rush into her tent and bring out her blankets
And throw them into the lake,
Screaming demented screams,
Dragging her treasures into the light,
Scattering them far on the water.
First of them all, her gramophone,
She hurled like a stone;
And they caught her and held her
Just as she swung aloft the next of her treasures
Her little hand-sewing-machine.
They threw her down on the rock
And five men held her until,
Not conquered by them,
But subdued by her will
She lay still.

The trader looked at the boy,
"He's done for," he said.
He covered the head
And went down to the Post;
The Indians, never glancing,
Afraid of the ghost,
Slouched away to their loafing.
After a curious quiet
The girls began the play
Of gathering the last of the hay.

She knew it was all in vain;
He was slain by the foe
That had slain his father.
She put up her hair that had fallen over her eyes,
And with movements, weary and listless,
Tidied her dress.
He had gone to his father
To hunt in the Spirit Land
And to be with Jesus and Mary.

She was alone now and knew
What she would do:
The Trader would debit her winter goods,
She would go into the woods
And gather the fur,
Live alone with the stir
Alone with the silence;
Revisit the Post,
Return to hunt in September;
So had she done as long as she could remember.

She sat on the rock beside Matanack
Resolute as of old,
Her strength and her spirit came back.
Someone began to hammer down at the Trader's house.
The late August air was cold
With a presage of frost.
The islands had lost
Their mirage-mooring in air
And lay dark on the burnished water
Against the sunset flare—
Standing ruins of blackened spires
Charred by the fury of fires
That had passed that way,
That were smouldering and dying out in the West
At the end of the day.
(1935)

At Gull Lake: August, 1810

Gull Lake set in the rolling prairie—
Still there are reeds on the shore,
As of old the poplars shimmer
As summer passes;
Winter freezes the shallow lake to the core;
Storm passes,

Heat parches the sedges and grasses,
Night comes with moon-glimmer,
Dawn with the morning-star;
All proceeds in the flow of Time
As a hundred years ago.

Then two camps were pitched on the shore,
The clustered teepees
Of Tabashaw Chief of the Saulteaux.
And on a knoll tufted with poplars
Two gray tents of a trader—
Nairne of the Orkneys.
Before his tents under the shade of the poplars
Sat Keejigo, third of the wives
Of Tabashaw Chief of the Saulteaux;
Clad in the skins of antelopes
Broidered with porcupine quills
Coloured with vivid dyes,
Vermilion here and there
In the roots of her hair,
A half-moon of powder-blue
On her brow, her cheeks
Scored with light ochre streaks.
Keejigo daughter of Launay
The Normandy hunter
And Oshawan of the Saulteaux,
Troubled by fugitive visions
In the smoke of the camp-fires,
In the close dark of the teepee,
Flutterings of colour
Along the flow of the prairies,
Spangles of flower tints
Caught in the wonder of dawn,
Dreams of sounds unheard—
The echoes of echo,
Star she was named for
Keejigo, star of the morning,

Voices of storm—
Wind-rush and lightning,—
The beauty of terror;
The twilight moon
Coloured like a prairie lily,
The round moon of pure snow,
The beauty of peace;
Premonitions of love and of beauty
Vague as shadows cast by a shadow.
Now she had found her hero,
And offered her body and spirit
With abject unreasoning passion,
As Earth abandons herself
To the sun and the thrust of the lightning.
Quiet were all the leaves of the poplars,
Breathless the air under their shadow,
As Keejigo spoke of these things to her heart
In the beautiful speech of the Saulteaux.

The flower lives on the prairie,
The wind in the sky,
I am here my beloved;
The wind and the flower.

The crane hides in the sand-hills,
Where does the wolverine hide?
I am here my beloved,
Heart's-blood on the feathers
The foot caught in the trap.

Take the flower in your hand,
The wind in your nostrils;
I am here my beloved;
Release the captive
Heal the wound under the feathers.

A storm-cloud was marching
Vast on the prairie,
Scored with livid ropes of hail,
Quick with nervous vines of lightning—
Twice had Nairne turned her away
Afraid of the venom of Tabashaw,
Twice had the Chief fired at his tents
And now when two bullets
Whistled above the encampment
He yelled "Drive this bitch to her master."

Keejigo went down a path by the lake;
Thick at the tangled edges,
The reeds and the sedges
Were gray as ashes
Against the death-black water;
The lightning scored with double flashes
The dark lake-mirror and loud
Came the instant thunder.
Her lips still moved to the words of her music,
"Release the captive,
Heal the wound under the feathers."

At the top of the bank
The old wives caught her and cast her down
Where Tabashaw crouched by his camp-fire.
He snatched a live brand from the embers,
Seared her cheeks,
Blinded her eyes,
Destroyed her beauty with fire,
Screaming, "Take that face to your lover."
Keejigo held her face to the fury
And made no sound.
The old wives dragged her away
And threw her over the bank
Like a dead dog.

Then burst the storm—
The Indians' screams and the howls of the dogs
Lost in the crash of hail
That smashed the sedges and reeds,
Stripped the poplars of leaves,
Tore and blazed onwards,
Wasting itself with riot and tumult—
Supreme in the beauty of terror.
The setting sun struck the retreating cloud
With a rainbow, not an arc but a column
Built with the glory of seven metals;
Beyond in the purple deeps of the vortex
Fell the quivering vines of the lightning.
The wind withdrew the veil from the shrine of the moon,
She rose changing her dusky shade for the glow
Of the prairie lily, till free of all blemish of colour
She came to her zenith without a cloud or a star,
A lovely perfection, snow-pure in the heaven of
    midnight.
After the beauty of terror the beauty of peace.

But Keejigo came no more to the camps of her people;
Only the midnight moon knew where she felt her way,
Only the leaves of autumn, the snows of winter
Knew where she lay.
(1935)

Power

The wave plunges and the sea-gulls cry
Power is in the ocean and the sky—
The wind-driven tide
That would come whispering on still days
With a long ripple breaking in a sigh,
Now crashes down;
The wind-blown gulls

That stood on tranquil days
Like metal birds fixed on the lobster-floats
Mirrored, gray-silver in the glass tide,
Rush with the gale and, when they turn,
Struggle upright, tossed again back.

Heart, that once as still as they,
Idled with an unmeaning sigh,
Or gazed at bygone days in memory's glass,
Now with hard passion buffeted
Beats up against the gale,
Or crashes on the shattered glass of memory,
And cries that there is power in destiny
As well as in the ocean and the sky.
(1941)

Notes to the Poems

The purpose of these notes is twofold: first, to identify if possible both the first periodical appearance and the first book publication of the poems in this anthology, and to note emendations; second, to explain unfamiliar words and important allusions. I have made extensive use of *The Canadian Encyclopedia, The Canadian Oxford Dictionary* (*COD*), *The Compact Edition of the Oxford English Dictionary* (*OED*), *The New Strong's Concordance of the Bible*, and Pierre Grimal's *Dictionary of Classical Mythology*. All Biblical quotations are from the King James Version. More specific debts are recorded in the introductory notes to each author below.

Isabella Valancy Crawford

I have followed the texts in *"Old Spookses' Pass," "Malcolm's Katie" and Other Poems* (Toronto: Bain, 1884), except as noted. For the dates of the poems, I am indebted to Margo Dunn, "A Preliminary Checklist of the Writings of Isabella Valancy Crawford," *The Crawford Symposium*, ed. Frank M. Tierney (Ottawa: U of Ottawa P, 1979): 141-55.

"Canada to England" This poem first appeared in *The Mail* (Toronto), July 28, 1874. It was not included in Crawford's 1884 collection.

7 *Samson* In Judges 16, Samson loses his strength when the seven locks of his hair are shaved off.

9 *Apocalypse* Revelation.

14 *the Ind* India.

15 *Ambrosial* Heavenly; ambrosia was the food of the gods, in Greek and Roman mythology.

15 *furies* Spirits of punishment.

26, 27 "*Man hath dominion*" Several Biblical passages use this phrasing, notably Zechariah 9: 10: "and his dominion shall be from sea even to sea, and from the river even to the ends of the earth."

46 *diapason* Harmonious combination.

"The Roman Rose-Seller" This poem first appeared in *The Mail* (Toronto), Aug. 19, 1874. It was then included in Crawford's 1884 collection.

1 *Paestum* Coastal town famous for its roses and Greek ruins.

2 *nectaries* Parts of flowers that secrete nectar.

5 *Dian* Diana, Roman goddess associated with hunting, virginity, and the moon.

8 *Afric* African.

10 *Tiber* River that flows through Rome.

14 myrtle Evergreen plant associated with love.

18 *canker* Fungus or wound.

30 *Vesta* Roman goddess of the hearth whose temple fires were tended by Vestal Virgins.

33 *Hesperus* Venus; the evening star.

40 *Persepolis* Ancient capital of Persia.

40 *Helot* Slave.

42 *Hybla's* Belonging to the Sicilian town known for the production of honey.

43 *Eros* God of Love (Greek mythology).

44 *despot* Tyrant.

46 *cypress* Evergreen tree associated with death.

53 *From Campus Martius to the Capitol!* From the field of Mars at the boundary of the city of Rome to the hill at its center.

"War" This poem first appeared in *The Toronto Evening Telegram*, Aug. 4, 1879. It was then included in Crawford's 1884 collection.

2 *Titan* The 1884 text reads "Titian." I have followed the 1905 text, since the association with giant size seems more appropriate than the association with the Renaissance painter.

18 *featly* Remarkably.

36 *Te Deum* Latin expression of thanksgiving.

37 *chancel* Area of church near altar.

45 *festal* Of a feast.

68 *scion* Descendant.

70 *vassals* Feudal dependants.

"The Camp of Souls" first appeared in *The Toronto Evening Telegram*, Aug. 9, 1880. It was not included in Crawford's 1884 collection.

5 *wishton-wish* This native name for the prairie dog was used by James Fenimore Cooper for the whipporwill, and that seems to be Crawford's reference.

28 *Manitou* Supernatural spirit (from the Algonquian).

42 *calumet* Native pipe for smoking tobacco.

"The Earth Waxeth Old" This poem first appeared in *The Toronto Evening Telegram*, April 16, 1883. It was then included in Crawford's 1884 collection.

title, 11 *waxeth* Grows.

33 *lea* Meadow.

44 *scudding* Running lightly.

67 *c[lear]* Since the last letters are omitted in 1884, I follow the 1905 text.

"The Dark Stag" This poem first appeared in *The Toronto Evening Telegram*, Nov. 28, 1883. It was not included in Crawford's 1884 collection.

41 *Muskallunge* Muskellunge; a large pike (from the Algonquian).

"The Canoe" This poem first appeared in *The Toronto Evening Telegram*, Feb. 26, 1884. It was then included in Crawford's 1884 collection. It was given the title "Said the Canoe" in the 1905 *Collected Poems*.

1 *twain* Two (archaic).

11 I follow the 1905 text in placing a semi-colon at the end of the line.

34 *sere* Withered.

60 *scimitars* Curved swords.

68 I follow the 1905 text in placing a comma after "pine."

"The Lily Bed" This poem first appeared in *The Toronto Evening Telegram*, Oct. 30, 1884. It was not included in Crawford's 1884 collection.

39 *Manitou* Supernatural spirit (from the Algonquian).

"The Hidden Room" This poem first appeared in Crawford's 1884 collection.

30 *bier* Frame for a coffin.

"Gisli: the Chieftain" This poem first appeared in Crawford's 1884 collection. It was given the title "Gisli, the Chieftain" in the 1905 *Collected Poems*.

Both Margo Dunn and Catherine Sheldrick Ross note that Crawford draws from various myths in this poem, and that she is less interested in the truth of Norse myth in particular than in the truth of myth in general. There is no Lada in Norse mythology, for instance. Dunn finds a source in Russian folklore, which has a spring goddess called Lada. Dunn reads this poem as "a version of the universal fertility myth of the goddess-queen's choice of the most heroic male to aid her in the re-creation of spring in the world" ("Crawford's 'Gisli, the Chieftain,'" *Contemporary Verse Two* 2:2 [1976]: 48). Ross calls the poem "the most condensed and complete working out of the solar myth that informs all [Crawford's] writing" ("Isabella Valancy Crawford's 'Gisli the Chieftain,'" *Canadian Poetry: Studies, Documents, Reviews* 2 [1978]: 28).

Among many textual problems, the subtitle for Part I is missing in the 1884 text, and so are some of the quotation marks. When I have added any punctuation, I have used square brackets. When I have followed the wording of the 1905 text, I have so indicated in a note.

I.1 *Lada* See general note above.

I.2 *Gisli* The name means "sunbeam" in Icelandic (Ross).

I.5 *mead* Liquor made from fermented honey.

I.12 *chaunt* Chant (archaic).

I.18 *distaff* Holds wool for spinning.

I.42 *Weft and woof* Threads used to make fabric.

I.50 *quaff* Drink deeply.

I.59 *"Glass-Hill"* Hill that dead souls must climb to reach Paradise (Ross).

I.78 *Weft and woof* See note for I.42.

II.3 *loom* Device for weaving.

II.9 Both the word "shields" and the semi-colon are absent

from the 1884 text.

II.19 *this woman-lipped haze* Ross compares this haze to mists that imprison heroines in other legends ("Sleeping Beauty," the *Volsunga Saga*).

III.2 *cloven* Split.

III.3 *twain* Two (archaic).

III.5 *Valhalla* Hall to which the souls of dead warriors go to feast with Odin, the supreme god in Scandinavian mythology.

III.16 *know* The 1884 text reads "knows."

III.20 The 1884 text reads "Its breast spurned slowly his red eyes." The terminal punctuation leaves the next line without a grammatical subject, and so I follow the 1905 reading.

III.32 *Gods* The 1884 text has "God's".

III.32 *gyres* Gyrations.

III.54 *cygnet* Young swan.

III.56 *chaunted* Chanted (archaic).

III.60 *Brynhild* The woman Gisli desires; for Ross, a Valkyrie (handmaiden to Odin).

IV.1 *Hell-way* Hel is the underworld in Scandinavian mythology.

IV.2 *Hell-shoes* Dunn notes that "Hel-shoes" in Norse mythology "were tied to the feet of Vesteinna, Gisli's wife's brother," not to Gisli.

IV.4 *spandrils* Spandrels; the spaces between arches and the ceiling.

IV.7 *worlds* "World's" in the 1884 text.

IV.24 *benison* Blessing.

IV.39 This line ends with a period in the 1884 text.

IV.42 This line reads "upward a quivering" in the 1884 text.

IV.45 This line lacks a semi-colon and ends in a period in the 1884 text.

IV.46 *Refluent* Flowing back.

IV.59 *wassail* Alcoholic drink for festive occasions.

IV.60 *"Skoal!"* Scandinavian toast in drinking.

IV.72 This line ends with a period in the 1884 text.

IV.75 *Odin's* Belonging to the supreme God in Scandinavian mythology.

IV.84 This line ends with a period in the 1884 text.

IV.92 This line ends with closing quotation marks in the 1884 text.

IV.108 This line ends with a period in the 1884 text.
IV.110 *jet* Black.
IV.132 *bier* Frame for a coffin.
IV.135 This line ends with a period in the 1884 text.

William Wilfred Campbell

For the dates of the poems, I am indebted to Carl F. Klinck, "A Complete Bibliography of Wilfred Campbell (1858-1918)," Special Collections, Queen's University; and to Laurel Boone, "Notes," *William Wilfred Campbell: Selected Poetry and Essays*, ed. Boone (Waterloo, ON: Wilfrid Laurier UP, 1987): 205-26.

"Indian Summer" This poem was called "Autumn" on its publication in *Varsity* (University of Toronto), Oct. 21, 1881; and in *Poems!* (1881), a booklet of Campbell's poems. In this version, the poem had two additional stanzas. It was called "Indian Summer" when it appeared in *Lake Lyrics and Other Poems* (1889).

"The Winter Lakes" This poem first appeared in *Century* (Jan. 28, 1889). It was then included in *Lake Lyrics and Other Poems* (1889).

"Vapor and Blue" This poem first appeared in *Century* (July 1889) and *The Week* (July 19, 1889). When included in *Lake Lyrics and Other Poems* (1889), it constitutes the "Prelude" to the volume.

"How One Winter Came in the Lake Region" This poem first appeared in *Century* (March 1890). It was then included in *The Dread Voyage and Other Poems* (1893).

"Pan the Fallen" This poem first appeared in *Atlantic Monthly* (Dec. 1890). It was then included in *The Dread Voyage and Other Poems* (1893).

Pan is the Greek god of shepherds and flocks whose combination of human and animal features made him an apt symbol of our mixed condition. In Lampman's words (in "The Modern School of Poetry in England"), "Human nature may be represented by the ancient Pan—half human and half-beast--but the human is the mightier part, and the whole is ever striving to be divine." Since Pan is conventionally depicted with a reed pipe, it was easy to see him as a type of the poet; he plays that role in this and other poems by the Confederation poets. Other versions of the Pan myth in this anthology are Roberts' "The Pipes of Pan," Carman's "By the Aurelian Wall," and D.C. Scott's "The Reed Player" and "The Piper of Arll."

"The Mother" This poem first appeared in *Harper's Monthly* (April 1891); *The Week* (April 3, 1891); and various Canadian newspapers. It was then included in *The Dread Voyage and Other Poems* (1893). When it was included in *Beyond the Hills of Dream* (1899), Campbell added this footnote to the title: "This poem was suggested by the following passage in Tyler's *Animism*: 'The pathetic German superstition that the dead mother's coming back in the night to suckle the baby she had left on earth may be known by the hollow pressed down in the bed where she lay.'"

I.6 *kenned* Knew (Scottish and Northern English).

II.1-2 Campbell omitted these lines in subsequent editions.

II.26 *clomb* Past tense of climb (archaic).

"The Dead Leader" This poem was privately published in 1891. It was then included in *Poems of Wilfred Campbell* (1905).

Campbell worked in Prime Minister Macdonald's Department of Railways and Canals from May 18, 1891. Macdonald died on June 6, 1891.

7 *assoil* Solution (archaic).

9 *Laurelled* Honoured.

20 *elysian* Immortal, ideal. In Greek mythology, the Elysian fields were the place of the blessed after death.

24 *titan* Giant.

"The Dread Voyage" This poem first appeared in *The Dread Voyage and Other Poems* (1893).

"Morning on the Shore" This poem first appeared in *The Dread Voyage and Other Poems* (1893).

The ending of this poem recalls the emergence of the drowned man of Esthwaite in Book V of *The Prelude* (426-59).

"An August Reverie" This poem first appeared in *The Dread Voyage and Other Poems* (1893).

7 *Ere* Before (archaic).

25-30 This stanza contains several echoes of the opening stanzas of Wordsworth's "Resolution and Independence."

40-42 Cf. Wordsworth's "Ode: Intimations of Immortality," ll. 17-18: "But yet I know, where'er I go, / That there hath past away a glory from the earth."

"Bereavement of the Fields" This poem first appeared in *The Globe* (Toronto), May 27, 1899; and in *Atlantic Monthly* (June 1899). It was then included in *Beyond the Hills of Dream* (1899).

Campbell's title is an allusion to Lampman's "Comfort of the Fields." Lampman died on Feb. 10, 1899.

6 Cf. Lampman's "Among the Timothy," ll. 21-22: "And these high moods of mine that sometime made / My heart a heaven . . . ."

27 *Hesper's* The evening star's (Venus is known as Hesperus).

30 *grieves not* Cf. Wordsworth's "Ode: Intimations of Immortality," ll. 179-80: "We will grieve not, rather find / Strength in what remains behind."

43 *this prison-house* Cf. "Ode: Intimations of Immortality," l. 67.

49 *Wordsworth, Arnold, Keats* Lampman's admiration for these writers is apparent in "Poetic Interpretation" and elsewhere.

50 *Pan* See note to "Pan the Fallen."

"The Lazarus of Empire" This poem first appeared in *The Globe* (Toronto), Oct. 17, 1899; and in *The Living Age*, July 28, 1900. It was then included in *Beyond the Hills of Dream* (1899).

In Luke 16: 20-25, Lazarus is a beggar who wants "to be fed with the crumbs which fell from the rich man's table." After both die, the rich man goes to hell and Lazarus is taken to Abraham, who says to the former, "Son, remember that thou in thy lifetime receivdst thy good things, and likewise Lazarus evil things: but now he is comforted, and thou art tormented."

12 Cf. Luke 16: 21.

"Phaethon" This poem first appeared in *Beyond the Hills of Dream* (1899).

In Greek mythology, Phaethon is the son of Helios (the sun). When he dared to drive his father's chariot of fire across the sky, he did so in such a dangerous manner that Zeus struck him down with a thunderbolt. Accordingly, the myth is a story of hubris, but Campbell transforms it to emphasize Phaethon's noble aspirations. By the end, this poem resembles Tennyson's "Ulysses," to which it is generally indebted.

2 *Hephaistos* Hephaestus, god of fire, son of Zeus and Hera.

3 *Helios* The sun; father of Phaethon.

17 *steeds* Pyrois, Eos, Aethon, and Phlegon, the horses that pulled Helios' chariot.

49 *heraclean* Herculean, requiring great strength.

65 *flagon* Bottle, vessel.

66 Cf. Tennyson's "Ulysses," l. 70: "to strive, to seek, to find, and not to yield."

77 *ambrosial* Heavenly. Ambrosia was the food of the Gods, in Greek and Roman mythology.

84 *vermeil* Orange-red.

107 *asphodels* Immortal flowers.

115 *ethiope* Ethiopian, black person (archaic).

126 *drave* Drove (archaic).

129 *eidolon* Phantom.

131 *fetlocks* Part of a horse's leg.

133 *'Whelming* Covering.

136 *cyclops-like* Like the one-eyed giants of Greek mythology.

154 *adamant* Diamond or other hard substance.

162 *leviathan* Monstrously large, like the Biblical sea monster.

185 *Ocean* God of the oceans.

199 Cf. Tennyson's "Ulysses," ll. 8-9.

"Nature" This poem first appeared in *Ainslee's* 15 (July 1905). It was then included in *The Poems of Wilfred Campbell* (1905).

6	*fetid*	Foul.
14	*cark*	Burden (archaic).
14	*dole*	Sorrow (archaic).
15	*weft*	Threads woven across a warp to make fabric.

Charles G.D. Roberts

For the dates of these poems, I am indebted to John Coldwell Adams, "A Preliminary Bibliography," *The Sir Charles G.D. Roberts Symposium*, ed. Glenn Clever (Ottawa: U of Ottawa P, 1984): 221-49; and to Desmond Pacey and Graham Adams, "Notes," *The Collected Poems of Sir Charles G.D. Roberts*, ed. Pacey and Adams (Wolfville, N.S.: Wombat, 1985): 363-636. I have acknowledged specific indebtedness to the latter after the abbreviation "Pacey and Adams."

"Ode to Drowsihood" This poem first appeared in *Scribner's* (Nov. 1879), where it was titled "Ode to Drowsiness." It was then included in *Orion and Other Poems* (1880) as "Ode to Drowsihood."

15	*Druid*	Ancient Celtic priest.
17	*mistletoes*	Sacred to Druids.
22	*Naiad*	Water nymph (Greek mythology).
29	*grackles*	Blackbirds; spelled "grakles" in 1880.
35	*Javan*	Java is one of the Indonesian islands.
43	*Nereids*	Sea nymphs (Greek mythology).
45	*Baiae*	Roman town.
46	*Maggiore*	Italian lake.
50	*Tuscan*	Tuscany is an Italian region.
54	*Fain*	Gladly.

"To Fredericton in May-Time" This poem first appeared in *Later Poems* (privately printed, 1881). It was then included in *In Divers Tones* (1886).

"In the Afternoon" This poem first appeared in Later Poems (privately printed, 1882). It was then included in In Divers Tones (1886).

16 *Tantramar* The river and the marsh area, near the Nova Scotia border, where Roberts grew up. The name comes from "Tintamarre" (French for "din"), referring to the noise of wild geese.

17 *sniff* The 1886 text reads "snuff."
18 *Westmoreland* The county of the Tantramar.
25 *mullein* Plant with yellow flowers.
27 *convolvulus* Plant with trumpet-shaped flowers.
43 *fain* Gladly.
44 *quaff* Drink deeply.

"The Tantramar Revisited" This poem first appeared in *The Week* (Dec. 1883), where it was called "Westmoreland Revisited." It was called "The Tantramar Revisited" in *In Divers Tones* (1886) and "Tantramar Revisited" in later collections.

"The Tantramar Revisited" is a return poem in the tradition of Wordsworth's "Tintern Abbey," to which Roberts alludes at three points. As in his own "In the Afternoon," Carman's "Low Tide on Grand Pré," and Lampman's "Between the Rapids," the poet returns to a familiar landscape, then confronts the discontinuities in his life, and assesses the present in terms of the past. In "The Poetry of Nature" (included in this anthology), Roberts admires "the large, contemplative wisdom" of "Tintern Abbey," but "The Tantramar Revisited" achieves a contrary effect, in its concluding recognition of the pervasiveness of illusion. In the "Prefatory Note" to his *Selected Poems* (1936), Roberts spoke of the form of this poem and of "The Pipes of Pan" as "rigid Ovidian elegiac metre," and he called attention to the "formal alternation of hexameter and pentameter lines."

Tantramar As noted above, this is the region in which Roberts grew up. The Tantramar marshes (near the Nova Scotia border of New Brunswick) are marked by the sharply fluctuating tides of the Bay of Fundy waters.

5 *chance and change* The phrase occurs in Wordsworth's "The White Doe of Rylstone," 7: 1595.

15 *riband* Ribbon.

17 *dikes* Much of the land in this area is reclaimed.

18 *Westmoreland* The county of the Tantramar, and the area named in the original title of the poem.

22 *Cumberland Point* Town now known as Dorchester (Pacey and Adams).

25 *Minudie* Nova Scotia village across the Bay of Fundy from the Tantramar area (Pacey and Adams).

33 *at this season* This phrase, which also occurs in ll. 37 and 39, echoes "Tintern Abbey," l. 12.

"The Pipes of Pan" This poem first appeared in *In Divers Tones* (1886).

For the myth of Pan, see the general note on Campbell's "Pan the Fallen."

1 *Olympus* Home of the twelve greater gods in Greek mythology.

2 *Tempe* Valley in northeast Greece.

9 *Penëus* River in Tempe.

10 *sward* Lawn.

13 *Artemis* Greek goddess of chastity, childbirth, and hunting; daughter of Zeus.

14 *Phoebus* Apollo, god of the sun; brother of Artemis.

15 *dryad* Wood nymph.

19 *lote* Nettle.

"The Poet is Bidden to Manhattan Island" This poem first appeared in *In Divers Tones* (1886).

3 *Phyllis* Typical pastoral name.

3 *swains* Shepherds (as in Milton's "Lycidas," l. 186).

4 *Knickerbocker* Dutch settlers of New York.

6 *ballades* Intricate verse form, common in older French poetry, with three eight-line stanzas and a four-line envoi. Roberts included several ballades in *Orion.*

12 *bucolic* The word usually means pastoral, but Roberts is suggesting that the urban life is more idyllic (hence the play on "urbane" in this line).

14 *husbandmen* Farmers (archaic).

15 *stock* Roberts puns on the financial stock market

and livestock.

18 *Saturn* Roman god of agriculture.

20 *Arcadia* Paradisal rural area.

23 *bulls and bears* Stocks are bullish when rising and bearish when falling.

26 *Proteus* Greek sea god who could assume many different shapes.

31 *ducks and drakes* A game played by skimming stones.

35 *dead* Deadbeats are those who owe money (colloquial).

44 *"pastures new"* See "Lycidas," l. 193.

44 *Bowery* Area in Manhattan.

"Ave!" This poem was separately published in 1892, then included in *Songs of the Common Day, and Ave: An Ode for the Shelley Centenary* (1893).

Although this is a commemorative poem written one hundred years after the birth of Percy Bysshe Shelley, and not a conventional elegy, the poem does use elegiac conventions, and therefore it should be read with Roberts' fine essay on the elegiac tradition (in *Selected Poetry and Critical Prose*, ed. W.J. Keith).

1 *Tantramar* See the notes to "In the Afternoon" l. 16 and "The Tantramar Revisited."

14 *fain* Gladly.

33 *the secret fire* See Isaiah 6: 6-7: "then flew one of the seraphims unto me, having a live coal in his hand, which he had taken with the tongs from off the altar: / And he laid it upon my mouth, and said, Lo, this hath touched thy lips; and thine iniquity is taken away, and thy sin purged."

44 *Vetches* Plants used for fodder.

52 *River of hubbub* As noted above, Tantramar comes from the French "Tintamarre," meaning "din."

63 *Minudie* Nova Scotia village across the Bay of Fundy from the Tantramar area (Pacey and Adams).

64 *Chignecto* Northern part of Bay of Fundy (Pacey and Adams).

65 *refluent* Flowing back.

70 Beauséjour is either "the Acadian settlement near Sackville" or "the fort near the New Brunswick-Nova Scotia border."

Tormentine is the cape "on the extreme eastern tip of New Brunswick. The distance between the two points is approximately 30 miles" (Pacey and Adams).

87 *him* Shelley (born in 1792).

103 *avatar* Incarnation of a god.

106 *fain* Gladly.

108 *bays* Wreathes of bay leaves worn by a poet.

114-20 Shelley admired the atheistical and republican ideas associated with the French Revolution.

133 *Thy venerable foster-mother* Oxford University. The following lines refer to Shelley's expulsion for refusing to recant his sceptical tract, "The Necessity of Atheism."

142 *Alastor* Shelley published "Alastor; or, the Spirit of Solitude" in 1816. The protagonist and the settings are described in the rest of the stanza.

151 *the lark* As in Shelley's "To a Skylark."

152 *Protean* Assuming many different shapes (like the god Proteus in Greek mythology).

152 *cloud* As in Shelley's "The Cloud."

156 *wild west wind* As in Shelley's "Ode to the West Wind."

159 *Arno* Italian river.

161 *thy mightiest creation* *Prometheus Unbound* (1820).

163 *all-forgiving* Prometheus forgives Jupiter at I.i.53 of *Prometheus Unbound*.

171 *Baths of Caracalla* Roman ruins that inspired Shelley while writing *Prometheus Unbound*.

172 *rhapsodies of green* In his preface to *Prometheus Unbound*, Shelley wrote of the "flowery glades, and the thickets of odoriferous blossoming trees, which are extended in ever winding labyrinths upon its immense platforms and dizzy arches in the air."

181 *Pisa* Shelley moved to Pisa in Jan. 1820.

182 *myrtles* Evergreens associated with love.

182 *ilexes* Hollies.

183 *San Giuliano* Shelley's Pisan residence.

184 *aziola* Owl; the subject of Shelley's "The Aziola."

185 *The Serchio* Tuscan river, the setting of Shelley's "The Boat on the Serchio."

188 *espousal psalm* "Epipsychidion"; Shelley called it "an idealized history of my life and feelings."

196 *thy supreme lament* "Adonais" (1821), Shelley's elegy for John Keats, who died on Feb. 23, 1821.

200 See "Adonais," ll. 379-80, where Adonais becomes "a portion of the loveliness / Which once he made more lovely."

201 *would not abide* See stanza 52 of "Adonais."

203 *has not died* See "Adonais," l. 361.

205 *swan-song mystical* Since the swan was believed to die singing, Roberts is implying that "Adonais" foreshadows Shelley's own death. Shelley implies as much in the last stanza of "Adonais."

211 *Lerici* Site of Shelley's last residence, the Casa Magni.

213 *Spezzia* With his friend Edward Wiliams, Shelley drowned in the Gulf of Spezzia on July 8, 1822. This stanza is Roberts' version of the elegiac convention of the sympathetic lament of nature.

221 *fateful bark* The *Don Juan*, Shelley's boat. See also "Lycidas," l. 100: "That fatal and perfidious bark."

230 *Casa Magni* Shelley's last residence.

241 *face to face* See I Corinthians 13: 12: "For now we see through a glass, darkly; but then face to face; now I know in part; but then shall I know even as also I am known."

251 *He of the seven cities* Homer.

255 *The Thunderous* Aeschylus, who wrote *Prometheus Bound*.

257-58 *Judah's crowned / Singer and seer divine* David.

259 *the Tuscan* Dante.

261 *whelming* Overpowering.

264 *thy kindred flame* Shelley was cremated on Aug. 15, 1822.

275 *Trelawney* Edward John Trelawney (1792-1881), friend of Shelley and Byron, and author of *Recollections of the Last Days of Shelley and Byron* (1858).

276 *that gentlest sage* Leigh Hunt (1784-1859), Keats' friend. Hunt did not get along so well with Lord Byron, the third of the "close companions" who attended the cremation.

294 *vasts* Immense areas.

307 *the keen stars* Shelley's late lyric "To Jane" begins "The keen stars were twinkling."

"Marsyas" This poem first appeared in *Songs of the Common Day* (1893).

In Greek mythology, Marsyas was a satyr who was so proud of his skills as a flautist that he challenged Apollo to a musical contest, with the winner to punish the loser. After winning, Apollo tied Marsyas to a tree and flayed him alive. As in Tennyson's "Tithonus," "Marsyas" focusses on one intense moment in a myth.

7 *Pontic* Of the Black Sea (Pacey and Adams).
11 *satyr* A woodland god with some goatish features.
22 *hern* Heron (archaic).
32 *the young God* Apollo.

Songs of the Common Day Many of these sonnets had been written much earlier and published discretely, but Roberts carefully arranged them into a twenty-six sonnet sequence that followed the course of a year on a Maritime farm. His very title is an allusion to Wordsworth's Preface to *The Excursion* l. 55: "A simple produce of the common day." I include 15 of these sonnets here; all of the titles are listed, and Roberts' changes are noted, in Susan Glickman's essay in this anthology.

"The Furrow" This poem first appeared in *Century* (April 1890). It was then included in *Songs of the Common Day* (1893).

5 *glebe* Field.
8 *lea* Meadow.
12 *cloven* Split.
13 *share* Ploughshare.

"The Sower" This poem first appeared in *Manhattan Magazine* (July 1884). It was then included in *In Divers Tones* (1886) before it appeared in *Songs of the Common Day* (1893).

9 *glebe* Field.
13 *churl* Peasant (archaic).

"The Waking Earth" This poem first appeared in *The Independent* (May 23, 1889). It was then included in *Songs of the Common Day* (1893).

13 *fetterless* Unshackled.

"The Cow Pasture" This poem first appeared in *Songs of the Common Day* (1893).

"Frogs" This poem first appeared in *The Dominion Illustrated Magazine* (Nov. 1888). It was then included in *Songs of the Common Day* (1893).

"The Salt Flats" This poem first appeared in *The Independent* (March 19, 1891). It was then included in *Songs of the Common Day* (1893).

1 *clove* Split.

5 *samphire* Maritime plant.

"The Pea-Fields" This poem first appeared in *The Atlantic Monthly* (Aug. 1891). It was then included in *Songs of the Common Day* (1893).

"The Mowing" This poem first appeared in *The Independent* (Aug. 21, 1890). It was then included in *Songs of the Common Day* (1893).

8 *timothy* Fodder grass.

10 *chemic* Pertaining to alchemy, the "science" that tried to turn base metals to gold.

11 *cordial* Warm.

"Buckwheat" This poem first appeared in *Songs of the Common Day* (1893).

"The Potato Harvest" This poem first appeared in *In Divers Tones* (1886). It was then included in *Songs of the Common Day* (1893).

14 *wain* Wagon.

"The Oat-Threshing" This poem first appeared in *Songs of the Common Day* (1893).

3 *cinnabar* Red.

8 *husbandries* Cultivation.

"The Autumn Thistles" This poem first appeared in *Canada* (Jan. 1891). It was then included in *Songs of the Common Day* (1893).

9 *amethystine* Violet.

"The Pumpkins in the Corn" This poem first appeared in *Songs of the Common Day* (1893).

11 *gadding* Wandering.

"The Winter Fields" This poem first appeared in *Century* (Jan. 1890). It was then included in *Songs of the Common Day* (1893).

11 *glebes* Fields.

"The Flight of the Geese" This poem first appeared in *The Independent* (April 17, 1890). It was then included in *Songs of the Common Day* (1893).

"The Vengeance of Gluskâp" This poem first appeared in *The Independent* and *King's College Record* in November, 1894. It was then included in *The Book of the Native* (1896).

Pacey and Adams note that Gluskâp is a "giant and a cultural hero of the Micmac Indians." Roberts wrote three other poems about him: "The Departing of Gluskâp," "The Quelling of the Moose," and "The Succour of Gluskâp." In his *Poems* (1901) and subsequently, Roberts changed the subtitle to "A Melicite Legend."

29 *sea-mews* Gulls.

The New York Nocturnes. This sequence of sixteen poems was not fully preserved after its original publication. Nonetheless, the sequence is one of Roberts' most ambitious works, for he attempts "to arrive at a vision of sanctified and eternal human love which would reconcile the disparate and conflicting elements—the urges towards both the profane and the sacred—which he found in his own divided nature" (58). That quotation comes from an article on which I have drawn extensively in my annotations: D.M.R. Bentley, "Half Passion and Half Prayer: *The New York Nocturnes*," *The Sir Charles G.D. Roberts Symposium*, ed. Glenn Clever (Ottawa: U of Ottawa P, 1984): 55-75.

"The Ideal" This poem first appeared in *New York Nocturnes* (1898).

10 *lilies* Associated with the Blessed Virgin and with Easter (Bentley).

Epigraph From a lost play of Sophocles; translated by Dryden as "O gods! what Venus or what grace divine, / Did here with human workmanship combine?"

"In the Crowd" This poem first appeared in *Lippincott's Magazine* (Sept. 1898). It was then included in *New York Nocturnes* (1898).

"Night in a Down-town Street" This poem first appeared in *Century* (Dec. 1897). It was then included in *New York Nocturnes* (1898).

7 *bourneless* Without goal or limit.

13 *cañon* Bentley argues that the Spanish spelling provides a pun on "canyon" and "canon" (law).

"At the Railway Station" This poem first appeared in *Harper's* (Feb. 5, 1898). It was then included in *New York Nocturnes* (1898).

title In addition to the literal meaning, "station" also carries religious overtones (as in the Stations of the Cross).

"Nocturnes of the Honeysuckle" This poem first appeared in *New York Nocturnes* (1898).

"My Garden" This poem first appeared in *Munsey's Magazine* (Jan. 1898). It was then included in *New York Nocturnes* (1898).

16 *tryst* Secret meeting of lovers.

"Presence" This poem first appeared in *Munsey's Magazine* (Feb. 1898). It was then included in *New York Nocturnes* (1898).

"Twilight on Sixth Avenue" This poem first appeared as "Twilight on Sixth Avenue at Ninth Street" in *Maple Leaf* (April 1895). It was then included in *The Book of the Native* (1896) before it appeared in *New York Nocturnes* (1898).

3 *diaphanous* Nearly transparent; delicate.

"The Street Lamps" This poem first appeared in *New York Nocturnes* (1898).

6 *fain* Gladly.

"In Darkness" This poem first appeared in *New York Nocturnes* (1898).

"In the Solitude of the City" This poem first appeared in *The Independent* (Feb. 10, 1898). It was then included in *New York Nocturnes* (1898).

3 *trysting* Meeting secretly.

"A Nocturne of Exile" This poem first appeared in *The Bookman* and *The Living Age* (Feb. 1898). It was then included in *New York Nocturnes* (1898).

13 *Ere* Before (archaic).

"A Street Vigil" This poem first appeared in *The Chap-Book* (Jan 15, 1898). It was then included in *New York Nocturnes* (1898).

title A vigil is when one foregoes sleep to maintain a watch; it is also the eve of a holy day.

3 *myrrh* Fragrant gum that was one of the gifts of the three wise men (Matthew 2: 11); later used for perfume (Bentley).

4 *washed with tears* Mary Magdalene washed Christ's feet with her tears (Luke 7: 38).

"A Nocturne of Trysting" This poem first appeared in *The Bookman* (Feb. 1898). It was then included in *New York Nocturnes* (1898).

title *Trysting* Secret meeting of lovers.

"In a City Room" This poem first appeared in *Munsey's Magazine* (Feb. 1898). It was then included in *New York Nocturnes* (1898).

"A Nocturne of Consecration" This poem first appeared in *The Independent* (Dec. 2, 1897). It was then included in *New York Nocturnes* (1898).

title *Consecration* To make sacred.

9 *lilies* Associated with the Blessed Virgin and with Easter (Bentley); see "The Ideal," l. 10.

31 *drain life to the lees* See Tennyson, "Ulysses," ll. 6-7: "I will drink / Life to the lees." "Lees" means "dregs," as of wine.

86 *chrismal* Mixture of oil and balsam used for anointing.

"The Skater" This poem first appeared in *Poems* (1901).

"The Unknown City" This poem first appeared in *Scribner's* (Sept. 1903). It was then included in *New Poems* (1919).

11 *jettied* Protected with a pier.

12 *enskied* Placed in the sky.

20 Cf. Wordsworth's "Immortality Ode," ll. 202-03: "To me the meanest flower that blows can give / Thoughts that do often lie too deep for tears." In both cases, "blows" means "blossoms."

29 *emprize* Undertaking.

36 *bournes* Limits.

"Philander's Song" This poem first appeared in *The Vagrant of Time* (1927).

title *Philander* To philander is to have casual affairs with women.

subtitle *"The Sprightly Pilgrim"* Pacey and Adams identify this as "apparently a projected work which was never completed."

1 *Anacreon* Sixth-century B.C. Greek poet of hedonistic themes.

"To a Certain Mystic" This poem first appeared in *Queen's Quarterly* (July 1931). It was then included in *The Iceberg and Other Poems* (1934).

According to Martin Ware, this poem was addressed to William Blake.

6 *shallop* Boat.

7 *Elysian* Heavenly.

11 *Tree Eternal* The Holy Cross.

"Two Rivers" This poem first appeared in *Dalhousie Review* (1937). It was then included in *Canada Speaks of Britain and Other Poems of the War* (1941).

18 Cf. "Ave!" stanzas 2 and 3.

33 *Midgic* Village north of Sackville (Pacey and Adams).

35 *studious halls* Mount Allison University.

36 *Westcock* Roberts grew up here.

63 *Temiscouata* Quebec lake off Maine border (Pacey and Adams).

64 *Allegash* Maine lake that is the origin of the St. John river (Pacey and Adams).

68 *alien* Roberts provided this footnote: "The sources of the St. John are in Maine."

69 *confluent* Flowing together.

78 Pacey and Adams note that "the first Loyalists landed at the city of St. John, and the city still bears the appellation The Loyalist City."

Archibald Lampman

For the dates of the poems, I am indebted to George Wicken, "Archibald Lampman: An Annotated Bibliography," *The Annotated Bibliography of Canada's Major Authors*, Vol. 2, ed. Robert Lecker and Jack David (Downsview, ON: ECW, 1980): 97-146. I have acknowledged specific indebtedness (with the word "Gnarowski") to the notes in *Selected Poetry of Archibald Lampman*, ed Michael Gnarowski (Ottawa: Tecumseh, 1990): 106-11.

"The Railway Station" This poem appeared in *The Week* (Toronto), Dec. 22, 1887. It was then included in *Among the Millet* (1888).

8 *bourneless* Limitless.

"In October" This poem first appeared in *Among the Millet* (1888).

3 *dolorous* Sad.

27 *runes* Secret objects.

"Among the Timothy" This poem first appeared in *Among the Millet* (1888).

3 *reaper* Gnarowski notes that D.C. Scott changed this word to "mower" in his 1900 edition of Lampman's poetry.
24 *Begirt* Encompassed.
34 *unbournèd* Without limit.
57 *maenads* Revellers.
64 *sere* Withered.
67 *anon* Shortly.
83 *sweet unrest* See Keats, "Bright Star," l. 12: "Awake forever in a sweet unrest" (Bentley).

"Among the Millet" This poem first appeared in *Among the Millet* (1888).

9 *sward* Field.

"Morning on the Lièvres" This poem first appeared in *Among the Millet* (1888).

Gnarowski notes that this Ottawa area river was known as the Rivière aux Lièvres," though D.C. Scott changed the spelling to "Lievre" in 1900.

2 *matins* Morning prayer.
3 *amethyst* Violet precious stone.
24 *plight* Pledge.

"Between the Rapids" This poem first appeared in *Among the Millet* (1888).

9 *five years* Cf. Wordsworth, "Tintern Abbey," ll. 1-2: "Five years have past; five summers, with the length / Of five long winters!"

"The Frogs" This poem first appeared in *Among the Millet* (1888).

10 *wrapt* Enveloped. D.C. Scott changed the word to "rapt" (Gnarowski).
35 *lucent* Shining.
47 *wrapt* See note to l. 10.
53 *antiphonies* Alternate singing.
66 *wrapt* See note to l. 10.

"Heat" This poem first appeared in *Among the Millet* (1888).

22 *midge* Insect.

"Winter Hues Recalled" This poem first appeared in *Among the Millet* (1888).

13 *garner-house* Storehouse.
63 *Ere* Before.
85 *sapphire* Blue.
88 *amethysts* Violet precious stones.
94 *athwart* Across.
95 *sapphire* See note to l. 85.

"In November" This poem first appeared in *Harper's* (Nov. 1890). It was then included in *Lyrics of Earth* (1896).

10 *mullein* Plant with yellow flowers.
21 *compline prayer* Said before retiring at night.
40 *sere* Withered.
43 *reverie* Spelled "revery" in 1896.

"A Sunset at Les Eboulements" This poem first appeared as "A Sunset on the Lower St. Lawrence" in *The Independent* (Oct. 1, 1891). It was then included in *The Poems of Archibald Lampman* (1900).

title *Les Eboulements* On the north shore of the St. Lawrence, across from Kamouraska (see l. 13).
6 *wattled* Fenced with interlaced woodwork.
10 *ere* Before.
13 *Kamouraska* On the south shore of the St. Lawrence.

"Comfort of the Fields" This poem first appeared in *Scribner's* (Feb. 1892). It was then included in *Lyrics of Earth* (1896).

25 *marguerite* Daisy.
30 *mullein* Plant with yellow flowers.
32 *vervain* Plant with purple flowers.
38 *meres* Lakes.
44 *wains* Wagons.
45 *thresher* "Thrasher" in 1896.

Notes to the Poems

"An Autumn Landscape" This poem first appeared in *Harper's* (Oct. 1892). It was then included in *Lyrics of Earth* (1896).

35 *haply* By chance.

"On the Companionship with Nature" This poem first appeared as "Nature Love" in *Youth's Companion* (Dec.1, 1892). It was then included in *Poems* (1900).

"September" This poem first appeared in *Harper's* (Sept. 1893). It was then included in *Lyrics of Earth* (1896).

8 *sere* Withered.
14 *marguerite* Daisy.
28 *threshers* "Thrashers" in 1896.
33 *ere* Before.
43 *vervain* Plant with purple flowers.
44 *aster* Plant with daisy-like flowers.
49 *russet* Reddish brown.
60 *elixir* Mythical substance able to change metals to gold.

"Indian Summer" This poem first appeared in *Scribner's* (Nov. 1893). It was then included in *Alcyone* (1899).

1 *sooth* Truth (archaic).

"The City of the End of Things" This poem first appeared in *Atlantic Monthly* (March 1894). It was then included in *Alcyone* (1899).

See D.M.R. Bentley's essay in this anthology for an account of the literary and social contexts of this poem.

4 *Tartarus* Underworld place of punishment.

"To an Ultra Protestant" This poem first appeared in *The Week* (Nov. 30, 1894). It was then included in *Poems* (1900).

title *Ultra* Extremist.
2 *sacerdotal* Of a priest's duties.

"To a Millionaire" This poem first appeared in *The Week* (Nov. 30, 1894). It was then included in *Poems* (1900).

11 *"the good, the beautiful, the true"* Often associated in Platonic tradition.

"Beauty" This poem first appeared in *The Week* (Nov. 30, 1894). It was then included in *Poems* (1900).

"Alcyone" This poem first appeared in *The Atlantic Monthly* (Jan. 1895). It was then included in *Alcyone* (1899).

title The "brightest star in the constellation Taurus" (Gnarowski).

10 *Pleiad* One of the seven daughters of Atlas and Pleione who were "changed into stars by the gods when they were pursued by the amorously inclined hunter, Orion" (Gnarowski).

"White Pansies" This poem first appeared in *Scribner's* (July 1897). It was then included in *Alcyone* (1899).

This poem is an elegy for Lampman's son Arnold, who was less than three months old when he died on August 4, 1894.

11 *changers* Money-changers.

13 *heartsease* Another name for pansies.

"The Largest Life" This poem first appeared in *The Atlantic Monthly* (March 1899). It was then included in *Poems* (1900).

"The Land of Pallas" This poem first appeared in *Alcyone* (1899). I have followed Lampman's corrected proofs in the Lampman Papers, Public Archives of Canada, Ottawa.

This poem is based on Lampman's socialist ideals, and it should be read in conjunction with his essay on "Socialism."

title *Pallas* One of the names, of unknown origin, of Athene, daughter of Zeus and goddess of wisdom (Greek mythology).

4 *eyots* Small islands.

10 *vesper* Evening.

12 *wist* Know (archaic).

87 *canons* Laws.

104 *beryl* Precious stone.

142 *anarch* Cause of anarchy (disorder).

145-48 E.K. Brown discovered that the poem originally ended

with this stanza:

Then I returned upon my footsteps madly guessing,
 And many a day thereafter with feet sad and sore
I sought to win me back into that land of blessing,
 But I had lost my way, nor could I find it more.

"Winter Uplands" Believed to be Lampman's last poem, this was published in *Poems* (1900).

"Epitaph on a Rich Man" This poem first appeared in *At the Long Sault and Other New Poems* (1943).

title *Epitaph* Either a tomb insciption or a poem that resembles one.

"At the Long Sault" This poem first appeared in *At the Long Sault* (1943).

When E.K. Brown published this poem for the first time in 1943, he claimed that it reflected a "widening" of Lampman's interests. As Brown also noted, however, "It is all too easy for the discoverer of a poem such as this to exaggerate its merit" (see *On Canadian Poetry* 107-08). Of the 1660 incident on which the poem is based, Brown said that Adam Dollard des Ormeaux (Daulac) "and his little band of French Canadians held a dilapidated fort for about ten days against an overwhelming number of Iroquois, continuing to fight till all but four were dead." The survivors (actually nine) were later tortured to death by the Iroquois.

15 *palisade* Defensive enclosure.

21 *Daulac* Adam Dollard des Ormeaux (1635-60). He had sixteen soldiers and 44 Hurons and Algonquins under his command.

26 *town* Daulac set out from Montreal for the Long Sault rapids.

42 *Iroquois* 300 Iroquois met them initially, with more arriving later.

66 *pales* Fencing.

68 *thews* Endowments.

Bliss Carman

For the dates of the poems, I am indebted to Muriel Miller, "Appendix B: Yearly Output of Carman's Poetry," *Bliss Carman: A Portrait* (Toronto: Ryerson, 1935): 120-34; to John Robert Sorfleet, "Notes on the Poems," *The Poems of Bliss Carman*, ed. Sorfleet (Toronto: McClelland and Stewart, 1976): 164-69; and to the notes in *Letters of Bliss Carman*, ed. H. Pearson Gundy (Kingston: McGill-Queen's, 1981).

"Low Tide on Grand Pré" This poem first appeared in *The Atlantic Monthly* (March 1887). It was then included in *Low Tide on Grand Pré: A Book of Lyrics* (1893).

On the genre of the return poem, see the general note to "The Tantramar Revisited." Carman has added an erotic context by addressing his poem to a lover; "Tintern Abbey," by contrast, is addressed to Wordsworth's sister.

title Grand Pré is a marshland area in the Minas basin of Nova Scotia. In the seventeenth century, it was settled by the Acadians, who were expelled in 1755.

"A Windflower" According to Miller, this poem appeared in 1889 before it was privately printed in 1890. It was then included in *Low Tide* (1893).

"In Lyric Season" According to Miller, this poem appeared in 1888. It was then included in *Low Tide* (1893).

3 *leaguer* League, in the sense of a measure of about 3 miles.

4 *Auroral* Of the dawn.

"The Pensioners" This poem appeared in *Harvard Monthly* (May 1889). It was then included in *Low Tide* (1893).

3 *vassal* Dependent (feudal).

6 *almoners* Those who distribute alms.

38 *whitethroat* Bird with white patch on throat.

"Carnations in Winter" According to Miller, this poem appeared in 1888. It was then included in *Low Tide* (1893).

1	*carmine*	Crimson.
7	*martins*	Swallows.
11	*antiphonal*	Singing alternately.

"A Sea-Drift" This poem appeared in the second edition of *Low Tide* (1894).

"The Eavesdropper" This poem appeared in *The Atlantic Monthly* (Feb. 1893). It was then included in *Low Tide* (1893).

11 This line originally read "With small innumerable sound," which is strikingly similar to l. 36 of Lampman's "Heat": "A small innumerable sound." When Peter McArthur brought the matter to his attention, Carman changed the line for the second edition of *Low Tide on Grand Pré* (1894) and apologized to Lampman. In Carman's words, the change made him "the saddest man in New York, not because I feared a charge of plagiarism, but because I must lose such a good line." Nonetheless, William Wilfred Campbell used this and other details to accuse Carman of plagiarism as well as "log-rolling" (favouritism) in what became known as "the war among the poets." See Alexandra J. Hurst, *The War Among the Poets: Issues of Plagiarism and Patronage Among the Confederation Poets* (London: Canadian Poetry Press, 1994), especially 35, 70, and 91.

"In Apple Time" According to Miller, this poem appeared in 1888. It was then included in *Low Tide* (1893).

11	*russet*	Reddish brown.
13	*runnels*	Brooks.
14	*undern*	Midday (archaic).
19	*prime*	Christian prayer said at 6 a.m.

"In the Heart of the Hills" This poem appeared in *The Independent* (June 16, 1892). It was then included in *By the Aurelian Wall and Other Elegies* (1898).

Carman wrote this elegy for his cousin, and Charles G.D. Roberts' brother, Goodridge Bliss Roberts, who died suddenly of pneumonia on Feb. 4, 1892.

21 *tern* Gull-like birds.
22 *skreel* Variant of "skreigh" (shriek).
28 *martin* Swallow.

"The Grave-Tree" According to Miller, this poem appeared in 1892. It was then included in *By the Aurelian Wall* (1898).

As an elegy for himself, this poem echoes back to such poems as Christina Rossetti's "'Song' ('When I am dead, my dearest')," and ahead to such poems as W.B. Yeats' "Under Ben Bulben." Carman placed the poem last in *By the Aurelian Wall.*

45 *Scarlet Hunter* A spirit of Carman's invention.

"By the Aurelian Wall" This poem first appeared in *The Independent* (Feb. 23, 1893). It was then included in *By the Aurelian Wall.*

Hardly an elegy in the conventional sense, this commemorative poem for John Keats (1795-1821) opens *By the Aurelian Wall.*

1 *Aurelian Wall* Roman arches that survive intact.

3 *Caius Cestius' tomb* On the edge of the Protestant Cemetery in Rome, where Keats was buried.

24 *some god* See Roberts, "The Pipes of Pan."

35 *whitethroats* Birds with white patches on throats.

43-46 Carman blends the myth of the pied piper with the Pan myth.

67 *his splendid name* Keats

72 *Grand Pré* See note to "Low Tide on Grand Pré."

72 *Margaree* Nova Scotia town.

74 *Gaspareau* Nova Scotia town.

"A Vagabond Song" This poem appeared in *The Bookman* (Nov. 1895). It was then included in *More Songs from Vagabondia* (1896).

8 *asters* Plant with daisy-like flowers.

"To P.V." According to Miller, this poem appeared in 1896. It was then included in *By the Aurelian Wall* (1898).

Carman wrote this elegy for Paul Verlaine (1844-96), the French symbolist poet.

8 *caporal* Tobacco.

10 *roistered* Revelled. The most notorious incident in Verlaine's sensational life was his affair with Arthur Rimbaud, which ended when he shot and wounded Rimbaud.

25 *mien* Look.

48 *Nunc dimittis* "Let your servant depart" (Latin; Luke 2: 29).

Poems from *Sappho*. The selections are from *Sappho: One Hundred Lyrics* (1903)

Sappho was a Greek lyric poet of the seventh century B.C. Although most of her surviving poems are fragments, her reputation as a genius of passionate, bisexual lyric poetry is secure. As Charles G.D. Roberts explains in his introduction to *Sappho*, Carman attempts to imagine the lost poems of Sappho: his method "has been to imagine each lost lyric as discovered, and then to translate it; for the indefinable flavour of the translation is maintained throughout, though accompanied by the fluidity and freedom of purely original work" (xv). Approaching *Sappho* as a sequence expressing Carman's Unitrinian ideal of "a love that combines the physical, the mental and the spiritual" (33-34), D.M.R. Bentley divides the book into five groups: an invocation in poems I-V; three sequences concerning Sappho's loves of Atthis (VI-XXXVIII), Phaon (XXXIX-LXI), and Gorgo (LXII-LXXXVII); and a concluding return to Atthis (LXXXVIII-C). In these notes, I have drawn frequently on Bentley's article, "Threefold in Wonder: Bliss Carman's *Sappho: One Hundred Lyrics,*" *Canadian Poetry: Studies, Documents, Reviews* 17 (1985): 29-58.

III

1 Bentley connects these qualities to the three divinities in the next line.

2 *Pan* God of flocks, he had a combination of goatish and human features.

2 *Aphrodite* Goddess of love.

2 *Hermes* God of merchants, thieves, and oratory; messenger of the gods.

8 *Lesbos* Island on which Sappho lived.

12 *Threefold* As in the triplets of each of the first two

lines, as well as in Carman's Unitrinian interest in harmonizing spirit, body, and mind (Bentley).

IV

2 *Protector* Pan was the god of flocks.

17-18 *secret / Learning* Carman is thinking of Hermes Trismegistus, the legendary source of occult (hermetic) wisdom.

30 *vernal* Spring.

VI

Bentley notes that this poem is largely "a translation of one of Sappho's larger fragments."

2 *thy* As yet unnamed woman (later called Atthis).

VII

1 *The Cyprian* Aphrodite.

XXIII

1 *Atthis* The woman addressed but not named in VI, VII, and XVIII.

2 *oleanders* Mediterranean shrub.

XXXIV

5 *Haply* By chance.

XLI

1 *Phaon* A male lover.

6 *coolth* Coolness.

XLV

In this poem, Phaon is thinking of Sappho in her absence (Bentley).

LIV

Sappho is the speaker again.

6 *oreads* Mountain nymphs.

LV

Phaon's response to the previous poem.

5 *deigned* Condescended.

9 *fettered* Limited.

LXI

2 *thou* Phaon, now dead (Bentley).

LXXVI

1 *Marsyas* See note to Roberts' "Marsyas."

4 *the great god* Apollo.

5 *fond* Foolish.

10 *ere* Before.

10 *thee* Gorgo (see LXXXVII)

LXXXIV

4 *sea-pharos* Beacon.

8 *your* Gorgo's.

LXXXVII

As Bentley notes, the relationship with Gorgo that started in LXXVI ends in this lyric.

LXXXVIII

7 *frondage* Leaves.

13 *thy* Atthis' (named in LXXXIX)

XCII

3 *you* Atthis.

7 *Eleusinian mother* Demeter, Goddess of agriculture.

10 *Great Mysteries* The Eleusinian mysteries: the annual celebrations in honour of Demeter at Eleusis.

XCIII

7 *thou* Atthis.

C

Bentley notes that the "Lityerses song" is "associated with harvest rituals on account of its namesake's ferocious fondness for reaping contexts," but that here we have "a spring ritual that does

not awaken the human dead."
17 *Mitylene* On the island of Lesbos.

"The World Voice" According to Miller, this poem appeared in 1915. It was then included in *April Airs: A Book of New England Lyrics* (1916).

"Vestigia" This poem appeared in *Later Poems* (1921).
title Variant of vestige (trace).

"The Ships of St. John" This poem appeared in *Later Poems* (1921). An earlier poem with this name appeared in *Ballads of Lost Haven* (1897).
9 *barkentine* Ship (usually spelled barquentine).
29 *insensate* Unfeeling
43 *capstan* Cylinder used to wind anchor cable.
53 *tide-rips* Rough waters.

"Victoria" This poem appeared in *Far Horizons* (1925).

Carman travelled across Canada on a reading tour in 1921. In a letter of Dec. 5, 1921, to Peter McArthur, Carman writes that "Vancouver turned out a splendid result, . . . though it was not until I struck Victoria and Government House that the old Scotch kindredness made its appearance."
1 *Saanich* Victoria suburb.
5 *broom* Shrubs with yellow flowers.
12 *Juan de Fuca Strait* Between Victoria and Washington state.

Duncan Campbell Scott

For the dates of these poems, I am indebted to Laura Groening, "Duncan Campbell Scott: An Annotated Bibliography," *The Annotated Bibliography of Canada's Major Authors*, Vol. 8, ed. Robert Lecker and Jack David (Toronto: ECW, 1994): 469-576. Where indicated, I am indebted to Stan Dragland, *Floating Voice: Duncan Campbell Scott and the Literature of Treaty 9* (Concord, ON: Anansi, 1994), and to the notes in Leon Slonim, "A Critical Edition of the Poems of Duncan Campbell Scott," Diss. Toronto, 1978.

"The Magic House" This poem first appeared in *Scribner's* (June 1890). It was then included in *The Magic House and Other Poems* (1893).

5 *myrrh* Fragrant gum used for perfume.
13 *Irised* Regulating light (as in the eye).
16 *casement* Window.
18 *swart* Dark.
26 *turret* Small tower.

"The Reed Player" This poem first appeared in *Scribner's* (Dec. 1890). It was then included in *The Magic House* (1893).

subtitle *B.C.* The initials stand for Bliss Carman, to whom Scott called attention to the poem in a letter of 16 Dec. 1890. When he reprinted the poem in his *Poems* of 1926, he dropped the dedication. The subtitle implies that Carman is a kind of Pan, much as Carman saw Keats in "By the Aurelian Wall." On Pan, see the general note to Campbell, "Pan the Fallen."

7 *bittern* Marsh bird with a loud call.
11 *Uriel* An archangel.
19 *Tyre* Mediterranean port and ancient trading center.
24 *argent* Silver.

"At Scarboro' Beach" This poem first appeared in *The Canadian Magazine* (June 1893). It was then included in *The Magic House* (1893).

title *Scarboro'* "Scarborough is a town in Maine, just south of Portland" (Slonim).
9 *Richmond* A "town in Maine, on the Kennebec River, north-east of Portland" (Slonim).
18 *main* Ocean.

"In the Country Churchyard" This poem first appeared in *The Magic House.*

Scott's very title is an allusion to Thomas Gray's "Elegy Written in a Country Churchyard" (1751), itself a highly allusive poem. Scott is attracted to the pastoral tradition because its conventions have worked so well for so long; in this poem, they enable him to approach the basic fact of mortality without other distractions. Unlike its predecessors, Scott's elegy is concerned with the problem created by a morbid attraction to death. Working through that problem, the poem ends with a renewed interest in everyday rural labour, much as Milton's "Lycidas" ends by turning to "fresh woods, and pastures new" (l. 193).

subtitle *Father* William Scott, a Methodist minister (1812-1891).

1-7 Cf. the opening stanza of Gray's "Elegy."

16 *Hepaticas* Plant with reddish-brown leaves.

17 *bloodroots* Plant with white flowers.

36-42 Cf. Gray's "Elegy," ll. 33-36.

39 *motley* Jester's costume.

50-56 Cf. Gray's "Elegy," ll. 81-84.

50 *swains* Shepherds.

95 *demesne* Estate.

"The Cup" This poem was privately printed in 1894, then included in *Labor and the Angel* (1898).

"The Onondaga Madonna" This poem originally appeared as "An Onondaga Mother and Child" in *The Atlantic Monthly* (Sept. 1894). It was renamed when it was included in *Labor and the Angel* (1898).

title *Onondaga* One of the Iroquois peoples.

title *Madonna* Conventional name for Virgin Mary, and for a picture of her.

"The Piper of Arll" This poem originally appeared in *Truth* (New York), (Dec. 14, 1895). It was then included in *Labor and the Angel* (1898).

title *Arll* Perhaps a contraction of Argyll, or a pun on "All," mistakenly seen as the derivation of Pan's name (Bentley).

9 *comb* Projection on rock.

11 *reaving* Carrying off.

19 *pennon* Flag.

20 *prore* Prow (archaic).

22 *spars* Ship's poles.

29 *gunwales* Ship's edges.

44 *Braird* Grass.
53 *lawny* Made of cotton or linen.
58 *Limned* Painted.
60 *wraith* Ghost.
67 *mead* Reward.
98 *exequy* Funeral ceremony.
110 *cordage* Rigging.
126 *ere* Before.
127 *prore* See note to l. 20.
135 *pennon* See note to l. 19.
144 *aye and aye* Forever and forever (archaic).
151 *gloaming* Twilight.

"Watkwenies" This poem first appeared in *Labor and the Angel* (1898).

title The 1898 text has this footnote: "The Woman who Conquers".

7 *hamlet* The name indicates a European settlement (Dragland).

8 *Iroquois* Confederacy of Cayuga, Mohawk, Oneida, Onondaga, Seneca, and Tuscarora peoples.

11 *interest-money* Some kind of government payment.

14 *snow-snake* Game played by throwing javelins "into a raised launching pad made of ice. The snakes, carved in pairs from the same sapling, have been cured, weighted at the front, polished, and then waxed for the day's weather conditions. They might slide as much as a mile, depending on the terrain, though a groove dragged in the snow by a log" (Dragland 191).

"Night Hymns on Lake Nipigon" This poem first appeared in *Atlantic Monthly* (Aug. 1900). It was then included in *New World Lyrics and Ballads* (1905). In both versions, the title appeared as "Night Hymns on Lake Nepigon." The last word was changed to "Nipigon" (now the standard spelling) in *The Poems of Duncan Campbell Scott* (1926).

title *Lake Nipigon* 100 km. northeast of Thunder Bay.

15 *pellucid* Clear or pure.

15, 17 *Nipigon* Spelled "Nepigon" in 1905.

20 *Adeste Fideles* Eighteenth-century hymn written by

John Francis Wade.

23 *Ojibwa* Spelled "Ojibeway" in 1905. The Ojibwa (or Ojibway) are the Algonquian people living in the vicinity of Lake Superior.

37 *Whelms* Overpowers.

"The Ghost's Story" This poem first appeared in *Acta Victoriana* (June 1902). It was then included in *Lundy's Lane and Other Poems* (1916).

"The Forsaken" This poem first appeared in *The Outlook* (April 25, 1903). When it was included in *New World Lyrics and Ballads* (1905), it featured this note: "This story is true. The fact may be of interest and value, perhaps, as proof of a well-known Indian characteristic, although the incident, as material for poetry, gains nothing in value from its truth. It was told me by the Hudson's Bay Company's factor at Nepigon House. 'Tikanagan' is the Ojibeway word for the Indian cradle, about the construction and uses of which a little chapter might be written. Huskies are sledge dogs, a corruption of Eskimo."

I.6 *Chippewa* Ojibwa; this spelling is "normally used to refer only to the Ojibwa living to the east, south, and southwest of the Great Lakes" (*COD*).

I.22 *tikanagan* See Scott's comment in the general note.

"On the Way to the Mission" This poem first appeared in *New World Lyrics and Ballads* (1905).

47 *Montagnais* The Innu people who live between Hudson Bay and the Labrador coast.

53 *bloodroot* Plant with white flowers.

53 *windflower* Plant with flowers of various colours.

"An Impromptu" This poem first appeared in *Via Borealis* (1906).

title *Impromptu* Improvisation.

2 *tamarac* Coniferous tree (usually spelled "tamarack").

4 *vireo* Small songbird.

18 *tabors* Small drums.

"Lines in Memory of Edmund Morris" This poem was privately printed in 1915, then included in *Lundy's Lane and Other Poems* (1916).

title *Edmund Morris* Morris (1871-1913) was a painter who took Native life as his subject. As a commissioned artist, he accompanied Scott to northwestern Ontario on the trip to negotiate Treaty 9 in 1906. He drowned in the St. Lawrence on August 26, 1913. See Jean S. McGill, *Edmund Morris: Frontier Artist* (Toronto: Dundurn, 1984).

5 *Nantucket* Scott was in New England when he heard (in a letter from Rupert Brooke) of Morris' death.

6 *Isle of Orleans* Island east of Quebec City where Morris was visiting at the time of his death.

13 *famous scribble* The difficulty of Morris' handwriting was legendary among his friends.

15 *Cuneiform* Writing used in Babylonian inscriptions.

15 *Chaldaic* Language of southern Babylon.

22 *Touchwood Hills* Near Fort Qu'Appelle, Saskatchewan (Dragland).

25 *Phimister Proctor* Canadian sculptor who moved to New York.

43 *Ere* Before.

76 *Titian* Sixteenth-century Venetian painter.

77 *Pellucid* Clear or pure.

81 *snood* Hair-band worn by unmarried women.

91 *Crowfoot* Chief of the Blackfoot Confederacy (Dragland).

95 *marked the site* Morris actually "painted an inscription on a stone for Crowfoot" (Dragland).

96 *Old Napiw* Napi, the Blackfoot trickster (Dragland).

100 *Sakimay* "Chief of the Sakimay Indian Reserve . . ., about seventy-eight miles east of Regina" (Slonim).

102 *kinnikinick* Smoking mixture (Dragland).

134 Ne-Pah-Pee-Ness Nepahpenais was a Saulteaux chief whom Morris painted (Dragland). The Saulteaux are "a branch of the Ojibway Tribe, so-called because they were centered near the falls ('sault') of Sault Ste. Marie" (Slonim).

142-45 American folksong (Dragland).

150-51 Cf. Ariel's speech in Shakespeare's *The Tempest*, I.2.403-05: "Nothing of him that doth fade / But doth suffer a sea change / Into something rich and strange."

157 *whorl* Coil.

218 *clomb* Climbed (archaic).

225 *Akoose* Accose ("Man Standing Above Ground") was the father of the chief of the same name whom Morris painted. Morris believed the father to be 103 years old, and he described him as follows: "His mind is quite clear & I talked with him in French. He is blind & his skin looks like parchment. His name was known far & wide in his time. Acoose was the fleetest of the Saulteaux. He used to compete with the whites in races & always outrun them. He went to hunt moose once & fell in with 9 elk. His bullets had slipped through his pocket so he ran them down the first day then drove them 60 miles to his own camp at Goose Lake & killed them" (qtd. from Morris' diary in Dragland 212).

222 *great-grandchildren* Not hyphenated in 1916.

254 *tenebrous* Gloomy.

279 *wraith* Ghost.

"The Height of Land" This poem first appeared in Lundy's Lane (1916).

title A height of land is the area between two watersheds. In this case, the title "refers to the ridge which separates the waters flowing north into James Bay from those flowing south into Lake Superior" (Slonim).

7 *Ojibway* See note for l. 23, "Night Hymns on Lake Nipigon."

10 *Chees-que-ne-ne* Cheesequini, the name of a chief whom Scott met on the 1906 Treaty 9 negotiations.

33 *bracken* I follow the spelling used in the 1926 *Poems*. In 1916, the word is spelled "braken."

33 *dwart-cornel* Dogwood.

52 *inappellable* "That cannot be appealed against; from which there is no appeal" (*OED*).

121 *Eft-minded things* Cf. Browning's Caliban, who feels "eft-things course" about his spine in "Caliban upon Setebos; or Natural Theology in the Island," l. 5.

140 *romaunt* Romance.

145 *whelms* Overpowers.

150 *susurrus* Whisperings.

"The Closed Door" This poem first appeared in *Lundy's Lane* (1916).

This poem is an elegy for Scott's daughter, to whom *Lundy's Lane* is dedicated as follows: "To the Memory of My Daughter Elizabeth Duncan Scott 1895-1907.'

"The Fragment of a Letter" This poem first appeared in *Beauty and Life* (1921).

According to E.K. Brown's "Memoir," this poem was "originally called, when it was written in May, 1919, 'A Note to Pelham Edgar.'" Pelham Edgar (1871-1948) was an English professor at the University of Toronto and a friend who accompanied Scott on his travels in northwestern Ontario to negotiate Treaty 9 in 1906.

29 *antiphonal* Sung alternately.

37 *impromptu* Improvisation.

58 *irrefrangible* Inviolable.

63 *sables* Blackens.

"En Route" This poem was privately printed in Scott's Christmas cards for 1930. It was then included in *The Green Cloister* (1935).

19 *Vagaries* Whims.

"Chiostro Verde" This poem first appeared in *The Green Cloister* (1935).

title Italian for "green cloister" (Slonim).

1-2 "The Chiostro Verde . . . is a part of the Dominican Church and Convent of Santa Maria Novella," in Florence (Slonim).

15 *Arno* The "river which runs through Florence" (Slonim).

28 *in the crannied wall* Cf. Tennyson's brief lyric,

"Flower in the Crannied Wall."

33 *Palestrina* "Giovanni Pierluigi da Palestrina (1525-1594), Italian composer of church music" (Slonim).

50-51 Paolo Uccello (1397-1475) made two frescoes on themes from the Creation "on the east wall of the Chiostro Verde" (Slonim).

"A Scene at Lake Manitou" This poem first appeared in *The Green Cloister* (1935).

For a reading of this poem, see Stan Dragland's essay in this anthology.

title *Lake Manitou* The difficulties in identifying a specific location for this poem are discussed by Dragland.

1 *fur-trader's* The apostrophe is missing in 1935.

9 *cocks* Small piles of hay.

70 *Nanabojou* Ojibway trickster.

71 *Manitou* Supernatural spirit.

81, 84 *Scapular* Cloth worn over shoulders as a sign of devotion.

90 *Manitou* See note to l. 71.

"At Gull Lake: August, 1810" This poem first appeared in *The Green Cloister* (1935).

title *Gull Lake* Either the Gull Lake north of Red Deer, Alberta (Slonim), or the Gull Lake in Saskatchewan (Dragland).

title *1810* Scott said that this poem "is founded on an incident narrated by Alexr. Henry Jr. in his journal of 1810" (qtd. in Dragland 198).

14 *Saulteaux* See the note for l. 134 of "Lines in Memory of Edmund Morris."

17 *Orkneys* The Orkney Islands in Scotland.

24 *Vermilion* Bright red.

28 *ochre* Brownish yellow.

30 *Normandy* Part of northwest France.

127 *the beauty of terror* Scott said that Emily Brontë discovered in the countryside around Haworth "the beauty and terror of *Wuthering Heights* and brought to life the Shakespearean Heathcliff" (qtd. in Dragland 205).

"Power" This poem first appeared in *Poetry* (Chicago) (April 1941; this was a special Canadian issue edited by E.K. Brown). It was then included in *The Circle of Affection* (1947).

Contexts

The Poetry of Nature

by Charles G.D. Roberts

"The poetry of earth is never dead," wrote Keats; and, though the statement sounds, at first thought, a dangerously sweeping one, there is no doubt that if he had been called upon to argue the point he would have successfully maintained his thesis. Regarded subjectively, the poetry of earth, or, in other words, the quality which makes for poetry in external nature, is that power in nature which moves us by suggestion, which excites in us emotion, imagination, or poignant association, which plays upon the tense-strings of our sympathies with the fingers of memory or desire. This power may reside not less in a bleak pasture-lot than in a paradisal close of bloom and verdure, not less in a roadside thistle-patch than in a peak that soars into the sunset. It works through sheer beauty or sheer sublimity; but it may work with equal effect through austerity or reticence or limitation or change. It may use the most common scenes, the most familiar facts and forms, as the vehicle of its most penetrating and most illuminating message. It is apt to make the drop of dew on a grass-blade as significant as the starred sphere of the sky.

The poetry of nature, by which I mean this "poetry of earth" expressed in words, may be roughly divided into two main classes: that which deals with pure description, and that which treats of nature in some one of its many relations with humanity. The latter class is that which alone was contemplated in Keats's line. It has many subdivisions; it includes much of the greatest poetry that the world has known; and there is little verse of acknowledged mastery that does not depend upon it for some portion of its appeal.

The former class has but a slender claim to recognition as

poetry, under any definition of poetry that does not make metrical form the prime essential. The failures of the wisest to enunciate a satisfactory definition of poetry make it almost presumptuous for a critic now to attempt the task; but from an analysis of these failures one may educe something roughly to serve the purpose. To say that *poetry is the metrical expression in words of thought fused in emotion*, is of course incomplete; but it has the advantage of defining. No one can think that anything other than poetry is intended by such a definition; and nothing is excluded that can show a clear claim to admittance. But the poetry of pure description might perhaps not pass without challenge, so faint is the flame of its emotion, so imperfect the fusion of its thought.

It is verse of this sort that is meant by undiscriminating critics when they inveigh against "nature poetry," and declare that the only poetry worth man's attention is that which has to do with the heart of man.

Merely descriptive poetry is not very far removed from the work of the reporter and the photographer. Lacking the selective quality of creative art, it is in reality little more than a presentation of some of the raw materials of poetry. It leaves the reader unmoved, because little emotion has gone to its making. Poetry of this sort, at its best, is to be found abundantly in Thomson's "Seasons." At less than its best it concerns no one.

Nature becomes significant to man when she is passed through the alembic of his heart. Irrelevant and confusing details having been purged away, what remains is single and vital. It acts either by interpreting, recalling, suggesting, or symbolizing some phase of human feeling. Out of the fusing heat born of this contact comes the perfect line, luminous, unforgettable, with something of mystery in its beauty that eludes analysis. Whatever it be that is brought to the alembic—naked hill, or barren sand-reach, sea or meadow, weed or star,—it comes out charged with a new force, imperishable and active wherever it finds sympathies to vibrate under its currents.

In the imperishable verse of ancient Greece and Rome, nature-poetry of the higher class is generally supposed to play but a small part. In reality, it is nearly always present, nearly always active in that verse; but it appears in such a disguise that its origin is apt to be overlooked. The Greeks—and the Romans, of course, following their pattern—personified the phenomena of nature till these, for all purposes of art, became human. The Greeks made their anthropomorphic gods of the forces of nature which compelled their adoration. Of these personifications they sang, as of men of like passions with themselves; but in truth it was of external nature that they made their songs. Bion's wailing "Lament for Adonis," human as it is throughout, is in its final analysis a poem of nature. By an intense, but perhaps unconscious, subjective process, the ancients supplied external nature with their own moods, impulses, and passions.

The transitions from the ancient to the modern fashion of looking at nature are to be found principally in the work of the Celtic bards, who, rather than the cloistered students of that time, kept alive the true fire of poetry through the long darkness of the Middle Ages.

The modern attitude toward nature, as distinguished from that of the Greeks, begins to show itself clearly in English song very soon after the great revivifying movement which we call the Renaissance. At first, it is a very simple matter indeed. Men sing of nature because nature is impressing them directly. A joyous season calls forth a joyous song:—

> Sumer is icumen in,
> Lhude sing, cuccu.
> Groweth sed and bloweth med
> And springth the wude nu.

This is the poet's answering hail, when the spring-time calls to his blood. With the fall of the leaf, his singing has a sombre and foreboding note; and winter in the world makes winter in his song.

This is nature-poetry in its simplest form,--the form which it chiefly took with the spontaneous Elizabethans. But it soon became more complex, as life and society became entangled in more complex conditions. The artificialities of the Queen Anne period delayed this evolution; but with Gray and Collins we see it fairly in process. Man, looking upon external nature, projects himself into her workings. His own wrath he apprehends in the violence of the storm; his own joy in the light waves running in the sun; his own gloom in the heaviness of the rain and wind. In all nature he finds but phenomena of himself. She becomes but an expression of his hopes, his fears, his cravings, his despair. This intense subjectivity is peculiarly characteristic of the nature-poetry produced by Byron and his school. When this Titan of modern song apostrophizes the storm thundering over Jura, he speaks to the tumult in the deeps of his own soul. When he addresses the stainless tranquillities of "clear, placid Leman," what moves him to utterance is the contemplation of such a calm as his vexed spirit often craved.

When man's heart and the heart of nature had become thus closely involved, the relationship between them and, consequently, the manner of its expression in song became complex almost beyond the possibilities of analysis. Wordsworth's best poetry is to be found in the utterances of the high-priest in nature's temple, interpreting the mysteries. The "Lines Composed a Few Miles Above Tintern Abbey" are, at first glance, chiefly descriptive; but their actual function is to convey to a restless age, troubled with small cares seen in too close perspective, the large, contemplative wisdom which seemed to Wordsworth the message of the scene which moved him.

Keats, his soul aflame with the worship of beauty, was impassioned toward the manifestations of beauty in the world about him; and, at the same time, he used these freely as symbols to express other aspects of the same compelling spirit. Shelley, the most complex of the group, sometimes combined all these methods, as in the "Ode to the West Wind." But he added a new note,—which was yet an echo of the oldest,—the note of nature-worship. He saw continually in nature the godhead which he sought and adored, youthful protestations and affectations of atheism to the contrary notwithstanding. Most of Shelley's nature-poetry carries a rich vein of pantheism, allied to that which colours the oldest verse of time and particularly characterizes ancient Celtic song. With this significant and stimulating revival, goes a revival of that strong sense of kinship, of the oneness of earth and man, which the Greeks and Latins felt so keenly at times, which Omar knew and uttered, and which underlies so much of the verse of these later days.

That other unity—the unity of man and God, which forms so inevitable a corollary to the pantheistic proposition—comes to be dwelt upon more and more insistently throughout the nature-poetry of the last fifty years.

The main purpose of these brief suggestions is to call attention to the fact that nature-poetry is not mere description of landscape in metrical form, but the expression of one or another of many vital relationships between external nature and "the deep heart of man." It may touch the subtlest chords of human emotion and human imagination not less masterfully than the verse which sets out to be a direct transcript from life. The most inaccessible truths are apt to be reached by indirection. The divinest mysteries of beauty are not possessed exclusively by the eye that loves, or by the lips of a child, but are also manifested in some bird-song's unforgotten cadence, some flower whose perfection pierces the heart, some ineffable hue of sunset or sunrise that makes the spirit cry out for it knows not what. And whosoever follows the inexplicable lure of beauty, in colour, form, sound, perfume, or any other manifestation,— reaching out to it as perhaps a message from some unfathomable past, or a premonition of the future,—knows that the mystic signal beckons nowhere more imperiously than from the heights of nature-poetry.

Forum (Dec. 1897)

Canadian Poetry in its Relation to the Poetry of England and America

by Charles G.D. Roberts

I have no words to thank you—no words to half express my deep and heartfelt appreciation of the very great honour done me here tonight and of the more than generous gift with which I am overwhelmed. You have given a most eloquent and emphatic contradiction to that old whining complaint about a prophet not being without honour except in his own country. For you have made it plain that in his own country a prophet may have both honour and—profit. May I try to show my appreciation, and to justify myself in the role of prophet, by prophesying a distinguished and distinctive future for Canadian Poetry.

I have taken as the subject of my address tonight, "Canadian Poetry in its relation to the Poetry of England and America." I purposely refrain from saying "of the rest of the English-speaking world," because the poets of Australia, New Zealand and South Africa seem to be linked more closely and more exclusively with the Mother Country than we are in Canada. Their poetry has less of a separate corporate existence than ours, has a more decided tendency to look to the Mother Country for recognition than has ours. This, for two main reasons, is only to be expected. They are, all three, much younger and less populous peoples than Canada. For all practical purposes they are under but one stream of influence, they inherit from but one source, the Mother Country; while we inherit from three sources, in varying degree,—from the Mother Country, America, and France. The influence of France has been, as yet, comparatively slight upon the poetry of English-speaking Canada, which alone I am considering here,—though I hope it may be greatly extended in the future, when the cultural characteristics of the two great races from which we spring may come to be more intimately interfused. But American influence, though altogether secondary to that of England and growing more so as our national consciousness matures, has been strong upon us in two ways. The mass immigration of that strong and dominant Loyalist American stock, influential out of all proportion to its numbers, provided us with a great proportion of our spiritual and intellectual endowment, that element of *character* which is the ultimate test of a people's stature; and our social relations with modern America have had their effect, not invariably a happy one, upon our verse structure and forms.

Our English Canadian Poetry may be divided, very loosely and for the purposes of this address, into two periods,—the pre-war and the post-war. The pre-war period may be considered as beginning in the 80's, with the publication of Crawford's *Old Spookses' Pass*, and Lampman's *Among the Millet*, 1888. At this point, if you will forgive me, I am compelled to become personal for a moment. In the course of this survey I am going to disregard entirely my own various books of verse and their influence, if any, on the development of Canadian Poetry. But it is necessary, to avoid misunderstanding, that I should refer to my little volume of juvenilia, *Orion and Other Poems*, which appeared in 1880. This book, which obtained in Canada and abroad a recognition out of all proportion to its merits, has been accepted as a sort of landmark. All the verses it contains were written between the ages of sixteen and nineteen,—most of them before I was eighteen. They are the work of practically a schoolboy, drunk with the music of Keats, Shelley, Tennyson and Swinburne. They are distinctly 'prentice work, distinctly derivative, and without significance except for their careful craftsmanship and for the fact that they dared deliberately to steer their frail craft out upon world waters,—certain of these youthful efforts appearing in the pages of the chief English and American magazines. But the only importance attaching to the little book lay in the fact that it started Lampman writing poetry and was the decisive factor in determining Carman to make poetry his career.

The distinctively Canadian poetry, of significance beyond the borders of Canada, therefore, may be considered as beginning with Isabella Crawford's *Old Spookses' Pass*, 1884;

Charles Mair's *Tecumseh*, 1886; Archibald Lampman's *Among the Millet*, 1888; F.G. Scott's *The Soul's Guest*, 1888; W.W. Campbell's *Lake Lyrics*, 1889; D.C. Scott's *The Magic House*, 1893; Bliss Carman's *Low Tide on Grand Pré*, 1893; Pauline Johnson's *White Wampum*, 1894; [and] Arthur Stringer['s] *Watcher of Twilight*, 1894; but it must be borne in mind that for seven or eight years previous to 1893 Carman's poems had circulated widely in privately printed broad-sheets, and had exerted an immense influence, before his first publication in book form.

Though Mair's *Tecumseh* appeared in 1886, it seems to stand apart from the new movement inaugurated by Crawford, Lampman, Carman and Scott. It marks the end of the old period,—Mair's first and only other volume of verse, *Dreamland and Other Poems*, having appeared in 1868. It looks backward rather than forward. Deriving, in its conception and its structure, straight from Shakespeare himself, but with its verbal music borrowed from Keats, it is a dignified and massive closet-drama, dramatic in form but narrative in spirit; and it stands up as a great isolated rock against the incipient tide of Canadian lyric verse. Isabella Crawford, on the other hand, seems to me to be looking forward rather than back. Her verse, though so different, belongs with that of Lampman, Carman, and D.C. Scott. It has a distinction and strength which have not yet been sufficiently recognized. Her early death was a great misfortune to our literature.

Now, having thus cleared the way, I will try to trace the influences which affected Canadian verse during this first period, and to point out wherein Canadian verse was distinctive from the verse of England and of America. Of course it is obvious to us all, that Canadian verse, like American verse, is but a branch of the one splendid parent stem. American verse, beginning to thrust forth from the parent stem nearly two hundred years ago, has by now attained a stature which fairly rivals that of its parent. Today it would be hard to say which shows the loftier and more sturdy growth. It is my claim that Canadian Poetry, a young shoot which began to bud forth not fifty years ago, started under happier auspices, developed more rapidly, and has already attained an authentic separate existence. It is of course overshadowed by its great rivals, but it is not obliterated by them. When the long but beneficent tyranny of the Tennysonian tradition in England—buttressed rather than shaken by Swinburne, Arnold, Morris, Rossetti (rudely assaulted but not overthrown by Browning) at last began to fall into saccharine decay, English poets seemed somewhat at a loss for guidance. Masters of craftsmanship like Stevenson, Le Gallienne, John Davidson, William Watson, Henley, Wilde, seemed to be groping in all directions for themes on which to exercise their craft. Francis Thompson wrote one magnificent and immortal poem; Alice Meynell produced a tiny sheaf of exquisite and stringently reserved verse, but both sounded their poignant notes upon approximately one theme. The choir had brilliant individual singers, but there was no leader, and the result was a mere confusion of sweet sound. To be sure there were no blatant discords. These were to come later!

Meanwhile, how was it faring with poetry in Canada? For one thing, there was singularly little confusion of purpose, or casting about for themes. In the main it was Nature poetry, of one sort or another. The Canadian scene and the Canadian atmosphere, were always present, sometimes as a very conspicuous background to the subject, sometimes as the subject itself. It was frankly enthusiastic. It was patently sincere. There was never any need to whip up the inspiration. From the "Bite deep and wide, O axe, the tree," of Isabella Crawford, to the "There is something in the autumn that is native to my blood," of Carman, there is the note of looking forward, of the optimism of a young and confidently aspiring people. The pervasiveness of this note gave a certain unity to the work of all the otherwise differentiated Canadian singers. It was a note that had practically faded out from the infinitely louder American chorus.

The influence of Tennyson—with the one brief exception already noted,—is not evident in this Canadian Poetry. It is descended rather from Wordsworth, Milton of the earlier poems, Landor, Keats, Shelley, Blake, and from Arnold in form and language though manifestly not in spirit. It also drew one strong stream of influence from Emerson and the New England school of transcendentalists, to whom it is heavily in debt for its philosophy and for its employment of the plain, blunt words of common speech. It owes something also to that very great American poet, Sidney Lanier. Whitman's influence both in thought and in form upon our poetry of this period is entirely negligible. And if I may be permitted to differ flatly from a very distinguished critic, Dr. Cappon, the wonderful poems of Edgar Allan Poe, were almost as negligible in their effect upon us. Even Carman, contrary to Dr. Cappon's thesis, was not greatly interested in Poe's form, and with Poe's philosophy of life he was emphatically out of sympathy. I can detect Poe's influence upon one only of our Poets, Tom MacInnes, and he belongs to our later period. Carman was influenced in one portion of his career by Browning, but that influence ultimately worked itself out. And Duncan Campbell Scott now and again shows traces of having fallen under the spell of George Meredith's more inspired verse. And it may be noted here that our poets were doing thirty or forty years ago what certain of the quieter and more serious poets of England have been doing since the war.

There is another consideration which gives unity to our Canadian poetry of this period. In doctrine, in dogma, in creed, our poets may differ very widely, from strict orthodoxy, through a sort of mystical theosophy, to a Neo-Platonic pantheism or Nature worship. But they all worship. They are all religious, in the broad sense, in their attitude toward this life and the future. They are all fundamentally antagonistic to everything that savours of materialism, and even of such high and stoical pessimism as that of Matthew Arnold. They are all incorrigible and unrepentant idealists.

I think I have traced the chief sources from which our poetry has sprung, and indicated, in the main, those characteristics which differentiate it from the work of contemporaries in England and America. I will conclude the survey of this first period by reading a sonnet of Lampman's and a lyric of Carman's, two poems which, of their kind, have not been surpassed by any of their contemporaries in England or America. They may serve to illustrate certain of the points which I hope I may be considered to have made:

Outlook

Not to be conquered by these headlong days,
But to stand free: to keep the mind at brood
On life's deep meaning, nature's attitude
Of loveliness, and time's mysterious ways;
At every thought and deed to clear the haze
Out of our eyes, considering only this,
What man, what life, what love, what beauty is,
This is to live, and win the final praise.
Though strife, ill fortune and harsh human need
Beat down the soul, at moments blind and dumb
With agony; yet, patience—there shall come
Many great voices from life's outer sea,
Hours of strange triumph, and, when few men heed,
Murmurs and glimpses of eternity.

A. Lampman

"Exit Anima"

"Hospes comesque corporis
Quae nunc abitis in loca?"

Cease, Wind, to blow
And drive the peopled snow,
And move the haunted arras to and fro,
And moan of things I fear to know
Yet would rend from thee,
Wind, before I go
On the blind pilgrimage.
Cease, Wind, to blow.

Thy brother too,
I leave no print of shoe
In all these vasty rooms I rummage through,
No word at threshold, and no clue
Of whence I come and whither I pursue
The search of treasures lost
When time was new[.]

Thou janitor
Of the dim curtained door,
Stir thy old bones along the dusty floor
Of this unlighted corridor.
Open! I have been this way before;
Thy hollow face shall peer
In mine no more . . . .

Sky, the dear sky!
Ah, ghostly house, good-by!
I leave thee as the gauzy dragon-fly
Leaves the green pool to try
His vast ambition on the vaster sky,--
Such valor against death
Is deity.

What, thou too here,
Thou haunting whisperer?
Spirit of beauty immanent and sheer,
Art thou that crooked servitor,
Done with disguise, from whose malignant leer
Out of the ghostly house
I fled in fear?

O Beauty, how
I do repent me now,
Of all the doubt I ever could allow
To shake me like an aspen bough;
Nor once imagine that unsullied brow
Could wear the evil mask
And still be thou!

Charles G.D. Roberts

Bone of thy bone,
Breath of thy breath alone,
I dare resume the silence of a stone,
Or explore still the vast unknown,
Like a bright sea-bird through the morning blown,
With all his heart one joy,
From zone to zone.

B. Carman

Between the first and second periods in Canadian poetry there is no break, but rather a very gradual transition. Some members of the first group are in full singing vigour today, as in the case of Duncan Campbell Scott, and have, indeed, more or less identified themselves with the mood and temper, even the external forms, of the second period. Others were already becoming well known in the decade preceding 1914. Preeminent among these is Tom MacInnes, standing somewhat apart from the stream of our poetry, and tracing the inheritance of his very individual talent to François Villon and Edgar Allan Poe, with an occasional dash of Keats. And I must mention here that remarkable woman Mrs. Harrison, known as "Seranus," who began her poetical career with "the stretchèd metre of an antique song" in *Pine, Rose and Fleur de Lis*, 1891, using old French verse forms and seeking to interpret the spirit of French Canada to English Canada; and who now, in *Songs of Love and Labor* and in *Penelope and Other Poems*, brings herself thoroughly abreast of modern movements and methods.

During and since the War new forces began to make themselves felt in Canadian verse, influencing both its matter and its manner. But in our verse, as in our painting and sculpture, the pervading sanity and balance of the Canadian temperament, its obstinate antagonism to extremes, saved us from the grotesque excesses indulged in by some of our English and American contemporaries. Modernism, so called, came without violence to Canada. It was with us not revolution but evolution. The slender but exquisite genius of Marjorie Pickthall seemed to flourish apart, hardly affected by latterday changes. I can do no more in this paper than touch upon some half dozen of the many singers who now form our choir. Katherine Hale, with her extremely meager output, is nevertheless very significant, because thoroughly modern in theme and treatment. Nature, with her, is always strictly subordinate to human nature. Charlotte Dalton treats big themes in a big way, her intellect and her genius being of the major order. A.M. Stephen, in the breadth and variety of the subjects which he treats, combines both the younger and the older schools. He is at times a Nature poet, at times a poet of humanity. But in the matter of form he has not as yet fully escaped the influence of Amy Lowell and Carl Sandburg. There are many others of whom I would wish to speak but the familiar "exigencies of time and space" forbid. And, of course, my lips are sealed in regard to the poetry of Lloyd Roberts and Theodore Roberts, my son and my brother.

But there are three poets whom I feel called upon to discuss more in detail, because they represent three distinct trends in modern Canadian poetry, and differ from each other fundamentally. I refer to Doctor E.J. Pratt, Mr. Wilson MacDonald, and the late Dr. Robert Norwood.

Dr. Pratt is the most predominantly intellectual. Under whatever he writes the thought processes are definite and precise, whether the writing be lyrical or narrative. Yet the thought is always adequately fused in the emotion. And he has the saving gift, the vital gift, of humour. He is easily the greatest master of pure narrative that Canada has produced. In *The Witches' Brew*, with its vast Rabelaisian humour and grotesque fantasy; "The Cachalot," with its splendidly robust and red-blooded imagination; and "The Roosevelt and the Antinoe," with its sustained strength, its gripping directness, its severity of diction and its unflagging interest,—he has given us poetic narratives hardly to be matched in contemporary letters. He is almost exclusively *objective*.

Mr. Wilson MacDonald is purely a lyrist, with a very wide range of form and theme. His best work is forged in the white heat of emotion, and is always definitely stamped with his own personality. It is primarily *subjective*. In his shorter, personal lyrics, such as "Exit," he achieves at times an unforgettable poignancy. In his passionately humanitarian poems he is modern in spirit, but in form he is distinctly classical. He has been so bold as to experiment frankly with Whitman's peculiar form and content, and he has justified the experiment. He has succeeded at times in breathing into that harsh form a beauty of words and cadences which Whitman never achieved.

The late Robert Norwood is, first, last, and always a mystic. His great narrative poem, "Bill Boram," is a lyrico-mystic creation masquerading under a thin disguise of realism. Its emotional fervour is always breaking through the disguise. His religious dramas, *The Witch of Endor* and *The Man of Kerioth*, are great lyrical poems rather than pure drama. His book of dramatic monologues, Browningesque in form but at the opposite pole from Browning in thought, content, and approach, are mysticism intellectualized. That peculiarly individual poem, "Issa," is a mystical autobiography in lyrical form, sustained with almost unflagging fervour throughout seven cantos. It is a remarkable *tour de force*. The three volumes of lyrics and sonnets contain poems of varying merit, from mediocre religious rhetoric to the highest quality of craftsmanship and lyric significance. But always in the web and texture of them is the pervading sheen of that mysticism which was Norwood's breath of life. The keynote to all his work is in the line "And let there be a going up to stars."

And now let me conclude with a few words about our younger poets, those who are just winning their spurs. And let me say at once that I survey their work with the profoundest satisfaction, feeling that the future of our poetry is in safe hands. It is the prerogative of youth to rebel. But our Canadian youth has sufficient sanity to save it from the extravagant and grotesque excesses of rebellion. I find here and there among the young poets a tendency to hark back to the artificiality of the post-Elizabethans,—a tendency, also, to stress the intellectual at the expense of the equally important emotional side of poetry. Some of them show the effect of a study of the works of the so-called metaphysical school, which derives from Ben Jonson rather than from Shakespeare. But I am not sure that this is altogether to be deplored, as a reaction against over sentimentalism. To Beauty, however, if not always to simplicity, they are faithful. There is none of that deliberate sabotage of beauty, that adulation of ugliness in the name of realism, in which certain wild-eyed extremists in other lands are wont to riot. I find traces of T.E. Brown, de la Mare, and Hopkins,--the influence of Emily Dickinson, Elinor Wylie, Edna Millay. I do not, God be thanked, find the influence of E.E. Cummings or Marianne Moore. Among these our younger poets I will not take the responsibility of selecting any names for mention here, lest I should do some an injustice by omitting them,—or prove myself a false prophet. I will only say that I believe some of them will go very far. Indeed, I think I will even go with them a little way, if my years—and my decrepitude—will permit!

"The old order changeth, yielding place to new."

March 18, 1933 address to the Eldon Club, Toronto; ed. D.M.R. Bentley, *Canadian Poetry: Studies, Documents, Reviews* 3 (1978): 76-86. Reprinted by permission of D.M.R. Bentley.

from Two Canadian Poets [:] a Lecture

by Archibald Lampman

In the last twenty years great advances have been made in this country, and many things have been accomplished which are a source of hope and comfort to those who are beginning to feel for Canada the enthusiasm of Fatherland[.] Already there are many among us whose fathers and grandfathers have lived and died upon this soil, who are neither British, French nor German, but simply Canadians. For them everything connected with the honour and well-being of their country has come to be a matter of daily interest. The enthusiasm of Fatherland, the attachment to native soil, the love of the name of our country[,] is one of those generous impulses which have always been a moral necessity and an encouraging help to people who do not live by bread alone. It is getting rather customary in our time to underrate patriotism as one of the virtues, and to substitute in its place cosmopolitanism or the enthusiasm for the advancement of all mankind, making no distinction in favour of any country. Nothing could be finer than that; but unfortunately our energies, if made to cover too wide a ground, are apt to lose themselves in mere speculation, and to fall short of practical effect. Perhaps it is safer therefore to be interested chiefly in the well fare of our own country, provided that we do nothing to hinder the just advancement of that of others. At any rate the true spirit of patriotism has always been a considerable factor in the best upward movements of the human race. Let us however discountenance blatant patriotism as we would discountenance everything that is suspicious and ridiculous. Dr. Johnson's old saying about patriotism holds true in a new country like ours more markedly than in any other, and there are a greater number of those who find that it pays to be extremely zealous about their Fatherland. Already there is a good deal of talk in the public press which reminds one a little of Elijah Pogram and Jefferson Brick. At this time when our country's destiny, its very independent existence perhaps, is a matter of doubt and anxiety, it behooves us to be silent and do no boasting, but look seriously about us for the wisest thing to be said and done at each crisis.

A good deal is being said about Canadian Literature, and most of it takes the form of question and answer as to whether a Canadian Literature exists. Of course it does not. It will probably be a full generation or two before we can present a body of work of sufficient excellence as measured by the severest standards, and sufficiently marked with local colour, to enable us to call it a Canadian Literature. It is only within the last quarter of a century that the United States have produced anything like a distinctive American Literature. There was scarcely any peculiar literary quality in the work of the age of Longfellow, and Hawthorne to mark it decidedly as American[.] But within the last twenty five or thirty years, along with the evolution of a marked American race, certain noticeable American peculiarities of mind and character have been developed, which have strongly affected literary expression. Our country is still in the house-building land-breaking stage, and all its energies must go to the laying of a foundation of material prosperity upon which a future culture may be built. Those capable minds, which in old and long-civilized countries might be drawn into literature, in Canada are forced into the more practical paths[.] They are engaged in making fortunes and founding families. Their descendants, the people who shall inherit the fortune, leisure, station secured by them will be the writers or the readers of the age when a Canadian Literature comes to be. At present our people are too busy to read, too busy at least to read with discernment, and where there are no discerning readers there will be no writers. Also our educational institutions—even our best universities—are yet too raw to develop a literary spirit. All they can now be expected to do is to furnish the country with smart lawyers, competent physicians, able business men. As we advance in age and the settled conditions of life, these things will be gradually changed[.] There will arise a leisured class, a large body of educated people, who will create a market for literature and a literary atmosphere. And when that happens a literature will be produced for them. If our country becomes an independent compacted, self-supporting nation, which is, or ought to be, the dream of all of us, its social and climactic conditions will in the course of time evolve a race of people, having a peculiar national temperament and bent of mind, and when that is done we shall have a *Canadian* literature[.]

It is no doubt futile to speculate on the character of a thing as yet so remote as a Canadian Literature; yet one might hazard a thought or two on that subject. We know that climactic and scenic conditions have much to do with the moulding of national character. In the climate of this country we have the pitiless severity of the climate of Sweden with the sunshine and the sky of the north of Italy, a combination not found in the same degree anywhere else in the world. The northern winters of Europe are seasons of terror and gloom; our winters are seasons of glittering splendour and incomparable richness of colour. At the same time we have the utmost diversity of scenery, a country exhibiting every variety of beauty and grandeur. A Canadian race, we imagine, might combine the energy, the seriousness, the perseverance of the Scandinavians with something of the gaiety, the elasticity, the quickness of spirit of the south. If these qualities could be united in a literature, the result would indeed be something novel and wonderful.

But if we have not yet anything that we can call a full Canadian literature, we are not without out writers. Every Canadian who has read no further than the newspapers has heard of Judge Haliburton, Charles Heavysege, Dr. Kingsford, Dr. Bourinot, W.D. Lesueur, Abbé Casgrain, Sir William Dawson, Octave Cremazie [sic], Louis Frechette, Professor Alexander, Professor Roberts[,] Miss Machar, Hunter Duvar. These are names of which we have reason to be proud. In the last decade or two a small quantity of work of very decided excellence has been produced by Canadians. If we confine our view to pure literature a great part of this small quantity of excellent work has been done in verse. It is natural that the poet should be the most conspicuous product of the awakening literary impulse in a new country like ours. The philosopher, the historian, the critic, the novelist are more likely to represent a long established civilization. In a new and sparsely settled land the urgent problems of life do not force themselves on the attention of men as they do in the midst of dense populations. Consequently though they may interest themselves in the study of philosophy as a matter of culture, they are not likely to produce much original work of that sort. The field for the historian is also not very extensive. The critic has no place because he has nothing to examine. Even the novelist is likely to be a later product; for it is in the press of the older civilizations, where life in all its variety throngs about him, that he finds birth, food and stimulus. But for the poet the beauty of external nature and the aspects of the most primitive life are always a sufficient inspiration. On the border of civilization the poet is pretty sure to be the literary pioneer[.] For the poet of external nature no country is richer in inspiration than ours. For the balladist or the narrative writer we have at least as good a field as our neighbours of the United States. For the dramatic poet, if a dramatic poet could be produced in our age, there are I should think several excellent subjects in [the] history of old French Canada.

In searching for a subject for this paper I could not think of any upon which I could have greater pleasure in writing than the one I have chosen; viz., the writings in verse of two Canadians, Professor Charles G.D. Roberts and the late George Frederick Cameron. The first is a writer, whose marked quality of imagination and powerful gift of style have gained him attention both in England and the United States; but what specially prompted me to choose this subject was a desire to say something of the late Mr. Cameron, a writer of a higher order of excellence as judged from the purest standpoint, of some very remarkable qualities of feeling and expression, who has not, as far as I can learn[,] attracted the attention he deserves.

As regards Mr. Roberts['] work I have always had a personal feeling which perhaps induces me to place a higher estimate upon it in some respects than my hearers will care to accept. To most younger Canadians, who are interested in literature, especially those who have written themselves, Mr. Roberts occupies a peculiar position. They are accustomed to look up to him as in some sort the founder of a school, the originator of a new era in our poetic activity. I hope my hearers will pardon me, if I go out of my way to illustrate this fact by describing the effect Mr. Roberts' poems produced upon me when I first met with them.

It was almost ten years ago, and I was very young, an undergraduate at College. One May evening somebody lent me *Orion and Other Poems* then recently published. Like most of the young fellows about me I had been under the depressing conviction that we were situated hopelessly on the outskirts of civilization, where no art and no literature could be, and that it was useless to expect that anything great could be done by any of our companions, still more useless to expect that we could do it ourselves. I sat up all night reading and re-reading "Orion" in a state of the wildest excitement and when I went to bed I could not sleep. It seemed to me a wonderful thing that such work could be done by a Canadian, by a young man, one of ourselves. It was like a voice from some new paradise of art calling to us to be up and doing. A little after sunrise I got up and went out into the College grounds. The air, I remember, was full of the odour and cool sunshine of the spring morning. The dew was thick upon the grass. All the birds of our May-time seemed to be singing in the oaks, and there were even a few adder-tongues and trilliums still blossoming on the slope of the little ravine. But everything was transfigured for me beyond description, bathed in an old world radiance of beauty, the magic of the lines that were sounding in my ears, those divine verses, as they seemed to me, with their Tennyson-like richness and strange, earth-loving Greekish flavour. I have never forgotten that morning, and its influence has always remained with me.

I am now able to discern Mr. Roberts' deficiencies. I know that he lacks tenderness, variety, elasticity and that he never approaches the nobler attitudes of feeling; yet that early work of his has a special and mysterious charm for me—and it is indeed excellent, of an astonishing gift in workmanship, with passages here and there which in their way are almost unsurpassable.

Almost all the verse writing published in Canada before the appearance of *Orion* was of a more or less barbarous character. The drama of *Saul* by Charles Heavysege and some of Heavysege's sonnets are about the only exceptions, which can be made to this statement. Mr. Roberts was the first Canadian writer in verse who united a strong original genius with a high degree of culture, and an acute literary judgment. He was the first to produce a style, strongly individual in tone, and founded on the study of the best writers. Mr. Cameron, although a poet of greater spontaneity, a more passionate force, and a much higher range of feeling, than Mr. Roberts does not equal him in perfection of style. He neither aimed at, nor attained the same artistic excellence of workmanship.

Mr. Roberts' work, so far as it is available for purposes of criticism, is contained in two small volumes; the first *Orion and Other Poems*, published in 1880, when he was still an undergraduate of the University of New Brunswick, and not yet twenty years of age; the second *In Divers Tones*, published in 1887[sic], when he was in his 27th year. The first volume was of course immature, but it was an immaturity full of promise, and full of exhilaration for the poet's younger countrymen. Some of the work in it is astonishing work for a Canadian Schoolboy of eighteen or nineteen. Two of the poems included in this volume, "Memnon" and the "Ode to Drowsihood"[,] had already attracted the admiration of Dr. Holland, the late editor of the *Century*, and had been published in that magazine. The second volume, that of 1887, may be considered the work of Mr. Roberts' maturity, for he has published nothing as good since. In this the promise of the first was strengthened and in part fulfilled. A few of the poems were remarkable accomplishments, and the workmanship of them all excellent enough to secure Mr. Roberts a high place among the writers of the continent.

All Mr. Roberts' writing is of a very scholarly character; it is the work of an artist and a student, possessed of a decided original tone of feeling. In each of his volumes the longest and most important work is a poem in blank verse, the subject chosen from Greek classic legend; "Orion" in the first, and "Actaeon" in the second. In these poems Mr. Roberts has won the rare distinction of having succeeded admirably in blank verse—a severe test. The blank verse of "Orion" and "Actaeon" is an interesting study. It has a highly original quality, and at the same time shows a curious mingling of many influences. It is the workmanship of a student of Homer, influenced largely by Milton and Tennyson, somewhat also by Keats and Matthew Arnold. I do not know of any writer, with the exception of Matthew Arnold in his "Balder Dead," who has given to blank verse a more charming touch of Homer than Mr. Roberts. His verse is [not] quite so Homeric in its lightness and a swift movement as that of "Balder Dead," but it has more weight and a greater fulness of music. It is touched somewhat with the halt and restraint of Milton, corrected with a spice of the rich impulsiveness of Tennyson's "Oenone." On the whole it is very fine; probably no better has been done on this side of the Atlantic.

"Orion" is the story of the gigantic huntsman, who made a compact with Oenopion, King of Chios, to rid his island of wild beasts in exchange for the hand of his daughter Merope. When Orion had performed the task, deemed impossible, Oenopion, fearing his terrible strength, intoxicated him with drugged wine, and in his sleep deprived him of sight. Orion however managed to make his way by divine direction to a neighbouring mountain height, where as he stood fronting the

East at dawn, the first rays of the rising sun falling upon his eyes restored him to sight. Several passages in the poem in which Mr. Roberts retells this tale are so picturesque, and so thoroughly well written that I cannot pass without quoting one or two.

Out of the foamless sea a heavy fog
Steamed up, rolled in on all the Island shores,
But heavier, denser, like a cloak, where lay
The Hunter; and the darkness gathered thick,
More thick the fog and darkness, where he lay,
Like as a mother folds more close her child
At night when sudden street brawl jars her dreams[.]
But now the folding vapors veiled him not,
The ineffectual darkness hid him not,
For one came with the king, and bare a torch,
And stood beside the Hunter where he lay;
And all the darkness shuddered and fled back
Sullenly into the grim visaged crags,
Beneath their battered foreheads; and the fog
Crept up a chilly horror round the King,
Made huge the writhed and frowning mountain brows,
Till cliff, and cloud, and chaos of thick night
Toppled about the place, and each small sound
Of footstep or of stealthy whisper rang
Tortured and shrill within the cavernous hollows.
Before the King, before the torch-bearer,
Stood one beside the Hunter's head,—a slave
Beside the god-begotten,—and he bare
Back with one arm his cloak, and in his hand
He bare a cup—with such like juice in it
As slew Alcmena's son—above the face,
The strong, white, god-like face, more deathly white
Even than death; then into each close lid
He dropped the poison with a loathing hand,
While he whose light made manifest the deed,
Winced in his eyes and saw not, would not see,
Those eyes that knew not of their light gone out.
And heavy drops stood forth on all the rocks,
And ocean moaned unseen beneath the fog;

But the King laughed—not loud—and drew his cloak
Closer about him and went up the beach,
And they two with him.

Another, when Orion on the mountain summit, fronting the dawn, awaits the healing presence of the sun.

The cliffs are rent and through the eternal chasm
A far-heard moan of many cataracts,
With nearer, ceaseless murmur of the pines,
Came with the east wind, whilst the herald gold
From cloven pinnacles on either hand
On gradual wings sank to that airy glen;
And many-echoed dash of many waves
Rose dimly from the cliff-base where they brake,
Far down, unseen; and the wide sea spread wan
In the pale dawn-tide, limit-less, unportioned—
Aye sentinelled by these vast rocky brows
Defaced and stern with unforgotten fires.

But he intent leaned toward the gates of dawn
With suppliant face, unseeing, and the wind
Blew back from either brow his hair and cooled
His eyes that burned with that so foul dishonor
Late wrought upon them, whispering many things
Into his inmost soul. Sudden the day
Brake full. The healing of its radiance fell
Upon his eyes, and straight his sightless eyes
Were opened. All the morning's majesty
And mystery of loveliness lay bare
Before him; all the limitless blue sea,
Brightening with laughter many a league around,
Wind-wrinkled, keel-uncloven, far below;
And far above the bright sky-neighboring peaks;
And all around the broken precipices,
Cleft-rooted pines swung over falling foam,
And silver vapors flushed with the wide flood
Of crimson slanted from the opening east
Well-ranked, the vanguard of the day,—all these
Invited him, but these he heeded not

I think that that is very remarkable writing for a lad of nineteen.

The style which in its immaturity showed so much imagination and intellectual force in "Orion," is developed, pruned, and compacted in "Actaeon." Here the verse is full of strength and melody, clearly wrought and excellently balanced. While reminding one of the Greek, of Tennyson, and of Matthew Arnold, it is so penetrated and coloured by Mr. Roberts' own peculiar picturesque quality as to form an altogether original style. The "Actaeon" is certainly the best poem of that kind that has been written in America, and as regards workmanship I think it will stand comparison favourably with Tennyson's "Oenone."

Actaeon you will perhaps remember, was that prince of Thebes, the pupil of Chiron the Centaur, who, as he was hunting with his fifty hounds on Mount Cithaeron, came upon Diana and her nymphs bathing in a mountain pool. The Goddess, stirred with sudden anger at the intrusion, turned him into a stag, and he was torn to pieces by his dogs. Mr. Roberts['] story is put into the mouth of an old woman of Plataea who tells how she saw the fate of Actaeon with her own eyes, as she was searching upon the mountain for herbs. This is the conclusion of her tale:—

> I have lived long and watched out many days,
> Yet have not seen that ought is sweet save life,
> Nor learned that life hath other end than death.
> Thick horror like a cloud had veiled my sight,
> That for a space I saw not, and my ears
> Were shut from hearing; but when sense grew clear
> Once more, I only saw the vacant pool
> Unrippled,—only saw the dreadful sward,
> Where dogs lay gorged, or moved in fretful search,
> Questing uneasily; and some far up
> The slope, and some at the low water's edge,
> With snouts set high in air and straining throats
> Uttered keen howls that smote the echoing hills.
> They missed their master's form, nor understood
> Where was the voice they loved, the hand that reared;
> And some lay watching by the spear and bow

Flung down.
        And now upon the homeless pack
And paling stream arose a noiseless wind
Out of the yellow west awhile, and stirred
The branches down the valley; then blew off
To Eastward toward the long grey straits, and died
Into the dark, beyond the utmost verge.

Mr Roberts' genius has in it a strongly pagan, earth-loving, instinct[,] a delight in the mere presence of life and nature for their own sake, a delight half intellectual, half-physical, touched with a passionate glow. This quality is most strongly marked in two poems which are also noticeable for their success in an unusual form of verse. The "Tantramar Revisited" and "The Pipes of Pan" are written in the Elegiac Distich of Tibullus and Ovid, a form which has been transferred into English with good effect. There is a certain passionate stress in it, which makes it specially applicable to descriptive writing of an emotionally meditative and reminiscent character. Lines like the following from "Tantramar Revisited" illustrate our poet's keen sympathy with nature and his strenuous and scholarly gift of expression.

Miles on miles beyond the tawny bay is Minudie.
There are the low blue hills; villages gleam at their feet[.]
Nearer a white sail shines across the water, and nearer
Still are the slim gray masts of fishing boats dry on the flats.
Ah, how well I remember those wide red flats, above
    tide-mark
Pale with scurf of the salt, seamed and baked in the sun!
Well I remember the piles of blocks, and ropes and the
    net-reels
Wound with the beaded nets, dripping and dark from the sea!
Now at this season the nets are unwound; they hang from
    the rafters
Over the fresh-stowed hay in upland barns, and the wind
Blows all day through the chinks, with the streaks of sunlight
    and sways them
Softly at will; or they lie heaped in the gloom of a loft.

What a vivid naturalistic expression there is in some of the following lines from the "Pipes of Pan"—a beautiful poem. You will observe what artifice of phrase the poet uses to convey to all the senses of the reader the rank warm luxuriant aspect of the spot he is describing.

> Here is a nook. Two rivulets fall to mix with Peneus,
> Loiter a space and sleep, checked and choked by the reeds[.]
> Long grass waves in the windless water, strown with the lote-leaf;
> Twist through dripping soil great alder roots and the air
> Glooms with the dripping tangle of leaf-thick branches, and stillness
> Keeps in the strange-coiled stems, ferns, and wet-loving weeds.
> Hither comes Pan to this pregnant earthy spot, when his piping
> Flags; and his pipes outworn breaking and casting away,
> Fits new reeds to his mouth with the weird earth melody in them,
> Piercing, alive with a life able to mix with the god's.

It is possible that some of these lines are in a slight degree over done, reminding one in that respect of the American poet Edgar Fawcett, who is very fond of reaching natural effects by artifices of this kind. The idea in the "Pipes of Pan" is that Pan, coming to this "pregnant earthy spot" when his pipes are worn out, plucks new reeds from the river and flings the old ones away, and the old pipes, in which the "God-breath" still lingers, float with Peneus to the Ocean, and are scattered over the whole world.

> And mortals
> Straying in cool of morn, or bodeful hasting at eve,
> Or in the depths of noonday plunged to shadiest coverts,
> Spy them, and set to their lips; blow and fling them away!
> Ay, they fling them away—but never wholly! Thereafter

Creeps strange fire in their veins, murmur strange tongues in
their brain,
Sweetly evasive; a secret madness takes them,—a charm-struck
Passion for woods and wild life, the solitude of the hills.
Therefore they fly the heedless throngs and traffic of cities,
Haunt mossed caverns, and wells bubbling ice-cool; and their
souls
Gather a magical gleam of the secret of life, and the god's
voice
Calls to them, not from afar, teaching them wonderful things.

The fancy is a beautiful one, and there is a sort of silvery joyousness in the movement of all the poem, which causes it to grow upon one's like the more frequently it is read[.]

The ode is a kind of verse in which Mr. Roberts is perhaps not qualified to be very successful[.] He has not sufficient ease and flow to work well in complicated stanzas[.] His talent applies itself best to blank verse for which a certain self-retardative, almost cumbrous tendency of movement, peculiar to him, is an excellent qualification. Nevertheless in his first volume there is a very good ode, that to "Drowsihood[.]" It is a purely sensuous production and rests its claim to distinction entirely upon the beauty of its workmanship. Two of the stanzas in particular I will quote as being remarkable for some happy phrases[.]

The startled meadow-hen floats off, to sink
Into remoter shades and ferny glooms;
The great bees drone about the thick pea-blooms;
The liquid bubblings of the bobolink,
With warm perfumes
From the broad-flowered wild parsnip, drown my brain
The grackles bicker in the alder-boughs;
The grasshoppers pipe out their thin refrain
That with intenser heat the noon endows:
Then my weft weakens, and I wake again
Out of my dreamful drowze.

Ah, fetch thy poppy baths, juices expressed
 In fervid sunshine, where the Javan palm
 Stirs, scarce wakened from its odorous calm
By the enervate wind, that sinks to rest
  Amid the balm
And sultry silence, murmuring, half asleep,
 Cool fragments of the ocean's foamy roar,
And of the surge's mighty sobs that keep
 Forever yearning up the golden shore,
Mingled with songs of Nereids that leap
  Where the curled crests down-pour.

Occasionally Mr. Roberts' work is spoiled by an effect of strain and elaborate effort, the movement of the scarcely successful labourer. A stanza like the following from "The Isles," an ode in his second volume, leaves no satisfactory impression upon the ear, even if the sense be grasped.

One moment throbs the hearing, yearns the sight,
 But though not far, yet strangely hid—the way,
 And our sense slow, nor long for us delay
  The guides their flight!
The breath goes by, the word, the light, elude;
 And we stay wondering. But there comes an hour
Of fitness perfect and unfettered mood,
 When splits her husk the finer sense with power
  And—yon their palm-trees tower!

"In the Afternoon," a truly beautiful little poem, is an illustration of Mr.Roberts' most noticeable faculty, the power of investing a bit of vivid landscape description with the musical pathos of some haunting reminiscence or connecting with it a comforting thought, some kindly suggested truth.

Wind of the summer afternoon,
Hush, for my heart is out of tune!

Hush, for thou movest restlessly
The too light sleeper, Memory!

Whate'er thou hast to tell me, yet
'Twere something sweeter to forget,—

Sweeter than all thy breath of balm
An hour of unremembering calm!

So he begins, and there follow many descriptive couplets, full of happy and life-like touches—here are some of them:—

Waist-deep in dusty blossomed grass
I watch the swooping breezes pass

In sudden, long, pale lines, that flee
Up the deep breast of this green sea.

I listen to the bird that stirs
The purple tops, and grasshoppers

Whose summer din, before my feet
Subsiding, wakes on my retreat.

Again the droning bees hum by;
Still-winged, the grey hawk wheels on high.

In "On the Creek," another happy poem, we find such stanzas as these

For scents of various grass
  Stream down the veering breeze;
Warm puffs of honey pass
  From flowering linden trees.

And fragrant gusts of gum,
  From clammy balm-tree buds
With fern-brake odours, come
  From intricate solitudes.

This last stanza is an instance of our poet's tendency to clog his lines with clusters of consonants. It is not the result of carelessness with him, but a whim of his own ear. Sometimes he carries it too far, and writes a stanza like the following, which is hard to articulate.

> From off yon ash-limb sere
>   Out thrust amid green branches,
> Keen like an azure spear,
>   A king fisher down launches. [ll. 41-44 of "On the Creek"]

I cannot help calling particular attention to a single quatrain from a poem entitled "Off Pelorus," in which Mr. Roberts retouches the old story of Ulysses and the Syrens, putting his song into the mouth of one of the sailors of the wandering king. You remember that the sailors bound Ulysses to the mast and caulked their own ears. As they pass the shore where the Syrens are singing

> See the King! He hearkens,—hears their song,—strains forward,—
> As some mountain snake attends the shepherd's reed.
> Now with urgent hand he bids turn us shoreward,—
> Bend the groaning oar now; give the King no heed!

I quote this stanza as an illustration of Mr. Roberts' picturesque power and his genuine poet's capacity for getting the utmost musical and dramatic effect out of words.

One can hardly open Mr. Roberts' book anywhere without meeting with some richly descriptive phrase or happy stroke of the imagination. Such lines as the following, transcribed here and there at random, stand out even from the excellence of the poems in which they occur, and touch the fancy with a delighted surprise[:]

> Oh tenderly deepen the woodland blooms
>   And merrily sway the beeches
> *Breathe delicately the willow blooms,*

And the pines rehearse new speeches [from "The Maple," Lampman's italics]

The yellow willows, full of bees and bloom [from "To Fredericton in May-Time"]

The sleepless ocean's ceaseless beat,
The surge's monotone [from "Out of Pompeii"]

Low down the south a dreary gleam
Of white light smote the sullen swells,
Evasive as a blissful dream,
Or wind-borne notes of bells [from "Out of Pompeii"]

A yellow-sanded pool, shallow and clear,
Lay sparkling, brown about the further bank
From scarlet-berried ash-trees hanging over [from "Actaeon"]

But this mount
Cithaeron, bosomed deep in soundless hills,
Its fountained vales, its nights of starry calm,
Its high chill dawns, its long-drawn golden days,

Was dearest to him [from "Actaeon"]
The everlasting gods, . . .
Girt with their purples of perpetual peace [from "Actaeon"]

yellow beach-grass, whose brown panicles
Wore garlands of blown foam [from "Orion"]

The echo-peopled crags [from "Orion"]

The star-consulting silent pinnacles [from "Orion"]

The sun, far-sunken o'er the wold,
Through archèd windows sluicing gold
In sloping moted rows [from "Launcelot and the Four Queens"]

The wealth of the poet's thought,
  Tho sweet to win, is bitter to keep [from "Ballad of the Poet's
      Thought"]

When the veering wind hath blown
A glare of sudden daylight down [from "To Winter"]

But one must read the entire poems in which these scraps occur in order to fully appreciate the gift of the poet.

As a sonnet-writer Mr. Roberts has been unevenly successful. Two or three of his sonnets are impressive in thought and excellently modulated: but others bear traces of effort and consequently do not thoroughly capture the ear. I think the following sonnet entitled "Reckoning" is his best [:]

What matter that the sad grey city sleeps,
  Sodden with dull dreams, ill at ease, and snow
  Still falling chokes the swollen drains! I know
That even with sun and summer not less creeps
My spirit thro' gloom, nor ever gains the steeps
  Where Peace sits, inaccessible, yearned for so.
  Well have I learned that from my breast my woe
Starts,—that as my own hand hath sown, it reaps.

I have had my measure of achievement, won
  Most I have striven for; and at last remains
  This one thing certain only, that who gains
Success hath gained it at too sore a cost,
If in his triumph hour his heart have lost
  Youth, and have found its sorrow of age begun.

Another of Mr. Roberts' sonnets "The Sower," apparently a transcript in verse of François Millet's famous picture of the same title, has received just praise[:]

A brown sad-colored hillside, where the soil,
  Fresh from the frequent harrow, deep and fine,
  Lies bare; no break in the remote sky-line,
Save where a flock of pigeons streams aloft,

Startled from feed in some low-lying croft,
  Or far-off spires with yellow of sunset shine;
  And here the Sower, unwittingly divine,
Exerts the silent forethought of his toil.

Alone he treads the glebe, his measured stride
  Dumb in the yielding soil; and tho' small joy
  Dwell in his heavy face, as spreads the blind
Pale grain from his dispensing palm aside,
  This plodding churl grows great in his employ;—
  Godlike, he makes provision for mankind.

Amongst other things Mr. Roberts has tried his hand at writing some rousing patriotic poems; with the degree of success which usually attends deliberate effort of that kind. They are clever, but heavy, pompous, and more of the tongue [than] the heart. The time has not come for the production of any genuine national song. It is when the passion and enthusiasm of an entire people, carried away by the excitement of some great crisis, enters into the soul of one man specially gifted, that a great national poem or hymn is produced. We have yet to reach such an hour, and we may pray that it will not come too soon or too late.

It is always difficult to form an estimate of any contemporary writer; but I think that that anyone who has read through Mr. Roberts' two volumes, particularly the second, will conclude that he has been in contact with a very clever man, a scholar, a man of wide culture, variously appreciative, evincing especially a sort of deep physical satisfaction in the contemplation of nature, united to a strenuous and original gift of expression. He will find in him passion, strong, though not of the finest ring, a rich and masterful imagination, the genuine faculty of verse, an ear intolerant of any failure, and a cool and subtle literary judgment, but I think he will also find him wanting in spontaneity, in elasticity, in genuine tenderness, and in delicacy of feeling. His want of tenderness and genuine delicacy appear most strongly in two love poems, included in his second volume "Tout ou Rien" and "In Notre Dame"; the first, a declaration which could only proceed from the most boundless and pitiless egotism; the other, to me a still more disagreeable poem, an expression of brawny passion, pitched in an exaggerated and oversensuous key.

In Mr. Roberts' work, notwithstanding the great ability that has gone to the making of it, there is often a certain weightiness and deliberateness of phrase, which suggests too strongly the hand of the careful workman, and robs it of the fullest effect of spontaneity. Although his poems are written upon many various subjects, and either of his books might appear upon a cursory glance to be somewhat remarkable for variety, only three or four really different notes are struck, and all the poems are found to be attuned to these. Mr. Roberts is purely an emotional and artistic poet like Poe or Ros[s]etti, and never attempts to lead us to any of the grander levels of thought and feeling. He has nothing to teach us beyond some new phases of the beauty of nature, which he has interpreted admirably; and altogether his work impresses one as the product of a strong artistic talent, rather than of a soul accustomed to the atmosphere of the nobler and severer beauty.

[Lampman then turns to an extended discussion of the poetry of George Frederick Cameron]

Feb. 19, 1891 lecture, Library of the Literary and Scientific Society, Ottawa; ed. D.M.R. Bentley in *The Essays and Reviews of Archibald Lampman* (London, ON: Canadian Poetry Press, 1996): 91-107. Reprinted by permission of D.M.R. Bentley.

Poetic Interpretation

by Archibald Lampman

There is nothing in the world, whether in nature animate or inanimate, or in the phenomena of human life, which has not connected with it some sense of beauty, either in itself or in its relation to the whole of life. Only those who have been gifted in some degree with the bright instinct which we call poetic feeling, can at all times be brought to see this; and those who have received this gift in such a high degree that they cannot be at peace with themselves or find any rest in the enjoyment of life, until they have made known to mankind the beautiful things they have seen and felt; these are the men whom we call poets.

Every phenomenon in life, every emotion and every thought produces a distinct impression of its own upon the soul of the poetic observer. The impression produced by a Mayday sunrise is very different from that produced by an October sunset. The feeling left upon the soul by the contemplation of a full-blown rose is not the same as the sense which it gathers from the beauty of a bunch of sedge. The latter is perhaps not less beautiful than the former, but the essence of its beauty is different.

Every feeling thus produced has what may be called its musical accompaniment—its own peculiar harmonic value, and in every poetic soul lies hidden an answering harmony, which may be aroused either by the presence of the impression itself, or by the more potent interpretation of the poet. The poetic soul is like a vast musical instrument, every chord in which represents the perfect musical value of some one of these separate impressions. Most of these innumerable chords have never been sounded; but there they will lie, as long as the soul remains, awaiting the touch of emotion either from within or from the hand of the interpreting poet.

The poet's reproduction of any impression must be effected not by a vivid picture only or by a merely accurate description, but also by such a subtle arrangement of word and phrase, such a marshalling of verbal sound, as may exactly arouse, through the listening ear, the strange stirring of the soul, involved in every beautiful emotion, which we feel to be akin to the effect of music. If the poet should undertake to reproduce the impressions of the summer sunrise, the October sunset, the rose and the bunch of sedge, not only must the pictures be different, but the tones must be different too. The perfect poet would be one in whose soul should be found the perfect answering harmony to every natural or spiritual phenomenon. He would be one who should go about the world gathering the impressions of life, not with sight and thought only, but with the inner ear of the intently listening soul. In creating his pictures of life he would weave into each of them its own peculiar harmony so perfectly that we should have no doubt whatever as to its degree of truth, but we should know it instantly for what it is. This of course has never been completely done, and no man has ever been a perfect poet.

The perfect poet, it may be said, would have no set style. He would have a different one for everything he should write, a manner exactly suited to the subject, for the style involves to a certain extent what I have been speaking about, the musical accompaniment. But almost every original poet has had his own easily recognizable method of imagination and expression, that which we call his style; for almost every poet has been dominated by some one special thought, feeling or musical instinct, which has overshadowed every other, and left an unalterable mark upon his imagery and his phraseology. This would not be the case with the perfect poet. He would not consent to be permanently influenced by any single impulse, however noble, but would arrive unerringly at the perfect rendering of everything. Often the single dominating instinct, guided by the longing for truth, impels the poet invariably to a choice of subjects of a kind exactly consonant with his mood, as in the case of Poe or Ros[s]etti, or he may endeavor to apply a peculiar form of imagination and musical feeling to a variety of subjects, and in such an effort he becomes invariably untrue.

Special purposes and special instincts have produced great

poets but not perfect ones. For the perfect poet would not necessarily be great. Many things beside the capacity to reproduce every beautiful impression in all its poetic truth, go to the making of a great poet. He must have noble thought, lofty purposes and great fertility, and these things in their worth and majesty far outweigh the charm[,] glorious as it is, which we sometimes find in poets of a lesser calibre as men, but gifted with a finer instinct and a more various susceptibility. Keats was not as great a poet as Wordsworth, but he was a more perfect one.

Style has generally been in the way of all poets in their efforts at exact poetic interpretation; indeed just in so far as they have subjected the ear and the imagination to the governance of settled method and tone, have they failed to render the pure and absolute impression produced by the phenomena of material nature and the movement and emotion of human life. Their work may be supremely noble and beautiful like Spenser's, or passionately alluring like Swinburne's, but not many passages can be pointed to as fair interpretations of the things which they are intended to represent.

Of all poets of the present century Keats, it seems to me, was the most perfect. He was governed by no theory and by no usurping line of thought and feeling. He was beyond all other men disposed to surrender himself completely to the impression of everything with which his brain or his senses came in contact. He died very young and before he had had time to work upon many things; but everything that his imagination handled came from it in a shape so nearly perfect, that whenever we have contemplated any one of those exquisite creations we have been almost compelled to say—this is indeed its absolute beauty and this is its absolute harmony.

Of the eight best known poems of Keats seven are almost faultless. The first and longest, *Endymion*, is the only one, in which the tones are not quite sound. But this was the work of an inexperienced and over-abundant youth, too eager to wait for the perfect musical fulfillment of its imaginings, content to set each thing down incompletely as it came, and then hurry on to the next. In "Lamia" we observe at once the advance to development. Here he had caught and mastered before he began the full harmonic complement of his subject, with all its action, its imagery, its beauty and its emotion. He did not, as many poets have done, endeavor to apply to a new creation an already well-used style and tone, which had served for a hundred other subjects. He knew that it must have a tone of its own, and that only by yielding to the answering echo of that tone in his own heart could the reader live for a moment with him in the full and beautiful reality of the things he had created. His theme was a semi-mythological tale of Corinth, and he told it like an inspired Corinthian. The painting is Greek. The harmony is Greek; and our imaginations involuntarily assume the Greek pose as we follow the flow of the story, watching the beautiful Lamia turning into the beautiful woman, passing from the bright and noisy stream of traffic between Cenchreae [sic] and Corinth to observe the meeting of Lamia and Lycius, threading the streets of the twilight city with their joyous activity, their luxurious plenty, and the murmur of their soft and fluent tongue, dwelling in that mysterious marble palace of languor and delight, holding a place at Lycius' bridal banquet with its sparkling merriment and teeming luxury, till in the end we are chilled to the heart by the gathered horror of the piteous catastrophe. All these things we feel as beautiful realities, not through the action and the imagery alone, but through the subtle music of the verse. The tone of that joyous Corinth is everywhere woven into it, but over all hangs the terrible fate of the story, the shadow of the cynic Apollonius, austere and saturnine. This too runs in an undercurrent through the melody, giving to the complete poem a tone, which could be assumed by nothing else, and without which the thing would be a body without a soul or a body but half alive.

So much for "Lamia"; then consider the complete change of tone in *Hyperion*. No other English poet ever had such an ear as Keats. He seems to be intently listening as he writes, listening at the heart of his subject, transcribing rather than creating his song. In *Hyperion* again the subject is Greek, but it is of the older mythology. We are among the elder Gods, discomfited and dethroned, gigantic primeval shapes, huddled together, or wandering in impotent gloom and desolation. The soft luxurious music of "Lamia" with its undersong of tragic anticipation would never do for this. Nothing would do for it but what the poet found—a tone that was deep and full and solemn, with a sound in it sometimes huge, hollow, Cyclopean, almost ponderous. The syllables fall at times like the footsteps of Enceladus, and even the timid complaining of Clymene is deeper and fuller, and bears in it a huger gloom, than the laments of earthly women. Listen to this from the description of Thea, the "tender spouse of gold Hyperion," who comes to the aged Saturn in his bowed despair, touches his wide shoulders and speaks to him—

> But Oh! how unlike marble was that face:
> How beautiful if sorrow had not made
> Sorrow more beautiful than beauty's self.
> There was a listening fear in her regard,
> As if calamity had but begun;
> As if the vanward clouds of evil days
> Had spent their malice, and the sullen rear
> Was with its stored thunder laboring up.

That is the tone—surely worthy of the Titan Gods! so large and solemn. The poet thus describes the place where the followers of Saturn meet in gloomy consultation.

> It was a den where no insulting light
> Could glimmer on their tears; where their own groans
> They felt, but heard not, for the solid roar
> Of thunderous waterfalls and torrents hoarse,
> Pouring a constant bulk, uncertain where.
> Crag jutting forth to crag, and rocks that seemed
> Ever as if just rising from a sleep,
> Forehead to forehead held their monstrous horns;
> And thus in thousand hugest phantasies
> Made a fit roofing to this nest of woe.

Listen to the tremendous fall of the syllables in those wonderful lines describing how Enceladus broke in upon the trembling lamentations of Clymene.

> So far her voice flowed on, like timorous brook
> That, lingering along a pebbled coast,
> Doth fear to meet the sea: but sea it met,
> And shuddered; for the overwhelming voice
> Of huge Enceladus swallowed it in wrath:
> The ponderous syllables, like sullen waves
> In the half-glutted hollows of reef-rocks,
> Came booming thus, while still upon his arm
> He leaned; not rising, from supreme contempt.

At last Enceladus arouses the wrath and courage of the Gods; and as the final words of that vast utterance fall from his lips, a light gleams in upon the faces around him. It is the pallid splendor of Hyperion, the only one of the primeval deities still left in the possession of his sovereignty. Thus his coming is described:

> Suddenly a splendor like the morn
> Pervaded all the beetling gloomy steps,
> All the sad places of oblivion
> And every gulf, and every chasm old,
> And every height, and every sullen depth,
> Voiceless, or hoarse with loud-tormented streams:
> And all the everlasting cataracts,
> And all the headlong torrents far and near,
> Mantled before in darkness and huge shade,
> Nor saw the light and made it terrible,
> It was Hyperion.

The poet is painting Titans and his harmony is Titanic. Sentence after sentence it falls upon the ear and satisfies us. It is the poetic truth. It satisfies us not by the grouping[,] the action, the imagery, the thought[,] alone, but by the melody which is to these things as the living soul. Consider again these marvellous lines[:]

There was a listening fear in her regard,
As if calamity had but begun;
As if the vanward clouds of evil days
Had spent their malice, and the sullen rear
Was with its stored thunder laboring up.

All these lines might be changed, or a single pause might be removed. The thought, the image would perhaps be the same; but the harmony would no longer belong to the idea, and the beautiful truth would be destroyed or mutilated. A perfect poetic utterance is like a human body of perfect physical beauty showing the life of the beautiful soul within in the movement of every feature, every limb, every muscle, every nerve. If a simple finger be paralysed or shrunken, the splendid harmony is disturbed, and the expression of the soul is made incomplete. So it is with the perfect poetic utterance. If a single living word is changed for a dead one—one that is dead in its place—the harmony is shattered; the musical soul no longer perfectly expresses itself. Let us take a few more examples from Keats, for even his small bulk of work is a storehouse of poetic perfections. "The Eve of St. Agnes," for instance; that wondrous poem that weaves about us irresistably the strange ringing charm of mediaeval phantasy, touching the ear in every syllable with the imaginative flavor of things old and long bygone—the story of a lover who met his mistress once by a quaint device on a wintery St. Agnes Eve, when there was wind and sleet without and revelry within and enemies on every hand—wooed and won her and carried her away with him into the storm and the night. The music and imagery of the very first lines are enough to make one shiver. They are the musical expression of the thought of numbing cold, combined with the mediaeval witchery of the theme[.]

St. Agnes' Eve—Ah, bitter chill it was!
The owl, for all his feathers, was acold;
The hare limped trembling through the frozen grass,
And silent was the flock in woolly fold:
Numb were the beadsman's fingers while he told

His rosary, and while his frosted breath,
Like pious incense from a censer old,
Seemed taking flight for heaven without a death,
Past the sweet Virgin's picture, while his prayer he saith.

The vivid harmony of these other lines, when the lovers make their way down the darkling stairway—

In all the house was heard no human sound.
A chain-drooped lamp was flickering by each door;
The arras, rich with horseman, hawk and hound,
Fluttered in the beseiging wind's uproar;
And the long carpets rose along the gusty floor[.]

And the last stanza with its tone of ancientness and of lives and dreams that have been ages buried in the tomb.

And they are gone; aye, ages long ago,
These lovers fled away into the storm.
That night the baron dreamt of many a wo,
And all his warrior guests, with shade and form
Of witch, and demon, and large coffin-worm,
Were long be-nightmared. Angela the old
Died palsy-twitched, with meagre face deform;
The beadsman, after thousand aves told,
For aye unsought-for slept among his ashes cold.

Turn then to the "Ode to a Nightingale." Read it over and over. Gather into the ear the whole of its sad deep yearning tone —the pure outpouring of that mood of melancholy, so strange an interweaving of joy and sorrow, when the poetic soul flags and falls from its dream, for a moment well-nigh broken and sore wearied with the iron necessities of this earthly life, yet finding in the very strength of its glorious desire a kind of shadowy joy, a mournful delight, whereby even the bitterness of its situation is transfigured and made to wear the semblance of something grand and poetic. The poet wishes that he might become like the nightingale, and with her "Fade away into the forest dim"

Fade far away, dissolve, and quite forget
  What thou among the leaves hast never known,
The weariness, the fever, and the fret
  Here, where men sit and hear each other groan;
Where palsy shakes a few, sad, last grey hairs,
  Where youth grows pale, and spectre-thin and dies;
    Where but to think is to be full of sorrow
      And leaden-eyed despairs;
 Where Beauty cannot keep her lustrous eyes,
  Or new love pine at them beyond to-morrow.

The tone of this stanza is the tone of the whole. The poet describes such things as might breed despair, but there is none of the strident accent of despair. They should not make men fail, but they are nevertheless mournful. He has therefore found for his thoughts their own proper music—a music that is deep and sorrowful, but too beautiful to be desperate.

In the "Ode to [sic] a Grecian Urn" we find another complete change in the harmony. It is the expression of the attitude to the poet's mind in the intense contemplation of some work of antique art, something calmly and perfectly beautiful; and the tone of the verse, so quiet and at the same time so ecstatic, is the pure musical expression of rapt and enchanted reverie[.]

Oh Attic shape! Fair attitude! with brede
  Of marble men and maidens overwrought,
With forest branches and the trodden weed;
  Thou silent form! dost tease us out of thought
As doth eternity: Cold Pastoral!
 When old age shall this generation waste,
  Thou shalt remain, in midst of other wo
Than ours, a friend to man, to whom thou say'st,
  "Beauty is truth, truth beauty"—that is all
 Ye know on earth, and all ye need to know.

"Dost tease us out of thought as doth eternity." There is in that the tone of the whole poem. It is a beautiful commentary on those other well-known words of Keats "A thing of beauty is a joy for ever." The smallest thing that is perfectly beautiful in form and hue, may seem at first glance to satisfy us, but in a little while, we find that we can never fill our souls with the entire sense of its beauty and perfection. It is something that is eternal and illimitable. Our finite mind cannot contain it. Lift and expand as it may, it is still conscious that there are breadths and heights even in this little thing that it can never reach. It will "tease us out of thought as doth eternity."

> Oh Attic shape! Fair attitude! with brede
>   Of marble men and maidens overwrought.

Can we not hear in every syllable of these two blameless lines the clear yet dreamy utterance of the purest surrenderment to the spirit of serene beauty, that mood of contemplation, which is so still, so passionless and yet so strangely full—the emotion of perfect rest.

I have illustrated my subject so abundantly from Keats, because he seems to me to have been the most perfect of later poets. His work is a storehouse of musical perfections. Next to Keats in the truth of poetic interpretation stands Wordsworth, who in his moods of inspiration was the most spontaneous of all our later poets, and in the loftiness of his nature was the greatest. Wordsworth's subjects, especially those in which he was successful, were humble. Very young people do not care for them. He never flatters or allures the imagination; and it is his glory that he has rendered the quiet musical feeling of very homely things with such a touching truth, that they grow in favour with us as we grow in years and in the knowledge of life. Often when we weary of the flowerier utterances of those who deal with more splendid scenes and more romantic passions, we turn to the work of this wise poet, with an ineffable sense of health and rest.

Wordsworth's work is very uneven; but it seems to me that the very fact that a few of his poems stand out in such fine and glorious contrast to the rest, is the strongest evidence of the genuine spontaneity of his gift. A great lyric poem is a thing which is written if one may so speak it in a dream. The emotion comes upon the poet and almost before he is conscious of it, the thing stands there on paper before him. It is done and he knows not how it was done. It has passed from him as the perfume from a flower. Wordsworth must have been hardly conscious of the great disparity of his work. He wrote steadily and serenely[.] Sometimes the great passion came over him, and he created things that were rarely beautiful, thrilled with the brightest life and tuned with the most accurate music. But he did not wait for these moments. He had a theory by the light of which he labored on incessantly, believing that every thought, that entered his mind, and was dear to him, might be run out into lines and stanzas, and so made to stand for a poem. His theory however was noble, and to aim at the highest level, with a partial failure is greater than to attain to an absolute perfection in a lower one. Wordsworth aimed at the loftiest, now and then he succeeded, and in his success he was the noblest of later English poets. Yet even in his best passages the rendering of the subtle melody of his idea is never perfect. He had not the imperious ear of Keats, who could not have rest[ed] till he had caught and mastered the fullness of every harmony. Wordsworth's finest utterances are always a little broken. They weaken and fall somewhere; but there is enough of them in every case to make us feel most vividly the beauty and truth of the conception[.] They awaken without doubt the answering harmony in our own souls. Such poems as "Michael," "The Leech-gatherer," "Ruth," seem to him who reads them for the first time quite unmusical; only after long acquaintance do we learn that they not only have a harmony but that it is exquisitely true. After having once learned to take delight in the quiet tones of Wordsworth, we begin to value at their true worth many things which had before so unreasonably mastered us.

One of Wordsworth's finest poems is "The Leech-gatherer," or as it is otherwise entitled "Resolution and Independence." The opening stanzas convey very perfectly the poetic impression of a blithe bright morning after a night loud with rain and storm[.]

There was a roaring in the wind all night;
  The rain came heavily and fell in floods;
But now the sun is rising calm and bright;
  The birds are singing in the distant woods;
  Over his own sweet voice the stock-dove broods;
The jay makes answer as the magpie chatters
And all the air is filled with pleasant noise of waters.

All things that love the sun are out of doors;
  The sky rejoices in the morning's birth;
The grass is bright with rain-drops; on the moors
  The hare is running races in her mirth.

"And all the air is filled with pleasant noise of waters." How simple and how perfect? Have we not a hundred times felt those words, though we have never expressed them? In the description of the aged and lonely leech-gatherer, wandering about the moors, there are several examples of the *curiosa felicitas* of expression noted by Coleridge, and of the most faithful and delicate musical interpretation[.]

  I saw a man before me unawares
The oldest man he seemed that ever wore grey hairs[.]
            . . . Not all alive nor dead,
Nor all asleep, in his extreme old age:
His body was bent double, feet and head
Coming together in their pilgrimage,
As if some dire constraint of pain, or rage
Of sickness felt by him in times long past,
A more than human weight upon his frame had cast.

Himself he propp'd, his body, limbs, and face,
  Upon a long grey staff of shaven wood;
And still as I drew near with gentle pace,
  Beside the little pond or moorish flood,
  Motionless as a cloud the old man stood;
 That heareth not the loud winds when they call,
And moveth altogether, if it move at all.

There is something, not in the ideas alone, but in the very choice and grouping of the syllables, in these strange lines, which causes us to feel irresistibly that we are in very truth face to face with an object of extreme feebleness, bent with the burden of an almost lifeless old age. They have a keen, strange force together with a curious dragging effect in the tone, that is altogether unique and lingers in the ear with a growing assertion of its mysterious truth.

As a total change we may turn to the little poems on the "Small Celandine." A little flower is no doubt a small subject for great poetry; yet is not the frailest thing that is sweetly beautiful worthy of a song? At any rate Wordsworth thought so, and honored the Small Celandine with two of the most charming efforts of his genius. Indeed after wandering through the loose and redundant verbiage of such poems as "The Thorn" and "Goody Blake," so extravagant in their homeliness, we are almost startled by the musical sweetness and compact cutting of these rare stanzas. They express, with a delicate brightness, and loving sincerity of music, the poet's happy contemplation of a little starlike blossom, which was to him not only a harbinger of spring, but the emblem of many humble things that are of more value than their gaudier neighbors[.]

E'er a leaf is on a bush,
In the time before the thrush
Has a thought about its nest,
Thou wilt come with half a call,
Spreading out thy glossy breast
Like a careless prodigal;
Telling tales about the sun,
When we've little warmth or none[.]
Prophet of delight and mirth,
Scorned and slighted upon Earth!
Herald of a mighty band,
Of a joyous train ensuing,
Singing at my heart's command,
In the lanes my thoughts pursuing,
I will sing, as doth behove,
Hymns in praise of what I love!

Soon as gentle breezes bring
News of winter's vanishing,
And the children build their bowers,
Sticking kerchief plots of mould
All about with full-blown flowers,
Thick as sheep in shepherd's fold!
With the proudest thou art there,
Mantling in the tiny square[.]

These are only three stanzas out of fourteen, all of them exquisite; but they perfectly represent the tone.

As an example of an unsuccessful attempt at poetic interpretation, I may quote from Wordsworth's "The Thorn."

Like rock or stone, it is o'ergrown
  With lichens to the very top,
And hung with heavy tufts of moss,
  A melancholy crop;
Up from the earth these mosses creep
And this poor Thorn they clasp it round
So close, you'd say that they were bent
With plain and manifest intent
  To drag it to the ground;
And all had joined in one endeavor
To bury this poor thorn forever[.] [Lampman's italics]

The picture intended to be painted in these lines is a strong one, but the ear at once informs us that the attempt has failed. It awakens no answering harmony in the soul. It has in fact no harmony at all, either true or false. The best examples of false harmonies are to be found in Byron, whose musical range was very narrow. The opening lines of the third canto of *The Corsair*, so magnificent and stately, but so untrue and so really unsympathetic, are a striking example.

One of the most interesting of Wordsworth's poems is that which begins "She was a phantom of delight." Its lofty masculine tone of noble praise, its serious, rapid, concise descriptive movement remind us wonderfully of Tennyson—so much so that one is led to imagine that Tennyson might have caught the keynote of his style from the reading of this poem. There are the lines in "Isabel" which seem like a richer echo of the music of Wordsworth's grander and simpler ones. The final stanza will be enough to quote.

> And now I see with eye serene
> The very pulse of the machine;
> A being breathing thoughtful breath,
> A traveller betwixt life and death;
> The reason firm, the temperate will,
> Endurance, foresight, strength and skill;
> A perfect woman, nobly planned,
> To warn, to comfort, and command;
> And yet a spirit still, and bright
> With something of an angel light.

Turn then to that other poem, also without a title, beginning "Three years she grew in sun and shower." This is the musical expression of sympathy with a more impassioned spirit. He is describing not the calm-minded noble woman of the former poem, but a figure glowing with the spirit of poetry, the light of a mind akin to his own. The measure is therefore no longer keen cut and stately, but swift and vehement[,] ringing with a sweeter and wilder intonation. This is the musical difference in the poet's interpretation of the two characters. Listen to the passionate melody, the flash of imagination in these lines—

> "The stars of midnight shall be dear
> To her; and she shall lean her ear
> In many a secret place,
> Where rivulets dance their wayward round,
> *And beauty born of murmuring sound*
> Shall pass into her face[.] [Lampman's italics]

In "Michael" and a great many parts of the *Prelude* and the *Excursion* we find a tone, which is the purest rendering imaginable of whatever musical sense attaches to those pictures and emotions of homely rustic life, which were dearer to Wordsworth's heart than any more complex development of human society could ever be. In his best treatment of these simple things he indulges in no pomp. His lines are direct and homely in their music; but there is in them a noble dignity which is due to all nature in her simple elements. What a sense of healthful content and rustic industry there is in the following lines from the description of Michael's cottage[.]

> Down from the ceiling, by the chimney's edge,
> Which in our ancient uncouth country style,
> Did with a huge projection overbrow
> Large space beneath, as duly as the light
> Of day grew dim, the housewife hung a lamp,
> An aged utensil which had performed
> Service beyond all others of its kind.
> Early at evening did it burn and late,
> Surviving comrade of uncounted hours,
> Which, going by from year to year, had found
> And left the couple neither gay, perhaps,
> Nor cheerful, yet with objects, and with hopes,
> Living a life of eager industry.
> And now when Luke was in his eighteenth year,
> There by the light of this old lamp they sat,
> Father and son, while late into the night
> The housewife plied her own peculiar work,
> *Making the cottage through the silent hours*
> *Murmur as with the sound of summer flies*[.]
> [Lampman's italics]

Some very noble examples of poetic interpretation are to be found in Wordsworth's sonnets. It seems strange at first thought that a poet whose utterance was often so loose and irregular, at times even garrulous, should have succeeded so well in a species of verse, requiring in the highest degree the artistic instinct for beautiful form, and the musical instinct for the most delicate and at the same time the largest harmonies; yet this looseness and irregularity in his methods was to a great extent a matter of principle with him, not of feeling, and it was no doubt often with a sense of fine comfort that he betook himself in easier hours to the sonnet, humouring the bright artistic instinct, which was certainly his, and which must have been always hungering within him. Some of his sonnets are the best in the English language. They are rhythmically finer than Shakespeare's or Milton's. His prefatory sonnet on the sonnet is perhaps from an artistic point of view the most perfect work of the kind ever written in our tongue. It could hardly be improved. It is so well known that I need not quote it. Let me rather draw attention to one of the beautiful sonnets on sleep. I will give it in full. The sense and melody of the first lines are curiously interpretive of that strange uncertain condition between sleep and waking, when we lie for hours haunted by innumerable images that pass before the mind in blind unreasoning succession, persuading us to the sleep, that is ever upon us, but never comes.

> A flock of sheep that leisurely pass by,
> One after one; the sound of rain, and bees
> Murmuring; the fall of rivers, winds, and seas,
> Smooth fields, white sheets of water, and pure sky,
> I've thought of all by turns; and still I lie
> Sleepless; and soon the small birds' melodies
> Must hear, first uttered from my orchard trees;
> And the first cuckoo's melancholy cry.
> Even thus last night, and two nights more, I lay,
> And could not win thee, Sleep! by any stealth:
> So do not let me wear to-night away:
> Without thee what is all the morning's wealth?
> Come, blessed barrier betwixt day and day,
> Dear mother of fresh thoughts and joyous health!

I have illustrated my subject altogether from Keats and Wordsworth because they furnish the most perfect and most abundant examples. No other of our later poets has had such an exquisite ear for all delicate harmonies as Keats, and no other has had such an eager and loving one for the sweet and simple harmonies of free healthy nature as Wordsworth. Next to these, I believe, comes Matthew Arnold. His "Forsaken Merman" with its strange haunting pathos, the grand endings of "Mercerinus" and "Sohrab and Rustum," many passages in "Empedocles on Etna" and various other poems are matchless interpretations of things that echo with a pure and solemn music. Tennyson though a splendid poet and a noble nature is by no means so faithful a poetic interpreter. Through all his work there is the grasp of a settled system of phrase and melody. The style is powerful and noble, but it does not always accurately interpret. The poet's ear is not sufficiently simple and ingenuous. Shelley failed often for a somewhat similar reason. Into every picture that he drew, into every thought that he expressed, he wrought the strange unreal color and the wild spiritual music, natural to his own beautiful but fantastic imagination. It is not actual nature that he interprets, but Shelley's wonderful re-creation of it. In all such pictures of life as are vehement, intense, passionately imaginative and tender, Robert Browning is a wonderful master; but he is too rapid, too rough, and has too much of a fixed way of talking about things to have a complete musical range. He is not one of the patient listeners for all of nature's secret harmonies. Rossetti interpreted some things, that were in consonance with his own life-long mood, strangely well. Coleridge succeeded perfectly in two poems, "Christabel" and "The Rime of the Ancient Mariner" but in the rest of his work he seems to have been laboring in the dark, far away from his natural bent.

Byron expressed admirably enough one of his own moods, that of romantic and melancholy self-contemplation. Swinburne is without variety[,] being absorbed and carried away by a single strain of riotous melody which he applies to everything. Such things as can be expressed in his manner he has interpreted as no other man has ever interpreted them, or ever will[.]

Perhaps the world shall some day have a poet who will interpret tenderly passionate dreams like Keats, simple and lofty ones like Wordsworth, strong and passionate pictures of life like Browning, ethereal imaginings like Shelley, grave and manly thought like Tennyson, and everything else with the best truth of the special poet who has handled it best. But we shall not look for such a poet for many a long [age].

Undated ms, first published in its entirety in *The Essays and Reviews of Archibald Lampman*, ed. D.M.R. Bentley (London, ON: Canadian Poetry Press, 1996): 126-41. Reprinted by permission of D.M.R. Bentley.

Contemporaries—V. Mr. Charles G.D. Roberts

by Bliss Carman

Mr. Roberts is one of those writers who must be regarded in their environment, to be justly estimated. Born and reared in the maritime provinces of Canada, with the blood of the loyalists in his veins; he is one of the patriots of the Dominion who, whether they look to an Imperial Federation or an Independence of rule, are before all else devoted to the honor and progress of their native land. The acknowledged laureate of this vigorous young nation, his poetry is in large measure the product of his enthusiasm and patriotism.

> "O Child of Nations, giant-limbed,
> Who stand'st among the nations now
> Unheeded, unadored, unhymned,
> With unanointed brow!" ["Canada" ll. 1-4]

So he opens his dignified ode on Canada. And in his verses on Canadian streams he weaves the story and legend of each with its musical name.

> "O rivers rolling to the sea
> From lands that bear the maple-tree,
>   How swell your voices with the strain
> Of loyalty and liberty!
> . . . .
>
> "Thou inland stream, whose vales, secure
> From storm, Tecumseh's death made poor!
>   And thou small water, red with war,
> 'Twixt Beaubassin and Beauséjour!
>
> "Dread Saguenay, where eagles soar,
> What voice shall from the bastioned shore
>   The tale of Roberval reveal,
> Or his mysterious fate deplore?" ["Canadian Streams" ll. 1-4, 21-28]

Then too the every day aspect of country life and the common-place things of the Canadian landscape have moved Mr. Roberts to love and sympathetic expression. "The Sower," "The Fir Woods," "Burnt Lands," "The Potato Harvest," "The Herring Weir,"—such are the themes that he has treated in a series of sonnets and published, along with other poems, in his most recent volumes[sic], *Songs of the Common Day*. And it is, of course, rather in these and similar themes that such a poet will find his happiest expression. For however the noble and brave and devoted story of his own country may move him, it must still fail to touch his work with fire unless he have himself personally heard the clash of arms and drum-roll at his own door. In times of peace the world is one; and the more philosophic and meditative subjects touch the artist fervently. I shall not quote here any of those sonnets I have mentioned, but give preference to two others which illustrate Mr. Roberts in two admirable ways.

The first sonnet I shall quote is an example of the simplicity—the value of treating simple human themes in the simplest way.

The Deserted City

"There lies a little city leagues away.
Its wharves the green sea washes all day long.
Its busy sun-bright wharves with sailors' song
And clamor of trade ring loud the live-long day.
Into the happy harbor hastening, gay
With press of snowy canvass, tall ships throng.
The peopled streets to blithe-eyed peace belong,
Glad housed beneath these crowding roofs of grey.

'Twas long ago this city prospered so,
For yesterday a woman died therein.
Since when the wharves are idle fallen, I know,
And in the streets is hushed the pleasant din;
The thronging ships have been, the songs have been;--
Since yesterday it is so long ago."

The other sonnet is an example of the writer's power in coping with the largest subjects. It is just here that Mr. Roberts is at his best. His hand is too heavy for bric-a-brac verse, but the most serious aspects and aspirations of life are plastic in his sure grasp. There is a dignity and fineness in his attitude towards the problems of this little earth, characteristic of the amplest-minded artists of all times. He is never petty and never vindictive. Without superstition of any sort, he is yet imbued with the ancient worship of Nature; the quiet of a northern pantheism pervades all his deeper work. For example, in these very lines:

"In the wide awe and wisdom of the night
I saw the round world rolling on its way,
Beyond significance of depth or height,
Beyond the interchange of dark and day.
I marked the march to which is set no pause,
And that stupendous orbit, round whose rim
The great sphere sweeps, obedient unto laws
That utter the eternal thought of Him.
I compassed time, outstripped the starry speed,
And in my still soul apprehended space,
Till, weighing laws which these but blindly heed[,]
At last I came before Him face to face,—
And knew the Universe of no such span
As the august infinitude of Man."

Mr. Roberts places in the front of his book an invocation that reveals the aim of his work:

"Across the fog the moon lies fair.
Transfused with ghostly amethyst,
O white Night, charm to wonderment
The cattle in the mist!

"Thy touch, O grave mysteriarch,
Makes dull familiar things divine.
O grant of thy revealing gift
Be some small portion mine!

"Make thou my vision sane and clear,
That I may see what beauty clings
In common forms, and find the soul
Of unregarded things!"

And yet, it is not in "common forms," and "unregarded things," that he touches his most consummate heights of song. For the larger, more wondrous and dim, pulses of life beat through his imagination like the lift and fall of the sea.

"That in my veins forever must abide
The urge and fluctuation of the tide," ["Ave" ll. 49-50]

This sums up the sentiment for nature, the sympathy with the outer world and passion for its perfection of loveliness, which makes Mr. Roberts akin to Keats and the Greeks; a sentiment that reveals itself in such minute an[d] human expression as in the two lyrics beginning

"Oh, purple hang the pods
On the green locust tree!" [Oh, Purple Hang the Pods!" ll. 1-2]

and

"The valley of the winding water
Wears the same light it wore of old." ["The Valley of the
Winding Water" ll. 1-2]

And then this sentiment for the beauty of the world is touched with pathos, with an unstrained ancient childlike pathos, in the "Epitaph for a Sailor Buried Ashore," perhaps its author's finest and most appealing brief lyric.

"He who but yesterday would roam
Careless as clouds and currents range,
In homeless wandering most at home,
Inhabiter of change;

"Who wooed the west to win the east,
And names the stars of north and south,
And felt the zest of Freedom's feast
Familiar in his mouth;

"Who found a faith in stranger-speech,
And fellowship in foreign hands,
And had within his eager reach
The relish of all lands,—

"How circumscribed a plot of earth
Keeps now his restless footsteps still,
Whose wish was wide as ocean's girth,
Whose will the water's will!"

It is in a still higher flight, however, a still more ambitious sphere of poetry, that we shall find our author at his best. Matthew Arnold has said [in "Maurice de Guérin"] that poetry "interprets in two ways; it interprets by expressing with magical felicity the physiognomy and movement of the outward world, and it interprets by expressing, with inspired conviction, the ideas and laws of the inward world of man's moral and spiritual nature." In a few of his poems, in the sonnet I have quoted above, and in one or two lyrics lately published in the magazines, Mr. Roberts shows, as it seems to me, "the faculty of both kinds of interpretation, the naturalistic and the moral" [Arnold, "Maurice de Guérin"]. In the opening of a lyric called "Afoot,"

"Comes the lure of green things growing,
Comes the call of waters flowing—
    And the wayfarer desire
Moves and wakes and would be going.

"Hark the migrant hosts of June
Marching nearer noon by noon!
    Hark the gossip of the grasses
Bivouacked beneath the moon!"

and in the closing of another lyric, a prayer to Nature, entitled "Kinship,"

> "Tell me how some sightless impulse,
> Working out a hidden plan,
> God for kin and clay for fellow
> Wakes to find itself a man[.]
>
> "Tell me how the life of mortal,
> Wavering from breath to breath,
> Like a web of scarlet pattern
> Hurtles from the loom of death.
>
> "How the caged bright bird, desire,
> Which the hands of God deliver,
> Beats aloft to drop unheeded
> At the confines of forever;
>
> "Faints unheeded for a season,
> Then outwings the furthest star
> To the wisdom and the stillness
> Where thy consummations are."

In passages like these poetry is at its best; it is doing for us what nothing else can; it is interpreting for us the beauty of the outward world and the inward mysterious craving of the human mind. Poetry, the poetic quality in all art, has in it something of the hushed wonder of a child in the face of the unknown; it is the rapt, not quite coherent, exclamation of the spirit, awaking to a consciousness of itself, allured at once by the outward passion for beauty, and teased by the inward curiosity for knowledge. To translate the cryptogram of Nature, that strange traditional record in an unknown tongue, whose cypher has not come down to us, is the joyful self-rewarded labor of the poet; then to this translation so magically divined, to add the comment of his own meditation. For poetry is to be a commentary on nature as well as a criticism of life. It is no scant praise, then, and yet I think it is not unjust, to say that Mr. Roberts in the work he has so far done has shown power in both these directions, both as a loving prophet of Nature and as a critic of the human aspiration. It is just so, by devotion to both these aims, that he will come to earn a secure place in English poetry.

I have said that Mr. Roberts had best be considered in connection with his national surroundings. There is in Canada a small body of men, the more earnest perhaps for their very isolation from the centers of thought and civilization, who are keeping alive a very real and pure worship of Nature. The *ennui* of a closing age has not sapped their enthusiasm; the discouraging triumph of a corrupt plutocracy has not yet touched their country; and while they are cut off from the mental activity which underlies the scientific and socialistic and philosophic speculation of London, they are also saved from the deadly blight of New York, that center of American letters, that gangrene of politics on the body of democracy. With their Loyalist traditions, their romantic history, their untold resource, their beautiful land, their vigorous climate, their future all to make, their days of immeasurable leisure, it is little wonder their songs should have all the genuine assurance of youth, the freshness of the fields. And with these conditions, it is a matter of course, too, that their poetry should deal chiefly with Nature and the interpretation of her signs.

The names of Mr. Archibald Lampman and Mr. Duncan Campbell Scott, along with Mr. Roberts's, have attracted our attention from time to time, and all three will be found, I think, not only devoted but imaginative interpreters of the beautiful outward world, not unworthy children of Keats and Emerson and Wordsworth. Upon its sensuous side their interpretation is near to that of Keats; upon its spiritual side it is near to the disinterested idealism of Emerson. And in the small but choice and significant body of verse which this school of young writers has given us, nothing will be found, I think, more perfect than the two lyrics I have quoted from above. Indeed, it is only in poets of the first order that we will find the haunting quality of the couplet,

"Hark the migrant hosts of June
Marching nearer noon by noon,'

or the terse penetration of the stanza,

"Tell me how some sightless impulse,
Working out a hidden plan,
God for kin and clay for fellow,
Wakes to find itself a man."

In these two poems the note which the Canadian cult is sounding so sincerely, if not very forcefully as yet, reaches its clearest utterance, the note of a worship of Nature from which modern knowledge has cast out fear, the note of a religion that was on the earth before Paganism had a name. To keep this note unstrained and pure will not be easy; to make it distinctly audible, not to say dominant, in English letters even for a season, would be a task for Byron's force or Browning's unquenchable vigor; and this is the task set my friends by their love of the outward world, by their bent for blithe seriousness; yet there are influences at work in their aid, so that in the end their devotion will not be altogether fruitless or unavailing. "He that believeth shall not make haste."

The Chap-Book 2:4 (January 1, 1895): 163-71.

This is the fifth article in a series that Carman wrote for this journal. Previous articles are on Gertrude Hall, William Sharp, Gilbert Parker, and Louise Imogen Guiney.

A Decade of Canadian Poetry

by Duncan Campbell Scott

Modern Canadian poetry may be said to have begun with the publication, in 1880, of *Orion*, by Charles G.D. Roberts. It struck the original note that had been absent, or present only fitfully, in the work of the poets that had preceded him. It connected the poetry of Canada with all that is excellent in English poetry the world over. It maintained the traditions of form and diction that must be respected if poetry is to continue as the art through which the utmost aspiration of the human spirit is to be expressed.

Looking back over the years that went before the publication of *Orion*, there is only one name that represents the same spirit, Charles Heavysege.

With this exception there is scarcely any work of the elder period that is remarkable for original power. But in the main, judged by the highest standards, this early Canadian poetry is by no means contemptible or unworthy of attention.

It is not worse in kind nor less in quantity than the mass of American verse produced at the same time under like conditions.

Anyone who at that period had been used to read Canadian poetry and lament its lack of power must have recognized in the work of Mr. Roberts a new and potent force; the academic imagery, the forced cadence, the lack of invention had disappeared. Almost for the first time a Canadian reader whose ear was attuned to the music of Tennyson, Keats and Arnold might, in quoting one of his own poets, do so with the feeling that here at last was verse flowing with the stream of general poetical literature. Six years later Mr. Roberts published *In Divers Tones*, and at that time, so far as books of verse are concerned, he was the sole representative of the now existing school of Canadian poetry.

It was during the next year that the poems of George Frederick Cameron were collected. They proved the great loss that Canadian letters sustained by the untimely death of this brilliant man.

One year later, in 1888, Archibald Lampman joined Mr. Roberts with *Among the Millet*; Frederick George Scott with *The Soul's Quest*, and in 1889 William Wilfred Campbell with *Lake Lyrics*. Previous to the year 1890 there appear to be no other books of importance whose authors have contributed to the poetry of the last ten years.

The term, School of Canadian Poetry, might be accepted with hesitation and some diffidence had not various competent critics adopted it uniformly. As applied to the group of writers usually mentioned under the appellation it may be too pretentious. It is valuable in that it conveys the idea of nationality, and if the Canadian people cannot thank its poets for immortal verse it may thank them for having forced the recognition of a growing national literature separate from that of the American Republic.

The decade of 1890 was in its second year before Mr. Roberts added another to the books I have mentioned. "Ave, an Ode for the Centenary of the Birth of Shelley," was published in 1892 and was included in *Songs of the Common Day*, issued during the following year. The latter book included also a series of sonnets dealing "with the aspects of common outdoor life." They exhibit Mr. Roberts in one of his happiest moods and they show the kinship that exists between the most prominent of this group of writers.

The remainder of *Songs of the Common Day* was occupied by lyrics and ballads, that repeated with a firm and unfailing touch the accent to which the earlier volumes had accustomed his readers. There was but one reminiscence in "Marsyas" of that earlier, classical manner that has unfortunately in succeeding books quite disappeared.

In 1891 Mr. J.F. Herbin, of Wolfeville, made his appearance with a small group of poems, and in 1893 and 1899 added *The Marshlands* and *The Trail of the Tide* to this first venture.

Mrs. J.W.F. Harrison, under the pen-name of "Seranus," had been a frequent contributor to periodical literature, and in the year 1891 she published *Pine, Rose and Fleur de lis*, a collection of old world forms, for the most part, with a Canadian and French-Canadian atmosphere, the result being happily suggested by the title. The book contains a tribute to Isabella Valancy Crawford, that fine genius who by her fiery temperament and her natural gift of expression must be counted the most richly endowed of our native poets.

While mentioning Mrs. Harrison's deft verse the performances of her sister-poets comes to mind. Miss Pauline Johnson and Miss Ethelwyn Wetherald published their volumes in the same year, 1895. Their verses occasionally published in the magazines had prepared the public for the very great poetic pleasure that these books gave. Miss Johnson's virile touch and strong imagination may be contrasted with the delicacy and shyness of Miss Wetherald's genius.

Mrs. Jean Blewett, whose verse has that warm human touch that has given infinite pleasure to her readers, added to their delight by collecting her scattered poems in 1897 under the apt title of *Heart Songs*.

Much of the charm of the book entitled *Northland Lyrics*, breathes from Mrs. Elizabeth Roberts MacDonald's share in it. Her lyrics are equal in power with those of her brothers, Theodore Roberts and W. Carman Roberts. The three have joined powers to produce what is, even considering its source, a noteworthy book. Miss Machar, whose excellent verse has been admired by a generation of readers, also collected her scattered poems in a volume called *Lays of the True North*.

By its lamentable finality the complete edition of the poems of Archibald Lampman is the most important addition to our poetic literature in the last decade. I do not feel called upon to state his rank with his contemporaries or to attempt a forecast of what the future has in store for his present fame. He was himself careless as to the one and unthinking as to the other. As regards everything worldly connected with his art, he had a perfect innocence; his one great concern was to produce his best.

The memorial edition of his poems was made up with the most catholic spirt. Consulting my own taste and with an eye to a final judgment, I might have omitted a few things that seem to me not to add to its value. But the most of those were included in books that had already seen the light, and I felt that they might be missed by many who had an equal right with myself to be pleased with poetry.

The narrative poem, "The Story of an Affinity," while weak in construction and lacking the invention of incident that is the life of such work, has many fine qualities, and is set in a framework of such beauty that it stands against any adverse criticism.

The Drama ["David and Abigail"], or Poem in Dialogue, contains much of his finest blank verse; the characters are clearly differentiated, and the whole treatment is cogent and sincere. His sonnets are, of course, everywhere glorious, and hardly another poet since Wordsworth can show so many of the highest quality, or a whole series of such varied interest.

I trust the collected poems dispelled the illusion that had arisen, that he was a poet occupied altogether with descriptions of nature. Nature in his interest came very near to man, but did not occupy the foremost place.

In his work, however, the use made of natural phenomena is very large, either where the matter is treated in a descriptive way, purely, or where it comes in by way of illustration to the *human* nature.

But this has been largely the practice of poets from all time and will continue so to be. A great proportion of the poetry that holds a very lofty place in the estimation of the world depends for its effect upon the happy blending of images and similes drawn from external nature with the thought-substance or emotion of the poem.

There are but few of Lampman's poems that do not lead from nature by a very short path to human life. The first impulse of his genius was the interpretation of nature, no doubt, but the desire to deal with human emotion, with the springs of human action, with the great hopes and desires of the human soul, was implicit in his mind. From the earliest of his writings to the latest this secondary quality demands attention, will be heard, keeps gaining strength and importance.

A year or two before he died he had begun to observe a more just balance between the divisions of his genius. In such grave, noble and suggestive poems, as "The City of the End of Things," "The Land of Pallas," "The Largest Life," and very many others that I might mention we possess his natural accent not less than in such pieces of realism as "Heat," or "Among the Millet."

There are several attributes in which his genius resembled that of Keats, and no one of them is more striking than the power of growth and development which may be determined from a study of his poems. That other attribute, a generous nobleness of soul, and its various confederate qualities, he shared in degree with his more gifted forerunner. Where a discerning reader finds the greatest cause to lament the broken work of Keats is in his letters. There may be seen vestiges of the deep mentality upon which the poems were based. Lampman left no such record, but another in the hearts of his friends. There it exists. To the mind of one of them, at least, it is clear that the power for growth and the solid philosophy which possessed his mind would together have produced a finer, more spiritual poetry, a poetry giving more of comfort and more of insight into life than any he has left.

While closing the last paragraph the thought of another, who shall no more draw upon his genuine gift for our profit, springs to mind. Dr. Theodore Rand, who for years had been associated with all that was purest in Canadian poetry, died in 1900.

During his last years he gave much of his leisure to the compilation of an exhaustive anthology of Canadian poems which was published in 1900 under the title, *A Treasury of Canadian Verse*.

Another distinct loss to letters was that occasioned by the death of Sir James D. Edgar, whose last work was published in 1893, *This Canada of Ours*.

Mr. E.B. Brownlow's scholarly verse may be found in the volume published posthumously in 1896, entitled *Orpheus*.

But I must complete the record of Mr. Charles G.D. Roberts' achievement during the decade by mentioning that delightful book which holds between its covers so much of Canada as to be called *The Book of the Native*. It was published in 1896. *New York Nocturnes* followed two years later, a collection of striking *genre* pieces, having for motive, chiefly, the turbulent life of the great city.

The whole of Mr. Bliss Carman's production in book form falls within the period with which I am dealing. *Low Tide on Grand Pré* appeared in 1893; two years passed and *Behind the Arras* was published; in 1897 came *Ballads of Lost Haven*; in 1898 *By the Aurelian Wall*; and *A Winter Journey* in 1900 [Scott is thinking of *A Winter Holiday*, which was published in 1889]. With the help of a kindred spirit he produced three books that are unique in their way and that have received much attention from a public that cares for a definite attitude. The *Songs from Vagabondia* were closed just the other day by the issue of the third and last volume, for Richard Hovey is lost forever to his companion and fellow-craftsman, and to us who admired his genial power. Each separate volume of Mr. Carman's has a distinctive tone. *Low Tide on Grand Pré* is given over to the spirit of unrest, to the longing that looks "before and after and pines for what is not"; *Behind the Arras* is taken up with allegories of human fate; *Ballads of Lost Haven* with the concern of the sea, its mystery and the mystery of those who traffic upon it; *By the Aurelian Wall* is a book of Elegies; *A Winter's Journey* [sic] contains tropical pictures, and recollections of the northland from the equator. Each of these books, so diverse in content, is permeated with the charm of Mr. Carman's manner, a manner that came in with him and that remains inimitable.

Mr. William Wilfred Campbell's first book belongs to the earlier decade, but *The Dread Voyage*, which was issued in the year 1893, better displays the essentially dramatic quality of his gift and the rare instinct that he possesses for a sympathetic interpretation of nature. None of our poets have so frequently grappled with the greatest problems of life and destiny and the humanism of his poems is their most striking quality. After *The Dread Voyage* came a book of tragedies in 1895; one, "Mordred," upon the Arthurian legend, and the other, "Hildebrand," dealing with the life of Pope Gregory VII, his character and his aims. After this book, in 1899, appeared a collection of Mr. Campbell's poems under the aegis of Houghton, Mifflin & Co., bearing the title of the initial poem "Beyond the Hills of Dream." The selection was happily made; it includes such notable work as "Lazarus" from *Lake Lyrics* and "The Mother," "Pan the Fallen," "An August Reverie," from *The Dread Voyage*. It comprises newer pieces, some of the strongest of which appeared first between covers in this volume. I refer to the powerful poems, "Peniel," "The Vengeance of Saki," and "Phaethon," and those others, less forceful but not less important, the elegy, "The Bereavement of the Fields [sic]," and that charming idyl, "The Wayfarer." The book contains also several stirring contributions to national poetry under the titles "England," "The World-Mother" and "The Lazarus of Empire."

In the natural selection of strenuous subjects Mr. Campbell has a companion in the Rev. Frederick George Scott. In the three books he has given to the public, *My Lattice* in 1894, *The Unnamed Lake* in 1897, and *Poems Old and New* in 1899 [actually 1900], the greater space is occupied by poems that deal with stormy motives, such as "Thor," "Samson," "The Frenzy of Prometheus." Such subjects are full of opportunity for vigorous writing and are dealt with by Mr. Scott in a direct and forcible style.

The only Canadian poet who can be said to stand in a class by himself is Dr. W.H. Drummond. Long before *The Habitant* made its appearance in 1897 his name was a household word in Canada and the humours of the "Wreck of the Jule Leplante" [sic] were known even where his name had not penetrated. Popular clamour led to the collection of the poems that had appeared in the newspapers from time to time. The book had an instantaneous success. It was purchased as no other book of verse published on this continent has been, and its success was deserved. The quaint dialect in which it is written had something to do with *The Habitant*'s good fortune, but it was the least potent factor in the case. It is true the dialect throws about the book a native and essential atmosphere, but that constituent is so mingled with deep humour and fine pathos that the vehicle and the matter expressed cannot be divided. The dialect we may liken to *etoffe du pays*, the substance and spirit of the poems to the flesh and soul of Jacques Bonnehomme. The result of this union is, that we have reproduced, in variety, a most lovable individuality, whose heart is easily moved, whose humour is contagious because it is so natural, and whose pathos is piercing from the same cause. *Phil-o-rum's Canoe* and *Madeline Vercheres* were issued in 1898 and repeated the triumphs of the earlier volume.

Merely as a matter of record I may here interject that in 1895 [sic] I published *The Magic House [actually 1893]* and in 1898 *Labor and the Angel*.

Mr. Francis Sherman commands attention by his first book *Matins* issued in 1896 and by several privately-printed booklets. The most remarkable of the latter is that entitled "In Memorabilia Mortis," a series of sonnets in memory of William Morris whose work is re-called in more than a superficial way in reading that of Mr. Sherman. The latter's work unrolls itself in a tapestry glowing with subdued but deep colours and shrouded in an atmosphere of romance.

Another book that I recall with an impression that it has not had the attention it deserves, is Mr. John Henry Brown's *Poems Lyrical and Dramatic*, which was issued in 1892. The sonnets contained in this volume are of excellent workmanship, and throughout the book gives the impression of high ideals and deep thought.

Another poet who has shown great progress during the last few years is Mr. John Stuart Thomson. His first volume was *Estabelle* issued in 1897, his second, *A Day's Song*, in 1900. In reviewing this last book, in these columns, a few months ago I took occasion to point out its power. It appeals to the highest standards of technique and has a fine restraint. Mr. Thomson possesses a manner that is somewhat rare; a manner that combines native strength with classical unity of purpose and expression.

Mr. Arthur J. Stringer has lyrical power of a very exceptional quality. His style is concise and aphoristic. He fills his verses with striking suggestions and situations. His three books, *Watchers of Twilight*, *Pauline*, and *Epigrams*, followed each other at intervals of a year, the first being issued in 1894.

I recall also with pleasure Mr. Bernard McEvoy's volume, *Away from Newspaperdom*, which appeared in 1897 and made available the poems which from time to time he had contributed to various periodicals and journals. They have an idyllic touch and a wide range of human interest.

It was within the decade just closed that Rev. A.J. Lockhart issued *Beside the Narraguagus*, which contains several ballads of excellent quality.

Mr. Gilbert Parker, whose verse is infrequent, produced in 1894 *A Lover's Diary*, in sonnet-sequence, a well-developed series of much psychical interest.

Dr. Thomas O'Hagan also added to the general fund his two books, *In Dreamland* and *Songs of the Settlement*.

Altogether about fifty books of verse have been published within the last decade. The record is remarkable when the difficulties that beset the author who offers matter for which there must always be a limited sale, are understood. It is difficult to appraise the value of this verse production, but it has surely not been without some result.

To glance at the effect beyond our boundaries, it may be ventured that a slight impression has been produced in England by the foremost of the poets I have mentioned. No encouragement has been given to any Canadian poet in that country either in a demand for editions of his poems, or in any extensive acceptances for periodical publication. In the main, our verse remains a matter of very little moment to the English public.

The United States, with whom we have mental affinities, has welcomed the work of Canadians, given it space and treated it seriously. The standing of Canadian literary men at home has depended largely upon the commendation of this support. Without that there would be less distinction or discrimination. Mr. William Dean Howells made the success of Lampman's first book. His genial criticism forced the recognition of that writer upon his own countrymen. Mr. Edmund Clarence Stedman showed the breadth of his view by including in the *Victorian Anthology* a selection of Canadian verse. This generous act did much to gain acknowledgment for our poets as worthy to rank in a final summing up of the work of the era.

When helped by foreign opinions our people have been quick in their interest and support, and, considering the conditions, it may be hazarded that appreciation has kept pace with performance.

So far as I am aware, there has been no single piece of verse that has spoken with so sure an accent as to become current among the Canadian people. Amid all this multitude of poems there has not been one that has entered deeply into very many hearts and become an epitome of individual longing or national hope. Using popular in one of its least hackneyed meanings, we must confess that there is no Canadian poetry that is popular with the Canadian people. This statement at first will wear a condemnatory face. If our poets cannot win the people to sing with them, of what use is the song?

The question has been asked and must be satisfied. Such poetry as we nearly all demand, poetry that will stir the heart, poetry that will enthral, poetry that will lead and support great deeds is not written under the conditions that now obtain. The poet is the bondman of his time, and must serve, moulding bricks without straw, as the demand is made.

Our time, if not out of joint, is at least thewless. It is the uncertain aim, the lack of any national solidarity that acts and reacts upon everything thought and done.

The uses of such poetry as we have are, however, sufficiently evident. In the first place it stands for progress; in the second it begins to form the basis of tradition. Advance is essential in art; and tradition is most valuable. At present it is wise to judge this poetry in the mass, and not by particular examples. So judged it gathers into a sphere of very considerable importance. It is inspired by wholesome ideals and filled with the genuine spirit of nature; it is an advance upon pre-Confederation poetry, and it forms a standard and reference for future Canadian writers.

The Canadian Magazine 17 (June 1901)

Poetry and Progress

Presidential Address delivered before the Royal Society of Canada, May 17, 1922

by Duncan Campbell Scott

I have the honour to deliver this evening the forty-first presidential address of the Royal Society of Canada. It is the custom of our Society that the presidency shall devolve in turn upon each of our Sections, and the Section Literature last year claimed the privilege of nominating the president of the Society.

I have thought to speak on this occasion of ideals and progress; first, and briefly, on the ideals of the Society,—those who formed it and gave it body and constitution, and then, in a more discursive fashion, about ideals in poetry and the literary life, and their relation to progress. There is, I claim, something unique in the constitution of a society that comprises Literature and Science, that makes room for the Mathematician and the Chemist, the Historian and the Biologist, the Poet and the Astronomer. Every intellectual type can be accommodated under the cloak of our charter, and we have survived forty-one years of varied activity with a degree of harmony and a persistence of effort towards the end and purpose of our creation that is worthy of comment. We are unique also in this, that two languages have equal recognition and *authority* in our literature sections, and that the premier place is occupied by the first civilized language heard by the natives of this country, which is ever the pioneer language of ideals in freedom and beauty and in the realm of clear logic, criticism and daring speculation. It here represents not a division of race, but a union of nationality, and joins the company of intellectuals by the dual interests of the two great sections of our people. We find our scientific sections welcoming essays in the French language and our literary sections interchanging papers and holding joint sessions on folk-lore and history. The ideal which possessed the founder of this Society and its charter members was undoubtedly that such an organism could live and flourish, that it could become a useful institution in Canadian life. We have progressively proved that, we prove it tonight, and we shall, I am confident, continue our demonstration in the future. Is it too fanciful to think or say that the element of cohesion which made this possible is idealism, or that gift of ideality which all workers who use Mind as an instrument possess in varying degree? The mental process by which a poet develops the germ of his poem and perfects it is analogous to the process by which a mathematician develops his problem from vagueness to a complete demonstration, or to the mental process whereby the shadow of truth apprehended by the biologist becomes proven fact. The scientist and mathematician may proceed in diverse ways to give scope to the creative imagination, and their methods are inherent in their problems. They proceed by experiment and by the logical faculty to a point of rest, of completion. The poet is unsatisfied until his idea is cleared of ambiguity and becomes embodied in a perfect form. The art of the poet is to clothe his idea with beauty and to state it in terms of loveliness, but the art of fine writing—style—need not be absent from the record of scientific achievement: it is, in fact, often present in marked degree. I doubt whether the satisfaction of the poet in finishing his work and perfecting it is essentially different or greater than the satisfaction of the scientist who rounds out his experiment and proves his theory. Such delights cannot be weighed or measured, but they are real and are enjoyed in common by all workers who seek perfection. I now boldly make the statement, which I at first put hesitatingly, in the form of a question, that it is ideality that holds our Society together, and that it was founded truly in the imagination of those who thought that such an institution could flourish in our national life.

During the past forty years many distinguished men have joined in this Fellowship—some have passed from this to greater honours, and others have passed away, but our methods of election and the keenness which our Fellows show in choosing their future colleagues ensure a steady stream of vigorous thought.

The subjects comprised in Section II, to which I have the honour to belong, are certainly varied,—English Literature, History, Archaeology, Sociology, Political Economy and allied subjects; and some of the allied subjects are most important, such as Philosophy and Psychology. While we have this wealth of subject matter, the scientific sections have an advantage over us in that they have greater solidarity of aim, that their groups have clearly-defined objects of study and investigation, and their results are more tangible. We must envy the scientists the excitement of the intellectual world in which they live. Consider for a moment the changes in scientific theory, method, and outlook since the charter members of this Society met together in 1882. It would not become me to endeavour to mention even the most important, but the realm of science appears to an outsider to be a wonderland. By comparison, literature seems to be divorced from life, and we would need to point to some book that had altered definitely the course of the world's thought to match some of the discoveries of Science which have changed our conceptions of the nature of life and of the universe. Perhaps, in making this remark, I am confusing for a moment the function of pure literature with the functions of Science. Literature in its purest form is vowed to the service of the imagination; its ethical powers are secondary, though important; and it cannot be forced to prove its utility. Literature engaged with the creation of beauty is ageless. The biological notions of Elizabeth's day are merely objects of curiosity, but Marlowe, Webster and Shakespeare are living forces. Sir Thomas Browne's medical knowledge is useless, but his *Urn Burial* is a wonder and a delight. Created, beauty persists; it has the eternal element in its composition, and seems to tell us more of the secret of the universe than philosophy or logic. But Letters will always envy Science its busyness with material things, and its glowing results which have rendered possible many of the imaginative excursions which poetry, for example, has made into the unknown.

It would be difficult, nay, impossible, to change radically

the methods of pure literature working in the stuff of the imagination. New ideas can be absorbed, new analogies can be drawn, new imagery can be invented, but the age-old methods of artistic expression will never be superseded. Apart from pure literature, or Belles Lettres, those subjects allotted to our section which are capable of scientific treatment, for instance, History, show a remarkable development. The former story-telling function of History and the endless reweaving of that tissue of tradition which surrounded and obscured the life of a people has given place to a higher conception of the duty of the Historian and the obligation to accept no statement without the support of documentary evidence. The exploration and study of archives and the collation of original contemporaneous documents are now held to be essential, and the partisan historian fortified with bigotry and blind to all evidence uncongenial to his preconceptions is an extinct being. International effort and co-operation have taken the place of jealous sectionalism and the desire to unfold the truth has displaced the craze to prove a theory. The new Science of History has its material in archives and collections of original documents, and one must here refer to the growth of our own Dominion collections under the guidance of an Archivist who is one of us, and who is aided by other distinguished Fellows of the Society. It should be remarked that one of the objects set forth by our charter was to assist in the collection of archives and to aid in the formation of a National Museum of Ethnology, Archaeology and Natural History. Let us not weaken for a moment in the discharge of this obligation. The Archives and the Museum exist largely owing to the influence of our Society, exerted constantly with great pressure, and, in times of necessity, with grave insistence. The Museum needs we consider highly important, and, as you are all aware, we intend to assist the Government to come to wise conclusions in these matters, and to keep alive and vigorous all projects that aim at conserving and developing our intellectual resources.

We talk too often and too lengthily about Canadian poetry and Canadian literature as if it was, or ought to be, a special and peculiar brand, but it is simply poetry, or not poetry; literature or not literature; it must be judged by established standards, and cannot escape criticism by special pleading. A critic may accompany his blame or praise by describing the difficulties of the Canadian literary life, but that cannot be allowed to prejudice our claim to be members of the general guild. We must insist upon it. If there be criticism by our countrymen, all that we ask is that it should be informed and able criticism, and that it too should be judged by universal standards. Future critics will recognize the difficulties which oppress all artistic effort in new countries, as do the best of contemporary critics. As Matthew Arnold wrote, in countries and times of splendid poetical achievement: "The poet lived in a current of ideas in the highest degree animating and nourishing to the creative power; society was, in the fullest measure, permeated by fresh thought, intelligent and alive; and this state of things is the true basis for the creative power's exercise." When we seek in our contemporary society for the full permeation of fresh thought, intelligent and alive, we do not find it; we do not find it in America or elsewhere, and if the premise is sound we can say, therefore, we do not find an ample and glorious stream of creative power. It is casual, intermittent, fragmentary, because society is in like state. But we may be thankful that in our country there has been and is now a body of thought, intelligent and alive, that gives tangible support to the artist and that has assisted him in his creative work.

You will note that I am taking high ground, in fact, the highest, in dealing with literature and the highest form of literature—poetry. I am well aware that there is a great increase in our written word during the last twenty-five years, and our writers are now competently meeting the varied demand of readers whose taste does not require anything too finely wrought nor too greatly imagined. I heard one of our successful writers declare the other day that what we should do now is to get the "stuff" down somehow or other and never to mind how it was done so long as it was done. Well, that would give us all the rewards of haste, but would hardly assist in building a literature. There must ever be this contrast between the worker for instant results and the worker who toils for the last perfection. One class is not without honour, the other is precious beyond valuation. As time passes we shall find in this country, no doubt, a growing corpus of stimulating thought that will still more tend to the nourishing and support of creative genius.

While we do not wish to part Canadian Literature from the main body of Literature written in English, we may lay claim to the possession of something unique in the Canadian literary life,—that may be distinguishable to even casual perception by a peculiar blend of courage and discouragement. In truth, there is such lack of the concentration that makes for the drama of literary life that it is almost non-existent. But, nevertheless, our resident authors, those who have not attempted to escape from this environment, have done and are doing important work in imaginative literature. I have thought to touch briefly upon two such lives typical of the struggle for self-expression in a new country.

If there had existed in our Society a rule that is observed in the French Academy, it would have been my duty to have pronounced, upon taking my chair, a eulogy on Archibald Lampman, who had died the year previous to my election, and to whose chair I succeeded. I would hardly have been as competent then to speak of him and his work as I am now, for both were too near to me then, and now I have the advantage of added experience, and, after a lapse of twenty odd years, poetic values shift. But what is poetic truth does not change, and it is a high satisfaction to find that there was so much of poetic truth in the work of my friend, our colleague, truth that fortifies, and beauty that sweetens life. He felt the oppression of the dullness of the life about us more keenly than I did, for he had fewer channels of escape, and his responsibilities were heavier; he had little if any enjoyment in the task-round of every day, and however much we miss the sense of tedium in his best work, most assuredly it was with him present in the days of his week and the weeks of his year. He had real capacity for gaiety and for the width and atmosphere of a varied and complex life, not as an actor in it perhaps, but as a keen observer, and as a drifter upon its surface, one in whom the colour and movement of life would have created many beautiful and enchanting forms. But he was compelled to work without that stimulus, in a dull environment and the absence also of any feeling of nationality, a strong aid and incitement to a poet, no matter of how much we may talk nowadays about the danger of national feeling. This lack made sterile a broad tract of his mind; it was a discouragement that he could not know that he was interpreting the aspirations and ideals of a national life. We still feel that lack of national consciousness, but perhaps it is a trifle less evident now. His love of country was very strong and took form in his praise of nature, that unsoiled and untrammelled nature that we think of as Canada, and his work in this kind has a verity and vigour that is unmatched. He filled the rigid form of the sonnet with comments on the life of the fields and woods and waters that ring as true as the notes of birds. A single half-hundred of these sonnets of his may be placed in any poetic company and they will neither wilt nor tarnish. Towards the end of his life he chose by sympathy to write more imaginatively about stirrings in the mind and heart of man, and there is a deep and troubled note in these things that gave portent of a new development. His career was closed too soon, and we have but to cherish what is left and rejoice over it as a treasure of our literary inheritance.

It is twenty-three years since Lampman died, and the period is marked by the death of Marjorie Pickthall, which occurred during April of this year at Vancouver. Hers was a literary life of another and contrasted kind. She was of English parentage, born in England, but educated in Canada, and she was in training and sentiment a good Canadian.

If one were looking for evidence of progress in Canadian literature during the period just referred to, one positive item would be the difference in the reception of the first books published by these two authors. Until the generous review by William Dean Howells of Lampman's book had been published in *Harper's Magazine*, it was here considered, when any consideration whatever was given to the subject, a matter of local importance. But the warm-hearted welcome of Howells led to sudden recognition of the fact that the book was an acquisition to general literature, and was not merely parochial. After that incident, and others like it, we find that recognition of Miss Pickthall's first book took place at once, and from our independent judgment, as an important addition to poetical literature. Advance is clearly shown by this fact; for until we have faith in the power of our writers we can have no literature worth speaking about; our position in arts and letters will be secured when we find foreign critics accepting a clear lead from us. We accepted Miss Pickthall, and our opinion was confirmed very generally afterwards.

It is to be deeply regretted that her career is closed and that we shall not again hear, or overhear, that strain of melody, so firm, so sure, floating towards us, to use a phrase of Lampman's, "as if from the closing door of another world and another lovelier mood." "Overhear" is, I think, the right word, for there was a tone of privacy, of seclusion, in her most individual poems, not the seclusion of a cloister, but the seclusion of a walled garden with an outlook towards the sea and the mountains. Life was beyond the garden somewhere, and murmurously, rumours of it came between the walls and caused longing and disquiet. The voice could be heard mingling the real appearance of the garden with the imagined forms of life beyond it and with remembrances from dim legends and from the untarnished old romances of the world. Her work was built on a ground bass of folk melody, and wreathed about it were Greek phrases and glamours from the "Song of Songs." But composite of all these influences, it was yet original and reached the heart with a wistfulness of comfort. She had a feeling for our little brothers of the air and the woods that was sometimes classical, sometimes mediaeval. Fauns and hamadryads peopled her moods, and our familiar birds and flowers took on quaint forms like the conventional shapes and mellow colours of tapestries woven long ago. "Bind above your breaking heart the echo of a Song"—that was her cadence, the peculiar touch that gives a feeling of loneliness and then heals it, and if one might have said to her any words at parting, they would have been her own words—"Take, ere yet you say good-bye, the love of all the earth."

These two lives are typical of the struggle of those who attempt the literary life in Canada. Lampman existed in the Civil Service, and was paid as any other clerk for the official work he did. Neither his position nor his advances in that position were given in recognition of his literary gifts. From this bleak vantage ground he sent out his version of the beauty of the world. Miss Pickthall was more definitely in the stream of letters, and her contributions to the periodical press in prose and verse gave her an assured standing and due rewards.

There is no necessity here and now for an apology for poetry nor for a defence of anyone who in Sir Philip Sydney's words "showeth himself a passionate lover of that unspeakable and everlasting beauty to be seen by the eyes of the mind." I admire that ideal, set up by the Welsh saying for the perfect man, the man who could "build a boat and sail it, tame a horse and ride it, make an ode and set it to music." None of us could qualify for perfection under this hard and inclusive test. It covers, you will observe, mastery of several kinds,—mastery of craftsmanship, and fearless daring; mastery of a difficult and noble animal; and, finally, the crowning mastery of poetry and music. We find it true of all peoples that these two arts are the cap stones of their civilizations. We are as far as ever from an understanding of what poetry really is, although we are at one in giving it supremacy in the arts and we are as far as ever from a perfect definition of poetry. Perhaps the best, the only definition of poetry is a true poem, for poetry and the poetic is a quality or state of mind and cannot be described, it is apprehended by sensation, not comprehended by reason. This renders ineffectual all attempts to answer the question "What is poetry?", and makes futile the approved definitions.

These efforts to define what is undefinable inevitably tend to become creative attempts, approximate to poetic utterance, and endeavour to capture the fugitive spirit of poetry by luring it with a semblance of itself. But the question is answered perfectly by even the fragment of a true poem. We know instinctively and say, "This is poetry," and the need for definition ceases.

The finest criticism of poetry plays about this central quality like lightning about a lovely statue in a midnight garden. The beauty is flashed upon the eye and withdrawn. It is remembered in darkness and is verified by the merest flutter or flash of illumination, but the secret of the beauty is shrouded in mystery. I refer to such sayings as this of Coleridge: "It is the blending of passion with order that constitutes perfection" in poetry; that of Keats, "The excellence of every art is its intensity"; that of Rossetti, "Moderation is the highest law of poetry." There are numerous like apothegms written by poets and critics about the art of poetry that accomplish perfectly the necessary separation between the art and the spirit of the art, between the means and the effect. They are flashed upon the mystery and isolate it so that it may be apprehended by its aloofness and separation from things and appearances. We can apply Coleridge's words to any chosen passage of Keats, for example, the familiar "magic casements opening on the foam of perilous seas in faery lands forlorn." We acknowledge that the perfection of the passage lies in the romantic passion blended with the order that is the sense of balance and completion, but the poetic quality escapes, it is defined, by the effect of the passage and by that alone.

We quote the words that Shakespeare puts into Anthony's mouth—

> I am dying, Egypt, dying; only
> I here importune death awhile, until
> Of many thousand kisses the poor last
> I lay upon thy lips.

We recognize that the excellence of this passage comes from its intensity. And even such an outcry, poignant to the verge of agony, is not inconsistent with the saying of Rossetti;

for moderation is a question of scale. The high law of moderation is followed in such an utterance of Anthony's as competently as when Hamlet says simply "The rest is silence," because it is true in the scale of emotion.

Of a truth the ideals of our contemporary poets are not those of the masters of the past,—neither their ideals of matter, of manner, of content or of form. Tennyson's thought "of one far off divine event to which the whole creation moves" is not only inadequate to express what a poet of the present day feels about the destiny of man and about the universe; it fails in appeal, it is merely uninteresting to him; and no modern poet would say as Matthew Arnold said: "Weary of myself, and sick of asking what I am and what I ought to be." Tennyson and Arnold are comparatively recent leaders of thought and we are more akin to the Elizabethans with their spirit of quest than we are to Wordsworth and Arnold. In our ideals of technique we are farther removed from the eighteenth century, from Pope and Gray, than from Donne and Herrick and Vaughan. Our blank verse at its best shuns all reference to Milton and has escaped once again into the freedom of Shakespeare and the wilderness of natural accent. The best of the work shows it, and from the mouths of the poets themselves we sometimes gather their perception of kinship with masters whose influence was unfelt by the Victorians. I remember well an observation Rupert Brooke made to me one evening during his visit to Ottawa in July, 1913, as we strolled over the golf links. There was a heavy dew on the grass, I remember,—one could feel it in the air, and the sky was crowded full of stars; the night, and peculiarly the coolness of the dew-saturated air recalled some line of Matthew Arnold. "How far away that seems," Brooke said, "far away from what we are trying to do now,—John Donne seems much nearer to us." It is the intensity of Donne that fascinated Brooke. It was that intensity that he was endeavouring to reach in his poem "The Blue Room," or in the stillness of arrested time portrayed in "Afternoon Tea." The diffuseness in Wordsworth and Arnold was the quality that made them remote. Brooke was fated for other things than to pursue the cult of intensity. Now we think of him as the interpreter of certain emotional states that arose from the war, and we may select Wilfred Owen as the exponent of certain other sharply hostile states.

The contrast between these typical natures is the contrast between the traditional feeling for glory and the personal feeling of loss and defeat to be laid to the national debit. Brooke identifies himself with the magnificence of all the endeavour that has gone to create national pride; his offering is one of joy, all is lost in the knowledge that he continues the tradition of sacrifice for the national ideal. Wilfred Owen feels only the desperate personal loss, loss of the sensation of high living, the denial by the present of the right of youth to the future. The contrast is known when we place Brooke's sonnet "Blow Out Ye Bugle Over the Rich Dead," beside Owen's, "Apologia." The first glows with a sort of mediaeval ecstacy, the second throbs with immediate sincerity and ironic truth. It is the voice of a tortured human soul. There has been agony before in English poetry, but none like unto this agony. How far removed is it from echoes of the drums and trumpets of old time valour, how far away from such a classic as "The Burial of Sir John Moore"? Here is an accent new to English poetry. There is the old power of courage, the indomitable spirit of the forlorn hope, but the anaesthetic of glory is absent, and the pain of all this futile sacrifice based on human error and perversity is suffered by the bare nerve without mitigation.

Rupert Brooke's admiration of that bare technique, fitted to that strange and candescent intellect of Donne's was forgotten when he touched those incomparable sonnets of his. In them the intensity of feeling takes on a breath and movement which is an amalgam of many traditions in English poetry, traditions of the best with the informing sense of a new genius added, the genius of Rupert Brooke. In his case, as in the case of all careers prematurely closed, it is idle to speculate upon the future course of his genius. It may be said, however, that his prose criticism, his study of Webster and his letters show that his mind was philosophic and that his poetic faculty was firmly rooted in that subsoil and had no mere surface contact with life. Our faith that Keats would have developed had he lived, takes rise from our knowledge of the quality of his mind, as shown in his criticism and in his wonderful letters. We can say confidently that a poetic faculty based on such strong masculine foundation, with such breadth of sympathy, would have continued to produce poetry of the highest, informed with new beauty and with a constant reference to human life and aspirations. With due qualifications the same confidence may be felt in the potential power of Rupert Brooke. He had not Keats' exquisite gift, but he was even more a creature of his time, bathed in the current of youthful feeling that was freshening the life of those days, and he would have been able to lead that freshet of feeling into new and deep channels of expression. Close association for a week with so eager a mind served to create and enforce such opinions. He seemed, so far as his talk went, more interested in life than art, and there was a total absence of the kind of literary gossip that so often annoys. His loyalty to his friends and confrères was admirable, and he had greater pleasure in telling what they had done than in recounting his own achievements,—what their hopes were rather than his own. I remember his saying that he intended to write drama in the future and put himself to the supreme test in this form of art. One cannot think of his figure now except in the light of tragic events that were hidden then, when there was no shadow, only the eagerness of youth and the desire of life.

Wilfred Owen too, and others of his group, inherited that touch of intensity, but there was bitterness added and he had to bear the shock of actual war which Brooke did not experience, —the horrors of it and the futility. It is to be doubted whether such writers as Owen or Sorley could have assumed or continued a position in post war literature, whether they could have found subjects for the exercise of such mordant talents.

There was a tremendous activity of verse-writing during the war, and the hope was often expressed that there was to be a renaissance of poetry and our age was to be nobly expressed. But the war ceased; the multitude of war poets ceased to write;

the artificial stimulus had departed and they one and all found themselves without a subject. Whatever technique they had acquired for the especial purpose of creating horror or pity was unfitted for less violent matter. The ideals which they had passionately upheld received the cold shoulder of disillusionment. The millenium had not arrived, in very truth it seemed farther off than ever, and the source of special inspiration had dried up. But the elimination of these poets of the moment did not affect the main development of poetry. Those poets, who had been in the stream of tendency, and who were diverted by the violent flood of war feelings and impressions settled back upon the normal. They had not required subjects more stimulating than those ordinary problems or appearances of life and nature which are always present. Their technical acquirements were as adequate as ever and they took up the task of expression where it had been interrupted.

There are many mansions in the house of poetry; the art is most varied and adaptable; we must acknowledge its adequacy for all forms and purposes of expression,—from the lampoon, through the satire, through mere description and narrative, through the epic, to the higher forms of the lyric and the drama. Rhythm, being the very breath and blood of all art, here lends itself dispassionately and without revolt to the lowest drudgery as well as the highest inspiration. But when so often calling on the name of poetry, I am thinking of that element in the art which is essential, in which the power of growth resides, which is the winged and restless spirit keeping pace with knowledge and often beating into the void in advance of speculation; the spirit which Shakespeare called "the prophetic soul of the wide world dreaming on things to come." This spirit endeavours to interpret the world in new terms of beauty, to find unique symbols, images and analogies for the varied forms of life. It absorbs science and philosophy, and anticipates social progress in terms of ideality. It is rare, but it is ever present, for what is it but the flickering and pulsation of the force that created the world.

I remarked a moment ago upon the remoteness of that mood

of Matthew Arnold in which he expresses soul weariness and the need of self-dependence. Arnold advises the soul to learn this self-poise from nature pursuing her tasks, to live as the sea and the mountains live. But our modern mood does not seek self-dependence, having no knowledge of that lack, nor does it refer to the unconscious for comfort or example. It asks for deeper experience, for more intense feeling and for expression through action. Science has taught the modern that nature lives and breathes, and in looking at the mountains and the sea, he is moved to feelings based on growing knowledge, unutterable as yet in thought. The modern feels no sickness of soul which requires a panacea of quiescence; he is aware of imperfections and of vast physical and social problems, but life does not therefore interest him less but more. He has the will to live and persistence to grapple with the universal complexities. This becomes evident in the revolt against established forms and in the intellectual daring that forces received opinion before a new jurisdiction.

This is a critical age and has its peculiar tone of criticism. Compared with other times it more loudly and insistently questions and mocks at the past—the past exists merely "to be the snuff of younger spirits whose apprehensive senses all but new things disdain." Art that takes on new forms has more than ever a critical outlook, and the criticism seems to be based on irritation. The purpose of the effort is not so much, if at all, to create beauty, as to insult older ideas of beauty, to *épater le bourgeois*, to shock with unwholesome audacities, to insert a grain of sand into each individual oyster shell and set up an irritation, seemingly without any hope of ultimately producing pearls thereby, but with the mere malicious design of awakening protest, the more violent the better. I might continue my quotation of Shakespeare, and say of these ultra modern minds that their "Judgments are mere fathers of their garments, whose constancies expire before their fashions"; but no matter how long the present fashion lasts, it may be treated in retrospect as a moment of irony.

A virus has infected all the arts; the desire for rebellious, violent and discordant expression has invaded even the serene province of Music.

The extremists in this art invoke satire as their principal divinity. They set out to describe, for example, the feelings of the heir of a maiden aunt who has left him her pet dog instead of fifty thousand pounds. They write waltzes for the piano with the right-hand part in one key, and the left-hand part in another. Masses of orchestral sound move across each other careless of what happens in the passing.

Perhaps I might be pardoned a short digression on the subject of Music,—its true progress in the path of perfection; for Music is the art of perfection, and, as Walter Pater declared, all other arts strive towards the condition of Music. The rise and development of modern Music is a matter of barely five hundred years and parallels the growth of modern Science. The developments of both in the future cannot be limited. They may progress side by side,—Science expanding and solving the problems of the universe, and Music fulfilling the definition that Wagner made for it as "the innermost dream-image of the essential nature of the world." Wagner's music was once satirically called the "Music of the Future." It is now firmly and gloriously fixed in the past. But Music is truly the art of the future. Men will come to it more and more as the art which can express the complex emotions of life in terms of purest beauty. It is the art most fitted to give comfort and release to the spirit and to resolve scepticism as it resolves discords. Side by side with a tone of supersensualism that runs through modern Music we have intellectual developments and also a straining towards spiritual thoughts which restore the balance. It is gratifying to note that Britain is taking the place she once occupied as a leader in musical creation. The obstacle to the understanding of Music has not been the absence of natural correspondences in the mind. Music has universal appeal, but because of the fact that it must reach the understanding through the ear, it must be twice created, and the written stuff is dumb until awakened into vibrating life. The invention of mechanical means for the reproduction of Music and their gradual improvement has made

Music as accessible as the reproductions of fine paintings. The widespread use of these music machines proves the desire of the people to hear and to understand, and the effect upon the public taste will be appreciable. The style of amateur performances will be improved, and it may not be too much to claim for this wide distribution of beautiful and deeply felt music an influence on the creative side and a stimulation to eager youthful spirits to translate their emotions into sound. Music is the great nourisher of the imagination, and the prevalence of great music means the production of great verse. Over and against the poets who have been deaf to the stimulation of Music we can quote some of the greatest who have been sensitive to it,—Shakespeare, Milton, Keats, and I may quote the remark of Coleridge, made in 1833: "I could write as good verses as ever I did if I were perfectly free from vexations and were in the *ad libitum* hearing of fine music, which has a sensible effect in harmonizing my thoughts, and in animating and, as it were, lubricating my inventive faculties."

The leaders of what is called the "New Movement in Poetry" have some ground for argument, but make unconvincing uses of it. The most voluble centres of the New Movement are in the United States, and the subject is pursued with all the energy and conviction that we have learned to expect from the adoption of any cause to the south of us. We must willingly confess that Americans are an art-loving people, and that now they are immensely interested in all the arts. From the first they were hospitable to foreign production and absorbed all that was best in the work of other nationalities, and lately they have grown confident of their native artists and reward them with patronage and praise.

The protagonists of the Modern Movement in Poetry are most hospitable to the old poets; they are orthodox in their inclusions and throw a net wide enough to catch all the masters of the art from the earliest to the latest times. They approve of poets of our own day who use the established verse-forms as well as the writers of vers-libre and the innovators. Their quarrel, therefore, must be with the poetasters, with the slavish imitators, with the purveyors of conventional ideas and the innumerable composers of dead sonnets. But these people have always been among us and have always been intolerable to the children of light. The weariness they occasion is no new experience. They at once fastened themselves on the New Movement and welcomed vers-libre as the medium which would prove them poets. In proclaiming freedom as the war cry of the New Movement, the leaders admitted all the rebels against forms which they had never succeeded in mastering, and while they poured into vers-libre a vast amount of loose thinking and loose chatter, as if freedom were to include licence of all kinds, they were still unable to master the form or prevail in any way except to bring it into contempt. The avowed object of the Movement is "a heroic effort to get rid of obstacles that have hampered the poet and separated him from his audience," and "to make the modern manifestations of poetry less a matter of rules and formulae and more a thing of the spirit and of organic as against imposed rhythm." A praiseworthy ideal! But has the poet ever been separated from his audience? Can poetry be made more than it ever was, a thing of the spirit? Did Browning separate himself from his audience when he cast his poem "Home Thoughts from Abroad" into its irregular form? Can one create a poem of greater spirituality than Vaughan's "I Saw Eternity the Other Night"? To exorcise this senseless irritation against rhyme and form, those possessed should intone the phrases of that great iconoclast, Walt Whitman, written in the noble preface to the 1855 edition of *Leaves of Grass*. "The profit of rhyme is that it drops seeds of a sweeter and more luxuriant rhyme, and of uniformity that it conveys itself into its own roots in the ground out of sight. The rhyme and uniformity of perfect poems show the free growth of metrical laws, and bud from them as unerringly and loosely as lilacs and roses on a bush, and take shapes as compact as the shapes of chestnuts and oranges, and melons and pears, and shed the perfume impalpable to form."

All that I intend to inveigh against in these sentences is the cult that seeks to establish itself upon a false freedom in the realm of art. Sincerity, or, if you will, freedom, is the touchstone of poetry—of any and all art work in fact. Originality is the proof of genius, but all geniuses have imitated. Poetry is an endless chain of imitation, but genius comes dropping in, adding its own peculiar flavour in degree. Sainte Beuve has written it down,—"The end and object of every original writer is to express what nobody has yet expressed, to render what nobody else is able to render . . . ." This may be accepted as axiomatic, it governs production here and elsewhere, present and future, and any literary movement is doomed to failure if it attempts to pre-empt the conception that poetry should be original, should be freshened constantly by the inventions of new and audacious spirits.

The desire of creative minds everywhere is to express the age in terms of the age, and by intuition to flash light into the future. Revolt is essential to progress, not necessarily the revolt of violence, but always the revolt that questions the established past and puts it to the proof, that finds the old forms outworn and invents new forms for new matters.

It is the mission of new theories in the arts, and particularly of new theories that come to us illustrated by practice, to force us to re-examine the grounds of our preferences, and to retest our accepted dogmas. Sometimes the preferences are found to be prejudices and the dogmas hollow formulae. There is even a negative use in ugliness that throws into relief upon a dark and inchoate background the shining lines and melting curves of true beauty. The latest mission of revolt has been performed inadequately, but it has served to show us that our poetic utterance was becoming formalized. We require more rage of our poets. We should like them to put to the proof that saying of William Blake: "The tigers of wrath are wiser than the horses of instruction."

I may possibly have taken up too much time in referring to modern tendencies in poetry, which are only ephemeral, and in combating the claim, put forward with all gravity, to distinction that flows from a new discovery. Already many of these fads have faded or disappeared. The constancies of these bright spirits have expired before their fashions. They are already absorbed with a new fad. But let it pass,—modernity is not a fad, it is the feeling for actuality.

If I am ever to make good the title imposed on this address, I must soon do so, and trace a connection between Poetry and Progress, if there be any. Maybe we shall find that there is no connection, and that they are independent, perhaps hostile. It is certain that Poetry has no connection with material progress and with those advances which we think of as specialties of modern life—the utilization of electricity for example. Euripides living in his cave by the seashore, nourished and clothed in the frugalest and simplest fashion, has told us things about the human spirit and about our relation to the gods which are still piercingly true. Dante's imagination was brooding and intense within the mediaeval walls of Tuscany. Shakespeare, when he lodged in Silver Street with the Mountjoys, was discomfortably treated, judged by our standards, and yet he lives forever in the minds of men. It is useless to elaborate this trite assertion; if material progress, convenience, comfort, had any connection with poetry, with expression, our poets would be as much superior to the old poets as a nitrogen electric bulb is to a rush light. Poetry has commerce with feeling and emotion, and the delight of Nausicaa as she drove the mules in the high wain heaped with linen to the river shore, was not less than the joy which the modern girl feels in rushing her motor car along a stretch of tar-macadam. Nausicaa also was free of her family for a while and felt akin to the gull that turned on silver wing over the bay; felt the joy of control over the headstrong mules, and the clean limbed maidens who tossed the ball by the wine-dark sea.

The feeling of delight is the thing, not its cause, and if there be any progress in the art of poetry, it must be proved in the keenness with which we feel the expression of the emotion. But the emotion gives rise to correspondences. What were the trains of thought set up in the Greek hearers who listened to the recital of that little journey of Nausicaa to the swift running river with the family washing? We can imagine they were simple enough, and we can compare them with the collateral ideas set up by the description of a journey in a high-power car set forth in that profane poem on Heaven by one of the moderns. The power of poetry has here expanded to include a world unknown to Greek expression. Here is progress of a sort. The poetry of the aeroplane has yet to be written, but, when it comes, it will pass beyond the expressions of bird-flight in the older poets and will awaken images foreign to their states of feeling. Shakespeare wrote of "daffodils, that come before the swallow dares, and take the winds of March with beauty." The aeroplane has beauty and daring all its own, and the future poet may associate that daring with some transcendent flower to heighten its world-taking beauty. Here may be found a claim for progress in poetry, that it has proved adequate to its eternal task and gathers up the analogies and implications, the movement and colour of modern life—not as yet in any supreme way, but in a groping fashion. It is far-fetched to compare the work of Homer to that of a lively modern—an immortal to one of those who perish—but how many poets perished in the broad flood of Homer? Immortal! The idea becomes vague and relative when we think of the vestiges of great peoples, confused with the innumerable blown sand of deserts, or dissolved in the brine of oblivious oceans, lost and irretrievable. Art is immortal, not the work of its votaries, and the poets pass from hand to hand the torch of the spirit, now a mere sparkling of light, now flaming gloriously, ever deathless.

If this be one contact between Poetry and Progress there may be another in the spread of idealism, in the increase in the poetic outlook on life, which is, I think, apparent. The appeal of poetry has increased and the number of those seeking self-expression has increased. The technique of the art is understood by many and widely practised with varying success, but with an astonishing control of form. This may be regretted in some quarters. One of our distinguished poets was saying the other day that there are too many of us,—too many verse writers crowding one another to death. My own complaint, if I have any, is not that we are too many, but that we do not know enough. Our knowledge of ourselves and the world about us and of the spirit of the age, the true spring of all deep and noble and beautiful work, is inadequate.

There is evidence of Progress in the growing freedom in the commerce and exchange of ideas the world over. Poetic minds take fire from one another, and there never was a time when international influences were so strong in poetry as they are today. France and Italy have, from the time of Chaucer, exerted an influence on the literature of England. The influence is still evident, and to it is added that of the Norse countries, of Russia and of Central Europe. Oriental thought has touched English minds, and in one instance gave to an English poet the groundwork for an expression in terms of final beauty of the fatalistic view of life. Of late, mainly through the work of French savants, the innumerable treasures of Chinese and Japanese poetry have been disclosed and have led poets writing in English to envy them the delicate touch, light as "airy air," and to try to distill into our smaller verse forms that fugitive and breath-like beauty. English poetry has due influence on the Continent, and there is the constant inter-play of the truest internationalism, the internationalism of ideals and of the ever-changing, ever-advancing laws of the republic of beauty. National relations will be duly influenced by this free interchange of poetic ideals, and the ready accessibility of new and stimulating thought must eventually prevail in mutual understanding. We can resolutely claim for Poetry a vital connection with this Progress.

In these relationships between Poetry and Progress, Poetry is working in its natural medium as the servant of the imagination, not as the servant of Progress. The imagination has always been concerned with endeavours to harmonize life and to set up nobler conditions of living; to picture perfect social states and to commend them to the reason. The poet is the voice of the imagination, and the art in which he works, apart from the conveyed message, is an aid to the cause, for it is ever striving for perfection, so that the most fragile lyric is a factor in human progress as well as the most profound drama. The poets have felt their obligation to aid in this progress and many of them have expressed it. The "miseries of the world are misery and will not let them rest," and while it is only given to the few in every age to crystallize the immortal truths, all poets are engaged with the expression of truth. Working without conscious plan and merely repeating to themselves, as it were, what they have learnt of life from experience, or conveying the hints that intuition has whispered to them, they awaken in countless souls sympathetic vibrations of beauty and ideality: the hearer is charmed out of himself, his personality dissolves in the ocean of feeling, his spirit is consoled for sorrows which he cannot understand and fortified for trials which he cannot foretell. This influence is the reward of the poet and his beneficiaries have ever been generous in acknowledging their debt. The voices are legion, but let me choose from the multitude as a witness one who was not a dreamer, one who was a child of his age and that not a poetical age, one who loved the excitement of an aristocratic society, insolent with the feeling of class, dissolute and irresponsible, one whose genius exerted itself in a political life, soiled with corruption and intrigue but dealing with events of incomparable gravity. Charles James Fox said of poetry: "It is the great refreshment of the human mind" . . . "The greatest thing after all." To quote the words of his biographer, the Poets "consoled him for having missed everything upon which his heart was set; for the loss of power and fortune; for his all but permanent exclusion from the privilege of serving his country and the opportunity of benefiting his friends."

I should like to close this address upon that tone, upon the idea of the supremacy of poetry in life—not a supremacy of detachment, but a supremacy of animating influence—the very inner spirit of life. Fox felt it in his day, when the conditions in the world during and after the French Revolution were not very different from the confused and terrifying conditions we find around us now. He took refreshment in that stream of poetry, lingering by ancient sources of the stream, the crystal pools of Greece and Rome. The poetry of his day did not interest him as greatly as classical poetry, but it did interest him. The poetry of the 18th century was a poetry with the ideals of prose: compared with the Classics and the Elizabethans, it lacked poetic substance. The poetry of our day may not satisfy us, but we have, as Fox had, possession of the Classics and the Elizabethans, and we have, moreover, the poetry of a later day than his that is filled with some of the qualities that he cherished.

If the poetry of our generation is wayward and discomforting, full of experiment that seems to lead nowhither, bitter with the turbulence of an uncertain and ominous time, we may turn from it for refreshment to those earlier days when society appears to us to have been simpler, when there were seers who made clear the paths of life and adorned them with beauty.

From *The Circle of Affection and Other Pieces in Prose and Verse*. Toronto: McClelland and Stewart, 1947.

Criticism

The Poetry of Our Golden Age

By E.K. Brown

During the past decade there has been a revival of poetry and of interest in poetry without a parallel in the present century. The hard school of a lingering depression, a troubled international scene, a war which has strained everyone's energy to the last sinews, has been stimulating and purifying for poetry. It has also been stimulating and purifying, although inevitably to a less degree, for the people in general, whose ears are not so wholly closed to the words of the seer or the music of the craftsman as once they were. Every year has brought with it at least one volume excellent and original: 1935 E.J. Pratt's *The Titanic*; 1936 *New Provinces, Poems by Several Authors*; 1937 E.J. Pratt's *The Fable of the Goats*; 1938 Kenneth Leslie's *By Stubborn Stars*; 1939 Anne Marriott's *The Wind Our Enemy*; 1940 E.J. Pratt's *Brébeuf and His Brethren* and A.M. Klein's *Hath Not a Jew . . .*; 1941 E.J. Pratt's *Dunkirk*; 1942 Earle Birney's *David*; 1943 A.J.M. Smith's *News of the Phoenix*; 1944 A.M. Klein's *Poems* and Dorothy Livesay's *Day and Night*; 1945 Frank Scott's *Overture.* Anthologies large and small, comprehensive and sectarian, costly and cheap, have enabled the new poetry to circulate in many milieus. A group of critics sympathetic to the new poetry has come forward to interpret and recommend it. The beginnings, indeed rather more than the beginnings, of a renewed respect for our poetry in the United States are already perceptible. No one admires more than I the epic energy and resonant music of Pratt, the high-spirited spontaneity and curious learning of Klein, the severe emotion and careful art of Smith, the considered simplicity of Birney. On this occasion others will pay homage to their poetry.

It falls to me to examine the poetry which preceded the new movement. I confess to feeling some anxiety at discerning in the works of some of its leaders, in the verses of some of their imitators, and in the criticisms of some of their allies a tendency to dismiss the earlier poetry with indifference or to approach it with patronage. To the academic critic, familiar with the history of letters, it is a truism that the success of a new movement results in a passing injustice to the movement it has displaced. So it was when Malherbe succeeded the Pléïade, when the Romantics won the dubious victory of *Hernani*, when one of the symbolists described Leconte de Lisle as a *marchand de quinquaillerie*. Such knowledge makes one patient, but it need not reduce one to silence. There is no reason why one should not anticipate the judgment of posterity, at least in part, why one should not call for the old idols, or some of them, to be brought forth from the lumber-room and set in the niches which will later be theirs forever.

I

I do not hesitate to claim that the most admirable body of poetry which has yet been written in English-speaking Canada within a short period belongs not to 1935-1945, but to 1885-1900. It appeared at a time much less propitious to poetry than ours: when it was much harder to get one's verses published in Canada, when there was a much smaller audience, when there was a stronger tendency to be interested only in the product of the region in which one lived. The poets overcame these handicaps as best they could; their work made its way slowly, it did not tell upon the life of the community even in the limited degree in which the work of our poets tells today. But the work itself was authentic and graceful.

A recent poem [Raymond Souster's "To the Canadian Poets"] abusing the poets of the past ends with the line of reproach:

> And Lampman turning his back on Ottawa.

The author considers that instead of burying himself in the woods and meadows Lampman should have done something with the material that Ottawa offered. One has only to read Lampman's poetry with some care, not very much care but just a little, to know that he did not merely turn his back on Ottawa. He has written stinging sonnets on corrupt politicians and malefactors of great wealth—I do not think that in substance they have been surpassed, and I am sure that in form they have not been surpassed, by more recent social poetry. In longer works Lampman expressed his contempt for the material preoccupation he observed on all sides: he knew it was debilitating to the national society and he said so. He went further and formulated, in the tradition of Shelley and Morris, perhaps the noblest tradition of English nineteenth century social idealism, his conception of the right standards of life, the true quality of life, in human societies. "The City of the End of Things" is a passionate suggestion of what he found to be wrong, "The Land of Pallas" is an idyllic and utopian statement of what he thought to be right. Lampman was not a great social poet, he was no Whitman, no Hugo. What is significant is that he knew exactly what Ottawa was, what the society which it had called into being was, before he decided that his best (but not his only) subject lay in nature. "For the poet," he declared, addressing the Literary and Scientific Society of Ottawa in 1891 [in "Two Canadian Poets: A Lecture"], "the beauty of external nature and the aspects of the most primitive life are always a sufficient inspiration." What he meant was that he did not think himself crippled as a poet by the dismal condition of society as he found it about him; there was for him, as there was not for the novelist or the biographer, an escape, not a cowardly escape, not an ignominious flight—an escape into a world of permanent values, meaningful, beautiful, inexhaustible. His decision was not unlike that made in our time by Robinson Jeffers, similarly afflicted by the sense that the American society about him was an inadequate and a corrupt society. Mr. Jeffers observes in the forward to the selected edition of his verse:

> Prose, of course, is free of all fields; it seemed to me reading poetry and trying to write it, that poetry is bound to concern itself chiefly with permanent things and the permanent aspects of life . . . . Prose can discuss matters of the moment; poetry must deal with things that a reader two thousand years away can understand and be moved by. This excludes much of the circumstance of modern life, especially in the cities. Fashions, forms of machinery, the more complex social, financial, political adjustments, and so forth, are all ephemeral, exceptional; they exist but will never exist again.

Lampman would have liked that. He hoped that what he saw and divined in Ottawa would never exist again. It was one of the more dreary stretches in the growth of the nation. In the past there had been great deeds and thoughts; and there would be again. But he did not see expressions of greatness in Ottawa in the last two decades of the past century. I do not think he was myopic.

The landscape of Canada awaited him. To it he brought a mind stored with the visions of Wordsworth and the pictures of Keats; he brought too his sensitive and acute eyes and ears; and he brought his passion for Canada, his imperative need to discover and to celebrate something in Canada which was beautiful and intense—and unique. It was inevitable that his subjects should often be taken from the nature that lay about him, the hills on the Quebec side, the river in its varied moods and aspects, the fields on the outskirts of the town. Considered as a part of the Canadian social and economic structure, Ottawa itself assumed beauty and a satisfying meaning. Lampman was a hardy spirit, and he drove his body beyond its strength; he took pleasure in long tramps, sometimes on snowshoes, on the most nipping winter days. The beauty of snow, especially in the delicate light of dawn and sunset, is admirably caught in his poems. But the seasons in which the spectacle of nature aroused the deepest excitement in him were the quick violent northern spring and the dreamy lingering end of summer. They were Keats's seasons too. The sense of a threat suspended over the end of summer is beautifully expressed in the final stanza of his "September":

> Thus without grief the golden days go by,
>   So soft we scarcely notice how they wend,
> And like a smile half-happy, or a sigh,
>   The summer passes to her quiet end;
> And soon, too soon, around the cumbered eaves
>   Sly frosts shall take the creepers by surprise,
> And through the wind-touched reddening woods shall rise
> October with the rain of ruined leaves.

The last line is grand with the announcement of a resistless change to come, and poignant with the poet's lament. It makes a strong and immediate impression; but perhaps most readers will not immediately appreciate how much of its power comes from the strategy by which it has gradually been prepared. The rest of the stanza is exceedingly quiet; the poet strews through earlier lines sounds which are approaches to lamentation—in "soon, too soon," there is more than an approach, there is a lamentation itself—and in the penultimate line develops a preluding movement which is exciting and full of suspense.

In Lampman's work the note of "September" is repeatedly struck, and it is one of the finest notes in our poetry. He was also at home as man and as poet in the wilder parts of the country. He often devoted his vacations to canoe trips in the northland. In 1896 the trip was from Lake Temiskaming to the Hudson Bay post at Temagami. In 1898 on sick leave, in his last escape from the city, he made his way by La Tuque to Lake Wayagamack, though by now he was not strong enough for a veritable expedition. In the poems on the northland he used a starker diction and a more austere movement. Intimate as his treatment of this wilder nature could be, it was not Lampman but his friend Duncan Campbell Scott who expressed the fullness of the emotion that arose in a sympathetic temperament in contact with the northland.

The death of Lampman in the winter of 1899 was, in my opinion, the greatest bereavement our poetry has ever suffered.

As Duncan Scott has beautifully said, he was turning leaves in some book that Death forbade him to write. Among the new themes in the poems of his last years was his evocation of a great moment in Canadian history, the feat of Daulac at the Long Sault. It was my privilege to decipher in the delicate script of his notebooks the text of this narrative in which, more perhaps than in any other work, he shows that at the end his genius was renewing itself, as Tennyson's had done at about the same age. The image which dominates the central part of the poem is that of a moose beset by a pack of snarling wolves and in the end brought down. It is worked out with passion and vigour. But at the close the gentle spirit of Lampman reasserts itself. The Frenchmen are dead, the Indians in retreat, the scene is illuminated by a quiet May moon. The lyric begins at Montreal, the prize whose safety was assured by the sacrifice, and passes to the Long Sault, where the sacrifice was offered:

All night by the foot of the mountain
  The little town lieth at rest,
The sentries are peacefully pacing
  And neither from East nor from West

Is there rumour of death or of danger:
  None dreameth tonight in his bed
That ruin was near and the heroes
  That met it and stemmed it are dead.

But afar in the ring of the forest
  Where the air is so tender with May
And the waters are wild in the moonlight
  They lie in their silence of clay.

The numberless stars out of heaven
  Look down with a pitiful glance:
And the lilies asleep in the forest
  Are closed with the lilies of France.

This lyric, in which the anapests work so persuasively on the emotions, in which serenity and tremulousness are so perfectly fused, was written late in 1898. In the February of the following year the poet was dead.

II

A note very like that of the lyric which closed "At the Long Sault" had been sounded some years earlier by a poet of the same generation, Bliss Carman. Carman, whose fame outside Canada has been broader than any other English Canadian poet has yet won, brought out in 1893 his first collection, *Low Tide on Grand Pré*. The titular poem is, like Lampman's lyric, at once serene and tremulous. As was Carman's way, the way of Shelley and Swinburne, he developed his theme to a greater length than it required, and lost himself in exquisite music. The opening stanza shows what music there was in Carman:

> The sun goes down and over all
> These barren reaches by the tide
> Such unelusive glories fall,
> I almost dream they yet will bide
> Until the coming of the tide.

It is an incantation; and the key words of the charm are "unelusive glories fall." The poet's coinage "unelusive," "glories" —one of the most richly musical words in the language, and the dying note in "fall" are admirable taken individually, and as a group have a rich and liquid effect. They are moreover framed with the most cunning art both as to diction and movement. Carman was a more sensuous being than Lampman, and to the serenity and the tremulousness he adds, even in so simple a piece as this, something of luxuriance. The temptations of verbal and musical luxuriance he was unfitted to resist or control; he was all too often soft or vague; his ear was more acute than his eye, and thus his images lack the appropriateness he could give to his rhythms. Poetry like his is today under a specially heavy cloud; but the time will surely come when our present indifference to Carman will amaze both the general reader of poetry and the historian of Canadian letters. If a personal note may be permitted, I should like to say that I now believe that in the past I have been too grudging in estimating this poet, so attractive in the sweep of his music and the sensuous sincerity of his language. At all times in his long career, except perhaps at the very beginning, his performance was uneven; but we must forget the inferior work, which towards the end predominated, and make our way back until we can read the young enchanter without the painful consciousness of how the enchantment was to lose its power.

The later poetry of Duncan Scott in no way obscures the excellence of his early collections. Excellent these indeed were; but his talent developed slowly, and it is after 1900, and not before, that his finest work was written, in poems such as "The Height of Land," "Variations on a Seventeenth Century Theme," and "The Forsaken." For my present purpose I shall confine myself to *The Magic House*, which appeared in the same year with Carman's *Low Tide on Grand Pré*, and *Labor and the Angel* which followed after five years. Unlike Lampman and Charles G.D. Roberts, he has seldom used the sonnet, but there are few modern sonnets in which art and emotion are so admirably allied as in "The Onondaga Madonna." The sestet will show its quality:

> And closer in the shawl about her breast
> The latest promise of her nation's doom,
> Paler than she her baby clings and lies,
> The primal warrior gleaming from his eyes;
> He sulks and burdened with his infant gloom
> He draws his heavy brows and will not rest.

The solemn movement is appropriate; but the suggestive power, as is usual in Scott's poetry resides rather in the idea and the image than in the music. This is one of the many striking poems in which Scott has dealt with the Indian; and he has indeed treated the Indian theme with greater power than any other English-speaking Canadian writer. The Indian for him is not a noble savage, nor yet the sordid victim of the potlatch: the Indian is simply a human being belonging to a class which has had difficulty in adjusting to a complicated social structure for which its background has not been a preparation. The entire active career of Duncan Scott, from his appointment to the civil service in 1879 as a junior clerk to his retirement in 1932 was passed in the department of Indian Affairs, which for twenty years he directed. His Indian poetry is the fruit of long experience, deep wisdom, and serene benignity.

In reaching out towards the Indian theme Scott showed his sensitiveness not merely to a social class which was depreciated and which he sought to establish in the national society, but no less to the primitive elements in that part of Canada which civilization had barely touched. Not only the Indians, but the landscape of the Rockies and the Selkirks and the pre-Cambrian shield were congenial to his imagination. It is to him we must go for the most suggestive evocations of the terror and strangeness of the north and the northwest, as readers in French Canada have gone to *La Foret* and *Le Pin du Maskeg*, those remarkable works of M. Georges Bugnet.

But, always a devoted admirer of Rossetti, and the tradition that stems from him, there is in Scott no less than the primitive the subtly civilized. In his first collection the subtly civilized strain is dominant; and in the second appeared "The Piper of Arll," a work of extraordinary delicacy, which won John Masefield for poetry. This is one of those voyages into a dream world strange and intense in color and line in which the English poets of the later nineteenth century delighted. And the movement of the verses is as admirable as the imagery. "The Piper of Arll" is not the kind of poetry to which at this particular moment we first turn, or turn with the most eager delight. So much may be admitted; but it should also be firmly said that if there is a provincialism of place—the provincialism against which the poets now most admired inveigh—there is also a provincialism of time. To let one's taste in poetry take its limits from the vogue of the moment is to succumb to the provincialism of time.

Lampman, Duncan Scott, Carman, these are the great names of the fifteen years I have been considering. But they were not alone. The mellow classical idylls, the homely regional pictures of Charles G.D. Roberts; the stormy eloquence and dreamy landscapes of William Wilfred Campbell; the picturesque and racy narratives of W.H. Drummond—of which Louis Fréchette wrote with such generous and discerning appreciation—in all these the spirit of true poetry is sometimes present, and vital.

It was a romantic spirit. And for some years poetry has been insurgent against romanticism. The insurgence will end; in France, where so often a new movement takes form before any other culture is aware of it, strong romantic currents are flowing again. In the poetry of Pratt the romantic spirit is almost always recognizable. He will help us, and the poets of yesterday will help us, if we approach them with neither scorn nor indifference, to escape from the characteristic limits of the taste of our time. Escape is necessary if we are to read poetry as whole men, and escape is the only means by which we may win the respect of the future, and in our degree aid that future to come into being undistorted and sane.

Brown's original English version of "L'age d'or de notre poesie," *Gants du Ciel* 11 (1946): 7-17. Reprinted by permission of David Staines from Brown, *Responses and Evaluations: Essays on Canada*, ed. Staines (Toronto: McClelland Stewart, 1977): 87-96.

The Significance of the Sixties Poetry

by R.E. Rashley

The most striking characteristic of the sixties poets is their turning away from the survey of the group accomplishments and the group qualities to introspective study of the individual in relation to nature. There were two things that made necessary a new search; one, the new environment itself, and the other, the new concept of life which nineteenth century science required. Both were tremendously disturbing. The neat white church of Goldsmith's risen village was the symbol of a fixed belief which satisfied and comforted the clustering villagers. Brock, for Sangster, was the symbol of man who was himself the centre of importance. The impact of evolutionary theory was to shake both of these foundations of security and to leave the people groping in a world where old landmarks no longer gave safe journey. The effect of immigration to the new world had been to confront people with an environment with which their old cultures had been similarly thrown out of harmony. Physical conquest had given success in material comforts but it was a success built on separation and hostility. Canadian nature had not yet become the source of imagery, the substance of analogy, and, hence, the source and condition of thought. The settlements were still living on the spiritual capital of the old world. Both of these conditions created a people insecure in their environment. While there are some steps toward an integration of experience in Sangster and others it is not until the sixties poets that this need for understanding of their environment and themselves and their relation to environment becomes acute enough to force an intensive effort.

What the sixties poets thought of the material civilization the pioneers had created is clear enough. Campbell writes of nature as

> the door that opens wide
> From this close, fetid house of ill;

That lifts from curse of street to vast
Receding hill on hill. [from "Nature"]

and Agnes Ethelwyn Wetherald laments success which is

rotted o'er by envious eyes
And sickened by the human heat
Of hands that strove to clutch it fast.
[from "The Patient Earth"]

It is a common note and uttered with surprising vehemence. That it is also common in English literature of the nineteenth century does not mean that it is only literary in origin; it is also produced by conditions in Canada. These poets were developed from a youth of close association with relatively untouched nature and guided by the values of art in a search into the meaning of life. Where they did think consistently about the actual structure of society their thoughts tended to be socialistic as with Carman and Lampman. The origins of this dissatisfaction with material life are already in some of the pioneer poetry. With the sixties poets, however, pride in the physical success has disappeared and life falls far short of what seems possible.

The enthusiasm with which the sixties poets preach the efficacy of nature as spiritual release is correspondingly large. Agnes Ethelwyn Wetherald writes:

When Spring unbound comes o'er us like a flood,
My spirit slips its bars,
And thrills to see the trees break into bud
As skies break into stars; [the first stanza of "In April"]

Nature, for the poets of this group, was a release of energy, a discovery which, for a time, gave them a fresh, eager enthusiasm and a boundlessly idealistic concept of life. "We are overlords of change," says Carman [in "The Pensioners"], "in the glad morning of the world." "We of the sunrise," says Scott,

Joined in the breast of God, feel deep the power
That urges all things onward. [from "Lines in Memory of
Edmund Morris"]

Nature was, for them, a positive influence for good in the lives of men. "Let us be with her wholly at all hours," writes Lampman

So shall we grow like her in mould and bent,
Our bodies stately as her blessed trees,
Our thoughts as sweet and sumptuous as her flowers.
[from "On the Companionship with Nature"]

"The life we give to beauty," says Carman, "returns to us again." On the height of land Scott says he feels

The long light flow, the long wind pause, the deep
Influx of spirit. [from "The Height of Land"]

What accounts for this release of energy is the sudden feeling of these poets that they are at home in their environment; the two disturbing influences have been quieted. The conflict of science and religion has been adjusted in the new concept of man and nature which each of the poets carefully works over in at least one poem; Scott in "Lines in Memory of Edmund Morris," Lampman in "On the Companionship with Nature," Carman in "Vestigia," Roberts in "Kinship," and so on. Man is part of nature and nature is an expression of spirit. In contact with nature there is a heightening of sensitivity, a feeling of limitations having been lifted. If man is the vehicle of spirit he is most conscious of well-being when he is most completely abandoned to its influences. The new feeling for nature is not in itself a programme of thought. The function of nature is to increase the good, to expand the capacities, to make man nobler so that his guiding concepts and social organization will implement that nobility.

The other disturbing influence, the conflict with the environment, is also automatically removed. Man is not in conflict with nature but part of nature. The harmony is not simply a matter of formulating a statement that man and nature are not separate but one manifestation of spirit. It is a much more subtle and mutual possessing. Kirby's nature is quite unlike the nature of Carman.

> The flush of fading verdure, like the streak
> Of beauty on consumption's dying cheek,
> Paints all the woods, and fills the deep arcades
> Of vari-coloured leaves, with glowing shades
> Serene and holy, as the rays divine
> That through the pictured panes of some old Minster shine.

The beauty of nature, here, is understood in terms of human values. Arcades and stained glass windows are man made; the colouration is vivid in terms of man's disease. Man is the centre of reference; understanding spreads out from him:

> His unremitting labours, from the ground
> Had cleared the forests that enclosed him round;
> And year by year enlarging, backward threw
> The woody circle that around him grew.

Sangster's nature has a different use. "From Queenston Heights" opens with the Sunday church bells which combine the religious quiet and the ease of nature with the satisfaction that love responds though far away. From the extreme quiet of the opening lines, the poet proceeds to the fury of nature in Niagara's tumult. He then returns to the quiet, but it is a human quiet, and a quiet after destruction; age, the denuded field, the tombstones. Finally, in relation to the former fury of nature, the human fury and pain of battle are recalled and the whole is resolved; from the crucible of pain come refinement in peace, objectified in the skill of the mechanic, and love, re-expressed and enlarged in the closing line:

> Heaven bridge these people's hearts, and make them one.

The poem is thus a composite of themes which come together as the varying facets of an intelligent comprehension of life, chiefly religious. Nature is one of the facets, one evidence of sensibility which contributes its part to the development of the total effect. It is not apprehended in terms of human values, but the human value is apprehended partly because of one's experience of nature which can be used to illustrate or support the development of the thought.

Carman's use of nature is different again. "The Eavesdropper" opens with a simple statement:

> In a still room at hush of dawn,
> My Love and I lay side by side
> And heard the roaming forest wind
> Stir in the paling autumn-tide.

The real theme of the poem is unstated, but the forest wind that roams suggests impermanence and the paling autumn-tide suggests loss. The meaning of the stanza, at least its overtone of meaning, lies entirely in the description of nature. The poem goes on with a simple statement that love made these people happy:

> I watched her earth-brown eyes grow glad
> Because the round day was so fair;

For the quality of the happiness we must read on:

> Outside, a yellow maple tree,
> Shifting upon the silvery blue
> With tiny multitudinous sound,
> Rustled to let the sunlight through.

The quality of the happiness is the reaction one makes to these lines of description. The human values are communicated and understood in terms of nature. Nature has become the means by which life is apprehended. When this process has occurred the people cannot be out of harmony with their environment. Their sentience is the product of environment and spirit. They are native in the only sense in which the word has meaning in this context. Carman is not describing nature. He is saying as well as he can what the quality of life, or at least one moment of life, is in this environment. This is something which even the most minor poets of the group do with success. Pauline Johnson, for example, has such a realization of experience when she writes

> All the shade
> Is marred or made
> If I but dip my paddle blade;
> And it is mine alone.[from "Shadow River"]

It is a very individual thing, but its truth to the general experience of the people with nature is apparent enough.

As always, in poetry, the new sensitivity required a new means of expression. The poets of the sixties were driven to examine very carefully the work of other poets and to explore the resources of the language. They also seemed, frequently, to learn from each other. Carman and Scott, especially, were alert to contemporary influences, but the new manner was practised by all the poets of the group. It is characterized by greater clarity and accuracy in the presentation of the details of nature, greater exploitation of vowel harmonies and alliteration, a more suggestive and evocative type of imagery. These poets considered their function important and took themselves and their work seriously. Two of them devoted their lives to literary pursuits and others practised their art persistently. Howe, finding that his literary interests threatened his worldly success, obediently strangled them. The sixties poets did not. Their function in their time and place was sufficiently urgent to make them conscientious in the practice of their art.

The poetry of the sixties group has been criticized severely by succeeding writers eager to clear the way for a new reading of experience. Though he deals with them more fairly than any other recent critic and grants them their important function of interpreting life in this environment through its response to nature, A.J.M. Smith denies them "complete relevancy" to the Canadian scene for a failure of response to its social, commercial and industrial manifestations. It seems unreasonable to charge these poets with ignoring humanity in its busy and concerted aspects when a reading of their poetry shows that, in one sense, no group was ever more aware of it. Complete relevancy is a measure rather difficult to apply and not necessarily very meaningful when applied. There is an obvious lack of harmony between the social aims of the poetry of the period and the aims of the commercial civilization which it criticized. There is a separation implied in the act of criticism and it is made more noticeable by the introspective nature of the search for spiritual significance in life, but it is a separation from the materialism and commercialism of society, not from society. The assumption that it is a separation from society implies that the significance of society is contained within the materialism which the poets rejected. One cannot deny reference to life to a group of poets who believed that "rightly loved, nature must make us more responsible and apt in the practice of the complex art of living, more unexacting and humane."[1]

It is not necessary to give one's attention to problems of social experience to arrive at human truth. The one who turns out toward the wilderness and attempts to clarify his relationship to it is studying humanity just as fruitfully as the social worker who disappears into the slums and observes its group phenomena. The substance discoverable in one man's sensibilities must be that of humanity. If the one man happens to be nourished from birth to manhood on what sustenance Canada provides, it seems reasonable to assume that what is discovered is the Canadian spiritual substance. One might criticize this poetry on the grounds that it was imitative, that it reflected

---

[1] Bliss Carman, "The Magic of the Woods," *The Friendship of Art* (Boston: L.C. Page and Company, 1903), [230]. [Carman actually wrote "more resourceful," not "more responsible."]

movements from abroad, that it was at its best only a lyric poetry, that its function was weakly performed, but these would be criticisms of the whole of society, not of the poets alone. A body of poetry is not produced out of a social vacuum and the limitations of a poetry are not necessarily the limitations of the poets. The philosophy of this group appears to have been sufficient to have animated the entire body of worthwhile poets of the time, and most of the editors and critics.

The failure to arrive at large, original, or confident readings of life, except in Carman, whose synthesis is too loose and inclusive to be satisfying, brings its attendant penalty. As a result there are no major poets and there is a continuance of the fear and loneliness of the pioneer, transmuted from the physical into the spiritual, however, a reflection of uncertainty, of failure to establish a completely satisfying relationship with the world. Its expression is one of the things done well in the poetry of the group; it gives value to even the minor poetry. W.W. Campbell's description of the coming spring catches both the loneliness and the fear:

> No passionate cry came over the desolate places,
> No answering call from iron-bound land to land;
> But dawn and sunsets fell on mute, dead faces
> And noon and night death crept from strand to strand.
> [from "How Spring Came (To the Lake Region)"]

Helena Coleman's "Forest Tragedy" closes in despair:

> And in my restless heart the old, deep strain—
> The bitter doubt and wild rebellious pain
> I thought were laid—come surging up again.

There is often an isolation, an otherness, in the descriptions of the group. F.G. Scott's "Unnamed Lake" remains unrealized, and Lampman's winter is sometimes presented with an absence of human relation that is terrifyingly complete. What, for that matter, could be lonelier or more isolated than his objectively described trees:

Poplars pallid as the day,
In masses spectral, undefined,
Pale greenish stems half hid in dry grey leaves.
[from "An Autumn Landscape"]

or Scott's objectively studied Indians? Objective examination of man is surely the reduction to an absolute of lonely separation. This is not a failure to undertake a social need, but a failure to perform the search for spiritual significance successfully. It is an indication of a need for and a possibility of finding a real homeland, spiritual as well as physical, in the former wilderness.

It is this which accounts for the difference in the nature poetry of the sixties group. There had been nature poetry always, but with the sixties group the response to nature seems to take on a special significance. Lampman counts over his detailed gleanings with meticulous and delicate care as if they were of the utmost importance. Scott puts the life of the Indian, one or two instances of it, under an intensely deliberate light. Carman seems, once in a while, almost to verge on prescience so completely do his best phrases recover the secret feelings of one's own experiences with nature. The minor poets of the group all have poems or stanzas that come suddenly to convincing life. It is not simply the intelligent and sensitive mind responding to nature's influences that accounts for this sense of expectancy and the elation that attends it. It is the reaching for self-knowledge, not knowledge of nature but knowledge of human nature, as it is revealed in the light of the evolutionary concept of life, and the adjustment to the environment.

In "The Ghost's Story," Scott identifies the search:

All my life long I heard the step
Of some one I would know,

He describes the quest, through the degrees of loneliness, for the happiness of this companionship, until, finally,

Just upon the border land,
Where flesh and spirit part,
I knew the secret foot-fall was
The beating of my heart.

Carman has almost the same poem in "The World Voice," which concludes:

all that I had heard
Was my own heart in the sea's voice
And the wind's lonely word.

It was the discovery that one restricting wall of their room, the exterior nature of the pioneers, was, after all, a mirror through which they could see themselves in new perspectives, that gave these poets their release and their elation. The function of the group was to explore this new knowledge of themselves created by the interaction of environment and people and the concept of evolutionary growth, the consciousness of society created by its environment as well as conquering it. The need was local as well as universal. The validity of the function is demonstrated by these poets' relative success; there is no Canadian poetry before their time comparable to theirs.

Chapter 6 of *Poetry in Canada: The First Three Steps* (1958; Ottawa: Tecumseh, 1979): 89-98. Reprinted by permission of Laura E. Rashley.

Poets of the Confederation

by Malcolm Ross

It is fair enough, I think, to call Roberts, Carman, Lampman, and Scott our "Confederation Poets." Not that they were avowed and self-conscious prophets of the new Canadian nationalism. Roberts, it is true, had his fling at the "patriotic ode," but it is precisely this part of his work which one would most willingly let die. Charles Mair, perhaps, is our Confederation poet in the obvious political sense—the trouble being that he simply was not a poet. Our men *were* poets—at their best, good poets. And what is surely remarkable when one recalls our earlier cultural history, these men stood at the head of a lively company of compatriots, who, if not "good poets," at least managed to write a considerable number of good poems (one thinks of W.W. Campbell, Isabella Valancy Crawford, Theodore Goodridge Roberts, Marjorie Pickthall, Francis Sherman).

The point is that Roberts gave proof that we had a voice, that "the child of nations, giant-limb'd" was not a deaf mute after all. And the editors, preachers, and bookish lawyers who had been clamouring ever since 1867 for a sign that we were indeed a people and not just the jagged fabrication of a parliamentary act, had, by the 1880s, some real reason to rejoice. One remembers, here, Archibald Lampman's excitement over Roberts's first volume of poetry. It is, says Lampman, "a wonderful thing that such a work could be done by a Canadian . . . *one of ourselves*."

A new note, certainly. Only a few years had elapsed since it was even technically possible to call a New Brunswicker like Roberts "a Canadian." This is significant enough. Even more significant is the fact that Lampman is excited not because Roberts, in *Orion*, writes a "Canadian poem" (he does not) but because Roberts *is* a Canadian and nevertheless can write! For Lampman "had been under the depressing conviction that we were situated hopelessly on the outskirts of civilization where no literature or art could be, and that it was useless to expect that anything great could be done by any of our companions, still more useless to expect that we could do it ourselves. I sat up most of the night reading and rereading *Orion* in a state of the wildest excitement, and when I went to bed I could not sleep."

Should we smile indulgently at such boyish extravagance? The word "great," for instance. Surely *Orion* gave no proof that "greatness" was now within our reach. Yet after (just after) Heavysege, just after Sangster, just after Mair, *Orion* must have seemed much more mighty than it seems, at this distance, to us. Here, at least, was skill, the possession of the craft, the mystery. Here was *another*—one like oneself. Here was something stirring, something in a book "by one of ourselves," something as alive and wonderful in its own way as the words on the lips of the railway builders. Our empty landscape of the mind was being peopled at last. *Orion* proved to Lampman that this high landscape could be linked by a stronger, surer steel than John A.and Van Horne could ever lay down. Lampman exulted because he was no longer alone. And it was no longer "useless to expect that we could do it ourselves."

Lampman's note on *Orion* makes the right entry to the work of the whole Confederation group. Unquestionably Lampman here reflects the peculiar national spirit of the immediate post-Confederation period. This was a nationalism in search of a nation and Lampman, in his way, like Macdonald in his, learned which way to look. There is even a hint of "Canada First" in Lampman's excited pride of discovery. But it is an echo at some remove. No political statement, no practical pointers, nothing faintly like a manifesto. The air is charged, that is all. And the poet suddenly finds that he too can draw breath in this air. There will be no Whitmanesque gestures, no tub-thumping 100 per cent Canadianism. Even Roberts in his posture of national laureate is as much imperialist as nationalist. And even in Toronto he remains a New Brunswicker with one eye on London, the other on New York.

Canada does not have, did not have, will not have writers as specifically and identifiably Canadian as Whitman and Hemingway are specifically and identifiably American. Our leap from colony to nation was accomplished without revolution, without a sharp cultural and ideological break from Europe, without the fission and fusion of Civil War. Roberts and Carman learn as happily from Emerson and Royce as from Browning, Rossetti, and Verlaine. And Darwin is made to take on the look of a Miramichi backwoodsman! True, Lampman and Roberts suddenly find that they are Canadians. But they are also (and at the same time) thoroughgoing provincials (with a feeling for place), and thoroughgoing citizens of the world (with a feeling for time).

Our group of Confederation Poets is important for us (among other reasons) because already it shows forth the peculiar and inevitable "openness" of the Canadian culture. Indeed, our best writers today have much more in common with Roberts and the others than they would care to admit. It is natural enough that our recent writers have abandoned and disparaged "The Maple Leaf School" of Canadian poetry. Fashions have changed. Techniques have changed. But the changes have not really been ours—at least, we have not been the innovators. Our newest poets owe as much to Eliot, Auden, and Robert Graves as the Confederation Poets owed to the seminal writers of their day. The point is—the debt is assimilated now (as it was then) and therefore is *almost* paid back. Then as now the feeling for place checks and balances the feeling for time. Then as now, voices are heard with individual accent (Lampman, Layton, Carman, Klein—not one of them sits on the ventriloquist's knee).

With Roberts and his group, then, the broad design of our unique, inevitable, and precarious cultural pattern emerges. This pattern, by the force of historical and geographical circumstances, is a pattern of opposites in tension. From the very first there is, of course, the federal-regional tension. (Roberts is suddenly "one of ourselves." He is—and yet he is not.) There is also, inescapably, the American-British tension. (One remembers the pull of Emerson and Royce against the English Victorians. And one remembers Roberts's break from Goldwin

Smith over the question of our "North Americanism." We had to be British *and* American at once if we were to be Canadian . . .) There is (and always was) the French-English tension, affecting very little the poetic imagination of Roberts and Carman but evident to a degree in the work of Lampman and Scott.

Our poetry just after Confederation ceased to be *merely* regional and therefore could be *unashamedly* regional. One could be, with all one's heart, the singer of the parish if one could be sure of a hearing beyond the parish. The appearance of national magazines like *The Canadian Monthly*, *The Nation*, and Goldwin Smith's *The Week* let the local voices out. These magazines, and notably *The Week*, also provided the necessary link with the literary and intellectual life of New York and London. Thus all the shaping forces—regional, national, and international—were now at play. The separate (and rudimentary) colonial cultures of British North America had been caught up and transfigured in a new (if tentative and precarious) structure. Within this structure all the original elements remained alive and operative.

Obviously there were (and are) dangers in the peculiarly Canadian cultural situation. These tugs and pulls we have been considering do not and cannot guarantee equilibrium and "settled character." It is not only the case that Roberts is least Canadian when he tries to write a deliberately "national" poetry. It is also clear that while he is responsive to the fashionable religious and philosophical ideas of the late nineteenth century he tends to recite them rather than to use them poetically. His philosophical poems, like most of Carman's, are little more than second-hand ideas versified. This is not to say that a poet's "ideas" must be "original." But they must be experienced, incarnated. One suspects that the crosswinds of regional, national, and international impulse flurried Roberts and that he never really found his own poetic centre. The fatal temptation of the Canadian poet (then as now) is to write "over his head," to simulate, and to improvise à la mode. The philosophical poems of Roberts and Carman stand as warnings to us. It is well to reach out beyond the parish for the idea. But the idea must be made flesh—flesh of our flesh. For if parochialism has been our curse so has its opposite. The task for us has always been to find the centre.

Roberts repays study—for his failures as much as for his successes. One finds in him wonderful flashes of wit (as in "Philander's Song"); evidences of pure religious feeling (as in "When Mary the Mother Kissed the Child"); an engaging fancy (as in "The Unknown City"); above all, the painter's eye, as in the homely *Songs of the Common Day*. The elements of a major poetry are here, and they are here still to be enjoyed—and praised. The pity is that these elements were never fused in the single "emotive furnace."

Carman is a less complicated creature than Roberts and much less conscious of his Canadianism. He was seduced as easily as Roberts by the second-hand ideas and in later years his talent was dissipated in the pursuit of quite ludicrous "metaphysical" will-o'-the-wisps. Nevertheless Carman has an utterly individual voice. In his very early work like the "Low Tide on Grand Pré" and even in later volumes like the *Sappho* and *Pipes of Pan* he strikes a note of magic the like of which has never been heard in the land before or since. He cannot be called a "national poet." But his delicate, eerie seascapes and his lonely cadences will continue to haunt the Canadian imagination.

It is astonishing how unlike Roberts Carman really is—although without Roberts and the crosswinds of the post-Confederation years, Carman might not have written poetry at all. While we have tended at times to lump together all these Confederation poets as "landscape painters," it is nevertheless the fact that no one of these men could be mistaken for the other and, with the possible exception of Roberts in his simpler descriptive pieces, no one of these men is concerned with description for its own sake.

Carman is a lyrical impressionist whose images project ecstatic feeling. Duncan Campbell Scott, at his most typical, constructs fantasy or uses his landscape as a tragic stage for the dark human figures who seem to rise out of it. Lampman, it is true, has the camera eye. But Lampman is no mere photographer. With Scott (and more completely than Scott), he has, poetically, met the demands of his place and his time. He has all the regional poet's feeling for place. We have already noticed his feeling for the wider place—the nation—and we can guess what this meant to his energy as a poet. Like Roberts (and more intensively than Roberts) he searches for the idea, the philosopher's stone. He searches not in the abstract but in time, his time. And he searches within the self (as Roberts failed to do).

It is not just that in poems like "The City of the End of Things" and "Epitaph on a Rich Man" Lampman seems to have a social and political insight absent in his fellows. It is that he never appropriates an idea for mere recitation. Ideas are germinal for him, infecting the tissues of his thought, now driven off, now recalled, realized or discharged. His poems, even his "nature" poems, are tense with the shadows of opposite values. Like the existentialist of our day, Lampman is not so much "in search of himself" as engaged strenuously in the creation of the self. Every idea is approached as potentially the substance of a "clearer self" in the making. Even landscape is made into a symbol of the deep, interior processes of the self in motion, or is used, like the hypnotist's bauble, to induce a settling of the troubled surfaces of the mind and a miraculous transparency which opens into the depths. Thus the superb "landscape" poem "Heat" concludes:

> And yet to me not this or that
>   Is always sharp or always sweet;
> In the sloped shadow of my hat
>   I lean at rest, and drain the heat;
> Nay more, I think some blessèd power
>   Hath brought me wandering idly here:
> *In the full furnace of the hour*
>   *My thoughts go keen and clear* (Italics mine)

The purpose of this volume is to give the general reader a fuller selection of the four "large" Confederation Poets than is available in any of the current anthologies. It is not possible in such a short space to make an adequate critical comment on each (or any) of these poets. A brief critical bibliography is therefore appended. My hope is that the selection here presented will remind us that we possess a poetic tradition of considerable merit and of recognizable character—a tradition which endures because, as Canadians, we cannot and should not want to escape the conditions which shaped it and us.

Introduction to *Poets of the Confederation*, ed. Malcolm Ross (Toronto: McClelland and Stewart, 1960): ix-xiv. Reprinted by permission of Malcolm Ross.

The Problem of Crawford's Style

by Germaine Warkentin

Isabella Valancy Crawford is from one point of view a figure easily stereotyped. Though he wisely rejected any such pitfall, Northrop Frye nevertheless acknowledged that she was "an intelligent and industrious female songbird of the kind who filled so many anthologies in the last century." But Frye also called her "the most remarkable mythopoeic imagination in Canadian poetry,"[1] and (although he himself has written nothing extended on Crawford) in so doing gave direction to three decades of study which has recaptured from sentimental history one of the strangest and most powerful figures of Canadian literary life. To modernist poets and critics like Louis Dudek, Crawford's work seems "all hollow convention," "counterfeit."[2] But James Reaney, operating with Frye's critical assumptions in a bravura essay of 1959, successfully reconstructed the very sophisticated grammar of images that unifies Crawford's vision, and in so doing opened up her poetry to the serious readership it had long been uneasily felt she deserved.[3]

Yet despite this new audience, the reading of Crawford's poetry has been vulnerable to a charge made by W.J. Keith against critics of Reaney himself: that of not giving sufficient attention to the quality of the poetry.[4] Recently Robert Alan Burns in stressing Crawford's "ambiguity" has attempted to rectify the balance, but only by applying to Crawford a now dated critical paradigm, one which does not succeed in penetrating the sources of her style in the complex of historical and cultural forces within which she worked.[5] Some of these forces have been identified in a preliminary way by Dorothy Livesay, Elizabeth Waterston, John Ower, and Dorothy Farmiloe,[6] and with their help it is possible to evoke the texture of Crawford's cultural experience as reader of Tennyson, Victorian woman, Ontario villager, and working poet in a nineteenth-century city. But apart from recognizing that Crawford had to write for money, and that she both learned from and attempted to escape from Tennyson, not much has been done to isolate and consider the stylistic practices of her work. These practices originate, I contend, in the "conflictedness" which critics of every persuasion have observed in Crawford. In her poetry, however, they lead not to the ambiguities of a proto-modernist poetics, but to the inclusive strengths of a public and socially oriented vision, one which seeks to comprehend in dispassionate equilibrium the strengths and limitations of all her characters.

Crawford's poems, as Roy Daniells writes, "tend to invite two readings—a straightforward and an esoteric—with very different results." Daniells is less troubled by this divergence than some others: of *Malcolm's Katie* he observes, "there are some nice pictures of the struggles and satisfactions of clearing the land and building homes in the wilderness," yet at the same time the poem "has the ability to pull the raw landscape into an interior world of living passion and fulfillment."[7] However, if we turn away from that small masterpiece—a long poem in the manner of Tennyson's domestic idylls which succeeds in challenging the very terms of its models—we are likely to find that raw landscape and interior world are *not* fused by the poem but are severed from each other by an almost baroque improbability in the poet's stance toward her subject matter. It is hard to be just to a passage such as

> From shorn fields the victor comes,
>   Rolls his triumph thro' the streets;
> On his chariot's glowing sides
>   Sound of shout and laughter beats.[8]

when we are trying at the same time to keep in perspective the fact that the poem from which it comes is called "September in Toronto." The conflict between the visionary intensity and height of style aimed at, and the quite plausible but entirely humble subject—an Ontario town in harvest time—frustrates the reader, and drives the critic to such Churchillian stratagems as A.J.M. Smith's observation that "energy is the most outstanding quality of Miss Crawford's best poems."[9] Yet this conflict suggests that the problem of style in Crawford is at least in part the key to understanding fully what she was attempting in poetry. To answer Keith's challenge, in other words, we need a procedure for understanding why the style of her most convincing poems shows the characteristics it does, and for recognizing when this strong and interesting poet is her own worst enemy.

It is possible to read Crawford with real appreciation when the gap between subject and manner is less obvious than it is in "September in Toronto," for example in *Gisli the Chieftain*, where an austere lexicon and a racing verse form are employed to portray a cosmic landscape of heroic scale:

> A ghost along the Hell Way sped:
> The Hell shoes shod his misty tread;
> A phantom hound beside him sped.
>
> Beneath the spandrels of the Way
> Worlds rolled to night—from night to day;
> In Space's ocean suns were spray.
>
> Grouped worlds, eternal eagles, flew;
> Swift comets fell like noiseless dew;
> Young earths slow budded in the blue.[10]

But about the poems that begin Garvin's 1905 collected edition of her work even James Reaney had reservations; "when I first started to read this section," he writes dryly, "I remember thinking it was going to be a long time before I reached the passages I couldn't forget in *Malcolm's Katie*."[11] Interestingly Crawford's first volume (the only one published in her lifetime) produced a divided response in a Victorian reader, the reviewer of London's *The Spectator*:

> The first poem is written in a dialectic [*sic*] which we commonly associate with the Western States, and tells in a vigorous fashion (though not without a curious, and we should think inappropriate sprinkling of ornate literary English), the story of a stampede of cattle in a pass of the Rocky Mountains. *Malcolm's Katie* is a love story spoiled

> in a way by an immoderate use of rhetoric, witness Alfred's speech on pp. 66-7, (such a tirade as surely never was delivered over a camping fire in the woods), but still powerful.[12]

Elizabeth Waterston has justly attributed to the influence of Tennyson's Parnassianism some responsibility for Crawford's taste for the elaborate and rhetorical.[13] But the unease in the *Spectator* notice comes from other sources than an "eighties" reaction against Tennyson's manner. This critic was well aware of the strength of Crawford's poetry and the seriousness of her stance, as this and other statements in the same review show. At the same time there is a reluctance to admit Crawford's chosen situation—Alfred's debate with Max in the forest over the nature of time, chance, and immortality—as *probable*. Crawford has the mythopoeic confidence to enable her to situate a philosophical debate on the pioneer fringe but the critics' failure to understand this has undermined any attempt to consider the actual nature of her poetics. This divided response is representative: over the past century Crawford criticism has shown several tendencies not always productive: either to deplore her vision, or to deplore what is thought to be a disjunction between her poetic manner and that vision, or to assume that an understanding of the vision is sufficient to understand her as a poet. I will argue here that Crawford's mythopoeic confidence and her poetic strategies *are* related, though in a way unexpected for a proto-Symbolist poet, if not for a Canadian of her culture and generation.

Despite what I have just said, we must begin with Crawford's structural strength, and the iron logic of her vision, for these are what persistently urge us to approach her poems with more than their limitations in mind. Crawford resists the stereotype of songbird fiercely: she is not "all moody and glimmery like late romantic Chopin," as Reaney has said, but "tough like Bach."[14] The source of this toughness is the visionary grammar Reaney has described. It begins with "a huge daffodil which contained all reality." The image of the daffodil, which she seems to have picked up from Tennyson, is made—in an imaginative act which places her securely on a line between Blake and Yeats—to yield an entirely unTennysonian coherence. In the fallen world of experience, the daffodil breaks up into

> tree and lake, eagle and dove, eagle and swan, the queen of heaven looking at herself in a glassy lake, wind and ship, cloud and caged skylark, whip and stampeding herd, good brother and evil brother, paddle and lily bed, smouldering darkness and prickly starlight, aristocratic Spartan and beaten Helot, Isabella Valancy Crawford and King Street, Toronto.[15]

But when these elements are disposed in a narrative—in long poems like *Malcolm's Katie*, "Gisli the Chieftain," and "Old Spookses' Pass," or in Crawford's prose fairy tales—they assume romance form, as Barbara Godard puts it, a "movement from a state of innocence through an encounter with the fallen world of mortality and evil, a movement which, when assimilated and empowered by human love, allows the hero to be transformed to a higher state of perfection."[16]

Yet the total effect of Crawford's poetry is not to focus us on the moment of reconciliation, important though it is. Though at the level of abstraction Crawford's romance structure is as secure as Spenser's, in the poetry itself she keeps rewriting that romance over and over again. Instead of building a single poem like many romance writers, she enters and re-enters this world of intense oppositions, making palpable for us the restless energy which pours through the pivotal points that link upper and lower, good and evil, day and night. For good or ill—and sometimes it is for ill—her sense of the poet's capacity to control this moment of re-entry though style is what determines the character of much of her poetry.

In the draft which is all we have of the long poem now called *Hugh and Ion*, the painter Ion is depicted as one who

> . . . lov'd the wilds, Athenian-wise, so lov'd
> His little Athens more—his canvas best

His patient and impatient eyes beheld
The leprosies of Nature, and her soul
Of beauty hidden under twisted limbs
And so his spirit at his canvas stood
And painted spirit—never burst a vine
Of Spring beneath his brush, but men beheld
The grapes of Autumn on it, and foresaw
The vintages . . .[17]

This Browningesque moment may or may not provide Crawford's credo as an artist. But it does catch her in the act of articulating the artist's divergent worlds as she had experienced them: the wilds, the "little Athens," and the canvas; the vines of Spring, and the grapes of Autumn they foretell. But it also catches Ion's sense of the artist's *task*, and his desire for a controlled, unified and essentially persuasive effect. Such a sense of the poet's authority is reflected in unexpected ways in Crawford's own art; in an impersonal reserve that finds her refusing the use of the first person except as a dramatic device, in her dialect poetry, where there is a shrewdness beyond the conventions of folk sagacity, in the amused judiciousness she sometimes gives us to appease our desire for irony (Alfred, the quasi-villain of *Malcolm's Katie*, has "the jewels of some virtues set / On his broad brow").

We can see a symptomatic detachment and economy in two roughly contemporaneous passages which deserve to be set side by side. The first is from that long poem "in a dialectic which we commonly associate with the Western States," "Old Spookses' Pass." The aging cowhand who is the speaker there is describing the herd whose eventual stampede calls up a chaos which can only be controlled by divine intervention:

Ever see'd a herd ringed in at night?
 Wal, it's sort uv cur'us,—the watchin' sky,
The howl uv coyotes, a great black mass
 With here an' thar the gleam uv an eye
An' the white uv a horn, an' now an' then
 An old bull liftin' his shaggy head

With a beller like a broke-up thunder growl,
An' the summer lightnin', quick an red,
Twistin' and turnin' amid the stars,
Silent as snakes at play in the grass.[18]

The second is in *Malcolm's Katie*, published in the same volume:

Who journey'd where the prairies made a pause
Saw burnish'd ramparts flaming in the sun,
With beacon fires, tall on their rustling walls.
And when the vast, horn'd herds at sunset drew
Their sullen masses into one black cloud,
Rolling thund'rous o'er the quick pulsating plain,
They seem'd to sweep between two fierce red suns
Which, hunter-wise, shot at their glaring balls
Keen shafts with scarlet feathers and gold barbs.[19]

In both these examples Crawford picks up a single image—the black herd of animals—and illuminates it with glancing light: the domestic cattle of "Old Spookses' Pass," flickeringly lit by summer lightning, the buffalo herd in *Malcolm's Katie* like a black cloud more sharply delineated by the sunset red of beacon fires. The Tennysonian artifice of the second passage reaffirms what Waterston has termed Crawford's "openness to the strongest model of her day,"[20] but the same might be said of the response to dialect poetry in the first passage; in both cases we sense Crawford's awareness of genre, of type, of the value of the model. But what is of real interest is the use to which she puts that awareness: she creates two completely different sets of conditions within which the herd—"raw landscape" to begin with—can become a visionary possibility. In either case, the herd signifies the same thing in her mythopoeic system: unformed chaos. In "Old Spookses' Pass," it is rendered from the almost domestic point of view of an observer long familiar with the herd and its unstable ways. Yet despite this simplicity and exactitude, everything the old hand tells us intimates the presence of a larger scale as well. In *Malcolm's Katie* the goal is to create openly that effect of heroic grandeur which is required as its valid setting by the "machinery" of Indian legend that parallels the human action of the poem. Crawford has used a single repeated image to enter the world of warring opposites at two different points, and significantly, those two points are defined in terms of a purely verbal space.

"Said the Canoe," Crawford's most brilliant, suggestive, and complex poem, affords an extended example of how her method works. This is a poem in the first person, but employing a dramatized persona, the canoe of the title. Speaking in the voice of a beloved woman who has been put to bed by the hunters who are her "masters twain," the canoe watches in the campfire light as their slaughtered stag is

> Hung on forked boughs with thongs of leather:
> Bound were his stiff, slim feet together,
> His eyes like dead stars cold and drear.
> The wandering firelight drew near
> And laid its wide palm, red and anxious,
> On the sharp splendour of his branches,
> On the white foam grown hard and sere
>   On flank and shoulder.
> Death—hard as breast of granite boulder—
>   Under his lashes
> Peered thro' his eyes at his life's grey ashes.[21]

The effect of this extraordinary stanza depends, to begin with, on Crawford's exact feeling for the tensions between words: slim and stiff, dead and stars, foam and hard, boulder and lashes, life and ashes. Fundamentally this tension arises from the contrast between the dead animal swinging from its pole and the living fire, "red and anxious," whose light illuminates the scene. Yet all is not contrast; there are in fact three focal points within the stanza. At one extreme is the "raw landscape" of the hunting camp: two men, a deer carcass, the leather thongs, the hooves, the drying foam on shoulder and flank. The other is purely visionary and is represented by the image of death, "hard as breast of granite boulder," peering through the deer's eyes at the grey ashes of the deer's own life. Mediating between these extremes is the wandering firelight which in an astonishing and tender moment lays its anxious palm on the dead body of the deer.

The detail of the firelight's hand continues the series of purely physical images that is a noticeable motif of the stanza: feet, eyes, palm, flank, shoulder, breast, and then eyes again. But almost all of these are dead; the fire, like the canoe, is alive. Furthermore, it seems to observe, and thus participates in a life beyond the night routine of the camp. It is, as the canoe has already recognized, the "camp-soul," and from its light

> Into the hollow hearts of brakes—
> Yet warm from sides of does and stags
> Passed to the crisp, dark river-flags—
> Sinuous, red as copper-snakes,
> Sharp-headed serpents, made of light,
> Glided and hid themselves in night.

The fire's light and its mediating influence suffuse the whole poem, though in the end we meet with the boundaries of its realm, which are determined by a countervailing presence, that of night. We meet also with the other, imponderable entities that flutter at that boundary line:

> The darkness built its wigwam walls
> Close round the camp, and at its curtain
> Pressed shapes, thin, woven and uncertain
> As white locks of tall waterfalls.

Crawford has presented us not with two poles of existence, on the one hand that of the hunters and on the other that of the death they take so routinely, but with a whole set of nested worlds, each with its degree of vision: the dead stag, the men with their songs "loud of the chase and low of love," the watching canoe, the dreaming hounds, the bat that circles over the flames, the probing fire with its "thin golden nerves of sly light," and at the periphery, the influence of yet another world, perhaps (to come full circle) the one that looks through the dead stag's eyes.

All of this comes about initially because of Crawford's *awareness* of the extreme boundaries of vision and of the distance between them. In "Said the Canoe" the verbal texture of the poem is constantly creating an arena in which these extremes can meet and comment on each other. Early in the poem Crawford challenges us to accept, on her terms, the kind of control she has chosen to exercise over the creation of that verbal texture. From the "golden nerves of sly light" there rise

. . .faint zones,
Half way about each grim bole knit,
Like a shy child that would bedeck
With its soft clasp a Brave's red neck,
Yet sees the rough shield on his breast,
The awful plumes shake on his crest,
And, fearful, drops his timid face,
Nor dares complete the sweet embrace.

The epic simile is taken over from Homer (*Iliad* vi, 392 ff.), and its dignity is startling to a reader expecting something more rhapsodical (or wishing for something less so). But Crawford uses this dignity to tie the poem together in a characteristic way. The literary context so unexpectedly suggested hints that the 74 lines of the poem, though not epic in quantity, will have the cosmic range of epic, from heaven to earth. (It is a gravity of reach which suffuses *Malcolm's Katie* as well, and suggests a formal, public quality behind the superficial prettiness of the idyll which places that poem securely in the context of the settlement epic as Howe, McLachlan, and Kirby were practising it.) In "Said the Canoe" the Indian infant's hesitation is as plausible as the war-garb of its heroic parent, and while the simile—seen as mere device—is obviously directing us to pay attention to the seriousness of the poem, it is at the same time stating the poem's central preoccupation; the tentativeness with which different levels of vision meet, a tentativeness which is still with us at the poem's concluding image of white-locked presences trembling like falling water at the edge of the curtain of night.

This tentativeness is not the result of a Tennysonian sense that (as David Shaw puts it) "the ultimate nature of the world is necessarily hidden from any finite mind."[22] Crawford is creating in this poem a firmly bi-polar structure—light contrasting with dark, life with death—and for her it is the structure by which the world may be *known*. Indeed, the schemata of her vision may be recognized in "Said the Canoe" in as full a form as Yeats' is in "The Second Coming." But two contrasting passages suggest the nature of the poetic difficulty she poses herself in doing so. The hunters sing:

> "O Love! art thou a silver fish,
> Shy of the line and shy of gaffing,
> Which we do follow, fierce, yet laughing,
> Casting at thee the light-winged wish?
> And at the last shall we bring thee up
> From the crystal darkness, under the cup
> Of lily folden
> On broad leaves golden?"

This and the succeeding song "Oh love, art thou a silver deer?" have an ornateness which suits the loftiness of the poem, yet at the same time a witty hint of dramatic distance in the conscious lushness differentiates them from the impersonal brilliance and controlled *diminuendo* of the campfire picture which follows:

> They hung the slaughtered fish like swords
> On saplings slender; like scimitars,
> Bright, and ruddied from new-dead wars,
> Blazed in the light the scaly hordes.
>
> They piled up boughs beneath the trees,
> Of cedar web and green fir tassel.
> Low did the pointed pine tops rustle,
> The camp-fire blushed to the tender breeze.

> The hounds laid dewlaps on the ground
> With needles of pine, sweet, soft and rusty,
> Dreamed of the dead stag stout and lusty;
> A bat by the red flames wove its round.

Despite their differences, however, the passages share an important feature: what we might begin by thinking of as their pictorialism. The fish of the second passage are, quite explicitly, "slaughtered." We are aware of their scales, their silver colour, their blazing brightness, details which, however intense, are very exact. When Crawford seeks to intensify an already vivid picture, it is through comparison: the fish are like swords, then like freshly bloodied scimitars. The swords and the scimitars are themselves as exact as other details in the same passage: the slender saplings, the boughs, the pointed pine tops, the sleeping hounds, and the red flames. There is nothing suggestive, nothing allusive, in any of this; the only attempt at metaphoric extension is in "cedar web" and "green fir tassel," both of which seem to be minor decorative effects rather than true metaphors. The hunters' song, by contrast, is elaborately figurative; if "Said the Canoe" has an ironic dimension, it might well be in its implicit circumscribing of that kind of figure in the limits of the song.

This suggests that Crawford has a surprisingly rationalistic concept of poetic diction. Her images arise in that area Daniells calls "landscape," and they do not unfold themselves in the metaphoric gesture we might expect of a mythopoeic poet like, for example, Reaney. Instead her terms are precise, explicit, denotative; however intense the effect she desires, it has to be created syntactically, descriptively, and through comparison, rather than by using the resources of metaphor and allusion. As a result, her methods of creating intensity at the purely verbal level come closer to those of the orator, with his need to persuade, than to the mythmaker, with his network of ever-resonating analogies. It is this gap, the gap between her mythopoeic vision and a poetic method innately, rather than adventitiously, rhetorical, which Crawford must bridge in every poetic decision she makes. She may not have had to make such decisions in isolation; I suspect that Crawford's reading of Thomson's *The Seasons* must have been just as attentive as her reading of Tennyson. Unfortunately, without concrete evidence we cannot say.

In seeking an answer to the problem of stylistic strain in Crawford we might stop here, at that "Parnassianism," were it not that her preference for what might almost be called a neoclassical theory of diction is related very cogently to other poetic strategies we can see in her work: to her alertness to genre, to her masquing use of dramatic persona in preference to the unmediated first person, and to the tense awareness of dramatic situation which we can see even in the orderly composition—it might be called "After the Hunt"—we have been looking at in "Said the Canoe." Crawford's poetic technique at its best, I would argue, exhibits five features which can be expected to support each other in any poem of hers which commands our serious attention. To "read" her adequately we need to watch for her conception of the genre she is using, to accept the paradox of a symbolic poet who avoids the connotative, the ambiguous, the allusive, to recognize the impersonality which issues in her exploitation of dramatic monologue, to detect the presence of mythopoeia at every level of the mimetic, and to respond to her gift for shaping dramatic situations. These are the characteristics of a self-consciously public poet, one whom the inwardness of Romantic poetry has entirely passed by, and they account, I contend, for the seriousness with which she approaches her subject matter, and the essentially public rhetorical stance which she therefore adopts.

The most fully achieved effects in Crawford's poetry are arrived at when all five of the characteristic features of her poetic are operating in consonance. Curiously these five features are precisely what we need to be aware of in her less satisfying poems as well. When Crawford's poetry weakens, it is not from the *absence* of these qualities, but from an almost demonic *inversion* of them. Because she is attentive to genre, it is easy for her to allow the conventions of a poetic kind to overtake the vision of a particular poem, for example in the verse she wrote to celebrate the return of the troops from the second Riel Rebellion, in genteel "album verse" like "The Inspiration of Song," "Life," "Faith, Hope and Charity," "The Poet of the Spring" (one marvellous stanza here, amidst the dross), and even in the piously-admired but in my view completely meretricious "The Camp of Souls." Similarly, if Crawford's diction at its best is direct, explicit, pictorial, unallusive, at its worst it has a disconcerting violence, a lack of tact, and a troubling failure to consider the ear. The impersonal voice can become oppressively oratorical, the mythopoeic vocabulary transform itself into a restricted set of images exploited for their superficial colour, the inherent drama of a situation can be reduced to mere theatre. It is as if a pivot operated within Crawford herself, like the one on which her visionary universe turns. This creative pivot provides a controlling mechanism by which the diverse elements of her art can be made to cohere; when they are all in balance and answering to each other the integrating vision and the world of "landscape" are brought into a distinctive and Crawfordesque rapport, and the campfire scene claims its place as an arena for serious verse. When they are out of balance Crawford diminishes into a mere imitator of Tennyson like "Owen Meredith" or Sir Lewis Morris, and to a minor niche among minor poets.

The meeting within Crawford of her own opposites— songbird and visionary—cannot have been easy, particularly in view of the fact that she excelled not at the brief and marketable Romantic lyric but in the fuller scale of the nineteenth-century verse-narrative. What that collision was like we can only gauge indirectly; she left some manuscripts when she died so suddenly in the King Street boarding house, but nothing more personal. It is clear, however, that she sought an audience assiduously. The genres of polite verse were important to her, of course, for she and her mother lived on the money she made by selling poems to the *Globe* and the *Telegram*, but so was a serious readership. She sought out Susie Harrison ("Seranus") at *The Week*, and received an interested response.[23] She reached outward for patronage and recognition in a larger literary milieu: copies of *"Old Spookses' Pass," "Malcolm's Katie," and Other Poems* (1884) went not only to the London reviewers (who treated her very fairly) but to former Governor-General Lord Dufferin in India. Tennyson, to whom she is indebted for much in *Malcolm's Katie* is reported to have read with interest the copy of *Old Spookses' Pass* she sent him.[24] Crawford's sense of her social role as a poet, in other words, was one with the public stance of her poetic method; her actions all suggest that despite her intensely personal vision, she did not think of poetry as in any way a hermetic craft. For Crawford the mythopoeic mode, like Max in *Malcolm's Katie*, is "social-soul'd." If we must read her poems ". . . with the eyes close shaded with the hand, / As at some glory terrible and pure,"[25] it is because she seems to have been less interested in the increasing privatization of symbolic modes in her age than in impersonally, compassionately focussing the perilous equilibrium of her art on the radical dividedness of man himself.

Notes

1. Northrop Frye, *The Bush Garden: Essays on the Canadian Imagination* (Toronto: Anansi, 1971): 147-48.

2. Louis Dudek, "Crawford's Achievement," in *The Crawford Symposium*, ed. Frank M. Tierney (Ottawa: U of Ottawa P, 1979): 123-25; see especially the response by Elizabeth Waterston.

3. James Reaney, "Isabella Valancy Crawford," in *Our Living Tradition*, ed. Robert L. McDougall, Second and Third Series (Toronto: U of Toronto P, in association with Carleton University, 1959): 268-88.

4. W.J. Keith, "James Reaney, 'Scrutumnus,' and the Critics: An Individual Response," *Canadian Poetry: Studies, Documents, Reviews* 6 (1980): 25-34.

5. Robert Alan Burns, "Crawford and Gounod: Ambiguity and Irony in *Malcolm's Katie*," *Canadian Poetry: Studies, Documents, Reviews* 15 (1984): 1-30.

6. Dorothy Livesay, "Tennyson's Daughter or Wilderness Child: the Factual and the Literary Background of Isabella Valancy Crawford," *Journal of Canadian Fiction* 2, No. 3 (1973): 161-67;

Elizabeth Waterston, "Crawford, Tennyson, and the Domestic Idyll," in *The Crawford Symposium*, 61-77; John Ower, "Isabella Valancy Crawford and 'The Fleshly School of Poetry,'" *Studies in Scottish Literature* 13 (1978): 275-81; Dorothy Farmiloe, *Isabella Valancy Crawford: The Life and the Legends* (Ottawa: Tecumseh, 1983). See also Catherine Sheldrick Ross, "Isabella Valancy Crawford's 'Gisli the Chieftain,'" *Canadian Poetry: Studies, Documents, Reviews* 2 (1978): 28-37, and the interesting suggestions made about Crawford's reading by Burns, note 5 above. D.M.R. Bentley's review of *The Crawford Symposium* ("Letters in Canada," *UTQ* 49 (1980), 453-55), issues a general call for a cultural approach to Crawford's aesthetics.

7. Roy Daniells, "Crawford, Carman, and D.C. Scott," in *Literary History of Canada: Canadian Literature in English*, ed. Carl F. Klinck et. al., 2nd ed. (Toronto: U of Toronto P, 1976), 424.

8. Isabella Valancy Crawford, *Collected Poems*, ed. J.W. Garvin (1905; rpt. Toronto: U of Toronto P, 1972) 150. (Hereafter referred to as "Garvin.") On the limitations of Garvin's text see S.R. MacGillivray, "Garvin, Crawford, and the Editorial Problem," in *The Crawford Symposium*, 97-106, and Mary F. Martin, "The Short Life of Isabella Valancy Crawford," *Dalhousie Review* 52 (1972): 390-400.

9. A.J.M. Smith, ed., *The Book of Canadian Poetry* (Chicago: The U of Chicago P, 1943), 129.

10. Garvin, 184.

11. James Reaney, Introduction to Garvin, xix.

12. Quoted by Reaney, Introduction to Garvin, xxii.

13. Waterston, "Crawford, Tennyson, and the Domestic Idyll," in *The Crawford Symposium*, 61-77.

14. Reaney, Introduction to Garvin, xx.

15. Reaney, Introduction to Garvin, xxxi.

16. Barbara Godard, "Crawford's Fairy Tales," *Studies in Canadian Literature* 4 (1979): 109-35.

17. Isabella Valancy Crawford, *Hugh and Ion*, ed. Glenn Clever (Ottawa: Borealis, 1977), 19.

18. Garvin, 267.

19. Isabella Valancy Crawford, *Malcolm's Katie*, ed. David Sinclair, in his *Nineteenth-Century Narrative Poems*, New Canadian Library (Toronto: McClelland and Stewart, 1972), 163.

20. Waterston, "Crawford, Tennyson, and the Domestic Idyll," 66.

21. Garvin, 68. All further references to "Said the Canoe" are to this text.

22. W. David Shaw, *Tennyson's Style* (Ithaca: Cornell UP, 1976),

290.

23. Katherine Hale, *Isabella Valancy Crawford*, 10.

24. E.J. Hathaway, writing in 1895 in *The Canadian Magazine*, said "Lord Tennyson, the Poet Laureate, wrote, congratulating her on her work, making special mention of this particular piece ["Old Spookses' Pass"]." The passage is quoted by Dorothy Livesay, "Tennyson's Daughter or Wilderness Child," 161.

25. Garvin, 247.

From *Canadian Literature* 107 (1985): 20-32. Reprinted with permission of Germaine Warkentin and *Canadian Literature*.

The Poem in its Niche: Lampman's "The City of the End of Things" and its origins

by D.M.R. Bentley

Written in the summer of 1892[1] and first published in *The Atlantic Monthly* in March 1894,[2] Archibald Lampman's "The City of the End of Things" seems destined to become the demonic, Canadian equivalent of Coleridge's Xanadu: a city of the visionary imagination upon which converges a Lowesian and ever-growing road-system of influences. The first major contributor to this system was John Sutherland who, in "Edgar Allan Poe in Canada," makes a detailed case for the debt of "The City of the End of Things" to such Poe poems as "The City in the Sea" and "The Haunted Palace," arguing that Lampman's poem has "the air of a tour-de-force in the Poe manner."[3] Among the other influences frequently mentioned in discussions of "The City of the End of Things" are Milton's depiction of Pandemonium in the second Book of *Paradise Lost*, Arnold's "A Summer Night" and, of course, James Thomson's "City of Dreadful Night."[4] Yet other candidates that have been advanced as influences on Lampman's poem are Byron's "Darkness,"[5] the Wanderer's confrontation with evidence of the industrial revolution in Wordsworth's *Excursion*,[6] and a gloomy sub-system of eighteenth-century poems that depict demonic edifices: Pope's *Temple of Fame* and *The Dunciad* and Christopher Smart's "Materies gaudet vi Inertiae" and its translation by Francis Fawkes ("Matter rejoices in the force of Inertia").[7] In the monetary terms that frequently characterize traditional influence studies, the debts and borrowings of "The City of the End of Things" seem extensive enough to call into question its integrity and independence as a work of art. Does "The City of the End of Things" sustain Malcolm Ross' argument that Lampman "never appropriates an idea for mere recitation"? Does it support Ross's contention that in the work of the Confederation poets the "debt" to English and American literature is "assimilated . . . and therefore . . . *almost* paid back"?[8]

1

Of course, the monetary model is not the only means of coming to terms with the relationship between a poem and the works that it "appropriates" or resembles. An alternative, and currently very fashionable, way of dealing with such matters is to substitute the word "intertextuality" for "influence," thus, depending on one's perspective, transcending, avoiding, skirting, or fudging such traditional elements of influence study as external evidence and plausibility—ideally, a demonstration that the poet did in fact read the work that supposedly influenced him or, failing this, an inference to the same effect based on the availability of the "source" works and convincing echoes of them in the works that they supposedly influenced. In Canadian, and presumably in other secondary and, in places, insecure cultures, there is another alternative to dealing with the kind of influence under examination—the influence of English (or American, or French) writers on Canadian ones—and that is, of course, silence: the turning of a blind eye to the existence of indebtednesses that seem to disprize native writers of their originality and, by so doing, dispossess the culture as a whole of part of its claim to uniqueness. The corollary of this essentially nationalistic (and, more recently, regionalist) manoeuvre of ignoring, pretending to ignore, or drastically underplaying the matter of external influences on Canadian writing is a preference for studies of influence or intertextuality—some of them very good—among Canadian writers of the same region or different generations, with both approaches tending to concentrate on influences that operate forward in time from starting points well into the present century. (Since Modernists and Post-Modernists alike identify the maturation of Canadian literature with the arrival in Canada of the movement of which they are themselves a part, it is anathema for many of them to think of indebtedness of one of their own to, say, a poet of the Confederation period.)

Yet another way of dealing with influence and intertextuality is to treat them as hermeneutical issues—to speak, as T.S.

Eliot does, of "really new"[9] additions to the literary tradition as altering, modifying, or re-adjusting the relations among all previous elements in that tradition or, as Harold Bloom (himself under the influence of Eliot) does, of "strong" later writers influencing their literary precursors.[10] In practical terms, what this usually amounts to is that a new work (*The Waste Land* is a good example) alters our apprehension of earlier works to such an extent that we draw up a new map of the tradition that leads up to it, or—to formulate the matter in Bloom's terms—that a "strong" and relatively recent poet so conditions our approach to his precursors that they (in fact, our readings of them) are effectively influenced by him. The difficulty with such "metamorphic play"[11] in the Canadian context is that, having produced no "really new" or "strong" writers—that is, writers who have re-adjusted the tradition or influenced their precursors (and notice the circularity of all this)—we are excluded at the start from reversing the field, as it were, in the study of influence or the play of intertextuality. Or, if we are not excluded, then our attempts to assert retrospective tradition-formation or influence are doomed to appear ludicrous. Imagine the response of a Pope scholar to the suggestion that a poem by Archibald Lampman (Archibald who?) reorganizes the tradition in which *The Dunciad* appears or counts as an influence on *The Temple of Fame*. That a Canadian reader knows better, *knows* that "The City of the End of Things" *has* altered his or her apprehension of Pope's (and Poe's and Byron's) poems, *has* influenced his or her reading of "The City of Dreadful Night" (or *The Wanderer* or *Paradise Lost*) will not matter one iota to critics and theorists concerned with the "real" canon of English (or American or French) literature—the "really new" works and the "strong" writers, the "central" texts and the "great" authors.

What is needed, then, is an approach to influence and derivation which accepts the "minor" status of a writer such as Lampman and the secondary nature of a literature such as Canadian without depriving writers of their claims to intelligence and creativity or the culture of its need for admiration and attention. One approach, which has both the strengths and the limitations of a sort of mathematical equation, would be to attempt to gauge a borrower's "originality" by assessing the extent of his divergence from his influences. Though there is some question of "whether any author's originality can be measured by subtracting one poem from another,"[12] this approach has some potential, though probably only in those few, if any, cases where all the influences on a given work are known, a (hypothetical?) condition being reached, thanks to various Canadian scholars, by poems like Roberts' "Tantramar Revisited." A more general and attractive approach to influence in the Canadian context, however, involves an affirmation with Ross that even minor poets in a secondary culture are not the passive recipients of influences from "strong" writers in the "great" traditions, but, on the contrary, exercise considerable intelligence and creativity in their selection and manipulation, importation, and adaptation, of their models. "In the matter of influence," writes K.K. Ruthven, "it is the receptor who takes the initiative, not the emitter."[13] Or, as Michael Baxandall rephrases it in mathematical rather than electronic terms: Y [the influencee] does not exist in a passive relation to X [the influencer]; on the contrary, "responding to circumstances Y makes an intentional selection from an array of resources in the history of his craft,"[14] one of which is X (or a work by, or an element of a work by, X). The present argument, simply, is that the status of Y in Baxandall's equation should be accorded not merely to "great" writers and artists like Milton and Picasso but also to minor figures such as Lampman who should be considered as (in Ruthven's phrase) "tak[ing] the initiative," playing an active role, in the complex relationship known as influence.

Fortunately, several Canadian poets have addressed the matter of their relation to the great tradition(s) in ways that support the approach to influence just outlined. Probably the best known of these is A.J.M. Smith who, as long ago as 1960 in his "Introduction" to *The Oxford Book of Canadian Verse*, articulated his concept of "*eclectic detachment*"—that is, the ability of "the Canadian poet" (later "contemporary Canadian poetry") to "draw upon French, British, and American sources in language and literary convention" with "a measure of detachment that enables him to select and adapt what is relevant and useful . . . ."[15] Smith subsequently speaks of the Canadian poet's ability to "select and reject," to exercise "freedom of choice," "to pick and choose just those poets (or just those aspects of those poets) that can satisfy our needs"[16]—formulations that are attractive for their implications of activity, differentiation, intellectual discernment, and creative purpose. A similar emphasis on the "initiative" of the "receptor" writer (Y) can be discerned in Lampman's account of the "perfect poet" at the conclusion of his essay on "Poetic Interpretation": "Perhaps the world shall someday have a poet who *will interpret* tenderly passionate dreams like Keats, simple and lofty ones like Wordsworth, strong and passionate dreams like Browning . . ., and everything else with the best truth of the special poet who has handled it best" (emphasis added). That Lampman is too deferential for Modern (and Post-Modern) tastes to his Romantic and Victorian predecessors should not obscure either the quiet insistence in these lines on volition and creativity or their implicit recognition of the discernment and differentiation required of any poet, Canadian or otherwise, who would aspire to perfection.

In the course of the two preceding paragraphs there have passed into the discussion various words and phrases which may now be brought to the foreground as part of an attempt to articulate an approach to influence that takes full account of the intelligence and creativity of the Canadian poet. These words and phrases, all of which place an active conception of a poet's use of his predecessors firmly within a context of purpose, are "*responding to circumstances Y makes an intentional selection*" (Baxandall), "select and adapt what is *relevant and useful*" and "pick and choose . . . [what] can satisfy *our needs*"(Smith). "Circumstances," "intentional," "relevant," "useful," "needs"—all of these words point towards the necessity in any approach to importation and adaptation of taking into account the purposes for which a poet makes levies on previous writers, the whys and the wherefores—the intent —governing his selection of this poem for emulation or that detail for expropriation. For Smith (ever the aesthete),[17] there was no question but that any poet worthy of approval "chooses the true and rejects the false" in the tradition(s) available to him on the aesthetic ground of "seek[ing] to eliminate bad taste and encourage good . . . ."[18] For Lampman (here in the Keatsian mode), the basis for selection is fitness: the suitability of an available style to the topic at hand. "The perfect poet," he writes, "would not consent to be permanently influenced by any single impulse" but "would have a different [style] for everything he should write, a manner exactly suited to the subject. . ." (*ALSP*, 88). While encouraging good taste and seeking an answerable style have lost their critical currency in recent years, they should not be too hastily dismissed as irrelevant to the issue that is rising into view, namely the role of purpose (or intention) in the matter of what may be called elective influence. That Smith did not choose to emulate Mrs. Hemans or Rudyard Kipling (and, in so doing, encourage "bad taste") was because his self-assigned purpose as a poet, critic, and anthologist was to import into Canada and promulgate classic Anglo-American Modernism (what he called "cosmopolitanism").[19] That Kroetsch converses with Wiebe in *Seed Catalogue* on the correspondence between expansive forms and expansive landscapes (and the very thought of writing a sonnet on Saskatchewan still conjures up the figure of Sarah Binks) suggests that forms continue to be selected (and judged) in Canada according to their fitness or suitability for their subjects and circumstances. Needless to say, criteria of aesthetics and decorum are not in or by themselves sufficient to explain the dynamics of elective influence; they may, however, have given us enough of a sense of the complexities of the temporal, spatial, and personal issues involved to allow us to proceed further with the formulation of a model for the understanding of importation and adaptation in Canadian poetry, a model that we can then test by looking at various aspects of "The City of the End of Things" including its relation to the poems of Pope,

Wordsworth, Thomson, and others.

The model proposed arises from the recognition of a type of problem-solving activity at or near the centre of the process of importation and adaptation. Taking a cue from Baxandall's conception of the artistic Brief ("the terms of the immediate task the [artist] addresses"),[20] the suggestion is that in the background of all works of Canadian poetry (and prose, too, for that matter) there can be inferred or posited a "task" that the poet has set for himself (this will be called his Commission) and a problem, or series of problems, that he must solve in order to fulfill his Commission. A poet's Commission may be aesthetic (to write a poem of "good taste," for example) and the problems devolving from it may be largely of the same order (to ensure that art conceals artifice, for instance, or as Smith puts it: to do "a hard thing . . ./ Perfectly, as though without care" [from "To a Young Poet"]. But even such a superficially "pure" ("art for art's sake") Commission cannot be understood unless it is referred to a variety of factors, tendencies, and circumstances without which terms like "good taste" and "Perfectly" are almost meaningless. Thus, in Smith's case (and still very generally), the Commission and problem(s) of a given poem must be referred to such matters as the poet's historical and geographical situation—Smith's orientation towards classic Modernism from the perspective of a central Canadian culture striving (at least until the latter stages of his creative career) to move abreast of Modern poetry as it had developed in England and the United States. Of course, a host of more specific considerations must also be taken into account when approaching a particular poem such as—to stay with Smith for a moment—"The Lonely Land."

"I think success in verse is largely due to getting the right form for the right content," wrote W.W.E. Ross to Smith on April 14, 1944, "[and] fitting them together to produce something with a new dimension, so to speak." This is a characteristically, though not exclusively, Canadian construal of the aim of poetry within the typically Modern one of "making it new" (Pound) or making "a new thing"[21] (the latter being a phrase from Eliot that is echoed, not fortuitously, towards the conclusion of Klein's "Portrait of the Poet as Landscape"). In conjunction with "The Lonely Land" itself (and a good deal more that we know about Smith at the time of the poem's composition in the mid-to-late 'twenties—his recent completion of an M.A. on Yeats, for instance, and his growing knowledge of most of the major strains of classic Modernism, notably Imagism, Symbolism, and the new Metaphysicalism), Ross's remark enables us to construe the Commission of "The Lonely Land" as follows: to present (Smith's term [in "To Hold in a Poem"] is "hold") in a poem of a recognizably Modern (and, therefore, in Canadian terms, "new") style a vivid sense of the northern terrain ("Land") and spirit ("Lonely") of Canada. With almost seamless continuity this Commission becomes a series of problems to be solved, a series of decisions to be made in the realm of importation and adaptation. The most obvious of these is the decision about which of the various styles in the Modernist repertoire is most suitable or "right" (Ross's word) for a poem about the Canadian North. On the evidence of the published versions[22] of "The Lonely Land" Smith did not easily solve even the large stylistic problem presented by his self-appointed Commission: as it first appeared in *The McGill Fortnightly Review* in 1926, the poem speaks of a poet who has imported the style of the middle Yeats in his attempt to parallel in poetry the work of the "Group of Seven" (its subtitle on this occasion); on its subsequent appearance in *The Canadian Forum* in 1927, the poem shows the emergence of a double solution to the stylistic problems generated by Smith's Commission: imagistic free verse to capture the contours of the northern terrain and its creatures ("ragged / And passionate tones / Stagger and fall, / And recover . . .") and metaphysical generalization to convey the spirit of the Canadian North ("This is a beauty of dissonance / This is a desolate splendour"); and on its final appearance in *The Dial* in 1929, "The Lonely Land" reveals a poet who has chosen to stand pat on his choice of Imagism and the new Metaphysicalism as the stylistic solutions to the problems raised by his Commission, while also bringing his poem further into line with the cosmopolitan assumptions of Anglo-American Modernism by shedding the explicitly national references that were present in its previous printings, especially in *The Canadian Forum* ("These are the poems of Canada," "Long Lake").

The fact that, between its publication in *The McGill Fortnightly Review* and *The Dial*, "The Lonely Land" veered sharply towards nationalism with its publication in the *Forum* indicates at least two things of importance: (1) that a Commission must not be regarded as static, since it may change as a poem proceeds from its initial inception to its final form (in this case, absorbing and discarding components along the way); and (2) that, in so far as it can be determined by the place of a poem's publication (here a series of "native" and "cosmopolitan" periodicals), its intended audience must be factored into any accounts of its Commission and the ensuing problems and solutions. (Sometimes Commissions are quite literal and limiting, as was the case with pieces published in Purdy's *The New Romans* [1967], where contributors were asked to submit "personal" and "relatively brief" accounts of "how they felt about the U.S. and Americans" but left to choose an "aspect of the subject"[23] and a form for their views—that is, to solve the problems contingent upon the Commission. Atwood's "Backdrop Addresses Cowboy" is one of the works "especially written for *The New Romans*,"[24] and it should be read with an awareness of the circumstances of its Commission in Centennial Year for a volume to be published in Edmonton by the ultra-nationalistic Mel Hurtig). It can therefore be seen that the idea of the Commission that is being advanced here as a means of coming to terms with the components of Canadian poems should no more be conceived as necessarily static (though it may be this) than the factors, tendencies, and circumstances surrounding the resolution of the difficulties engendered by the Commission should be limited to a consideration of such "big" issues as aesthetics and literary movements; on the contrary, a Commission may be fluid and changing (as variant editions, not to mention manuscripts, frequently confirm), and there is no reason to eliminate, except when patently irrelevant, any factor—historical, economic, biographical, geographical, bibliographical . . .—that can shed light on the initiation and resolution of a Commission, the inception, creation, and achievement of any Canadian poem.

Before returning to "The City of the End of Things," it is worth taking a moment to restate the model being advanced for the study of importation and adaptation in Canadian poetry in terms of an analogy with Solitaire, a card game, or, rather, a series of card games, which appears to offer a more useful image of artistic activity than Baxandall's Eliotic billiard game (where Y, the influencee, is the cue-ball that hits X, the influencer, to produce a "rearrangement" of the relation of the two balls to each other and to "the array of all the other balls").[25] In the card-playing analogy, the poet's Commission is equivalent to his choice of a particular type of Solitaire to play (there are numerous varieties of the card game), and the ensuing problems and solutions are parallel to his drawing and deploying the cards in his pack—that is, the genres, styles, image patterns, and so on that are in his repertoire. An achieved Commission corresponds to getting the game of Solitaire "out," a happy condition that luck and skill may achieve quickly and elegantly or—as was the case of "The Lonely Land"—in a more indirect and "messy" way. The more experienced the Solitaire player, the more likely he or she is to attempt and "get out" a difficult game (a pastoral elegy, for example, or a long and intricate poem such bp Nichol's *The Martyrology*); the less experienced, the more likely to attempt easier games (three-stanza lyrics, for instance, or plot-based narrative poems) and to fail to bring even these to an elegant solution. Some players will choose to play the same variety of Solitaire repeatedly (as Bliss Carman did in *The Pipes of Pan* series [1902-05]), and will be judged accordingly. Others will exercise themselves (and us, their spectators and critics) by continually, and often simultaneously, playing different games and solving various problems. When a player goes beyond existing Solitaires to produce a significantly different version of the game, he can be considered as an innovator, as a talent who has "altered" the tradition in the manner valued by Eliot, Bloom, Baxandall, and others. Arguably, this has yet to happen in the field of Canadian literature, and may never happen, since the very idea of *the* tradition has fallen into disrepute under the pressure of such decentralizing forces as regionalism, feminism, and Post-Modernism.

2

In "The City of the End of Things," Lampman took as his Commission, selected as his game, the task of writing a poem about the negative consequences of materialism ("the End of Things") for the human spirit and for human society. The fact that in manuscript "The City of the End of Things" is subtitled "The Issue of the Things That Are" and paired with "The Land of Pallas" (subtitled "The Country of the Ought to Be")[26] allows us to situate the poem's depiction of the effects and results of materialism's elevation of matter over spirit within the humanitarian-socialist tradition that stretches back in the Victorian period through William Morris (whose *News from Nowhere* is a principal source for "The Land of Pallas")[27] to Ruskin, Carlyle, F.D. Maurice, Robert Owen, and others who had long since adopted a sceptical (and, by turns, trenchant and prophetic) attitude to industrialism and its parent individualism.

But, while a recognition of Lampman's continuity with the British humanitarian-socialist tradition is necessary to explain his concern with the consequences of elevating the material over the spiritual, it is not necessarily sufficient to explain his decision to focus his poem on a "City" (a location that contrasts markedly with the rural setting of the socialist utopia of "The Land of Pallas"). In order to appreciate the reasons for this decision, and, indeed, to come to a full understanding of the Commission behind "The City of the End of Things," it must be recalled that the poem was first published in 1894 in *The Atlantic Monthly*, which is to say, in a major "Magazine of Literature, Science, Art and Politics" (to quote its subtitle) emanating from Boston, in the heart of the Northeastern United States. This fact is of great importance because it suggests that, at some stage of its execution (perhaps at the outset, perhaps *in medias res*, perhaps on its completion: we may never know), Lampman conceived of "The City of the End of Things" as addressing an issue that was of great concern to Americans, especially those in the Northeastern States, in the 1890s: the rapid and fairly recent growth of the cities of Chicago and New York particularly into massive industrial centres whose social and physical environments were increasing causes for concern.[28] Of Lampman's interest in America's urban problems, their human consequences and their possible outcomes, there is evidence in "To Chicago," a poem written a little over a year after "The City of the End of Things" in the Whitman long-line, a form evidently regarded by the poet as suitable for a celebration of the urban renewal that seemed for many evident in the so-called "white city" or "dream city" of the 1893 Columbian Exhibition or Chicago World Fair. The publication of Lampman's "To Chicago" in 1894 in another Boston periodical, *The Arena*,[29] seems to support the speculation that part of the Commission of "The City of the End of Things" was to speak to urban problems and their human consequences with particular reference to the industrial cities of the Northeastern United States. To judge by the one published response to "The City of the End of Things," the poem hit its mark. "'The City of the End of Things,' Archibald Lampman's splendid poem in the March *Atlantic*, will scarcely be understood by the people who wish to tear down all things and build bigger and higher," wrote Joseph Edgar Chamberlin ("The Listener") in the March 3, 1894, issue of *The Boston Evening Transcript*; "[i]t is a gloomy vision of the future: suggestive of Coleridge's 'Kubla Khan' in its language and imagery, but having a different feeling and a different purpose, if the Listener reads it aright. In Chicago the poem will not be popular. In Boston it ought to be. We are not so near to dwelling in this City of the End of Things as we might be: let us hope that we shall not come nearer to it!"[30]

Of the role of *The Atlantic Monthly*, not only as an hospitable niche for "The City of the End of Things," but also as a factor in its Commission, there is evidence above and beyond the magazine's mere location in Boston. In the same issue as the first publication of Lampman's "Alcyone" (which should also be read in the context of the issues being raised here), an anonymous review entitled "The City in Modern Life" in *The Atlantic Monthly* urges Americans to undertake careful study in an area that was already becoming a focus of special interest for the magazine: "the phenomena of the life in [their] cities."[31] The fact that "The City of the End of Things" was published in March 1894, near the perceptible beginning of this special interest (Henry J. Fletcher's "American Railways and American Cities" appeared in June 1894, the three parts of Charles Mulford Robinson's "Improvement in City Life" appeared in January-June 1899, and Henry Van Brunt's not unrelated "Architecture Among the Poets" appeared in April 1893), helps to explain why Lampman offered the poem to *The Atlantic Monthly*, but with certain misgivings. "I enclose some verses which are rather different from anything I have hitherto sent you," he told the magazine's editor, Horace Scudder, in a letter of May 25, 1893; "[t]hey are intended to represent—in an exaggerated way of course—what we are coming to, if the present developments of machinery continue under the present social and economic conditions. But perhaps you do not go in for that kind of thing."[32] Although "The City of the End of Things" doubtless helped to create the audience for "that kind of thing," it had one crucial antecedent among the items in *The Atlantic Monthly* that were concerned with urban life and related matters: Walter Crane's essay on "Why Socialism Appeals to Artists," which appeared in the Janurary 1892 issue of the magazine only a few months before the composition of Lampman's poem in the period between "30 Jun[e]. . .Aug[ust] 1892."[33]

As eloquent in its analysis of the evils of industrialism as it is in its championship of the "larger faith"[34] of Socialism, Crane's very Morrissian essay contains what can easily be seen as the point of departure for Lampman's own depiction of "The City of the End of Things" in terms suggestive of a gigantic factory whose inhabitants, with their "clanking hands" and "iron lips," have come to resemble the machines that they serve. "Our century has seen the development of an enormous mechanical invention," writes Crane,

> and, by its industrial application, has established a system of machine labor which has taken the place of the older system of division of labor . . . . [I]n the great commercial centres . . . the struggle for existence grows ever fiercer and more tragic. . . . Interesting and characteristic local developments disappear, and . . . art has a tendency to become more and more cosmopolitan. This state of things may be pronounced a blessing or a curse according to one's mental standpoint.[35]

To pronounce "*[t]his state of things . . .a curse*": here, it may be, is the inciting moment of Lampman's Commission in "The City of the End of Things," the challenge that the poet chose to take up and play out in the summer of 1892. We can never know this for sure, of course, but it is an hypothesis that gains support from the similarity between the negative attitude towards industrialism in Crane's essay and that of Lampman's poem, and from the resemblance between the "carved idols" and the "grim Idiot" in "The City of the End of Things" and the following passage from "Why Socialism Appeals to Artists":

> The blind Gods of Cash and Comfort are enthroned on high and worshipped with ostentation, while there exist, as it were on the very steps of their temples, masses of human beings who know not either, or at the most scarcely touch the hem of their garments.
>
> We must bow down and worship the golden image which our kings of profit and interest have set up . . . . These be your gods, O Israel.[36]

There is even a verbal parallel of the sort usually adduced as proof of influence or indebtedness between Lampman's "ceaseless round / Of a gigantic harmony" (i.e., cacophony) and the "restless and inharmonious" "machinery of life" in an industrial society which, Crane contends, "engenders" an "atmosphere" that is neither "happy . . . for the artist" nor "healthy . . . for humanity."[37] And could it be that these last phrases provided Lampman with the idea for the "venomed air" of "Lean Death" that "blanch[es]" "whoso of our mortal race" should stumble unexpectedly on "The City of the End of Things"?

"Why Socialism Appeals to Artists" may have prompted the Commission of "The City of the End of Things," and it may also have provided some of the cards in the pack of images and ideas that Lampman would deploy in "playing out" the poem, but it did not (nor could it, being prose) either pose or solve all the problems encountered by the poet in realizing his Commission. Probably the most immediate of these problems was formal: what style would be "exactly suited to the subject" of the industrial city and the "curse" of "machine labor," and what sort (genre, length) of poem would be appropriate? To the second of these questions, the answer should have been obvious if Lampman, as seems to have been the case, was contemplating publication of his poem in an American magazine, specifically *The Atlantic Monthly*: he would have to write a piece of sufficient magnitude to do justice to his subject, but short enough to win acceptance in a venue with a decided preference for lyrics over long poems. [Harold] Innis' remark that the relationship between Carman's poetry and the "demands of space" in American magazines may be invoked again in this context, for it is certainly arguable that the space allotted to poetry in *The Atlantic Monthly* and similar publications was a factor in Lampman's decision to render "The City of the End of Things" in the form of a medium-length (eighty-eight line) lyric. To the other question of what style would be most suitable or fitting for the subject matter of the poem, an answer can only be given in terms of the traditional associations and general characteristics of a given literary form—in this instance, iambic tetrameter in cross-rhymed units (*abab*) that are incorporated into verse paragraphs rather than presented as separate stanzas. As thus described, the form of "The City of the End of Things" breaks conveniently into three components, each answerable to an aspect of the poem's subject matter: first, iambic tetrameter, a form relatively unaccommodating to adjectives and adverbs and correspondingly rich in nouns and verbs, furnishes a very suitable vehicle for the poem's emphasis on mere things and on constant movement; secondly, crossed (alternative, interlocking) rhymes, a form at once repetitive, enclosed, and quite highly ordered, constitutes a fitting reflection of the "hideous" and "monotonous" routine of the inmates of "The City of the End of Things"; and, thirdly, the verse paragraph, a form more continuous and relentless than a series of stanzas, provides an appropriate accompaniment to Lampman's account of the "ceaseless" movement and inexorable running-down of industrial civilization. (One further and final factor that might have dictated the form of "The City of the End of Things" may have been Lampman's desire to set his poem apart from other city-poems with which it might immediately invite comparison, most notably "The City of Dreadful Night," which is written mainly in six-line stanzas of iambic pentameter.)[38]

To apply "logic . . . to aesthetics" in this way will seem to some to be altogether too rational and cold blooded. Surely, some readers will have been thinking, poetry is not simply the product of rational choices and problem-solving in a world governed by such factors as the available publishing outlets and poetic forms. What about inspiration and intuition? The answer to such cavils and queries must be that, in approaching poems as Commissions with ensuing problems for solution, "inspiration" and "intuition" have not so much been denied (except in the most naïve, sophomoric senses of these words) as brought within the perimeters of critical inquiry, made part of an approach to "influence" (importation and adaptation) that assumes the control of any poet who is worth studying over his resources and his work. To assume otherwise of a poet is to place his *oeuvre* beyond the pale of serious consideration for its own sake, to designate his works as mere documents that are of little, if any, intellectual and aesthetic interest in and of themselves. If this section has done anything beyond establishing a context and a means of approaching "The City of the End of Things," it has removed from the poem and from Lampman the implication of being what the opening stage of the argument implied: a rather passive, and therefore uninteresting, recipient of materials from poems by Thomson and others.

Indeed, and in conclusion, it is now possible to recognize that Lampman's borrowings from various poets in "The City of the End of Things" are part of a complex and purposeful process of importation and adaptation in which what Lampman chose to reject or ignore is as important as what he chose to appropriate and deploy. In the latter category are a number of words and images that helped Lampman to fulfil some important aspects of his Commission, namely the poetic description of a demonic edifice, its tutelary inhabitants, and its spiritual effects. From Pope and Smart, for example, he may have derived the idea of a vast architectural structure presided over by four ominous figures, one of whom is associated with the "lightless north." But since Lampman's Commission was to address industrialism and its consequences rather than Dulness or literary pretension, the bulk of *The Dunciad*, *The Temple of Fame*, and "Materies gaudet vi Inertiae" fall into the category of what he chose to ignore or reject in writing "The City of the End of Things." A similar pattern is discernible in the relationship between Lampman's poem and *The Excursion*, where it is only what pertains to the Commission of "The City of the End of Things"—principally, Wordsworth's description of a factory town and the figure of "Gain, the master idol of the realm"[39]—that are imported and adapted by the Canadian poet. Since in all these instances (and, no doubt, in others), Lampman subdued his chosen materials to his own purposes and form, he can no more be accused of being uncreative than unintelligent in his importations and adaptations; on the contrary, "The City of the End of Things" is the product of a poet who is as actively creative in his use of his sources as he is discerningly eclectic in his choice of them—a poet who is not, in his own sense, "perfect" but whose best works are certainly worthy of serious attention in and of themselves, not least in these days when the issues that many of them address are more urgent than ever before Canadians and Americans.

Notes

1. See Early, "A Chronology of Lampman's Poems," *Canadian Poetry: Studies, Documents, Reviews* 14 (1984): 82.

2. See *The Atlantic Monthly*, 72 (March 1894): 350-52.

3. Sutherland's article was first published in *Northern Review* in 1951, and is conveniently reprinted in *Archibald Lampman*, ed. Michael Gnarowski (Toronto: Ryerson, 1970), 159-78, the text quoted here. For a discussion of Sutherland's approach to Lampman's poem, see my "A Thread of Memory and the Fabric of Archibald Lampman's 'City of the End of Things,'" *World Literature Written in English* 21 (1982): 86-95.

4. See *Ibid.*, 89-91.

5. See L.R. Early, *Archibald Lampman* (Boston: Twayne, 1986), 99.

6. See Bentley, "A Thread," 89-95.

7. See, for example, *The Temple of Fame*, 26-27, 67-70, and 119-23, *The Dunciad* I, 13-15 and 46 and IV, 653-56 and *The Poetical Works of Christopher Smart*, ed. Karina Williamson (Oxford: Clarendon, 1987), IV, 20-25.

8. Introduction, *Poets of the Confederation*, ed. Malcolm Ross, New Canadian Library (Toronto: McClelland and Stewart, 1960), xi and ix.

9. "Tradition and the Individual Talent," *The Selected Prose of T.S. Eliot*, ed. Frank Kermode (New York: Harcourt Brace, 1975), 43.

10. See *The Anxiety of Influence* (1979; rpt. Oxford: Oxford UP, 1985), 153-54.

11. George Steiner, *Real Presences: The Leslie Stephen Memorial Lecture* (Cambridge: Cambridge UP, 1986), 7.

12. K.K. Ruthven, *Critical Assumptions* (Cambridge: Cambridge UP, 1979), 121. See also W.E. Collin, *The White Savannahs*, ed. Germaine Warkentin, Literature of Canada: Poetry and Prose in Reprint (Toronto: U of Toronto P, 1975), 183-88 and Bentley, "A Thread," 91-95.

13. *Critical Assumptions*, 123.

14. *Patterns of Intention: On the Historical Explanation of Pictures* (New Haven: Yale UP, 1985), 59.

15. "Introduction," *The Oxford Book of Canadian Verse, In English and French* (Toronto: Oxford UP, 1960), li.

16. "Eclectic Detachment: Aspects of Identity in Canadian Poetry," *Canadian Literature* 9 (1961): 12. The following quotation from Lampman is from *Archibald Lampman: Selected Prose*, ed. Barrie Davies (Ottawa: Tecumseh, 1975), 91; hereafter cited as *ALSP*.

17. See Brian Trehearne, *Aestheticism and the Canadian Modernists: Aspects of a Poetic Influence* (Kingston: McGill-Queen's UP, 1989), 230-307.

18. "Eclectic Detachment," 12.

19. See "Introduction," *The Book of Canadian Poetry: A Critical and Historical Anthology* (Chicago: U of Chicago P; Toronto: Gage, 1943), 28.

20. *Patterns of Intention*, 30.

21. Eliot, *Selected Prose*, 43.

22. These can be most readily compared in Desmond Pacey, *Ten Canadian Poets: A Group of Biographical and Critical Essays* (1958; rpt. Toronto: Ryerson, 1969), 212-14 and Smith, *Poems: New and Collected* (Toronto: Oxford UP, 1967), 50-51. Subsequent quotations from "The Lonely Land" are taken from these sources.

23. Al Purdy, "Introduction," *The New Romans: Candid Canadian Opinions of the U.S.* (Edmonton: Hurtig, 1968), ii.

24. *Ibid.*, "Acknowledgements."

25. *Patterns of Intention*, 60. In *The Hitleriad*, Klein describes poetry as "the solitaire of wit and rhyme"; see *The Collected Poems of A.M. Klein*, comp. Miriam Waddington (Toronto: McGraw-Hill Ryerson, 1974), 186.

26. Lampman MS. Papers, MG29 d59 Vol. 3, National Archives of Canada, Ottawa.

27. See my "A Wizard to the Northern Poets: Notes on William Morris in Nineteenth-Century Canadian Poetry," *Victorian Studies Association Newsletter* (Ontario) 44 (1989): 12-14.

28. Adna Ferrin Weber, *The Growth of Cities in the Nineteenth Century: A Study in Statistics* (1899; rpt. Ithaca: Cornell UP, 1963), 131 notes that a "tendency towards concentration in the cities was noticeable in the 1890s," but, of course, this was on nothing like the scale of urban growth in the Northeastern United States.

29. See *The Arena* 9 (April 1894): 632. In "Archibald Lampman

and Hamlin Garland," *Canadian Poetry: Studies, Documents, Reviews* 16 (1985): 42-43, James Doyle describes *The Arena* as "the most widely circulated American magazine of its day to be concerned with questions of social reform" and contrasts its "socialistic" and "radical" bias with the "conservative and nationalistic publications of Chicago" in which Lampman had asked Garland to place the poem in November 1893.

30. Quoted in *An Annotated Edition of the Correspondence between Archibald Lampman and Edward William Thomson (1890-1898)*, ed. Helen Lynn (Ottawa: Tecumseh, 1980), 111.

31. "The City in Modern Life" (rev. of Albert Shaw, *Municipal Government in Great Britain* [1895]), *The Atlantic Monthly*, 75 (April 1895): 553.

32. Peter E. Greig, "A Checklist of Lampman Manuscript Material in the Douglas Library Archives [Part 2]," *Douglas Library Notes*, 16 (1967): 13.

33. Early, "A Chronology," 82.

34. "Why Socialism Appeals to Artists," *The Atlantic Monthly* 69 (January 1892): 115.

35. *Ibid.*, 111.

36. *Ibid.*, 112-13.

37. *Ibid.*, 113.

38. The debt of "The City of the End of Things" to "The City of Dreadful Night" has been often asserted, but never examined in detail; the resemblances are verbal (for example, Thomson's poem also includes the word "clanking" [215]) and thematic (for instance, both deal with the negation of memory), but the poems are very different in their primary focus, "The City of Dreadful Night" being concerned principally with the "Death-in-Life" that results from the demise of "Faith," "Love," and "Hope" (these quotations are from the text of the poem in the *Complete Poetical Works*, ed. Bertram Dobell [London: Reeves, 1895]). In his *At the Mermaid Inn* column for March 5, 1892, Duncan Campbell Scott calls attention to the publication of "The City of Dreadful Night" in the February issue of *The Fortnightly Review*, noting its "intensely gloomy" atmosphere and manner (*At the Mermaid Inn: Wilfred Campbell, Archibald Lampman, and Duncan Campbell Scott in* The Globe *1892-93*, Introd. Barrie Davies [Toronto: U of Toronto P, 1979], 29). If Lampman read Thomson's poem at this time, which is very likely, it must have been fresh in his mind (and a subject, perhaps, of Bloomian anxiety) when he began "The City of the End of Things" on June 30, 1892.

39. See Bentley, "A Thread," 89-90.

Section VIII of *The Gay] Grey Moose: Essays on the Ecologies and Mythologies of Canadian Poetry, 1690-1990* (Ottawa: U of Ottawa P, 1992): 187-200. Reprinted with permission of D.M.R. Bentley and the University of Ottawa Press.

Into the West: "A Scene at Lake Manitou"

by Stan Dragland

> In the course of his life [Eshkwaykeezhik / Last Sky / James Red Sky] had acquired considerable knowledge of the Christian lore and rites and could see no fundamental conflict between them and those of his people.
>
> Selwyn Dewdney, *The Sacred Scrolls of the Ojibway*

Hardly anybody anthologizes "A Scene at Lane Manitou." It doesn't even appear in Souster and Lochhead's selected poems, *Powassan's Drum*, which gathers a group of Indian poems in a section with the same title. Ever since I first read the poem in *The Green Cloister*, I have wondered why it isn't more popular. Janice Simpson calls it one of Scott's best poems (67), and I agree. In my own Scott canon I place it above "On the Way to the Mission" and "The Forsaken," though, as Gerald Lynch hints, "A Scene at Lake Manitou" is almost "The Forsaken" revisited. The structure is very different, and so is the narrative centre—a mother's grief over the death of her son —but there is a similar focus on the strength, resilience, and endurance of the Widow Frederick, another of Scott's Native heroines. Glenys Stow says that "the passionate energy usually present in the Indian verse is missing" (175) in "A Scene at Lake Manitou"; perhaps such perception accounts for its being so often passed over in anthologies and critical discussion in favour of its companion poem, "At Gull Lake: August 1810." I can understand that, but not the greater popularity of "The Forsaken."

"The Forsaken" is very important in Scott's career as an early success in the free verse variable line, with occasional rhyme, of which "A Scene at Lake Manitou" is a later example. But "The Forsaken" is not a better poem. In fact, there *is* a surge of passionate energy in the narrative of "A Scene at Lake Manitou" when the Widow Frederick breaks in her grief and begins to feed the lake with her Western possessions, and there is also a structurally important and mysteriously intense recurrent image of the view out into the lake. The function of this image needs a subtler interpretation than it has yet received and, in fact, the poem as a whole needs to be read less as an expression of the difficulties of mixing cultures and more as the human tragedy it is.

The details of the poem are specific to their time, place, and culture, but these contribute to the narrative texture that roots the emotion. "A Scene at Lake Manitou" has as much in common with "By a Child's Bed" and "The Closed Door" as with any of the other Indian poems. Scott wrote "A Scene at Lake Manitou" in 1933, long after the death of his daughter in 1907, but that loss stayed green in him for the rest of his life. It adds a touch of poignancy to Scott's grandfatherly welcome of other people's children, like E.K. Brown's Deaver. The uncanny thing is that he also "foresaw" his loss. "By a Child's Bed" is haunting enough before one discovers that it was written in 1902:

> These fairy kisses,
> This archness innocent,
> Sting me with sorrow and disturbed content:
> I think of what my portion might have been,
> A dearth of blisses,
> A famine of delights,
> If I had never had what now I value most;
> Till all I have seems something I have lost;
> A desert underneath the garden shows,
> And in a mound of cinders roots the rose. (*Poems* 188)

This poem shows that Scott carried a parent's fears with him into the North. Retrospectively his treaty-making summers must have seemed a criminal sacrifice of time with his daughter.

To suggest that only parents may identify with other parents whose children are taken from them would be to underestimate the othering power of imagination and love. Still, shared situations multiply the intensity of the identification. Scott was travelling through a land in which infant mortality was extremely high, owing especially to the tuberculosis that is probably the death of Matanack and his father in "A Scene at Lake Manitou." In fact, two of the journals of July 27, 1906, record a death at Brunswick House on Lake Missinabie that probably influenced the poem. Samuel Stewart is silent on the subject. [Pelham] Edgar is brief and inadvertently ironic: "Very hot day —Bishop leaves early. Doctor Meindl concludes his work & Indian dies in evening." If Edmund Morris hadn't been a member of the party at this point, there would have been no indication that the Indian who died was a boy.

Stewart says that on July 27 Morris was "busily engaged in completing sketches made by him of several of the Indians," but Morris wasn't too busy to notice what was going on around him:

> Dr. Meindl examined the Indians in the little church. Many of them have the cough which so often leads to consumption, and—far away from the others—all alone like a wounded animal there was a young boy dying of consumption. The tent was covered by boughs of trees. He died this evg. and the chief read the service in the native tongue. He had no near relations and appeared frightened. (Morris papers)

Figure 1

This seems likely to be what Morris wrote, though what I translate as "frightened" might actually be "neglected." To read his diary is to understand well why Scott begins "Lines in Memory of Edmund Morris" with a joke about his friend's handwriting. Morris seems to go on from where the above passage leaves off to describe a long and monotonous dance held to honour the deceased boy.[1] The sketch in Morris's diary (see figure 1) seems likely to be his drawing of the scene he described verbally, though it appears with other sketches after his last journal entry. He probably flipped forward a few pages when he wanted to sketch something. Some detail from this death scene recalls the poem ("boughs of trees" could be the "cedar screen," for example), but the death of a young boy with "no near relations" is clearly not the death of Matanack. It is interesting, though, that in his "Old Lords of the Soil," a Toronto newspaper article dated May 9, 1907, Morris recalls seeing "a squaw when her boy was dying offering up sacrifices to appease the Evil Spirit." This is to illustrate the general question that "How deep a hold the Christian religion has on these people it is difficult to say." Circumstantial evidence suggests that the young boy's death and the woman's sacrifice, even if separate occurrences (even if the latter were only recounted to Scott by Morris, who stayed in the North longer than the treaty party did), probably fed into "A Scene at Lake Manitou."

Suggestions have been made that Scott had a particular Lake Manitou in mind, either in Saskatchewan (Slonim) or on Manitoulin Island (Simpson). There is a perhaps likelier candidate just west of Lake Temagami—not on but near the treaty party's route. However, it seems just as likely to me that Scott picked or rather named his setting in the same spirit in which he rolled together a medley of actual experiences to create a single narrative. Manitou is a powerful word, after all, and one that most non-Native people would be likely to understand at least superficially. "A Scene at Lake Missanabie" would be as effective a title as "Night Hymns on Lake Nipigon," or "Spring on Mattagami," but it would be lacking in spiritual resonance.

Substituting Lake Missinabie for Lake Manitou doesn't

pinpoint the poem's origin, because both the Widow Frederick and her "hand-sewing-machine" derive from Abitibi Post on the first leg of the 1906 journey. Gerald Lynch mentions the sewing machine (see figure 2), although he doesn't describe it quite accurately (51n). This is the photograph labelled "Indian Family, Abitibi 1906." The next photograph in the sequence (see figure 3) is of "The Widow Frederick." In Pelham Edgar's "Twelve Hundred Miles by Canoe" she is the "poor soul" of 70, "childless and a widow [who] craved medicine for loneliness." Edgar doesn't identify the woman by name, but his article is illustrated with the photograph mentioned above, captioned "The squaw who craved medicine for loneliness."

Figure 2

Figure 3

What about the phonograph that the Widow Frederick actually throws into the lake? None is mentioned as the possession of a Native, but Stewart says that "At [Long Lake Post], as at almost all the others we visited, a gramophone was kept going most of the day for the amusement of the Indians, who appeared to be highly delighted with the performance (102). This would perhaps be the "Edison cylinder type of gramophone" mentioned by S.A. Taylor, in "Reminiscences of Lac Seul," as being ordered by post manager J.D. Mackenzie sometime after 1906. That was when Taylor was "transferred to the Lac Seul Post as book-keeper and assistant" (46). Scott says in an undated letter to Florence Leslie Jones "that all my poems dealing with Indians are true to aboriginal conditions; I dislike the words 'founded on fact,' but in truth there is fact in all these poems." He then goes on to say of "A Scene at Lake Manitou" that the poem "is very close to actuality" (Scott papers). Both of these statements are somewhat equivocal, but the second hints at a single source for the poem. Would this have been witnessed or heard about? Might "actuality" have been composite? I can't say for sure. At any rate, the second last item in Scott's 1900-1910 notebook (though the date "15 Novr 14" appears just before it) is a list of subjects bearing, most of them, on "A Scene at Lake Manitou." These notes for the poem appear to be Scott's first exploration toward what it might focus on:

> The boy going to hospital
> Death of lad [?] with consumption
> Starting [?] baby
> Attempt of HB Co to get girl
> The woman who tore everything to pieces
> Wounded boy; throwing the household goods into water

Since Edmund Morris says that many people wanted "medicine for loneliness," one wonders how Dr. Meindl responded to the request. The request may sound naïve as well as sad, but why would so many make it unless they had some expectation of getting satisfaction? Dr. Meindl seems to have been a regular doctor—nothing in his official report or in other accounts of his activities suggests otherwise—so he would have felt responsible for mending the body and practising preventative medicine to the best of his abilities. Indeed a non-Native doctor of the time would have felt that western medical science had outstripped Native healing in administering to the body (the irony being that white medicine was needed to combat imported white diseases—smallpox, measles, tuberculosis). Dr. Meindl would have been a remarkable medical man indeed had he felt, in 1906, any inkling of a need to address himself to the spirit, or even the mind, to use the term most westerners still conceive of as arranged in a binary relationship with body. Loneliness is depression. There is a clue to what might have been needed for loneliness in Thomas King's *Medicine River*: "'A hot shower,' said Harlen, turning on the dome light and looking at the map, 'is great for depressions. In the old days, we used to have regular sweats for just that reason. The old people were pretty smart, you know'" (106). A "sweat" is a session in a sweat lodge, a sort of sauna for the spirit practised by Ojibway as well as the Prairie Blackfoot of King's novel.

But the question of who heals Natives better, the white doctor or the shaman, is beside the point, isn't it? Yes and no. Healing is what the Widow Frederick is seeking for her son in the poem. Interestingly, no healer, white or Native, is mentioned in the poem as having been sought for Matanack, at least none other than Father Pacifique. The Holy Water came from him; Matanack "had worn his Scapular / always." Father Pacifique is an earthly representative of Jesus, a well-known healer whose healing is magic, though miracle is the name it goes under. Jesus defies physical mortality by simply recalling to its body the departed spirit of Lazarus. His story has understandably raised the Widow Frederick's hopes. Faith in holy water and scapular might seem either sense or superstition, depending on one's religion. But perhaps the active absence is that of the shaman. Would an expert shaman, administering to Matanack's spirit and body in concert, paying attention to the relationship between human spirit and the spirits at large, be able to cure the white disease, the "foe" that slays him? Here again there would be different answers, depending on one's conception of the body: matter, spirit, both?[2]

To entertain such speculations is to treat Matanack as an actual patient, not as a verbal construct; it is to address the poem not as a poem but as a jumping-off point for extra-literary inquiry. Scott's Indian poems almost always stimulate such thinking, and there would be nothing wrong with it if it didn't masquerade as literary criticism. Is "A Scene at Lake Manitou" a document relevant to the question of assimilation, for example, to "the pain and frustration resulting from the clash of two cultures" (Lynch 51)? Does the Widow Frederick represent "the possibility of a creative reconciliation of the two cultures" (Simpson 75)? A qualified yes to both questions. But is the poem *about* these matters? Yes again, as far as I'm concerned, though I think we are talking now about secondary or even tertiary themes, subordinate to the tragic theme of inevitable death. To say so is to invert the usual priority in criticism of Scott's Indian poems, the assumption that the function of the poem is to make a statement, rather than to dramatize something. Yes, the shaman's absence is significant; no, it isn't central to the poem as a poem.

The Widow Frederick's name has attracted comment. Gerald Lynch assumes that the deceased husband was a white man. Janice Simpson recognizes this as an assumption, but builds on it, anyway: "perhaps the death of the white man was a prefiguration of Scott's fear, implied in the poem's final image, that attempts to combine the two cultures creatively are doomed to failure" (72). The word "implied" doesn't qualify this questionable generalization enough. In the matter of names Simpson makes an assumption of her own, the perfectly understandable one that Matanack is an Indian name (72). After all, it doesn't sound European. Scott may well have assumed that his readers would take it that way. There *is* a small chance that he remembered and would have expected his most persistent readers to discover that he had said something else on the subject in the first paragraph of his story "Spirit River":

> These things happened in the country of the Ojibway, where English and French begin to be merged with that soft language, and where all sounds are corrupted by a sort of savage slurring, particularly proper names,—Frederick becomes Matenack, Thomas becomes Toma, Pays Plat is Peepla and Teresa, Trasey. (*Elspie* 63)

There is a Trasey in "Spirit River," but no Peepla, Toma, or Matenack. There is a Toma in "Labrie's Wife," another (with Pierrish and Arcange) in "Roses on the Portage," and yet another in "The Mission of the Trees," where Matenack is the name of an Indian boy who dies of hunger.[3]

In "Spirit River," Frederick and Matenack are versions of the same word, the same name. I doubt that it makes sense to identify the two names in "A Scene at Lake Manitou" (Frederick Frederick is no name to give a character whose death you want taken seriously), but it does seem necessary to introduce the evidence that Matanack (or Matenack) is no Indian name, but a hybrid produced by the pull of one language on another. "Corrupted" and "savage slurring" are uncomplimentary, suggesting degeneration and not the vitality of a language in flux. Scott could not have been expected to regard the relaxation of English pronunciation and spelling as progress. His own language may have shifted, in certain plain-speaking poems (like "A Scene at Lake Manitou," in fact), away from inherited poetic conventions, but it would not have occurred to him that anything positive might come of hybridizing standard English. Well, Scott was no William Faulkner, thinking of his work from one end to the other as a single body made of organic parts. Most likely we aren't supposed to know (maybe he himself had forgotten) what he made of Matanack elsewhere, and the fact that it means Frederick should slide into the background.

What about the other name issue? Frederick *is* a European name, anyway, but that doesn't mean that the husband was white. Most members of the various Treaty 9 crews had European and Indian names both, just as many of the lakes and rivers have both—or sometimes more than two; English, French, and Native. Some of the signatories of the treaties, officially all Indians, had English names; some had Indian names, whether or not they could write them. The Widow Frederick has an Indian name, Stormy Sky, given only in English translation; likely her husband had one, too. Since he died 12 years ago, it isn't necessary to introduce him by name. Part of the complication here is that Widow Frederick is less a name than a marker of relationship in patriarchy, a suppression of female identity. Scott has not fully restored the woman's Ojibway name (and he does use untranslated Native names in some poems and stories), but he at least has indicated something of her original identity.

Is Stormy Sky a symbolic name, then? Janice Simpson finds it a key to the Widow Frederick's character. A storm of sorts does erupt in the poem ("something broke in her heart") when the death vigil becomes insupportable and Stormy Sky explodes into action, throwing her "treasured possessions" into the lake in desperate barter for her son. But this is uncharacteristic. In the aftermath of her grief throes, resignation resurfaces ("She knew it was all in vain"), followed shortly by her old resolution. Retrospectively the outburst seems to have been (less for Matanack than for herself) a release from the tension of hopeless hoping. There is nothing stormy in her calm view of the future:

> She was alone now and knew
> What she would do:
> The Trader would debit her winter goods,
> She would go into the woods
> And gather the fur;
> Live alone with the stir
> Alone with the silence;
> Revisit the Post,
> Return to hunt in September;
> So had she done as long as she could remember. (*Cloister* 52)

What this phlegmatic woman will do now is what she has always done. Native names are not necessarily keys to character, and perhaps Scott is acting on that knowledge. Given what we know of the controlled Widow Frederick, anyway, the name is ironic. Pacifique would actually fit her better.

Reflecting on Matanack, on the Widow Frederick / Stormy Sky, makes a mere beginning on the subject of names in "A Scene at Lake Manitou." Along with the other proper nouns, so many that they stand out and alert the reader to examine the notational system they represent, names are doorways into this poem. To the general respectfulness lent the capitalized names just mentioned, including that of Father Pacifique, additional reverence is due to Jesus and Mary. Lake Manitou is capitalized as a place, but Manitou and Nanabojou are names parallel to those of Jesus and Mary. Indian is capitalized, as would be expected; so is Christian. But with Holy Water and Scapular we seem to be in a discretionary area. Scott is elevating the objects represented by these words, and balancing them on the Native or natural side with Powers, Earth, Air, Water.

These last pairings of capitalized words are, in fact, an index of the cultural balance of the Widow Frederick's mind. They also create a frame of sorts for the central episode in which she breaks down. Just before this her mind is rambling: "Fitfully visions rose in her tired brain, / Faded away, and came again and again"; "Nanabojou / And the powerful Manitou / that lived in the lake" are "Mingled with thoughts of Jesus / who raised a man from the dead" (50). Once she calms down, after her outburst, this balance of Ojibway and Christian elements reasserts itself. The Widow Frederick decides that Matanack has "gone to his father / To hunt in the Spirit Land / And to be with Jesus and Mary" (52). This mixture of cultures may seem ironic to either Native or non-Native readers, but it appears natural to the Widow Frederick. At least the absence of authorial comment suggests that she normally feels no strain of reconciliation. What wrenches this mingling, this unity of diversities, out of simultaneity and into sequence is the strain of her grief. Then the capitalized Christian words are superseded by the capitalized Indian ones. It's not insignificant that the new religion gives way to the old, of course (suggesting, depending on one's perspective, either a regression or a return to roots), but that the two reassemble and cohabit again as part of the Widow Frederick's resignation is also significant. It means that this woman is not, like the "Half-breed Girl," tortured by mongrelism. She is more like Charles Wabinoo, in Scott's account: "the Indian at the best point of a transitional state, still wild as a lynx, with all the lore and instinct of his race undimmed, and possessed wholly by the simplest rule of the Christian life" (*Circle* 122).

I made something in chapter 3 of the fact that Scott patronizes Charles Wabinoo. Perhaps his speaker is patronizing the Widow Frederick. After all, Jesus and Nanabojou may be parallel figures, dying and reviving gods in their respective mythologies, but there is a huge difference between the faultless teacher / saviour and the trickster who is powerful and foolish at once. There is a huge difference between monotheistic and polytheistic cosmology. When he refers to Powers in the plural, and to "*the* Manitou in the lake" (my emphasis), Scott shows an understanding that spirit in Ojibway cosmology has not been drawn out of nature to dwell solely in the central figures. The Widow Frederick's ecumenism is simplistic, but there is no need to think of her as passively ignoring these differences because she is an Indian. She may be no Nistonaqueb, no intellect, but her simple-mindedness is readable as simply human. Scott may have *thought* that the Widow Frederick was merging an inferior with a superior system; he may have expected his readers to feel that sort of irony. But he didn't direct the reader to it, which means that there is no basis for reading racism into that aspect of the poem. The sentence in which the men "slouched away to their loafing" might sound like the notorious editorializing word "slunk" in "The Forsaken," but on a hot and humid August day, lying around seems sensible to me. I don't see reproaching these men for letting the girls get in "the last of the hay," since that is a game, not work. I don't think race is much of a factor in the poem, though Scott certainly hasn't skirted the damaging stereotype of the lazy Indian.

There are three other capitalized words: Post, Trader, and West. Added to the rest, especially since Scott is not usually given to uppercase proliferation, these suggest a stressing of the convention. With Scapular and Holy Water they help swing the voice of the narrator away from Duncan Campbell Scott and toward a persona that seems partly composed of the innocence of the Widow Frederick. After all, Trader is capitalized only in a section in which the third person of the narrator is clearly near the thoughts of the Widow Frederick. In the first line of the poem we read "fur trader's house," and then "trader" appears at the beginning of section 8. The trader is unnamed, so his position is what is being elevated in "Trader." This Hudson's Bay Company functionary has virtual control of the Widow Frederick's life. Like the other Indians, she is tethered to the "Post" by the "winter goods" advance, or "debit," she depends on the trader to give her against the furs she will bring him in the spring. English business, French religion: between them the "founding races" own her, body and soul.

Why is West capitalized? All of the other words are easier to figure than this one. If I were one of those critical dinosaurs, a devotee of Practical Criticism, I'd be obliged to make sure that no speck or smidgen of the poem were left unattached to an armature of unitary interpretation. What a relief those days are over. Why is West capitalized? I'll circle around to a possible answer.

D.M.R. Bentley has noticed that the "scene" in the title refers both to the dramatic scene that is recounted and to scene as in scenery (40). Some critics have felt that the scenery, particularly the view of the lake, comments on the scene. Any reader of the poem is going to feel the importance of these descriptions, which (not quite symmetrically) frame the narrative action, but there's a tendency to overinterpret, to paraphrase what they do so as to make them almost explicitly explain the action. Here they are:

The lake was all shimmer and tremble
To the bronze-green islands of cedars and pines;
In the channel between the water shone
Like an inset of polished stone;
Beyond them a shadowy trace
Of the shore by the lake
Was lost in the veil of haze (lines 11-17).

Worn out with watching,
She gazed at the far-off islands
That seemed in a mirage to float
Moored in the sultry air (lines 30-33)

The islands had lost
Their mirage-mooring in air
And lay dark on the burnished water
Against the sunset flare—
Standing ruins of blackened spires
Charred by the fury of fires
That had passed that way,
That were smouldering and dying out in the West
At the end of the day (lines 145-52)

Gerald Lynch observes that the landscape, at the end, has become "a wastelandscape." "The Widow Frederick may be 'resolute as of old,'" he goes on,

> but we are left to wonder how she is to traverse such a landscape without a son to live for and with a religion that is a mixed bag of Christian and Indian—spiritless Christianity, weak medicine. Although she achieved a questionable consolation with the thought that Matanack "had gone to his father / To hunt in the Spirit Land / And to be with Jesus and Mary," what value can such a religion retain in the shadow of the burnt-out image of the pines as "ruins of blackened *spires* . . . ." In this sense, the landscape with which the Indian is left to contend is both exterior and interior. That the poem is generally concerned with the Indians' future is suggested in the image of the fire that has passed, now "dying out in the West"; east-to-west is not only the

> physical direction taken by this fire that is "smouldering and dying away in ashes"; it is also the direction in which civilization moved, subsuming Indian culture. (53)

Janice Simpson takes this further:

> The wasteland world with which "A Scene at Lake Manitou" concludes is obviously not a breeding ground for a creative cultural synthesis, and the poem thus leaves the reader with the uncomfortable feeling that the woman, like her husband and her son, is doomed to be destroyed. (69)

I don't think the complex final image of the poem should be considered in isolation from the earlier versions of it (in the poem, in the day). What is *in* the three-part image we are looking at, what it's doing in the poem, is mysterious enough to compel interest. I think it's wise to honour that mystery, rather than stretching connectives or inventing context to lower it into the merely intelligible. What happens as the image changes throughout the day?

Possibly the "veil of haze" that obscures the distance is a morning mist, but the poem opens in what feels like the full heat of an August day. Probably what we see is heat haze. Now all of the first five sections (section 6 begins "suddenly something broke") should be seen as taking place in pretty much the same moment. Those early sections set the scene and introduce the antecedent context; there is no narrative advance. They feel quite full, of course, because we are offered a lot in them—not only the view of the lake, but the activity of the hay-makers, the image of the death watch, the history of the watcher and her son, her thoughts. But nothing happens until section 6. What then happens, with its aftermath, takes until sundown. It's astonishing, when you think of it, how foreshortened this action is. The Widow Frederick reaches her crisis, recovers from it, and plans out her future in a matter of hours. No one has commented on the speed of this recovery, perhaps because it doesn't feel unnaturally rapid. After all, the poem has very economically filled in those 12 years of the life of Matanack and his mother.

I think Janice Simpson feels the great distance from "bronze-green islands" to "standing ruins of blackened spires," because she suggests that the "rising mist uncovers images of destruction" (69) on the far shore of the lake, presumably, of which only "shadowy traces" may be seen at the poem's opening. But clearly they are the same green islands, changed utterly, at the end of the poem. I don't take literally the image of the forest fire that follows the dash. After all, as dramatic as the day has been, there was no forest fire on the islands in the lake. The islands now *look* as though they have been burnt up, but the sunset does that. The visual effect is reminiscent of this stanza in "The Piper of Arll":

> There were three pines above the comb
> That, when the sun flared and went down,
> Grew like three warriors reaving home
> The plunder of a burning town. (*Poems* 35)

But there is a nearer analogue of sorts. The forest fire is uncannily reminiscent of this sentence in "The Last of the Indian Treaties": "The Indian nature now seems like a fire that is waning, that is smouldering and dying away in ashes . . ." (110). Perhaps some unacknowledged pressure from this statement leads Simpson and Lynch to their anticipation of a bleak future, either for the Widow Frederick or her race. I don't see that kind of bleakness in the poem. The only time the Widow Frederick is definitely looking out at the lake is in section 2. Even then, there is no necessary attachment of the view to her consciousness. I don't want to be inflexible about this, just precise. What is sad about the end of the poem is not simply a lament for the waning of the race, but a reframing of an earlier image that appears at the end of section 4:

> He was just sixteen years old
> A hunter crafty and bold;

But there he lay,
And his life with its useless cunning
Was ebbing out with the day.

Perhaps it seems perverse to possess quantities of cultural context (religious conflict or harmony, the decline of the red race) and not to press it all into service, but the function of context is never to bend a poem out of its natural shape. The sun as it sets at the end of "A Scene at Lake Manitou" temporarily blackens the trees outlined against it, creating a frightening *effect* of waste and destruction (distanced from a real forest fire by a mere dash) infused with deep emotion born of its gathering into itself the tragic waste of Matanack's youth.

Having said that, having dealt with the ending of the poem in the poem's own terms—that is, placing the emphasis on the emotional impact of the dénouement as a fulfilment of the emotional disturbance in the Widow Frederick and its echo in the reader—I want to acknowledge that a capitalized "West" does feel like more than a direction. The West (seen as the Occident) is capable of subsuming the English business and the French religion I spoke of. Keeping this possibility in mind, there are two potential takes on the preposition "in": when read as "dying away *in* the West"—in that direction, into—the phrase indicates absorption and assimilation—*if* one identifies the "the fury of fires" with the Widow Frederick and the Widow Frederick with her race. The West may also carry something of the traditional association with a Christian Heaven, or divine source, as in "Good Friday, Riding Westward," or "Ode: Intimations of Immortality." This interpretation would multiply the irony. It seems important, however, to preserve the iffiness of all this; any attempt to assemble the haze of contingencies and assert that "A Scene at Lake Manitou" is about assimilation might well dissolve. It's not mere hairsplitting that brings me around to qualified agreement with Gerald Lynch: death by absorption is in the poem, yes, but in a resonance, a nuance. It's a question of proportion, or to use a photographic metaphor, of depth of field. Each reader / lens will adjust to it, will adjust it, somewhat differently.

Is it possible that "A Scene at Lake Manitou" is neglected because Scott's reputation has rested mainly with academics and academics aren't exercised by relatively simple poems? Simplicity often seems to require little analysis. Perhaps that's not it; "The Forsaken," a much more famous poem, is also straightforward. Perhaps there is something else: in the attempt to gauge how Indian the so-called Indian poems are, shaving off points of authenticity for distance from the "real thing," it's possible to forget to feel the emotion these poems generate. In the absence of "compensating" complexity, the critical reputation of "A Scene at Lake Manitou" may have suffered from that tangential approach. I would like to see its Indianness muted and its lovely humanness praised.

Notes

1. Somebody, either myself or Jean S. McGill, is inventing a path through the passage just quoted. In *Edmund Morris: Frontier Artist*, McGill deciphers thus: "a young Indian was dying of consumption and we visited him. It was a picture of loneliness. His wigwam was placed by the lake, far removed from the others. Boughs of trees had been placed over it to keep off the scorching sun but they had become dried up. Day after day like a wounded animal he awaited the end. It came quickly that night. A bull strayed into his tent and the boy died of fright, doubtless thinking in the dusk that it was an evil spirit. He had no near kin. The Indians were afraid to enter the wigwam but the Chief knelt by his side and read a sermon from their syllable bible or prayer book" (64)

2. See David Young, et. al., *Cry of the Eagle: Encounters with a Cree Healer*, "an account of what a Cree medicine man [Russell Willer] was able to express to outsiders about the way he perceives the world and how he attempts to transform his vision into action" (vii)

3. "The Mission of the Trees" was written in November 1899, perhaps as a result of Scott's first Indian Affairs visit to Northern Ontario. The dying boy with almost the same name (Matenack / Matanack) suggests a comparison of the two poems, but they aren't much alike. "The Mission of the Trees" is a sentimental ballad metrically reminiscent of "Hiawatha"; "A Scene" is in free verse. There is something of the same pagan / Christian tension in both poems, but handled

very differently. The "bad guys" in "The Mission" are pagans who turn on "Mizigun, the mighty hunter, / And his dear son Matenack":

> "These two Christians,"—cried the pagans,
> "Breed our hunger and our woe,
> Let us kill them and their spirits,
> They are turning Wendigo" (*Poems* 309)

Christian faith wins out in the poem, even over death; "A Scene" places the two religions side by side, with no overt valorizing of either.

Works Cited

Bentley, D.M.R. "Drawers of Water: The Significance and Scenery of Fresh Water in Canadian Poetry." (Parts 2 and 3). *Contemporary Verse II* 7.1 (1982): 25-50.

Dewdney, Selwyn. *The Sacred Scrolls of the Southern Ojibway.* Toronto: U of Toronto P for The Glenbow Institute, 1975.

Edgar, Pelham. "Twelve Hundred Miles By Canoe: Among the Indians in Northern Waters." *Canada* IV (Nov. 24, 1906): 255; "Second Letter" (Dec. 22, 1906): 436; "Ottawa to Abitibi" (Jan 5, 1907): 515-16; "Latchford to Matachewan" (Jan. 19, 1907): 61-62; "Biscotasing to Fort Matagami" (Feb. 2, 1907): 156-57; "Fort Matagami" (Feb. 16, 1907): 245-46; "The Homeward Journey" (Mar. 16, 1907): 412-13.

King, Thomas. *Medicine River*. Markham, ON: Viking, 1990.

Lynch, Gerald. "An Endless Flow: D.C. Scott's Indian Poems." *Studies in Canadian Literature* 7, 1 (1982): 27-54.

McGill, Jean S. *Edmund Morris: Frontier Artist.* Toronto: Dundurn, 1984.

Morris, Edmund. Edmund Morris Papers. Queen's University Archives.

----------. "Old Lords of the Soil." Toronto, *The News*, Thursday May 9, 1907.

National Photography Collection, Ottawa. Acc. 1971-205, Box 3266 F1: Treaty No. 9 Photographs.

Scott, Duncan Campbell. *The Circle of Affection and Other Pieces in Prose and Verse*. Drawings by Thoreau MacDonald. Toronto: McClelland and Stewart, 1947.

----------. Duncan Campbell Scott Papers. MG 30 D 100. Public Archives of Canada, Ottawa.

----------. *The Green Cloister: Later Poems*. Toronto: McClelland and Stewart, 1935.

----------. "The Last of the Indian Treaties." *Scribner's* 40 (1906): 573-83.

----------. *The Poems of Duncan Campbell Scott*. Toronto: McClelland and Stewart, 1926; Introd. John Masefield. London: Dent, 1927.

----------. *Powassan's Drum*. Ed. Raymond Souster and Douglas Lochhead. Ottawa: Tecumseh, 1985.

----------. *The Witching of Elspie*. Toronto: McClelland and Stewart, 1923. Rpt. New York: Book for Libraries, 1972.

Simpson, Janice. "Healing the Wound: Cultural Compromise in D.C. Scott's 'A Scene at Lake Manitou.'" *Canadian Poetry: Studies, Documents, Reviews* 18 (1986): 66-76.

Slonim, Leon. "A Critical Edition of the Poems of Duncan Campbell Scott." Diss. U of Toronto, 1978.

Stewart, Samuel. Journal (June 30-Sept. 9, 1905; May 22-Aug. 15, 1906; June 15-July 1, 1908. Department of Indian Affairs Archives. RG10e RG10 Vol. 11, 399.

Stow, Glenys. "The Wound Under the Feathers: Scott's Discontinuities." *Colony and Confederation: Early Canadian Poets and Their Background*. Ed. George Woodcock. Vancouver: U of B.C. P, 1974. 161-77.

Taylor, S.A. "Reminiscences of Lac Seul." *Moccasin Telegraph* (Fall 1962): 46.

Young, David, Grant Ingram, Lise Swartz. *Cry of the Eagle: Encounters with a Cree Healer*. Toronto: U of Toronto P, 1989.

Chapter 8 of *Floating Voice: Duncan Campbell Scott and the Literature of Treaty 9* (Concord, ON: Anansi, 1994): 174-88. Reprinted with permission of Stan Dragland and the House of Anansi Press Ltd., 34 Lesmill Road, Toronto, M3B 2T6. Photographs PA-59520 and PA-59523, Acc.1971-205, Box 3266 F1: Treaty 9 Photographs, National Photography Collection, are reproduced with permission of the Public Archives of Canada.

New Provinces? or, In Acadia, No Ego

by Susan Glickman

In 1893 "Ave" was published in a volume called *Songs of the Common Day* after a sequence of sonnets which served to balance the elegy both in length (thirty-seven sonnets to the elegy's thirty-one sections) and in style (restrained rather than grandiose, or, in the terms of this study, picturesque rather than sublime).[1] We remember from stanza IV of "Ave" that "the deep surprise and rapture" of the sublime cannot endure for long (l. 36)—the poet always finds himself back on earth with "the common, kindly flowers" (l. 37). The solace of the familiar is intimated in that odd but beautifully apt adjective "kindly"; the same spirit of tenderness pervades Roberts' sonnets, elevating what might otherwise seem merely virtuoso description into psalm-like meditation. Throughout the sequence the poet finds, if not rapture, then profound satisfaction in contemplation of the quotidian.

At the same time, he does remind us, especially in the winter sonnets, that hidden in the ordinary is always a "cordial essence" ("The Mowing," l. 11) or "germ of ecstasy" ("The Winter Fields," l. 12), however "unwittingly divine" ("The Sower," l. 7). Taken as a whole, the "Songs of the Common Day" propose a different ethos than the Romantic one of "Ave," a more strenuous, agrarian moral, explicated here in the sestet of "The Cow Pasture."

> Not in perfection dwells the subtler power
>   To pierce our mean content, but rather works
>   Through incompletion, and the need that irks,—
> Not in the flower, but effort toward the flower.
> When the want stirs, when the soul's cravings urge,
> The strong earth strengthens, and the clean heavens purge.

A good example of how Roberts' absolute confidence in the sonnet form helps him illuminate an otherwise banal subject is "The Pea-Fields," wherein the yearnings of a herd of cows stand for the aspirations of the spirit for beauty just beyond its reach. It is more than a little audacious for a poet whose most ambitious work has *Shelley* represent this hunger to turn his attention to browsing cattle. But I believe he carries it off.

The Pea-Fields

These are the fields of light, and laughing air,
  And yellow butterflies, and foraging bees,
  And whitish, wayward blossoms winged as these,
And pale green tangles like a seamaid's hair.
Pale, pale the blue, but pure beyond compare,
  And pale the sparkle of the far-off seas,
  A-shimmer like these fluttering slopes of peas,
And pale the open landscape everywhere.

From fence to fence a perfumed breath exhales
  O'er the bright pallor of the well-loved fields,—
My fields of Tantramar in summer-time;
  And, scorning the poor feed their pasture yields,
Up from the busy lots the cattle climb,
  To gaze with longing through the grey, mossed rails.

One of the great pleasures of this poem is its sensuality: a sensuality not clumsily bovine, but, on the contrary, delicate and whimsical, and found as much in the rich interplay of consonance and assonance as in the impressionist discrimination of colour and light. The paratactic structure of the octave, with its breathless "and . . . and . . .and" construction, persuasively recreates the act of looking, as does the careful description with its simultaneous repetition and differentiation of shades of "pale."

The speaker steps into the frame in a more analytic mode in the sestet, claiming the view ("well-loved fields," "*my* fields of Tantramar") and commenting upon it. Inevitably one makes the association between the speaker and the cattle gazing "with longing," but this analogy does no disservice to either, because the movement and gaiety of the scene draws us in too. By the end of the poem, it's not just the air that's "laughing."

As with his reinterpretation of classical elegy in "Ave,"

Roberts' use of the sonnet is radical in two senses: as a return to roots, and a gesture of independence. Having accomplished so much with the elegy, it is perhaps not surprising that he should wish to test himself within the confines of another great poetic form. What is surprising, however, is his use of the sonnet to present the Maritime landscape. Indeed, a glance through a contemporary anthology like William Sharp's *Sonnets of this Century* (1887) reveals surprisingly few poems dealing directly with nature. In the nineteenth-century English sonnet, "Nature as a revelation of spiritual truth, nature however beautiful, is increasingly seen as disjoined from, and indifferent to, man; and increasingly the emphasis is on man's plight in an alien universe: 'I, a stranger and afraid, / In a world I never made.'"[2] Moreover, as W.J. Keith has observed, "the descriptive sonnet, a poem that uses the fourteen-line form not so much to say anything of importance as to isolate and evoke the particular mood of a particular landscape, is rare in the history of the sonnet in English."[3]

And although sonnets themselves had undergone a revival with the Romantics, sequences were rare until Elizabeth Barrett Browning's bestselling *Sonnets from the Portugese* (1847). Following her success, and in the tradition of the Elizabethans, later sequences such as George Meredith's *Modern Love* (1862) were "almost exclusively preoccupied with a novelistic delineation of amatory relations."[4] The only real model available to Roberts for a nature sequence such as "Songs of the Common Day" was actually Canadian: Charles Sangster's "Sonnets in the Orillia Woods" (1859).[5] Rather than expressing alienation, Sangster's sonnets suggest that "Our life is like a forest" (VII, l. 1), evoke the "Blest Spirit of Calm that dwellest in these woods" (V, l. 1) and, meditating on "eternal change" in nature, note that "Man is awed, / But triumphs in his littleness" (VIII, ll. 9-10).

Sangster's twenty-two sonnets, proem and epilogue do tell the story of a summer romance, in the context of a past thwarting of love, but details of the relationship are extremely vague. (We must rely on biography to inform us that the poet's wife had died the previous year, only eighteen months after their marriage.) But rather than amatory relations themselves, what interests Sangster is the way in which a retreat to nature helps a young man possessed by tumultuous feelings regain some perspective on his life. Indeed, every forest creature has a familiar lesson for him: in sonnet IV, the ant and the bee; in VIII, fossils; in X, the snail, "Christian-like" in patience and resignation.

As the animal analogies suggest, Sangster generally does not turn to nature to be transported, but to be instructed on how to improve himself. He evokes the picturesque rather than the sublime, another quality Roberts generally shares with him in this form. Indeed, Roberts' repertoire of images in his sequence includes picturesque touchstones such as winding roads, cattle, plough horses, "a little brown old homestead, bowered in trees" ("The Oat-Threshing," l. 1) and "stumps, and harsh rocks, and prostrate trunks all charred" ("The Clearing," l. 1). But Roberts claims he "did not consider Sangster seriously at all," being solely influenced by "the best work in Europe."[6] Certainly Roberts' sonnets, with their elegance of form and language, control of mood, and variety of description, go far beyond anything accomplished by Sangster, so it is perhaps no wonder he would wish to dissociate himself from his Canadian predecessor and evoke only Wordsworth by calling his sequence "Songs of the Common Day."

This title alludes to the poetic goals articulated in the preface to the 1814 edition of *The Excursion*. After the rhetorical inquiry why "Paradise, and groves / Elysian, Fortunate Fields" should be "A history only of departed things, / Or a mere fiction of what never was" the rhapsody unfolds:

> For the discerning intellect of Man,
> When wedded to this goodly universe
> In love and holy passion, shall find these
> A simple produce of the common day.
> —I, long before the blissful hour arrives,
> Would chant, in lonely peace, the spousal verse
> Of this great consummation: and, by words
> Which speak of nothing more than what we are,
> Would I arouse the sensual from their sleep

Of Death, and win the vacant and the vain
To noble raptures; while my voice proclaims
How exquisitely the individual Mind
(And the progressive powers perhaps no less
Of the whole species) to the external World
Is fitted:—and how exquisitely, too—
Theme this but little heard of among men—
The external World is fitted to the Mind;
And the creation (by no lower name
Can it be called) which they with blended might
Accomplish:—this is our high argument. (ll. 47-71)[7]

Wordsworth goes on to invoke the "prophetic Spirit" of inspiration, and to pray for "a gift of genuine insight" for his "Song" (ll. 83-88).

Roberts too opens his sequence with a prayer the portent of which is identical to Wordsworth's:

Make thou my vision sane and clear,
  That I may see what beauty clings
In common forms, and find the soul
  Of unregarded things! (Prologue, ll. 9-12)

In pursuit of this goal, Roberts avoids metaphor, preferring the occasional simile, or literal description leading to moralizing reflection. There are few hidden symbols in his work; rather, symbols are explicated as they might be to the thoughtful observer, who wonders to himself why certain sights and sounds interest him so much. Here again Roberts follows Wordsworth, who declares in his first sonnet that "Duddon, long-loved Duddon, is my theme" (l. 14). Even when not addressed directly, the river remains the standard against which human accomplishments are to be measured. He professes to discover everything he needs to know about life from the exploration of his native landscape. Therefore, *The River Duddon* may be seen as a more ample version of *An Evening Walk*, or perhaps Wordsworth's revision of *Descriptive Sketches*, transferring the expedition from the exotic Alps to the familiar Lake District. Sangster precedes Roberts in locating a sequence very specifically in a Canadian setting, describing the local flora and fauna, but both Canadian poets incarnate the Wordsworthian sense of one's native habitat as inexhaustible.[8]

And just as Wordsworth resolves to "with the thing / Contemplated, describe the Mind and Man / Contemplating; and who, and what he was" (ll. 93-99), Roberts includes in his original sequence a fair number of poems which aspire to "philosophy." Most of these, however, form a separate group at the end of the sonnet sequence—they have no seasonal identity, and are at once less concrete imagistically and more overtly emotional than the other pieces.

Thus, as Don Precosky notes, the sequence really consists of two parts. The first twenty-six poems are ordered

> upon a temporal or causal principle; they do not merely belong together: they belong together in a specific order . . . Together they tell the story of a year in nature in New Brunswick . . . The remaining eleven poems, beginning with "In the Wide Awe and Wisdom of the Night," constitute not a sequence, but a group. Their sequential ordering is not as important as the fact of their being deliberately put in close proximity to each other. In these sonnets, Roberts usually omits specific details of setting and deals directly with ideas.[9]

In fact, only one of these final sonnets, "The Herring Weir," was included in the sequence as reprinted in Roberts' 1901 *Poems*. The others were all moved out of "Songs of the Common Day" into a section entitled "Miscellaneous Sonnets."

The "Prefatory Note" to this volume remarks: "Of all my verse written before the end of 1898 this collection contains everything that I care to preserve."[10] Evidently, Roberts did not dislike these sonnets; he simply felt they were not integral to a sequence whose goal was described as to "find the soul / Of unregarded things" (Prologue). A comparison of "Songs of the Common Day" as it first appeared with successive versions in 1901 and 1936 shows a continuous process of simplification and clarification:

The Evolution of Roberts' Sonnets

	Songs of the Common Day	*Poems* (1901)	*Selected Poems* (1936)
	Prologue	Prologue	Prologue
1	The Furrow	The Furrow	The Flight of the Geese
2	The Sower (*DT*)	The Sower (*DT*)	The Sower (*DT*)
3	The Waking Earth	The Waking Earth	The Waking Earth
4	The Cow Pasture	*To Frederiction in May-Time* (*DT*)	When Milking Time is Done
5	When Milking Time is Done	The Cow Pasture	The Frogs
6	The Frogs	When Milking Time is Done	The Cow Pasture
7	The Salt Flats	The Frogs	The Herring Weir
8	The Fir Woods	The Herring Weir	The Salt Flats
9	The Pea Fields	The Salt Flats	The Fir Woods
10	The Mowing	The Fir Woods	The Pea Fields
11	Burnt LandsThe Pea	Fields	The Mowing
12	The Clearing	The Mowing	*Where the Cattle Come to Drink* (*DT*)
13	The Summer Pool	*Where the Cattle*(*DT*)	Burnt Lands
14	Buckwheat	Burnt Lands	The Clearing
15	The Cicada in the Firs	The Clearing	The Summer Pool
16	In September (*DT*)	The Summer Pool	Buckwheat
17	A Vesper Sonnet	Buckwheat	The Cicada in the Firs
18	The Potato Harvest (*DT*)	The Cicada in the Firs	The Potato Harvest (*DT*)
19	The Oat-Threshing	In September (*DT*)	The Oat-Threshing
20	The Autumn Thistles	A Vesper Sonnet	The Autumn Thistles
21	Indian Summer	The Potato Harvest (*DI*)	The Pumpkins in the Corn
22	The Pumpkins in the Corn	The Oat-Threshing	The Winter Fields
23	The Winter Fields	The Autumn Thistles	In an Old Barn
24	In an Old Barn	Indian Summer	*The Stillness of the Frost* (*BN*)
25	Midwinter Thaw	The Pumpkins in the Corn	

26	The Flight of the Geese	The Winter Fields
27	In the Wide Awe and Wisdom of the Night	In an Old Barn
28	The Herring Weir	*The Stillness of the Frost* (*BN*)
29	Blomidon	Midwinter Thaw
30	The Night Sky	The Flight of the Geese
31	Tides (*DT*)	
32	The Deserted City	
33	Dark (*DT*)	
34	Rain (*DT*)	
35	Mist (*DT*)	
36	Moonlight	
37	O Solitary of the Austere Sky	

NOTE: Those sonnets first published in *In Divers Tones* (Montreal: Dawson Brothers, 1887) are noted as (*DT*), those from *The Book of the Native* (Boston: Lamson, Wolfe, 1896) are noted as (*BN*), and a title in italics entered the sequence with the 1901 revision.
Songs of the Common Day (Toronto: William Briggs, 1893)
Poems (New York: Silver, Burdett, 1901)
Selected Poems of Sir Charles G.D. Roberts (Toronto: Ryerson, 1936)

In "The Poetry of Nature," published in the American journal *Forum* in 1897, Roberts declares that the power in nature "which moves us by suggestion . . . may reside not less in a bleak pasture-lot than in a paradisal close of bloom and verdure, not less in a roadside thistle-patch than in a peak that soars into the sunset. It works through sheer beauty or sheer sublimity; but it may work with equal effect through austerity or reticence or limitation or change."[11] Given that he himself wrote poems such as "The Cow Pasture" and "The Autumn Thistles"—and that sonnets such as these are among his most widely admired works—it is not surprising that many critics have considered the paragraph above to be Roberts' most telling *ars poetica*. And the gradual pruning of "Songs of the Common Day" in the direction of austerity supports this interpretation.[12]

As we have already seen, debate about what constitutes legitimate poetic material had become fiercer with the rise of landscape poetry, and the enlargement of aesthetic categories beyond those Roberts calls "sheer beauty or sheer sublimity" had brought new perplexities. Mimesis was no longer just a neo-classical conundrum; whether poetry represents objective reality or subjective impressions, and if it does so through denotative language or, instead, by the feelings it evokes, were issues of immediate concern.

This concern runs throughout the columns written by Roberts' contemporaries William Wilfred Campbell, Archibald Lampman and Duncan Campbell Scott in "At the Mermaid Inn." The on-going argument over the respective merits of "realistic" and "romantic" approaches to nature accelerated in the final weeks of the column—and perhaps contributed to its demise. On 17 June 1893, Campbell declares that "Wordsworth, who has been called the greatest nature poet, has never divorced nature from humanity in any of his work, and it is really, after all, man with whom he deals. The true greatness of Wordsworth lies in his simple, grand emotion, his power of entering into the humanities of the scene about him. He is not and never could be a minute scenic artist, such as the descriptive sonnet writers we have today."[13] Then in the very next column, Lampman praises Herbin's *The Marshlands*, quoting as an example of his excellence exactly the kind of sonnet Campbell depreciates. Scott picks up the discussion about Wordsworth in the penultimate column, before Campbell ends all possible dialogue rudely, if humorously, with the following raspberry, published on the first of July:

At Even

I sit me moanless in the sombre fields,
The cows come with large udders down the dusk,
One cudless, the other chewing of a husk,
Her eye askance, for that athwart her heels,
Flea-haunted and rib-cavernous, there steals

The yelping farmer-dog. An old hen sits
And blinks her eyes. (Now I must rack my wits
To find a rhyme, while all this landscape reels.)
Yes! I forgot the sky. The stars are out,
There being no clouds; and then the pensive maid!
Of course she comes with tin-pail up the lane.
Mosquitoes hum and June bugs are about.
(That line hath 'quality' of loftiest grade.)
And I have eased my soul of its sweet pain.
John Pensive Bangs, in *The Great Too-Too Magazine* for July)

As Pope showed us blithely in *Peri Bathous: or, The Art of Sinking in Poetry* (1728), failure of the sublime results in bathos. What Campbell demonstrates here, equally well, is that failure of the picturesque gives us kitsch.[14]

Because publication of "At the Mermaid Inn" was suspended after this column, some critics have taken Campbell's parody to be an attack on his colleague, Archibald Lampman. He certainly was attacking Lampman's point of view in their on-going discussion, but the style of the parody is quite unlike that of Lampman. It is much closer, in fact, to a parody sonnet Lampman himself had published in a "Mermaid Inn" column thirteen months earlier, on 2 June 1892, and attributed to his "friend the sonneteer." This mysterious personage argues that "The best way to impress your subject on the reader is to cast it in a totally unsuitable form. It's the contrast that does it, you know." Then he demonstrates his point by reading the following:

Reality

I stand at noon upon the heated flags
  At the bleached crossing of two streets, and dream,
  With brain scarce conscious, now the hurrying stream
Of noonday passengers is done. Two hags
Stand at an open doorway piled with bags
  And jabber hideously. Just at their feet

A small, half-naked child screams in the street.
A blind man yonder, a mere hunch of rags,
Keeps the scant shadow of the eaves, and scowls,
Counting his coppers. Through the open glare
Thunders an empty waggon, from whose trail
A lean dog shoots into the startled square,
Wildly revolves and soothes his hapless tail,
Piercing the noon with intermittent howls.

The ensuing dialogue is also recorded:

> "Certainly you have outdone yourself this time," I cried. "You have violated every law of moral dignity and literary decency. I prefer not to hear any more of your so-called sonnets." My friend instead of answering me broke out into a roar of coarse and offensive laughter. He crushed up his papers into a couple of pellets, and, filliping them into my face, strode rudely out of the room. The poor fellow has talent if he would only apply it in a serious and sensible way.

As F.W. Watt has commented, "it is obvious that Lampman was not so scandalized by his friend the sonneteer, his *alter ego*, his Satanic spirit, or whoever he was, as a literal reading of the scene would suggest; he perhaps regretted that decorum would not allow longer and more fruitful visits."[15]

At this time, the only book Lampman had published was *Among the Millet*; the only sonnet in it which resembles "Reality" in its confrontation with the more sordid aspects of urban life is "The Railway Station." By contrast, most of the other sonnets are subjective and emotional, with titles like "Perfect Love," "Despondency," "Music," "Solitude" and so on. Their language and imagery is conventional; they would scandalize no one. Others are given a natural context, such as "A Night of Storm" or "Winter Thought," but as the title of "An Old Lesson from the Fields" indicates, they do exactly what Campbell recommends: interpret nature as it relates to human endeavours. The isolated figure of the meditative poet appears in virtually every piece, to remind us who is putting together the scene and why it is important. Only a very few sonnets are primarily descriptive: "In November," "Solitude," "Autumn Maples," "The Dog," and "March." And even in these, the use of figurative language and point-of-view insists that we understand nature to be the context for the speaker's personal reflections rather than the locus of an exercise in aesthetic representation.

Moreover, Campbell himself seems to have valued Lampman's work for its idealism rather than seeing it as woodenly realistic. His "Bereavement of the Fields," an elegy for Lampman written shortly after the poet's death in February 1899, mourns that he will "No more, with eyes adream and soul aloft, / In those high moods where love and beauty reign / Greet his familiar fields, his skies without a stain" (ll. 5-7).[16] He imagines that, having been "enfranchised," Lampman now moves among "Wordsworth, Arnold, Keats, high masters of his song" (ll. 44-49). Given Campbell's view of Wordsworth as the ideal nature poet, placing Lampman among this company suggests admiration rather than disdain for his work.

Nonetheless, the modern editor of the "At the Mermaid Inn" anthology, Barrie Davies, comments that "At Even" bears "a cruel resemblance to Lampman's [poetry]," especially as it is followed by "tongue-in-cheek criticism, which refers to such poetry as 'millet-like in its terse realism.'"[17] But in fact, the text reads "*M*illet-like," so while Campbell may have been taking a dig at Lampman's volume *Among the Millet*, he was more likely targetting Roberts, whose sonnet "The Sower" alludes to Millet's most famous painting. Moreover, the "poet" of "At Even," John Pensive Bangs, is clearly a reference to "the American versifier John Kendrick Bangs [whose ditties] appeared regularly in important magazines such as *The Century*."[18] Not only were Roberts' sonnets in "Songs of the Common Day" more realistic than those of Lampman, but he was both more prolific and more frequently published in important American journals—and thus more likely to be lampooned by comparison with someone like Bangs. And *Songs of the Com-*

mon Day had just come out to great praise at the time of Campbell's column.

Whether or not Roberts was the intentional and Lampman the incidental target of Campbell's ire, we can be sure of one thing: he intended his comments to embarrass *all* those who persisted in writing nature lyrics once he had decided his own emphasis on description in *Lake Lyrics and Other Poems* (1889) had been misguided.[19] He was not alone in his disdain for the direction poetry was taking: Roberts himself was to write several articles deploring the vulgarity of modern poetry and applauding Canadian poets for resisting the excesses of imagist technique and socialist ideology. As late as 1931 he exclaimed that "Cubism, imagism, futurism, have had their fantastic way with the people, who, ashamed to acknowledge their bewilderment, have hastened to acclaim them lest they be thought conventional."[20] Nonetheless, as Campbell's parody makes clear, Roberts too was becoming increasingly "modern" —that is, terse and objective.

Roberts' 1901 revision of "Songs of the Common Day" is earlier than the date usually given for the beginning of Canadian modernism: the publication of Arthur Stringer's collection of free verse, *Open Water*, in 1914. But the movement towards restrained diction and concrete imagery in Roberts' sonnets can certainly be seen as going in a modernist direction, even if he had yet to dispense with closed form. By contrast, the tired sentiments and grandiose imagery of Stringer's poems are not up-to-date just because he *doesn't* rhyme.

Stringer's famous foreword argues passionately against "necrophilic regard for . . . established conventions"; he declares that modern poetry "is remote and insincere, not because the modern spirit is incapable of feeling, but because what the singer of today has felt has not been directly and openly expressed. His apparel has remained mediaeval. He must still don mail to face Mausers, and wear chain-armour against machine-guns."[21] And there are a few poems in this collection, particularly those which use anaphora for a paratactic structure reminiscent of Walt Whitman, which seem to be authentically enabled by their form. These include "Milkweed," "The Steel Workers," "At Charing-Cross," and the following:

> One Night in the North West
>
> When they flagged our train because of a broken rail,
> I stepped down out of the crowded car,
> With its clamour and dust and heat and babel of broken talk.
> I stepped out into the cool, the velvet cool, of the night,
> And felt the balm of the prairie-wind on my face,
> And somewhere I heard the running of water,
> I felt the breathing of grass,
> And I knew, as I saw the great white stars,
> That the world was made for good!

But this poem works as much because of patterned repetition in language and metre (especially in lines 1 and 3, as against 2 and 4) as because of unexpected liberations from form. Moreover, this kind of epiphanic moment is repeated so often, and sometimes so trivially in the book, and is so clearly counterpoised to "black hours" (in which "Blind fate has bludgeoned my bent head, / And on my brow the iron crown / Of sorrow has been crushed"), that both lose their persuasiveness and read as established conventions themselves. It is hard to see what is modern about such poems as "Black Hours," "Some Day, O Seeker of Dreams," "Before Renewal," "The House of Life," or "Life-Drunk."

In other words, Stringer's work rarely lives up to the expectations engendered by his foreword. It would be more accurate to say that most of the poems in *Open Water* escape tedium only because they are in free verse; open form, rather than allowing the poet to express new ideas, enables him to express conventional ones in a slightly new way.

It may be objected that prosody *is* the only aspect of poetry that can be made new. But the modernist thesis was—and remains—that the world underwent cataclysmic change during and after World War I, and that the old forms carried implicit values to which no one could (or ought to) subscribe anymore. According to this argument, all formal constraints, whether of rhyme and metre or of larger units like stanza or verse form (sonnet, sestina, and so on) are, by definition, reactionary. Louis Dudek, for example, while conceding that Lampman's sonnets are the best work of the period, argues that they are ultimately meretricious because they subscribe to an obsolete form. On the other hand, he describes Stringer's foreword to *Open Water* as "an early document of the struggle to free Canadian poetry from the trammels of end-rhyme."[22] He even discusses F.O. Call's preface to *Acanthus and Wild Grape* in identical terms, despite the fact that Call argues for increased poetic freedom rather than simply in favour of open over closed forms—and demonstrates the versatility he's after by offering works in both styles in the two halves of his collection.[23]

As R. Alex Kizuk notes, "Call pursues the same unities of concept and feeling in both parts of the book . . . in the two title poems 'Acanthus' and 'Wild Grape,' content is sublimely unaffected by form . . . Both announce that beauty is eternal."[24] Two other themes—love, and courage in the face of war—also unify the two halves of the book. Nonetheless, Munro Beattie asserts that the acanthus poems "illustrate conventional modes, and manage to be as inane and hackneyed as most other Canadian poems of the period. The wild grape poems are intended, on the other hand, to demonstrate the superiority of free verse."[25] But neither Call's foreword nor his poems "demonstrate" such a thesis. Nor can one imagine a writer publishing half a book of deliberately terrible poems without making it clear they were intended as parody! This is especially unlikely in Call's case, given that thirteen of these thirty-two "inane and hackneyed" poems are reprinted from his British chapbook *In a Belgian Garden* (1917).

Far from being in the vanguard of modernism, Call did not continue his experiments in *vers libre* for long; his next book,

Blue Homespun, consists of forty-three sonnets in three sequences. The first and longest of these, from which the collection takes its title, consists of twenty-three impressions of French Canada and its inhabitants. Unlike Roberts' views of the Maritimes, Call's sonnets are frankly emotional. They make no pretense to cool aestheticism in form or feeling. The other two sequences, "From a Walled Garden" and "Simples" are even more subjective, exploring the individual's relationship to nature in a familiar Romantic idiom.[26]

Another writer frequently described as the first modern poet in Canada is W.W.E. Ross. He too wrote sonnets that have been disregarded by critics anxious to argue that free verse is the only authentic modern prosody. Indeed, the introduction to *Shapes and Sounds: Poems of W.W.E. Ross*, in which Barry Callaghan makes the claim for Ross's pioneering status, misrepresents the poet in order to support this claim. First, Callaghan asserts that "Imagism, the kind of poetry Eustace wrote, is at the base of all modern verse," although in this very collection of 122 poems, only seventy-one can fairly be described as imagist.[27] The others include twenty-two free verse poems on abstract subjects like love, death, and art; six of Ross's own prose poems and eight translations of those of Max Jacob; eleven rhyming poems and one rhymed translation; and three sonnets. Second, the editors of *Shapes and Sounds*, say they "like to think that if W.W.E. Ross had lived to compile a collection of his own poems these are the ones he would have wished to preserve"—implying thereby that Ross would have conceded to their virtual rejection of his entire volume of sonnets, one of only three books published in his lifetime.[28] This would seem to go against what Ross himself has to say on the subject:

On Art

Art makes from time to time some form unseen
Before and fills it with a content true,
So that it stands triumphant in the view,

High beauty with no intervening screen;
We seek the mystery that lies between
The execution and the impulse new—
The starting,—and the exact method too
Whereby the hands of art their triumphs glean;—
But all in vain. The secret is not told
Even into the ears of wisest men,
Who stand perplexed before such mystery.
Art takes new forms and yet retains the old,
Efficient as at the very moment when
They were engendered in such secrecy.

As well as arguing for the continued efficacy of old forms, this sonnet is one of a group described as "Sometimes Quite Imitative," and echoing poets like Shakespeare and Shelley. Other pieces in the book on subjects like the persistence of classical mythology or the power of beauty support its argument.

However, by the time *Shapes and Sounds* was put together, Ross had recognized that his reputation as an early modernist was what had revived interest in his work, and was content to let his sonnets be overlooked. In effect, he became complicit in rewriting his own poetic history. For example, the three sonnets included in the book are all dated 1932, the date of publication, not of composition, and placed in the second section of the collection as though they were written later than the "laconics." This misrepresentation no doubt contributed to statements like that of George Woodcock that "Ross found his inspiration drying up around 1930 [and] turned unsuccessfully to the very traditional forms (sonnets and rhymed quatrains)."[29] But in his own foreword to *Sonnets* (1932), Ross notes that they were written from 1923-30; that is, contemporaneously with the free verse published in *Laconics* (1930).[30] He stated his goals for the sonnets as follows: "The general idea was to employ the 'clean' language of free verse without the lack of rhythm or pattern which offended me in [modern poets] except some of Pound etc. As regards Sonnets I had the notion that longer lines were needed to express ideas adequately and the sonnet form seemed suited to this purpose. I was ditched by my inability to carry over into them—the prestige of the models being so great—the aforesaid 'cleanness.'"[31] In other words, *Sonnets* and *Laconics* balance each other; together they constitute his version of *Acanthus and Wild Grape*.

It may be worth noting that Ross's sonnets are more regularly Petrarchan than those of any of his Canadian predecessors, including Sangster. And, on the other hand, most of his free verse wants to be dactyllic hexameters; frequently it gives in to almost complete regularity, whether in early poems like "Wild Rose," "Death Nearing" and "Pacific," or late ones like "Sounds" (1940) and "Autumn Maples" (1958). Ross's imagination was clearly possessed by formal conventions, as he seems to acknowledge in a letter to Ralph Gustafson of 23 September 1956: "The laconics form was developed in 1925 in an attempt to find one that would be 'native' and yet not 'free verse,' one that would be unrhymed and yet definitely a 'form.'"[32] Thus the free verse foreword of *Shapes and Sounds* argues for:

> These pieces in
> a style more "North American,"
> perhaps, or in
> a manner more "Canadian"
> than the most
> of what has been put down in verse
> in Canada,
> are not asserted to be so;
>
> But it is hoped
> that they will seemingly contain
> something of
> what quality may mark us off
> from older Europe,—
> something "North American"—
> and something of
> the sharper tang of Canada.

Unfortunately, to my ear, this unrhymed statement of poetic

intention is as clumsy, trite, and prosaic, as his sonnet on the sonnet. Granted, most of Ross's free verse poems are not as bad as this, but many are sufficiently banal that the huge claims made for his accomplishment become intriguing. In general, an obsession with novelty of technique has been the most unfortunate legacy of the modernist movement. But the reverence with which Ross is regarded today indicates something more particular: the extraordinary pressure the critical establishment in Canada has felt to derive a genealogy of local modernism.

When he revised "Songs of the Common Day" yet again for the 1936 *Selected Poems of Sir Charles G.D. Roberts*, Roberts followed the 1901 order very closely. However, he abandoned the presentation of the poems as a sequence, calling them simply "Sonnets of the Canadian Scene." This is a further stage in the elimination of the subject: without the structural continuity implicit in the idea of a sequence, the inference of coherence and point-of-view of a single speaker's ongoing experience of the scene cannot be made. In effect, he removes himself from the picture.

A tendency towards impersonality can be seen from Roberts' earliest work, which relies on Greek mythology, through his animal stories, to a late achievement like "The Iceberg." In "Ave," however, we saw something quite different: an exuberant, even defiant, appropriation of what M.H. Abrams has called "The Greater Romantic Ode" to describe a New Brunswick childhood as sufficient cause for the poetic vocation. "Ave" celebrates the individual, but it was hard for Roberts' generation to convince themselves or their readers of the legitimacy of this response at the end of the nineteenth century; self-consciousness about what Keats had called the "egotistical sublime" led to a withdrawal from such confident assertions of the mutuality of person and place, and an insistence on "objective" description as a chastening discipline. The dialectic enacted in Roberts' 1892 volume between the sublime ("Ave") and the picturesque ("Songs of the Common Day") is paradigmatic.

Still, virtually every poet drawn towards the sublime has been, at the same time, disturbed by the implications of valuing one's imaginative transformation of reality over reality itself. What Keats tried to do with his doctrine of negative capability was to resolve the dilemma by escaping subjectivity: the poet was to be receptive to sublimity, but to stay focused on its source outside rather than on its effect upon himself. He wanted "a life of sensations rather than thought." Indeed, Arthur Henry Hallam considered that Keats and Shelley should be described as "picturesque" because they were "poets of sensation." This was meant as praise, for he held that "this powerful tendency of imagination to a life of immediate sympathy with the external universe, is not nearly so liable to false views of art as the opposite disposition of purely intellectual contemplation."[33]

This observation, from Hallam's 1831 essay "On Some of the Characteristics of Modern Poetry," anticipates a central tenet of what *we* call "modern poetry," usually summed up by the Imagist motto *No Ideas But in Things*. But the theory was already implicit in the Romantics and explicit in the writings of many of Hallam's contemporaries. As Carol T. Christ has noted, the Victorians' "concern with what they feel are the dangers of Romantic subjectivity explains their various attempts to construct an epistemology which derives the feeling with which we respond to objects from the qualities of the objects themselves. 'To see the object as in itself it really is' is the business of the critical power, Arnold tells us.[34]

In other words, valorization of the image as the central feature of poetry derives from a conviction of the unreliability of the subject. This ethos led initially to Wordsworth's use of "spots of time": in order to anchor an instant of intensely personal feeling in the world of shared material experience, the poet tries to recreate the physical circumstances which provoked—or at the very least provided a context for—the private revelation. Walter Pater describes this procedure for the aesthetic movement as art's search for the "exquisite moment." And

James Joyce borrows from the language of the Church to redefine it for the modernists as "epiphany."

At the same time as they strove for objectivity in the representation of images, the Victorians also experimented with different poetic forms to find some way to lessen the dominance of the lyric subject. Browning donned the masks of dramatic monologue, Tennyson moved from confession to narrative, and Arnold from private to public utterance. All three explored the theme of the isolated spirit and its longing for release from the burden of consciousness; all three deplored the perils of solipsism. And they took the reading public with them: when the most comprehensive anatomy of the Romantic sublime, *The Prelude*, was finally published in 1850, Victorian retreat from its epistemology was already established. Tennyson's *In Memoriam*, appearing the same year, was a bestseller; Wordsworth's posthumous work was not.

According to C.K. Stead, the driving force of modern poetry since the Georgians has been away from discourse towards the image. This is the "new poetic" he describes in his book of that name.[35] It was not that earlier writers neglected imagery; it was that they blathered on before, around, and after its appearance. Thus Ezra Pound describes Wordsworth as "a silly old sheep with a genius, an unquestionable genius, for imagisme, for a presentation of natural detail." John T. Gage, who quotes this comment, notes that Pound's "reluctance to say the same for the poetry of the Victorians was not due to any fundamental disagreement about the ends of poetry as perception of an exquisite moment, but to the ostentatiousness . . . of their versification.[36]

Josephine Miles has traced the history of poetry from the Augustan sublime, full of high sentiment, through Wordsworthian directness of both observation and discursive statement, to the rejection of such directness as manifesting presumption—first in the Victorian movement towards implication and symbol, and later in imagism and a general preference for unmediated description.[37] Ultimately, modernists reverse Wordsworth's emphasis, preferring to trust the "eye" over the

"I." The retreat from the Romantic sublime leads to a revival of the picturesque, in its modern, free-verse incarnation: imagism.

Imagism, though a short-lived and rather disorganized movement in and of itself, has had a profound and lasting impact upon the way the natural world is represented in modern poetry. While the picturesque fashion had encouraged accuracy of description, it also perpetuated the medieval habit of "divine analogy": that is, all phenomena were seen to be part of a moral tableau the explication of which awaited the discernment of the poet. The physical world was of interest for what it could teach one about the metaphysical. But the imagists insisted on creating a mood in the reader through the *exclusive* use of imagery. No rhetorical flourish, no editorial comment, was to disturb the absolute pictorialism of method. As A.J.M. Smith put it, "the purpose of an imagist poem is to perceive and to present perception."[38]

Graham Hough observes that: "We know well enough what the Imagists are tired of. They are tired of Arnold's 'Dover Beach' . . . the melancholy nineteenth-century automatism by which no natural object can appear without trailing its inglorious little cloud of moralizing behind it."[39] Though they had already become uncomfortable with the position of the Romantic subject, Arnold, Tennyson, Browning, and their contemporaries did not have the twentieth-century prejudice against abstract or conceptual language (or against eloquence). Interested as they were in description, they did not expect it to carry the entire rhetorical burden of a poem. However, during the reign of what Eliot called the "objective correlative," the resources of poetry became increasingly limited to whatever could be portrayed as out there, in the world. But ironically, as Carol T. Christ has noted: "The dream that objects without interpreting discourse can carry their own meaning not merely for a single consciousness but for the whole mind of Europe commits Eliot to a poetry that contains a far greater amount of ambiguity than more Romantically based theories of poetic composition do."[40]

In his own comments on the rise of modernism, Roberts maintains that "the pervading sanity and balance of the Canadian temperament, its obstinate antagonism to extremes, saved us from the grotesque excesses indulged in by some of our English and American contemporaries. Modernism, so called, came without violence to Canada. It was with us not revolution but evolution."[41] Many recent critics have come to the same conclusion, and ascribed it to a similar reading of the Canadian character—although where Roberts sees "sanity and balance" they find fault. John Metcalf speaks for this camp when he declares: "Insularity, creaking conservatism, and ignorance delayed the impact of the 'modern' in Canada by some forty years."[42]

Canadian literature only became a subject of concerted scholarly inquiry in the second half of this century; Northrop Frye was a leader in this regard. But neither he nor his followers were frank about the strong modernist bias with which they approached works of earlier periods. At the same time, they were all too cognisant of their cultural insecurity. The result was that the only explanation they could imagine for the slowness of the modernist movement to catch on in Canada was that our writers were second-rate. The corollary to this assumption was that any writer who exhibited the correct (modernist) allegiance must be superior. Hence the apotheosis of Ross.

Louis Dudek provides an analysis of early nineteenth-century Canadian literature according to the modernist credo: "Bourgeois culture was languishing in an emotionless and decently smothered poetry of cosmic abstractions and abstract Christian virtues, at best of nature references which were unexperienced and unvisualized. Then came Imagism, Chinese poetry (as analyzed in a famous forgotten essay by Fenollosa), and finally even modern psychology, to tell us that this was death, not life. The real image is the live thing."[43] Besides the dismissive tone, and the speciousness of describing nature references in pre-Imagist verse as "unexperienced and unvisualized," we find also intellectual elitism via the reference to the Fenollosa essay (which, far from being forgotten, is constantly referred to and quoted from by Pound scholars). Unfortunately, Dudek is not the only writer to take this tone. Margaret Coulby Whitridge is another: "It is scarcely surprising to find Lampman moving away from the influences of Keats and Arnold, Wordsworth and Tennyson, to which he and most other Victorian poets originally succumbed. Lotus-land was left far behind when the poet faced reality with a sense of impending terror and tried to depict the coming age."[44]

The propensity of critics speaking from prejudice to make errors is well-known. An obvious example occurs in Jean Mallinson's essay on Roberts, when she recapitulates the syllogism that 1) a new country provides new experiences which 2) can *only* be expressed in a new language, so therefore 3) colonial poetry, availing itself of existing conventions, must inevitably be false. To let her speak in her own words:

> The weakness of colonial style is . . . its often timid reliance on traditional models which belong to the poet linguistically but which are not appropriate to the novelty of experience in a new setting. It is perhaps particularly unfortunate that Roberts and others in his time had or thought they had, not only a style but a philosophy of nature which was hard to evade. Had he been writing from eighteenth century models it might have been more apparent that pastoral poetry as it was then written in England was absurdly inappropriate as a model for writing about his experience in the Canadian bush, and he might have invented something new.[45]

She gets so carried away that she fails to notice that Roberts was *not* writing about "his experience in the Canadian bush," but about life on well-established Maritime farms. Among other caveats, Mallinson's lapse is a salutary reminder of how prevalent the "bush-garden" myth has become.

Finally, in *Aestheticism and the Canadian Modernists*, Brian Trehearne says that he hopes to establish "the profound continuity of Modernism with the prior literary traditions it appeared at first to have routed." Nonetheless, he too states that "the Canadian Modernists are set keenly apart from the poetasters of their time by virtue of their recent Aesthetic rather than late Romantic poetic derivation."[46]

So, according to Dudek, Canadian poets in the first quarter of this century wrote abstractly Christian poetry with ineffectual imagery; to Whitridge, their work was unrealistic and socially irresponsible; to Mallinson, it was hollowly derivative; to Trehearne, formally inept. All of these charges, and more, may be found in the manifestos and reviews of A.J.M. Smith ("Wanted: Canadian Criticism," *The Canadian Forum*, April 1928), Leo Kennedy ("The Future of Canadian Literature," *The Canadian Mercury*, December 1928), and F.R. Scott ("New Poems for Old," *The Canadian Forum*, 1931). Perhaps the most famous—and certainly the best-known—site of this criticism is Scott's poem "The Canadian Authors Meet." First published in the *McGill Fortnightly Review* in 1927 (the year after Roberts became the president of the Toronto branch of the Canadian Authors Association), it has had an extraordinarily wide and continuous dissemination. Scott reprinted it (minus the self-mocking conclusion) in the first anthology he published with Smith, *New Provinces: Poems of Several Authors* (1936), and included it again in their next joint effort, *The Blasted Pine: An Anthology of Satire, Invective, and Disrespectful Verse Chiefly by Canadian Writers* (1957). Even today the poem is anthologized as though it were credible as literary criticism, or even, as Desmond Pacey calls it, "a complex condemnation of a whole set of values, of a whole way of life."[47]

Chester Duncan is a rare dissenting voice, arguing that the poem "in its adolescence and unkindness, gets worse and worse with the years."[48] Perhaps the most offensive aspect of the poem is its characterization of the female members of the association as "virgins of sixty who still write of passion" by a callow observer whose remarks reveal him as equally ignorant of women, older people, and passion itself. But as Bentley notes of the poem, "its central satirical and critical tenets—that to be cosmopolitan, objective, high Modern and male is to be good and to be patriotic, subjective, Romantic and female is to be bad—have been enshrined by the high Modernist Munro Beattie in no less influential a place than the *Literary History of Canada*."[49]

On the other hand, it is precisely because of its "adolescence" that the poem can get away with such unkindness. As Dudek reminds us, "Scott's poetry . . . is an example in our literature of the turning away of one generation from another, in this case the son departing from the ways of the father."[50] Similarly, in the special Canadian issue of *Poetry* he edited in 1941, E.K. Brown remarked on the "bitter vengefulness" with which nineteenth-century writers were pursued by the generation of their grandchildren. In addition to the usual complaints that the older poets were too formal and only wrote about nature, he adds the observation that "much of what the younger generation deplored arose from a cause of which they still seem strangely unaware: the silence and sterility of the generation between."[51]

It is certainly true that Carman and Roberts got extra mileage out of the fact that there were no powerful young poets to challenge their pre-eminence during the first quarter of the century. On the other hand, the blandly uplifting rhetoric that passed for literary criticism on their part did not inspire any confidence that the old guard was as seriously committed to art as it fancied. Carman's silly lectures, Roberts' suave generalizations, and Duncan Campbell Scott's fixation on "beauty" were recognized by younger writers for what they were: attempts to smooth over any challenge to poetry in general and to their own work in particular.

Indeed, the scorn heaped on his predecessors by Smith in his original preface to *New Provinces* seems to respond as much to the public statements of the older generation about poetry as to their poetry itself. He declares complacently that: "The bulk of Canadian verse is romantic in conception and conventional in form. Its two great themes are nature and love —nature humanized, endowed with feeling, and made sentimental; love idealized, sanctified, and inflated. Its characteristic type is the lyric. Its rhythms are definite, mechanically correct, and obvious; its rhymes are commonplace."[52] But if we actually peruse the anthologies he singles out for blame—*The Oxford Book of Canadian Verse* and Garvin's *Canadian Poets* —we find a great many strenuous ballads and narratives based on aboriginal or folk materials, some satire, some elegy, and many works that simply do not fit his general descriptions. And in his 1976 "Confessions of a Compulsive Anthologist," Smith admits that "despite the tone of rather youthful arrogance" to be found in this preface, at the time he "knew practically nothing about the historical development of a genuine Canadian poetry."[53]

This is exactly why his preface was suppressed—E.J. Pratt, Robert Finch, and the publisher Hugh Eayrs disliked "the tone of it and the general impression which will be left on the public mind that Canadian literature had to wait for us to get its first historical success."[54] By contrast, the preface substituted by Scott makes only the most timid claim to "a development of new techniques and a widening of poetic interest beyond the narrow range of the late Romantic and early Georgian poets," and even admits that the "search for new content was less successful than had been the search for new techniques."[55]

Perhaps Scott was feeling beaten down by the two-year process of getting the anthology out, and he had warned Smith early on that "You will have to be careful not to make claims for a greater radicalism than this volume will show."[56] At any rate, his modesty proved prophetic of the book's lack of impact on the literary scene; of the eighty-two copies sold in the first ten months, ten were purchased by Scott himself, and reviews were equally sparse.

As with the canonization of Ross, it is extraordinary how reverent literary history has been with respect to *New Provinces*. John Ferns is a typical advocate in arguing that, although this odd anthology didn't come out until 1936, and although it was "little bought and read when it appeared," it somehow "helped to establish, albeit belatedly, a modern poetry movement in Canada."[57] Surely it would be more accurate to say that it has established, retroactively, a turning-point in Canadian culture: a point when a talented new generation of poets publicly dissociated themselves from the post-Romantic aesthetic. Although they had been preceded by Stringer and Ross, Smith and Scott have had far more impact through their long and active literary careers than had the earlier modernists. This is really why *New Provinces* has become so important: it portended the imminent triumph of modernist theory (and, to a lesser extent, practice) in Canadian literary life.

The book itself hardly lives up to the claims of its authors. As noted above, Smith objected to "the bulk of Canadian verse" for being lyrics with correct rhythms and commonplace rhymes. Yet almost every poem in the anthology rhymes, and many are in regular iambic pentameter. Moreover, the most daring moment is not to be found in the few unrhymed pieces like Finch's "The Hunt," or Scott's flat-footed cut-up prose in "Efficiency," but rather A.M. Klein's disguised sonnet in section V of the most ambitious piece in the collection, "Out of the Pulver and the Polished Lens."

In his rejected preface Smith had also complained that: "The most popular experience is to be pained, hurt, stabbed or seared by beauty—preferably by the yellow flame of a crocus in the spring or the red flame of a maple leaf in autumn."[58] Similarly, in his essay "Direction for Canadian Poets," published the same year as *New Provinces* itself, Leo Kennedy condemns his colleagues for producing "Jingo utterances from mental vacua; stereotyped descriptions of loons, lakes, pine trees, prairies and other natural Canadian phenomena," etcetera.[59] So we should not expect to find their anthology opening with the almost purely formal exercises of a Robert Finch. Nor should we expect any nature poetry, especially that deliberately evocative of the Canadian landscape. But what of Scott's "Trees in Ice" or "March Field," Pratt's "Seagulls," Kennedy's "Shore," or Smith's own "Creek"? Indeed, Mr. Cosmopolitan Smith himself employs most of Kennedy's detested stereotypes (substituting ducks for loons, it is true), in what is perhaps the best-known poem in the book, "The Lonely Land."

Desmond Pacey made available the three successive versions of this piece, from its first appearance in *The McGill Fortnightly Review* of 9 January 1926, the subsequent revision published in *The Canadian Forum* of July 1927, and the final version of *New Provinces*. He suggests that: "All these changes, with one possible exception, effect an improvement in the poem: they tighten it, make it more concrete and exact. The one exception is the addition of the final four lines, which seem to me merely to make explicit and abstract what was implicit and concrete."[60]

It is hard to disagree with his approval of Smith's revisions when one compares the pseudo-Yeatsian form of the original stanzas with those we know now:

> Hark to the wild ducks' cry
> And the lapping of water on stones
> Pushing some monstrous plaint against the sky
> While a tree creaks and groans
> When the wind sweeps high.
>
> It is good to come to this land
> Of desolate splendour and grey grief,
> And on a loud, stony strand
> Find for a tired heart relief
> In a wild duck's bitter cry,
> In grey rock, black pine, shrill wind
> And cloud-piled sky.[61]

However, the original poem is actually shorter, at twenty lines, than the final version, at thirty-eight. And the original is absolutely direct, both in its emotional presentation and in its physical details. So what happens in revision cannot be a matter of "tightening" or becoming more "concrete." The revision is really a matter of rhetorical emphasis: the old Romantic self-presentation, the tired heart seeking relief among the scenes of nature, is no longer persuasive to readers like Pacey. It's acceptable for the speaker to attribute bitterness to the spray, and passion to the cries of the wild duck—to animate the landscape with his feelings—but not to acknowledge them himself. Modern readers are uncomfortable with the explicit editorializing of the closing quatrain, but not with the first occurrence of this evaluative voice in the penultimate stanza, because there it is accompanied with lots of imagery. And in general, the imagery *has* improved: the language is fresher, more interesting, sharper.

In fact, what we see Smith doing here is exactly what we saw Roberts do before him: emphasizing description and, at the same time, trying to limit and control the reader's experience of the speaking subject so as not to evoke, too clearly, the tradition of Romantic sublimity implicit in any scene of an individual's colloquy with nature.[62] Smith goes much farther prosodically than Roberts does, creating the typographical illusion of free verse by breaking up a rhyming poem into short lines. But, oddly (in spite of himself?) he also evokes a memory of nature-sonnets like those of Roberts by dividing his poem into three equivalent stanzas (eleven lines, eleven lines, twelve lines) followed by a short rhetorical conclusion, not unlike the three quatrains and concluding couplet of the English sonnet. "The Lonely Land" even has the traditional "volta" or turn after the first two sections, where it moves from description to reflection upon the meaning of the scene. In its bones, it remembers sonnet form very well. So despite the novelty of its layout in 1936, there is a good deal that is conventional about "The Lonely Land."

Moreover, as George Woodcock remarks: "The familiar cedar and firs and wild ducks' calls in a poem like 'The Lonely Land' lead us into a landscape in its feeling as mythological as any painted by Poussin for the encounters of Gods and mortals."[63] Similar scenes can be found in many of F.R. Scott's poems, with a slightly different emphasis: the land is still inarticulate because, as he puts it in "Laurentian Shield" (1946), it has not yet been "written on by history," but eventually it will be transformed by "the full culture of occupation."

Curiously, though he speaks of "occupation," Scott, like Smith and other proponents of this nationalist vision, doesn't recognize that the land is empty neither of people nor of history. As Gary Boire notes, "from the midst of these declarations of a decolonized aesthetic, paens for an indigenous art, Canada's indigenous peoples are conspicuously absent. In the process of centring himself, the self-styled pioneering artist either marginalizes native people or renders them altogether invisible."[64] Scott's recourse to Greek mythology to summon new Canadian legends is, in this regard, particularly telling. To make the land less lonely, he and his modernist *confrères* summon the same Mediterranean zephyrs that whispered to [Thomas] Cary on the Plains of Abraham. To imagine a Canadian future, they evoke a European past.

In this regard, as in so many others, the modernist project is not nearly as new as its advocates like to believe. As D.G. Jones reminds us: "Except that it looks north rather than west, 'Laurentian Shield' recapitulates in miniature the nineteenth-century long poem; its pioneering theme, its basic figure whereby the land becomes articulate in a material syntax which will yet be a civil sentence in the pastoral mode."[65] Despite their belief that they were finally discovering an authentically Canadian poetic, Smith, Scott and their associates were actually rephrasing a traditional vision in the language of the day. Ignorant of their poetic forbears as they might have been, avid as they were to denounce them, they inherited an ideology in spite of themselves.

This is certainly one reason for the phenomenon Sandra Djwa notes: "The resonant image of the Twenties was 'The Solemn Land,' 'The Lonely Land,' the northern land, but not *The Waste Land.* Critical comments that Canadians did not produce poems analogous to 'Prufrock' or 'Mauberly' and hence a version of English and American modernism, do little to illuminate modern poetry in Canada. The cultivated disillusionment that characterizes such poems is simply not representative of the Canadian culture of the Twenties."[66] For as Thomas Weiskel remarks, "the wasteland motif of Romantic and

Modernist literature presents an abridgment of the sublime moment so that we . . . await futilely the restorative reaction which never comes, except ironically."[67]

Djwa's "cultivated disillusionment" is equivalent to Weiskel's "irony"; neither can coexist with the evocation of the sublime. And the sublime still had a powerful hold on the Canadian psyche, despite critical insistence on impersonality and objectivity. In fact, this impulse towards the sublime may add another dimension to Robert Kroetsch's famous witticism that Canadian literature "evolved directly from Victorian into Postmodern . . . the country that invented Marshall McLuhan and Northrop Frye did so by not ever being Modern."[68]

Notes

1. Charles G.D. Roberts, *Songs of the Common Day, and Ave: An Ode for the Shelley Centenary* (London: Longmans, Green, 1893). The edition used for the purposes of quotation, however, is *Selected Poetry and Critical Prose*, ed. W.J. Keith (Toronto: U of Toronto P, 1974).

2. Gertrude M. White and Joan G. Rosen, *A Moment's Monument: The Development of the Sonnet* (New York: Charles Scribner's Sons, 1972), 94.

3. W.J. Keith, "Charles G.D. Roberts and the Poetic Tradition," in *The Proceedings of the Sir Charles G.D. Roberts Symposium, Mount Allison University*, ed. Carrie MacMillan (Halifax: Nimbus, 1984), 60. Keith acknowledges the accomplishments of John Clare in this vein, but notes that "his writings were little known in Roberts' time" (60).

4. Maia Bhojwani, "'The Tides': Roberts' Sonnet about the Sonnet," *Journal of Canadian Poetry* 3 (1981): 20.

5. Charles Sangster, "Sonnets, Written in the Orillia Woods," in *The St. Lawrence and the Saguenay and Other Poems; Hesperus and Other Poems and Lyrics* (reprint, Toronto: U of Toronto P, 1972), 155-86. All quotations are from this edition.

6. Roberts dismisses Sangster in a 1927 interview, published as "Lorne Pierce's 1927 Interview with Charles G.D. Roberts (as Reported by Margaret Lawrence)," ed. Terry Whalen, *Canadian Poetry: Studies, Documents, Reviews* 21 (1987): 70. D.M.R. Bentley argues that "the sonnet, particularly the Petrarchan sonnet, with its spatial

division between a blocked octave and sestet, furnished Canadian poets of the 'Confederation' period and before with 'framing' or 'fencing' structures suitable to the features of the cultivated and civilized baselandscape." "A New Dimension: Notes on the Ecology of Canadian Poetry," *Canadian Poetry: Studies, Documents, Reviews* 7 (1980): 9. By the "ecology" of poetry, he means the innate decorum, or fit, between an aesthetic form and the landscape it describes; he seems to see Roberts' use of the sonnet as almost inevitable. Many of his explorations of this topos can be found in *The Gay]Grey Moose: Essays on the Ecologies and Mythologies of Canadian Poetry 1690-1990* (Ottawa: U of Ottawa P, 1992).

7. William Wordsworth, *The Excursion* in *Poetical Works*, ed Thomas Hutchinson, corrected by Ernest de Selincourt (Oxford: Oxford UP, 1936). Marshall McLuhan suggests that "the notion of this pre-established harmony between the individual mind and the external world is the key to the eighteenth-century passion for landscape. Wordsworth naturally underestimates the degree to which this 'theme' was rehearsed among men from 1730 onwards, if only because anybody tends to be least aware of the decades immediately before his own time. They are taken for granted, as known." See "Tennyson and Picturesque Poetry," *Essays in Criticism* 1 (1951): 272-73.

8. On the other hand, there is a great deal more description in Roberts' sonnets than in Wordsworth's, which are mostly excursions on human history and emotion rather than close observation of nature for its own sake. The only descriptions in *The River Duddon* which contain Roberts' kind of concrete imagery are those of the cows in XVIII, 1-3; the sheep-washing in XXIII, especially 5-8; the gloomy niche in XV; and the resting place in XXIV, 1-9. Even "Return," sonnet XVII, while full of unusually brilliant imagery, turns into historical speculation. And "Flowers," sonnet VI, is fourteen lines of Augustan platitudes. As Wordsworth himself notes: "There is scarcely one of my Poems which does not aim to direct the attention to some moral sentiment, or to some general principle, or law of thought, or of our intellectual constitution." Quoted by Josephine Miles in *Eras and Modes in English Poetry* (Berkeley: U of California P, 1964), 136.

9. Don Precosky, "'The Need That Irks': Roberts' Sonnets in *Songs of the Common Day*," *Canadian Poetry: Studies, Documents, Reviews* 22 (1988), 22-23.

10. Charles G.D. Roberts, *Poems* (New York: Silver, Burdett, 1901).

11. Roberts, "The Poetry of Nature," in *Selected Poetry and Critical Prose*, 276.

12. Jean Mallinson argues that it "describes accurately his own temperamental preference" even though the rest of the article proposes that the poetry of objective description is inferior to that of human experience. "Kingdom of Absence," *Canadian Literature* 67 (1976): 31. Precosky goes even farther, seeing "austerity," "reticence," "limitation," and "change" as the four moods which control both the tone and the content of "Songs of the Common Day." See "The Need That Irks," 28-30, for an over-ingenious exposition of how these terms apply to the sequence.

13. *At the Mermaid Inn: Wilfred Campbell, Archibald Lampman, Duncan Campbell Scott in* The Globe *1892-93*, ed. Barrie Davies (Toronto: U of Toronto P, 1979), 334. All further quotations are from this edition.

14. John Moss, arguing that colonialism inevitably sets up a barrier between the poet and nature, promotes this poem as a *serious*, if failed, attempt by Campbell in which "the poet seems to recognize that the only way he can get into the picture—that is, find language that will effectively merge consciousness with the landscape—is quite literally to climb in. The effect is bizarre, and only a little redeemed from the ridiculous by the wistful supposition that his irony is intentional." "Landscape, Untitled," *Essays on Canadian Writing* 29 (1984): 31.

15. F.W. Watt, "The Masks of Archibald Lampman," *UTQ* 27 (1958): 182. In his own person, Lampman had already remarked in his column of 10 December 1892 that "the quarrel between realism and romanticism is about as empty a one as that over the iota in the Nicene Creed. Between realists and romanticists, provided they be men of genius, there is very little difference that any but the professional critic can see. The aim of both is artistic truth, and the difference of method fades out of sight before the larger meanings and grander motives of their work."

16. "Bereavement of the Fields," in *William Wilfred Campbell: Selected Poetry and Essays*, ed. Laurel Boone (Waterloo: Wilfrid Laurier UP, 1987). All further quotations are from this edition.

17. Davies, *At the Mermaid Inn*, viii.

18. Boone, *William Wilfred Campbell*, 161. As well, not only are cows a recurrent motif in "Songs of the Common Day," but the other titles Campbell lists for Bang's fictitious volume (especially "The Lonely Clam" and "Bunchgrass") are more reminiscent of Roberts'

maritime milieu than of Lampman's Ontario. It may also be worth noting that Lampman's letter to his friend E.W. Thomson at the time remarks only that "Our 'Mermaid Inn' engagement with the 'Globe' has terminated; they do not want us any more. That makes me a little poorer than I was." He does not allude to any conflict between the columnists. See *An Annotated Edition of the Correspondence Between Archibald Lampman and Edward William Thomson (1890-1898)*, ed. Helen Lynn (Ottawa: Tecumseh 1980), 88.

19. In addition to his attack on realism in the *Globe*, he wrote several columns on the subject in an American publication, *The Evening Journal*: 3 September and 3 December 1904, and 23 January, and 25 March 1905, according to Carl F. Klinck in *Wilfred Campbell: A Study in Late Provincial Victorianism* (1942; rpt. Ottawa: Tecumseh, 1977), 221-23.

20. Roberts, "A Note on Modernism" in *Selected Poetry and Critical Prose*, 298.

21. Arthur Stringer, "A Foreword," *Open Water* (Toronto: Bell and Cockburn, 1914), 18; 10-11. All quotations from Stringer's work are from this volume.

22. *The Making of Modern Poetry in Canada: Essential Articles on Contemporary Canadian Poetry in English*, eds. Louis Dudek and Michael Gnarowski (Toronto: Ryerson, 1967), 3. For his comments on Lampman, see "Lampman and the Death of the Sonnet," *The Lampman Symposium*, ed. Lorraine McMullen (Ottawa: U of Ottawa P, 1976), 39-48.

23. F.O. Call, *Acanthus and Wild Grape* (Toronto: McClelland and Stewart, 1920).

24. R. Alex Kizuk, "One Man's Access to Prophesy: The Sonnet Series of Frank Oliver Call," *Canadian Poetry: Studies, Documents, Reviews* 21 (1987): 32.

25. Munro Beattie, "Poetry 1920-35," *The Literary History of Canada: Canadian Literature in English*, 2nd ed., ed. Carl F. Klinck (Toronto: U of Toronto P, 1976), 2:236. Ken Norris repeats Dudek and Gnarowski's view of Call's preface as a manifesto for free verse equivalent to that of Stringer in "The Beginnings of Canadian Modernism," *Canadian Poetry: Studies, Documents, Reviews* 11 (1982): 56.

26. F.O. Call, *Blue Homespun* (Toronto: Ryerson, 1924).

27. *Shapes and Sounds: Poems of W.W.E. Ross*, eds. Raymond Souster and John Robert Columbo (Toronto: Longmans, 1968), 4. All quotations from Ross refer to this edition. Bruce Whiteman also

ignores the sonnets in his column praising Ross, implying, by this omission, that the poet was an imagist *pure laine*. See "W.W.E. Ross: Imagism, Science, Spiritism," *Poetry Canada Review* 6:3 (1985): 9. Don Precosky acknowledges the existence of the sonnets, but dismisses them in half a page as completely failed, devoting the rest of his essay on the poet to the thesis that "Ross's poetry is probably the purest example of Imagism ever written by a Canadian." *Canadian Writers and Their Works*, Poetry Series: 4, eds. Robert Lecker, Jack David, and Ellen Quigley (Toronto: ECW, 1987), 168.

By contrast, Peter Stevens reports that, far from considering himself an imagist, Ross "felt hostile to, and irritated by, William Carlos Williams," and that his most profound influences were e.e. cummings and Marianne Moore. See "On W.W.E. Ross," *Canadian Literature* 39 (1969): 43; 45.

28. Editorial Note, *Shapes and Sounds*, 8. The three sonnets included here are "The Pythagorean Basilica," "On the Supernatural," and "The Nimble Fish."

29. George Woodock, Introduction to *Canadian Writers and Their Works* Poetry Series: 3, eds. Robert Lecker, Jack David, and Ellen Quigley (Toronto: ECW, 1987), 6.

30. W.W.E. Ross, *Sonnets* (Toronto: Heaton, 1932).

31. Quoted by Michael Darling, "On Poetry and Poets: The Letters of W.W.E. Ross to A.J.M. Smith," *Essays on Canadian Writing* 16 (1979-80): 95. Even Brian Trehearne, who declares that: "Unlike his Imagist poems, Ross's sonnets are behind his times by some thirty or forty years" recognizes that the "two distinct manners of verse he explored constitute a more substantial traditionalist-modernist tension in his artistic development than is generally recognized." *Aestheticism and the Canadian Modernists: Aspects of a Poetic Influence* (Montreal: McGill-Queen's UP, 1989), 33. A.R. Kizuk explores this tension in "Canadian Poetry in the 'Twenties: Dialectics and Prophesy in W.W.E. Ross's *Laconics* and *Sonnets*," *Canadian Poetry: Studies, Documents, Reviews* 18 (1986): 35-54.

32. Ross goes on to state that this prosody worked *best* with his "northern" poems. *A Literary Friendship: The Correspondence of Ralph Gustafson and W.W.E. Ross*, ed. Bruce Whiteman (Toronto: ECW, 1984), letter 36.

33. Arthur Henry Hallam, "On Some of the Characteristics of Modern Poetry," in *Victorian Poetry and Poetics*, eds. Walter E. Houghton and G. Robert Stange (Boston: Houghton Mifflin, 1968), 850.

34. Carol T. Christ, *Victorian and Modern Poetics* (Chicago: U of Chicago P, 1984), 6.

35. C.K. Stead, *The New Poetic* (London: Hutchison, 1964).

36. John T. Gage, *In the Arresting Eye: The Rhetoric of Imagism* (Baton Rouge: Louisiana State UP, 1981), 17.

37. See Miles, *Eras and Modes in English Poetry*. Norman Friedman also argues that the major difference between Romantic and Victorian poetry is that "the Romantic poem does not characteristically seek impersonality." See "From Victorian to Modern: A Sketch for a Critical Reappraisal," *The Victorian Newsletter* 32 (1967): 30.

38. A.J.M. Smith, "F.R. Scott and Some of his Poems" (1967), in *The McGill Movement: A.J.M. Smith, F.R. Scott and Leo Kennedy,* ed. Peter Stevens (Toronto: Ryerson, 1969), 93. On the other hand, as Don McKay notes, something of the sublime persists even at the heart of imagism: "the sudden angle of perception, the phenomenal surprise which constitutes the sharpened moments . . . in such defamiliarizations, often arranged by art, we encounter the momentary circumvention of the mind's categories to glimpse some thing's autonomy—its rawness, its *duende*, its alien being." "BALER TWINE: thoughts on ravens, home and nature poetry," *Studies in Canadian Literature* 18 (1993): 131-32.

39. Graham Hough, *Image and Experience: Studies in a Literary Revolution* (Lincoln: U of Nebraska P, 1960), 14.

40. Christ, *Victorian and Modernist Poetics*, 90.

41. Roberts, "Canadian Poetry in its Relation to the Poetry of England and America" (1933), *Canadian Poetry: Studies, Documents, Reviews* 3 (1978): 84.

42. John Metcalf, "The Curate's Egg," *Essays on Canadian Writing* 30 (1984-85): 43.

43. Louis Dukek, "F.R. Scott and the Modern Poets" (1950-51), in *The McGill Movement*, 70. Scott himself argues thus in his two-part article "New Poems for Old" in *The Canadian Forum* 11 (1931): 296-98, 337-39. More than fifty years later we hear the same message from Bruce Whiteman: "most of the poetry written in Canada before the First World War was jejeune, amateurish and, with the obvious exceptions, now all but unreadable. It was in the 20s that Canadian poetry really began to come of age." "The Beginnings of Modernism (1)," *Poetry Canada Review* 7 (1985): 44. Similarly, in a column commemorating Scott, David O'Rourke declares that "Canadian poetry properly begins with A.J.M. Smith." *Poetry Canada Review* 6 (1985):

8. But W.J. Keith goes even farther; according to him, "Canadian literature was still in its infancy" in 1943! See *Canadian Literature in English* (London: Longmans, 1985), 211.

44. Margaret Coulby Whitridge, introduction to *The Poems of Archibald Lampman* (Toronto: U of Toronto P, 1974), xxiv.

45. Mallinson, "Kingdom of Absence," 35-36. Mallinson appears indebted to Rashley for this argument; see *Poetry in Canada: The First Three Steps* (Toronto: Ryerson, 1958), 44-45. But whereas he saw the lack of fit between poetic style and the environment as a predicament of "pioneer" writers, Mallinson includes Roberts' generation. In this regard she is closer to Desmond Pacey who declares that "Canadian literature, and Canadian culture generally, suffered, during the last century and for the first two decades of this, from the fault of being 'derived.' It is a fault that all colonial cultures have in common, and it is a fault that is by no means easy to eradicate." Among the invidious sources derived from he cites Wordsworth, Tennyson and Arnold. See "At Last—A Canadian Literature" (1938), *Essays in Canadian Criticism: 1938-1968* (Toronto: Ryerson, 1969), 1-2.

46. Trehearne, *Aestheticism and the Canadian Modernists*, 21; 13.

47. Desmond Pacey, *Ten Canadian Poets: A Group of Biographical and Critical Essays* (1958; rpt. Toronto: Ryerson, 1966), 251. This evaluation is quoted approvingly by Stephen A.C. Scobie in "The Road Back to Eden: The Poetry of F.R. Scott," *Queen's Quarterly* 79 (1972): 314. See also the introduction on Scott and the notes to the poem in *An Anthology of Canadian Literature in English*, eds. Russell Brown and Donna Bennett (Toronto: Oxford UP, 1982), 1:346-48.

48. Chester Duncan, Rev. of Scott's *Selected Poems, The McGill Movement*, 75.

49. Bentley, *The Gay]Grey Moose*, 259. Bentley explores the implications of the name and characterization of "Miss Crotchet," and notes that the masculine bias of modernist criticism is implicit in the vocabulary of its proponents; for example, "manly" is "Smith's term for such traits as 'irony' and 'intellect'"(259). On the way in which this bias has shaped the Canadian canon, see Carole Gerson: "Anthologies and the Canon of Early Canadian Women Writers" in *Re(dis)-covering Our Foremothers: Nineteenth-Century Canadian Women Writers*, ed. Lorraine McMullen (Ottawa: U of Ottawa P, 1990), 55-76, and also "The Canon between the Wars: Field-Notes of a Feminist Literary Archaeologist," *Canadian Canons: Essays in Literary Value*, ed. Robert Lecker (Toronto: U of Toronto P, 1991), 46-56.

50. Dudek, "F.R. Scott and the Modern Poets," 58.

51. E.K. Brown, "The Development of Poetry in Canada, 1880-1940," *Poetry* 58 (April 1941): 39-40. Similarly, Smith notes that "The powerful influence of Roberts, Carman, and Lampman was both an inspiration and a handicap to their successors for at least two generations." Introduction to *The Book of Canadian Poetry: A Critical and Historical Anthology* (Chicago: U of Chicago P, 1943), 24.

52. A.J.M. Smith, "A Rejected Preface," in *New Provinces: Poems of Several Authors*, ed. Michael Gnarowski (Toronto: U of Toronto P, 1976), xxvii.

53. *On Poetry and Poets: Selected Essays of A.J.M. Smith* (Toronto: McClelland and Stewart, 1977), 108-09. As Robin Mathews remarks: "Since the McGill Movement the hallmark of general misunderstanding has been the tendency to lump good and bad poetry into 'the maple leaf school,' dismissing the whole without examining the parts." See "Poetics: The Struggle for Voice in Canada," *CVII* 2:4 (1976): 6.

54. Letter from Pratt to Scott, dated 20 Dec. 1935, quoted in the introduction to *New Provinces*, xiv.

55. *New Provinces*, v.

56. Letter of 17 Feb. 1934, quoted in the introduction to *New Provinces*, xiii.

57. John Ferns, *A.J.M. Smith* (Boston: Twayne, 1979), 107; 108.

58. Smith, "A Rejected Preface," xxvii.

59. Leo Kennedy, "Direction for Canadian Poets," in *The McGill Movement*, 12.

60. Pacey, *Ten Canadian Poets*, 214.

61. A.J.M. Smith, "The Lonely Land," in *Ten Canadian Poets*, 212.

62. Gary Shapiro suggests that, despite the fact that the New Criticism was a consistent effort to read all poetry in terms of the criteria of the beautiful ("coherence, autonomy and organic unity"), modernist poetics still tend to give a privileged position to what has traditionally been known as the sublime. See "From the Sublime to the Political: Some Historical Notes," *New Literary History* 16 (1985): 217. This might explain anomalies like "The Lonely Land" being published in *New Provinces*. On the other hand, Smith himself did not reprint the work in any of his three editions of the *Book of Canadian Poetry* (1943, 1948, 1957), nor in *The Oxford Book of Canadian Verse* (1960), and he told Michael Darling this was because the poem was too romantic, in "An Interview with A.J.M. Smith," *Essays on Cana-*

dian Writing 9 (1977-78): 59.

63. George Woodcock, Rev. of Smith's *Collected Poems (1963), The McGill Movement*, 123.

64. Gary Boire, "Canadian (Tw)ink: Surviving the White-Outs," *Essays on Canadian Writing* 35 (1987): 4.

65. D.G. Jones, "Private Space and Public Space," *On F.R. Scott: Essays on His Contributions to Law, Literature, and Politics*, eds. Sandra Djwa and R. St. J. Macdonald (Montreal: McGill-Queen's UP, 1983), 47. Sandra Djwa doesn't look back quite so far, but still notes the presence of traditional concerns: "In poems like 'Old Song,' 'Lakeshore,' and 'Laurentian Shield,' Scott wrote of a terrain first explored by Roberts and Duncan Campbell Scott—and, for that matter, by his father, F.G. Scott, in 'The Unnamed Lake.'" *Canadian Writers and Their Works* Poetry Series: 4, eds. Robert Lecker, Jack David, and Ellen Quigley (Toronto: ECW, 1990), 179.

66. Djwa, "'A New Soil and a Sharp Sun': The Landscape of a Modern Canadian Poetry," *Modernist Studies* 2 (1977): 16.

67. Thomas Weiskel, *The Romantic Sublime: Studies in the Structure and Psychology of Transcendence* (Baltimore: Johns Hopkins UP, 1976), 26.

68. Robert Kroetsch, "A Canadian Issue," *Boundary 2* 3 (Fall 1974): 1.

From *The Picturesque and the Sublime: A Poetics of the Canadian Landscape.* (Montreal: McGill-Queen's UP, 1998): 103-27. Reprinted with permission of Susan Glickman and McGill-Queen's University Press.

AGMV
MARQUIS
Québec, Canada
2000